SACRED SITES AND ·WAYS

STUDIES IN THE TOPOGRAPHY OF THE GOSPELS

·BY

GUSTAF DALMAN, D.D.

PROFESSOR OF THEOLOGY AT THE UNIVERSITY OF GREIFSWALD

AUTHORISED TRANSLATION BY

PAUL P. LEVERTOFF, D.D.

LONDON
SOCIETY FOR PROMOTING
CHRISTIAN KNOWLEDGE
NEW YORK: THE MACMILLAN CO.

First published 1935

MADE IN GREAT BRITAIN

TRANSLATOR'S NOTE

THIS translation of Dr. Gustaf Dalman's *Orte und Wege Jesu* has been made from the third German edition, with considerable additional matter by the Author and a few notes by the Translator, who wishes to make grateful acknowledgment of the assistance given him by his daughter in the compiling of the indexes and for careful reading of the proofs by Dr. Lowther Clarke.

This work of the foremost authority on the historical geography of the Holy Land is, in a sense, a sequel to his *Jesus-Jeshua*, which I was privileged to bring out in an English dress for the S.P.C.K. in 1929. The most exact knowledge of the land, the language, the Jewish literature, and the Church tradition, is combined here to produce a work of unusual richness and most solid thoroughness.

While indispensable to all serious students of the Gospels, it could be used as the most scientific " Guide " to the Land of Jesus.

PAUL P. LEVERTOFF.

Name of Jesus, 1934.

ABBREVIATIONS EMPLOYED

I.—GENERAL

PJB=Palästinajahrbuch.

ZDPV=Zeitschrift des Deutschen Palästina-Vereins.

PEFQ=Palestine Exploration Fund Quarterly.

RB=Revue Biblique Internationale.

ZDMG=Zeitschrift der Deutschen Morgenländischen Gesellschaft.

CIL=Corpus Inscriptionum Latinarum.

MGWJ=Monatschrift für Geschichte u. Wissenschaft des Judentums.

II.—TALMUDIC AND MIDRASHIC LITERATURE

Tos.=Tosefta.

p.=Palestinian Talmud. Names of the tractates without the addition of p. refer either to the Babylonian Talmud or to the Mishna. The abbreviations of the names of the tractates are those commonly used. Thus: Ber.= Berakoth, Sab.=Sabbath, Pes.=Pesachim.

Mech.=Mechilta; Gen. R., Ex. R., Lev. R., Num. R., Deut. R., refer to the Midrashim to these books.

CONTENTS

LIST OF ILLUSTRATIONS

Grateful acknowledgment is made to the Palestine Exploration Fund for their kind help in making the maps for this book.

xi

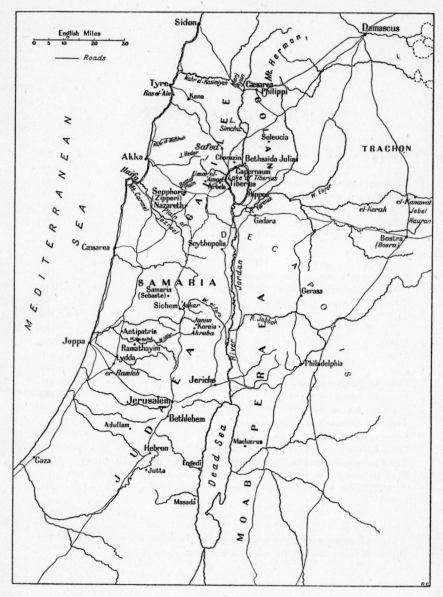

English Miles
0 5 10   20   30

— Roads

Sidon

Damascus

Tyre
Ras el-Ain

Nahr el-Kasimiyeh

Mt. Hermon

Cæsarea
Philippi

Kana

L. Simchu

MEDITERRANEAN SEA

Akka

Haifa

Mt. Carmel

Nahr el-Mukhuh

J. Heder

Safed

Chorazin

Seleucia

Bethsaida Julias

TRACHON

Plain of GALILEE

Umm el-'Amad
Arbela

Capernaum
Lake of Tiberias
Tiberias

Hippos

W. Ehrer

el-Kanawat
Jebel Hauran

el-Kerak

Sepphori
(Zippori)
Nazareth

Bittar Plain

Plain of Esdraelon

Yarmuk

Bostra
(Bosra)

Cæsarea

Scythopolis

Gadara

DECAPOLIS

SAMARIA
Samaria
(Sebaste)

Sichem   Askar

W. el-Farin

R. Jabbok

Gerasa

Jamin
Korata
Akraba

River Jordan

Joppa

Antipatris
Ramathayim
Lydda
er-Ramleh

PERAEA

Philadelphia

Jericho

Jerusalem

Bethlehem

Dead Sea

MOAB

Adullam

Hebron

Engedi

Machaerus

Gaza

Jutta

Masada

B.C.

xii

I

INTRODUCTORY : THE LAND OF JESUS

PALESTINE is the land in which the history of Israel has achieved, in the Person of our Lord, its aim and purpose for humanity. Consequently, as Jesus gathered up the significance of this land's history into Himself, it must have been an appropriate place for the upbringing both of the People of God and of the Son of Man.

It has been rightly suggested[1] that the external conditions which aid the deepening of the individual Christian's spiritual life are also of vital importance for a whole people destined to be trained for a life of communion with God. These include a certain degree of solitariness, combined, however, with the possibility of fruitful contact with the outer world ; a sense of dependence upon God in the struggle for existence, together with an overwhelming perception of the sublime and the universal. In fact, Palestine's narrow frontiers between a coast-line poor in harbours and the wide desert ; the broad vistas visible from its mountain-ridges ending in the boundless sea and high, snow-covered peaks ; its chalk precipices, which provide the patient toilers with the bare necessities of life, and which, without rain and dew, would be turned into arid deserts ; its blazing sky ; its terrible storms ; its raging sea ; its relationships to Egypt and Mesopotamia, to Greece and Rome—countries too far off to absorb her, yet sufficiently menacing to make flight to God her only salvation from extinction : all these are essential factors in the history and the faith of Israel. In the life and work of our Lord the external conditions were also factors which must not be overlooked. One familiar with Palestine realises that Jesus cannot be fully apprehended apart from her ; for the Child was a gift of God to her. His life-work was in the first place to be not only *in*, but also *for*, this land.

[1] Scovgaard-Petersen, *Landet hvor Kilderne sprang*, vol. i. (Copenhagen, 1923), p. 11.

I

The period of history in which Jesus was born was determined primarily by the Roman oppression ; out of the oppression grew the question, Where is the Redeemer ? And,
above all, Where is God ? And the answer which God gave
was found in the person and witness of Jesus. He was the
answer, since He was the Child of this country, and because
His becoming what He was, as the Son of Man, was determined by the results of its history. Consequently, the influence of Palestine's soil, climate, and geographical position
during Israel's long history belongs to those factors which
made Jesus, by the will of God, what He should *be* to His
people and what He should *become* to humanity.

Moreover, it was also provided by God that the revelation
of His character and will, intended as it was for all men,
should not, in the form of its appearance, be entirely foreign
to any human being. Therefore this revelation was unfolded
in Palestine and here the Word became Flesh. For this small
country, lying as it does where the temperate zone meets the
semi-tropical, displays unusual varieties of climate and soil-
formation. Not only can one experience within the compass
of a mere half year all possible temperatures from a cold almost
arctic to a heat little short of torrid, but the complexity of
this land of contrasts permits one to be, by just a slight change
of place, in all seasons and zones within the span of a few
hours. In the sub-tropical Jordan-valley grow bananas and
palms, as well as the vine. On the coast, dates no longer
ripen, but the mulberry, orange, lemon, and cactus-fig flourish
in rare luxuriousness. In the mountainous regions on both
sides of the Jordan-valley there is an abundance of ever-
green olive-trees and fig-trees, the foliage of which begins
to turn green only shortly before the summer comes,[1] apple
and pear trees also thrive here ; while on the northern slopes
of the heights, the cedar, now becoming rare, ascends to
the snow limit. About six miles east from Jerusalem no snow
falls, even when the mountain-summits are covered with snow
for days ; and a distance of about fourteen miles in the same
direction brings us from winter into summer. How varied
also is the configuration : the mountainous regions of Judæa,
with rounded heights and deep-cleft valleys ; the more open
Samaria, and lower Galilee with its plains between clear-cut
mountain-ridges ; then the table-land of Moab and of the
Golan, as well as the little undulating deep lowlands of the

[1] In April. See Mt. xxiv. 32 ; Mk. xiii. 28 ; Lk. xxi. 29.

coast. The normal slopes of the mountainous regions which, in the north, in the neighbourhood of the highest mountain-chains, are steeper, and the great dampness of the coastal region make it possible to cultivate small stretches of the chalk and volcanic soil. The wheat, which is scattered upon un-ploughed and unmanured land, and then ploughed in, then fills the " barns " (Mt. vi. 26 ; xiii. 30 ; Lk. xii. 24), *i.e.* nowadays the tall grain-chest of the Palestinian peasants. The drought strip of semi-desert (Aram. *madbera*), where only the herds of its nomadic inhabitants and the natives of its borderland find sustenance, must also be included—a spot which Jewish law wished to confine entirely to the pasturage of sheep and goats, a place into which a man could flee to be hidden or alone (Lk. i. 80 ; iv. 1 ; Mk. i. 12). And everywhere among the mountains there is no lack of rocky tracts only suit-able for grazing which are therefore differentiated from the cultivated land by being called " the desert places " (Aram. *atar madbar*, in the Christian Palestinian, Mk. i. 35). In the life of our Lord these " desert places " played a special rôle (Mk. i. 35 ; vi. 32, 35).

All these contrasts, which have come into being through the ruptures of the earth's crust in the length and the breadth of the land, and which are so sharply differentiated, have deter-mined the history of the population of Palestine at all times. Their influences in the past continued to operate in the time to which the life of Jesus belonged. The desert and the cultivated regions ; the Jordan-valley and the mountain-ridges ; the Judæan capital and Galilee, separated from it and therefore independent of its influence, where zeal for God and His Kingdom assumed such different aspects ; the land on either side of the Jordan and its lake—all these made their distinct contributions towards the shaping of the life of Jesus. The coast and the Mediterranean were a background destined to become significant for the effects of the life of Jesus only in the decades which were to follow. These natural lines of demarcation also prevented the pure Hellenism, which took root in the East especially, from influencing the Jewish region to such an extent as it would otherwise have done, and thus left for the gradual development of the Son of Man and His disciples a native soil where a genuine Israelitish spirit still predominated.

The egoistic self-complacency of Roman despotism, satirised in a Talmudic world-judgment-scene (Abodah z. 2b) with

bitter irony, had, after the death of Archelaus in 6 A.D., taken
the politically most developed West into its own administration, and left in the East and on the coast autonomous cities,
where Greek colonists, loyal to Rome, enriched themselves
at the expense of the native population, and gave over the
government of the rest, after deliberately splitting it up, to
the two sons of Herod, Antipas and Philip, who, although
natives, were racially aliens.

The western mountainous region, from the plain of Jezreel
to its southern slope towards the desert, thus formed Roman
Judæa in the widest sense of the word,[1] to which also belonged
the maritime district from Carmel to Joppa, with Cæsarea
(Jewish *Kesari, Kesarin*) which the Romans made into a capital.
The greater Judæa was divided again into two provinces :
Judæa in the narrower sense and Samaria.[2] This was due
to the Roman toleration of native jurisdiction among Jews
and Samaritans ; and besides, their opposition to one another,
caused by the different opinions concerning the legitimate
place of worship (Jn. iv. 20), necessitated separate treatment, and was useful to Roman administration. A curved
line formed the frontier, which probably ran from Antipatris
towards *Wady deir Ballut* and the *Ish'ar*, approached the plain
of *'Askar* near the mountain of *el-Ormeh*, and then descended
over *Janun* towards Koraia (now *Kerawa*) into *Wady el-Far'a*.
Since the regulation of the year 145 B.C., which moved this
frontier in the north-west and north towards the north,[3] to
include the districts of Lydda, Ramatha (Ramathaim) and
Ephraim, a later shifting of the line must have taken place,
which took in also Akraba in the north-east, a good day's
journey (about 25 miles) from Jerusalem,[4] to Judæa.[5] In
this way both districts were probably divided according to
the predominant character of the population in each. Because
of the attitude of the Jews to the Sabbath laws, the Romans
recruited their police-troops chiefly from among the Samaritans.[6] The Roman administration must have concentrated

---

[1] Hebrew *Jehuda*, Shebi ix. 2 ; Aram. *Jehud*, Dan. ii. 25 ; so also the Peshita.
[2] Hebrew *Shomeron*, Aram. *Shamerayin*, Ezra iv. 10 ; Pal. Ev. Lk. xvii. 11.
The Jews avoided to use this name and spoke of " the land of the Cutheans."
[3] 1 Macc. x. 30, 38 ; xi. 34 ; *Ant.* xiii. 4, 9. *Cf.* Haefeli, *Geschichte der Land-
schaft Samaria* (1922), p. 81.
[4] Maas. sh. v. 2.
[5] *Bell. Jud.* iii. 3, 5. It may be that the four districts which 1 Macc. xi. 57 ;
Ant. xiii. 5, 4 describe as having been confirmed by Antioch VI. to Jonathan
had already included Akraba. See *Bell. Jud.* iii. 3, 5.
[6] Schürer, *Geschichte* i., p. 459.

its attention upon the two capitals, Jerusalem and Sebaste, *i.e.* Samaria. The native administration had to collect and deliver the taxes, but the " letting " of the customs (Lk. xix. 2) and the guarding of the frontiers Rome kept in her own hands. Judæa was entirely cut off from the coast, because its maritime towns, controlling the former Philistine region, possessed, in various ways, autonomy under Roman supervision. The important Samaritan harbour, Cæsarea, built by Herod, was in the hands of the Roman administration.

The northern hinterland of Palestine, Galilee (Aram. *Gelila*, p. Sanh. 18d), was, like Judæa, cut off from the sea, but in addition was limited, in favour of Tyre, to the region south of the chain of the *Jebel Ḥeder*, so that the whole northern slope of the land as far as *Nahr el-Ḳasimiyeh* was separated from it. The administration carried on by Rome's submissive friend, Herod Antipas (the centre of which was at first Zippori and after A.D. 18 Tiberias), meant a weakening of Jerusalem's influence, and hence, an advantage to Rome.

For the same reason, the strip of land in the south-east, inhabited by Jews, the so-called *Peræa*,[1] or Transjordania (Mt. iv. 25 ; Mk. iii. 8), Aram. *'ibreh dejardena*,[2] was also apportioned to the same ruler, together with the obligation to protect Judæa from the advance of the Nabatæans, who were menacing the whole of eastern Palestine, even to Damascus (2 Cor. xi. 32). Anyone who pictures to himself the frontiers of Peræa, especially eastward from the Dead Sea, where it could only have consisted of mountain slopes, can realise that this task, in spite of the strong fortress of Machærus, must have been almost insuperable.

The north-east of the country was assigned to Herod's son, Philip. His domain included the Trachon,[3] and was therefore intended to form a barrier here and up to the farthest limit of land suitable for cultivation, against the Nabatæan pressure on Damascus, an object of ardent desire to Arabian power. In *Paneas* (Cæsarea Philippi), on the important road from Damascus to Tyre and Sidon, resided the Tetrarch, as its peaceable guardian, who was open to attack from either side at any moment. He could only enter his

---

[1] See Haefeli, *Samaria und Peräa*, p. 66 *f.*

[2] Pal. Ev. Mt. iv. 23. Hebrew *eber ha jarden*, Isa. viii. 23 ; Shebi. ix. 2. Also " Judæa beyond Jordan," Mt. xix. 1 ; *cf.* Mk. x. 1, if the text is to be altered (*cf.* below, ch. xii. 3).

[3] Aram. *Terakhona*, p. Shebi. 36c, Pal. Ev. Lk. iii. 1. *Cf. Ant.* xvii. 8, 1 ; Sifre on Dt. li. ; Tos. Shebi. iv. 11.

brother's domain from the upper course of the Jordan, and
when he desired that his burial-place should be in Bethsaida-
Julias, on the Lake of Tiberias (*Ant.* xviii. 4, 6), it was because
he felt that there, at least, he would lie somewhat nearer to
his native land.

The middle east was held by the federation of the Ten
Cities,[1] of the organisation of which we know nothing; nor
is Decapolis ever mentioned in Rabbinic literature. With
Scythopolis the federation reached over the Jordan, a wedge
between Galilee and Samaria. With Gerasa and Philadelphia
it embraced the east of Jewish Peræa. It formed thus a
complete protection to the eastern frontier. Being split into
ten autonomous cities, it was innocuous to western Palestine.
The common struggle with the Bedouins of the desert was a
most important bond of union for them all. That Augustus
apportioned Gadara and Hippos to the province of Syria
(*Bell. Jud.* ii. 6, 3) is probably to be considered as characteristic
of his policy in regard to the whole of the Decapolis, for it
was thus completely separated from the Jewish parts of
Palestine.

The fact that Nazareth was the native place of Jesus put
Him beyond the power of the Jerusalem authorities, as long
as He did not enter their sphere of influence. From Capernaum He could also easily avoid Herod Antipas, and He
could choose between the domain of Tyre in the north, the
principality of Philip in the east, and, in the south and south-
east, the parts about Hippos, Gadara, and Scythopolis, of the
Ten Towns. It was also easy to find privacy here, if He desired
it for Himself and His disciples. Moreover, Galilee was
eminently conducive to the development of a unique type of
Jew. Josephus praises the courage and pugnacity of the
Galilæans (*Bell. Jud.* iii. 3, 2). According to the Talmud
(Ned. 48a), it was their quarrelsomeness that made them put
limits to each other, by vows of prohibition, even in regard
to public properties (Ned. 48a). They set more store by their
honour than by wealth (*mammon*, p. Keth. 29b). That they
were not precise in their manner of speech and were careless
in the pronunciation of consonants[2] was due to the fact that
a non-Semitic language, Greek, was used frequently and
exercised a wide influence there.[3]

[1] Mt. iv. 25; Mk. v. 20; vii. 31. Aram. '*asarte medinata*, Pal. Ev. Mt. iv. 25.
See Guthe, *Die griechisch-römischen Städte des Ostjordanlandes* (1918), *Gerasa* (1919).
[2] Erub. 53a. See Dalman, *Gramm. d. Jüd. Pal. Aramäisch*, 2nd ed., pp. 57, 96.
[3] *Jesus-Jeshua*, English translation, pp. 2-6.

In the three territories of Jewish Palestine, Judæa, Galilee, and Transjordania, there were also certain differences in regard to the consumption of the fruit of the land in a Jubilee-year.[1] The question of doubtful tithing was differently handled.[2] There was also no small possibility of disagreement in the fixing of the Calendar by the intercalation of the leap-year, although the law emphasised that only the exigency of two countries should be decisive, and that Judæa, as the " dwelling-place of God," was to set the standard.[3] Concerning the form of the marriage-contract the Galilæans agreed with the Jerusalemites, but not with the Judæans.[4] In Galilee engaged couples were not allowed to be together alone, but, on the other hand, the nuptials were there exempt from the regulations current in Judæa.[5] In Galilee, but not in Judæa, the public domain was assigned to the princes.[6] Many Galilæans considered it permissible to keep the smaller cattle in other than " desert " places, even if this should necessitate their crossing arable land on the way to the groves which served as pasturage (Tos. Bab. k. viii. 14). The bestowal of the half-shekel for the Temple-sacrifices and the dedication of things for the use of the priests by a ban-formula were unknown among them (Ned. ii. 4) ; neither were they very scrupulous about making use of the things thus vowed away (p. Ned. 37c, cf. b. Sanh. 43b). Wine and oil coming from Galilee for Temple use were looked upon with suspicion from the point of view of ritual purity, because the Samaritan districts, through which they would have to be brought,[7] intervened. In the domain of worship, the consideration of the Day of Atonement as a feast,[8] the prohibition of work on the whole of the Passover eve,[9] and the special liturgical rite for the New Year's Day Service,[10] were peculiar to Galilee. At a funeral the professional mourners went behind the bier in Judæa, while in Galilee they went in front of it.[11] In Galilee the Sabbath interrupted the mourning regulations and customs, but not so in Judæa.[12]

Moreover, Galilee and Judæa had different weights,[13] different prices for cereals,[14] different kinds of soil,[15] different seasons of vintage, and, partially at least, different climates.[16]

[1] Shebi. ix. 2, 3 ; Tos. Shebi. vi. 10.   [2] p. Dem. 21d.
[3] Tos. Sanh. ii. 2, 13   [4] Keth. iv. 12.   [5] Keth. i. 5.
[6] Ned. v. 5.   [7] p. Chag. 79b.   [8] Chull. v. 3 ; Sifra Emor viii. (99c).
[9] Pes. iv. 5.   [10] p. R. h. 5, 59c.   [11] Sab. 153a.
[12] Mo. K. 23a.   [13] Keth. v. 9.
[14] Tos. Dem. v. 16.   [15] Bab. b. 122a.   [16] p. Bab. b. 15c.

All these differences made it possible for a Galilæan woman, for instance, to refuse to move with her husband to Judæa or Transjordania, or *vice versa*, and the husband had no redress.[1] It was even thought that animals used to the herbs of Galilee could not thrive in Judæa, even as an animal of the mountain could not prosper on the plains.[2] It was not unusual for a man to possess a wife in each of the three " lands," Galilee, Transjordania, and Judæa.[3]

The distance from the Temple and from the centre of jurisdiction had necessarily its consequences for Galilee. One can take it for granted that neither the Sadducean nor the Pharisaic type of piety was widespread there. Among the prominent scribes of the centuries before the destruction of the Temple, only Nittai of Arbel can be discerned as being a Galilæan.[4] At the time of the Emperor Claudius, a certain Galilæan, Eleasar, being well versed in the law, convinced Izates, the proselyte, of the necessity of circumcision (*Ant.* xx. 2, 4). When Jochanan ben Zakkai taught in the place Arab, in Galilee, he was once moved to utter the following admonition : " Galilee, Galilee ! Thou hatest the Law ; behold, robbers will one day come upon thee " (p. Sabb. 15d). At a later date, when Jose the Galilæan appeared among the scholars of Judæa, he was once called by a woman of whom he asked the way, "foolish Galilæan," because of his verbosity (Erub. 53b). The Pharisees and scribes who encountered our Lord wherever He appeared, in Capernaum (Mk. ii. 6, 16, 24), in Dalmanutha (viii. 11), even in the eastern region (ix. 14 ; x. 2), came probably from Jerusalem, and the Evangelist did not deem it necessary to point this out each time (*cf.* Mk. iii. 22 ; vii. 1). Thus it would seem that the piety of the Galilæans was not altogether of a Pharisaic brand, but that the Judæan "missionaries" did their best to convert them to their point of view. As no mention is made of them in regard to Nazareth, it is possible that this town was not considered by them of importance enough for their propaganda, and this accordingly was a matter of significance to our Lord's upbringing. But, after all, Jesus became what He was as Man, not through isolation from, but in His struggle with, Pharisaism.

---

[1] Tos. Ned. iv. 7.   [2] Keth. xiii. 10.   [3] Tos. Gittin viii. 5.
[4] Ab. i. 7.   That it was different in the time after the destruction of the Temple is evident from the list of twenty localities in Lower Galilee which Klein has shown to have been centres of scribes at that period (*Palästina Studien* i., p. 26 *f.*).   But it is significant that Upper Galilee is not represented in it.

The following references to Galilæans, however, although belonging to a later period, are connected with the various aspects, both natural and political, of northern Palestine, and help us to understand the reason why this region was chosen by God for the upbringing of Jesus and the training of His Apostles.

A certain Galilæan who, as such, was designated *min* (sectarian), reproached the Pharisees for mentioning in the date of a bill of divorcement the name of the alien ruler together with that of Moses.[1] It was the Galilæan Judas (Acts v. 37) to whom the rule of God and the rule of Rome seemed incompatible and whose passionate patriotism caused so much misery to his people.[2] The inhabitants of Kephar Nahum were not only conscious opponents of the Pharisaic interpretation of the Law, but were also " broad " in regard to the practice of certain religious customs. They declared, for instance, that it was permissible to ride on a Sabbath day.[3]

In Zippori we find a certain Jacob of Kephar Sechanya,[4] who was considered to have been a follower of Jesus.

A miracle-working sectarian exercised his practice in Guphta near Zippori (p. Sanh. 25d).

Elisha ben Abuya lost, in the plain of Gennesaret, his faith in the Law (p. Chag. 77b).

Of a certain Galilæan it is assumed that he was an expert in the secret lore dealing with the Throne of the Divine Glory (Sabb. 80b).

Jerusalem was, in itself, merely the centre for southern Palestine, thanks to its situation on the double spurs of the mountains, and on the main high-road leading from north to south through the central region of the country. But Galilee, despite its remoteness, was connected with it primarily by the strong sense of opposition to the Samaritan attitude

---

[1] Yad. iv. 8, ed. Riva di Trento 1559, Mantua 1561. Later editions have changed *min* into *sadduki* (Sadducee).

[2] *Ant.* xviii. 1, 6 ; xx. 5, 2 ; *Bell. Jud.* ii. 8, 1 ; 17, 8. According to *Ant.* xviii. 1, 1, he was a Gaulanite from Gamala, but as he is otherwise always called " Galilean," he must have come from the Galilean Gamala (Tos. Makk. iii. 2, 6 ; Arach. 32a), which Klein (*Monatsschrift*, lxi., p. 139) identifies with *Jebel Jamleh*, north of *Tibnin*, but which must be located more exactly in *el-Jehudiyeh*, south of this mountain. The designation " Gaulanite " by Josephus would thus be due to an error caused by confusing this Gamala with that of Gaulanitis.

[3] Eccl. R. i. 8 (70b). Riding on a Sabbath is a sign of " libertinism " (p. Chag. 77b ; b. Sanh. 46a).

[4] There are various readings of this place-name : Kephar Sechanya (Eccl. R. i. 8 ; Ab. z. 14a, 27b), Kephar Shechanya (Eccl. R. i. 8), Sichnin (Tos. Chull. ii. 24), Kephar Samma (Tos. Chull. ii. 22 ; p. Sabb. 14d ; Ab. z. 40d).

towards the proper place of worship, and thus also by the pilgrimages for the three festivals (Ex. xxiii. 14; xxxiv. 23; Dt. xvi. 16). According to Rabbinic Scriptural interpretation, women, the blind, the deaf, the lame, the sick, the aged, and children who could not either be carried on the father's shoulders or walk at his side from Jerusalem to the Temple, were exempt from this duty;[1] but it was absolutely imperative for all healthy male adults, in spite of all difficulties that might be connected with the journey. Our Lord belonged to a family which observed this duty (Lk. ii. 41 *f.*), and, according to the Fourth Gospel (Jn. vii. 10, 14), He Himself practised it. The same is true also of the Temple tax (Mt. xvii. 24 *f.*), although, as we have seen, the Galilæans were generally lax in regard to the payment of this.

True as it is that " the Son of Man had not where to lay his head " (Mt. viii. 20; Lk. ix. 58), there was one point which He considered as the goal of His wanderings, where "all will be accomplished " (Jn. xix. 28, 30). " To-day and to-morrow and the day after to-morrow must I wander," He said; but He added: " for it cannot be that a prophet perish out of Jerusalem " (Lk. xiii. 33). Whatever it was that urged Him to go to Jerusalem, it is certain that what He wrought and experienced there had to spread from this centre of the Jewish people into all parts of Palestine and into the whole of the Jewish Diaspora (Acts ii. 9 *f.*). The wide dispersion of the Jews had caused Jerusalem to become a centre of considerable magnitude in the Roman Empire. Whatever took place there, took place on the world's stage.

Of importance for the life of Jesus were, therefore, the ways of communication supplied by the natural routes of international thoroughfare—above all, the coast-road to Egypt, with its offshoots from the east and north-west (of graded importance according to the starting-points and natural position, among which the transverse valley of Palestine, the plain of Jezreel, played a unique rôle). Connected with these lines were the common routes of local communication which, in the central and southern Palestinian seaboard, ran mostly at the foot of the mountains and not near the coast; the western mountain-chain with its watersheds; and the Jordan-valley. In His wanderings He used the ways from north to south; the road along the Jordan towards Jerusalem, on

[1] Chag. i. 1.

the one hand, and towards the region of the coast, on the other; and the transverse roads of Galilee. According to the purpose of His journeys, He made use of the local possibilities of travel within the land. It is, however, significant that the *Via Maris*, one of the links connecting that centre of civilisation, Damascus, with the coast-road, and thence with the sea along which it passes, although it had never played any conspicuous rôle in the history of ancient Palestine, now came into prominence in connection with the spread of the Gospel in a most distinct fashion. To the author of the First Gospel it was of importance only in regard to the fulfilment of prophecy (Mt. iv. 14 *f.*). But also in other respects the highways were of vital importance for the planting of the Church by the Apostles, as related in the Book of Acts, and the road to Damascus acquired at that period a new unforeseen significance, whether St. Paul chose to travel along the western shore, or to turn off round the southern end of the Lake of Gennesaret and continue along the eastern shore, on his memorable journey to that city (Acts ix. 3 *f.*).

The sea-routes must also be numbered among the great thoroughfares. Palestine proper, however, having poor natural harbours, benefited little by them, until Herod, by supplying the artificial harbour of Cæsarea, at the spot where the *Via Maris* enters into the region of the coast, changed things for the better. This brought Palestine into close touch with the civilisation as well as with the despotism of the Roman Empire. Our Lord Himself had no part in this intercourse; the traces, however, of its consequences for the culture and political development of the land ran through His life from His birth to His death.

The fact that the references of the Evangelists to localities are more or less casual, without any connection with a larger background, and, moreover, their lack of first-hand knowledge of these places, make the task of the geographer rather difficult. Doubtless the vicissitudes of the transmission of the Gospel narratives up to the point when they were fixed in their present form have also influenced their geographical references. The form of a narrative would have often taken on a different shape if it had been written down by an eye-witness and one familiar with the district. Bultmann,[1] however, has no basis at all for his hypothesis that the " cult-legends " which the Christian Church needed for her " Christ-myth " consisted,

---

[1] *Die Geschichte der synoptischen Tradition*, pp. 35, 148.

apart from some descriptive matter, of "apophthegms,"[1] didactic sayings and miracle-stories, which, generally speaking, did not contain any names of definite places, as they are not according to the "style" of such subjects. Rabbinical literature which never shows any interest in making an historical person a centre of special portraiture yet contains a large number of place-references in connection with apophthegms, didactic sayings, and miracle-stories, although these are mostly without any importance for the subject-matter. Gamaliel, for instance, once refused to absolve a person from a vow as long as he, Gamaliel, was under the influence of Italian wine.[2] Now, from the point of view of the casuistic instruction concerning vows it was of no moment where this incident took place; yet the Midrash points out that the wine was drunk by Gamaliel in Kesib, and that he refused any treatment of the subject until he reached the "ladder" of Tyre : "As soon as they reached the ladder of Tyre, Rabban Gamaliel descended from the ass, rolled himself up in a cloak, and taught us many things."

A certain rabbi's saying is referred to in connection with a discussion concerning rain-seasons.[3] The transmitter of the saying, however, was not satisfied with the mere quotation, but introduced it with the evidently superfluous remark : "When I passed the synagogue of the Tarsians, I heard the voice of Rabbi Shemuel ben Nachman, who taught . . ."

In connection with the laws of witchcraft a number of miracle-stories are told (p. Sanh. 25d). One of these relates to the bath and lake of Tiberias ; the second is connected with Rome ; the third and the fourth took place either in or near Zippori. But all these localities have no particular significance in relation to the subject-matter as such, only just such miracle-narratives require this touch of realism.

According to Bultmann,[4] the localisation of the Zacchæus-narrative in Lk. xix. 1 is editorial fiction, because, as Wellhausen had pointed out, the tree on to which Zacchæus climbed could have stood only outside the city. But the Evangelist must also have known that one does not climb trees in the midst of a city in order to see someone. Hence when he writes that "Jesus entered and passed through Jericho" (xix. 1), he refers to the outskirts of the city, *i.e.* not

---

[1] [*I.e.* the short, pithy sayings or significant acts, enclosed in an historical setting, the purpose of which was to justify some point in the belief or practice of the Church.—TRANSLATOR.]

[2] Lev. R. xxxvii. (101a).   [3] *Ibid.* xxxv. (98a).   [4] *Loc. cit.*, p. 35.

to the small ancient town on the hill but to the greater Jericho
of the Herodian period, in the environs of which sycamores
grew on the road as they do even at the present time.   Moreover, the road from the Jordan to Jerusalem passed actually
through this greater Jericho, as the pre-Herodian Jericho on
the hill by the well had no direct connection with the only
possible ascent to the mountain.

Thus the whole assumption that the original apophthegma
did not contain any names of localities is based on a false
conjecture.   But above all, the early Church was not searching
for a " cult-legend " for her " myth " ; but, in contrast to the
Paganism which needed such a highly coloured basis, she
stood up before the world with a simple narration concerning
the historic actuality of a Person, in and through whom God
came to fulfil His eternal purpose.   Apart from the testimony
of the inner life of the Church, the concreteness of this Person's
manifestation in an earthly environment in the past was the
only external proof for its reality.   Hence the necessity of
connecting the story of the Saviour's life and work with the
actual soil, the scenes of His activity.

However, intelligent treatment of the place-references in
the Gospels could not consist merely in pointing them out
on the map.   Even a pilgrimage through Palestine does not
achieve its full purpose when it merely leads to the finding of
the places thus mapped out in the belief that the awakening
of the emotions at the sight of them is the chief object.   Such
a notion in regard to the value of the geographical orientation
leads, in the case of the Gospel story, to many disappointments,
as the character of that account does not as a rule supply us
with the necessary foundations for it, and the exact identifica-
tions given by Church tradition seldom deserve much confi-
dence.   But even were it otherwise, the result gained would
only be slight and of little value.

I have always answered the question as to whether this or
that place be historical by saying, " Here everything is historical," because of my conviction that while no isolated
spot in this land could have signified anything historically in
itself, but only in so far as it might be near to, or far from,
some other place of undoubted fame, yet in a sense each
individual place, even when unmentioned in history, did
indeed have a determining share in the whole course of the
history recounted in the Gospels.   Hence, the purpose of
this book is not to isolate the places and ways of the Gospel

story from the Holy Land as a whole, as if something of special moment were attached to them—in the manner of the man who walked on a road in Palestine with his feet so nearly placed the one to the other that he could only shuffle, in order to be sure that he missed no spot of ground which might have borne the foot-prints of our Lord.   On the contrary, our aim is to fit each place into the background and setting of the land in its entirety, and to contemplate every part in relation to the whole.   This ideal (which, I must confess, I have not perfectly realised) has urged me to concentrate on the portrayal of the places and ways mentioned in the Gospels, without discussing the historical value of the narratives in which they occur.

Apart from my own explorations during my wanderings through the whole of Palestine, which occupied a considerable number of years, I have naturally not neglected the witness of the local tradition of the early Church of the land.   It was, after all, based on familiarity with the places, and does not stand in the same category as the later conjectures of the Crusaders and the Franciscans, which do not deserve the appellation " tradition."   The references in Rabbinic literature had also to be considered.   Although the final formulation of this literature had not yet taken place in the time of Christ, its inception was on Palestinian soil, and belonged to an epoch in which the Jewish people and Judaism had not as yet detached themselves from their original centre.   Excavations which have as their chief aim the discovery of the monu- ments of Hellenistic and Herodian Palestine[1] can, and must, be used as supplementary sources of knowledge.   So far, little has been done in this direction.   Prehistoric, Canaanitish, Israelitish periods have been explored ; but the time of the Herodians, that most important epoch for Christians, has been neglected.   We are still, for instance, only partly in- formed concerning the architectural styles and technique of that period.   When this is remedied, we shall be in a better position to know the Land of Jesus.

[1] For what is known so far, *cf.* Thomsen, *Denkmäler Palästinas aus der Zeit Jesu* (1926) ; De Groot, *Jerusalem ten tijde van Jesus, Stemmen des Tijds,* viii., p. 223.

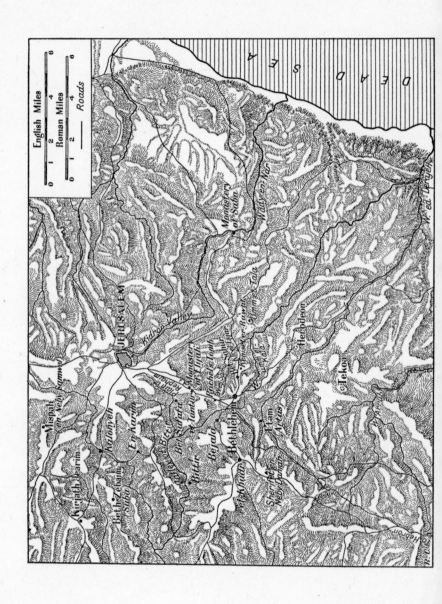

II

BETHLEHEM: THE SHEPHERDS' FIELD AND THE NATIVE PLACE OF JOHN THE BAPTIST

BETHLEHEM would not have become the place of the Nativity had it not been the native place of David. This is incontestable, even for those who consider the Nativity narratives to be legendary. David, however, *became* in Bethlehem the man that he was when he entered the scene of history, while to the Saviour Bethlehem was merely the manger where His Mother laid Him. Yet there were factors in the life of David as man and king, which set the pattern of what Jesus became to the world and are inseparable from our conception of Him. Therefore Bethlehem is to us both the city of David and the place of the Nativity, but our minds are focussed on the manger and on Him who lay there, for we have seen His star in the *West* and have come to worship Him.

Southern Palestine, known in the time of Christ as " Judæa " (Mt. ii. 1), is formed mainly by a central mountain range, with slopes to east and west. Its peculiarity is that its ridge, furrowed throughout, and nowhere forming a high tableland,[1] contracts, at the stretch of land which lies between Hebron and Jerusalem—about eight miles long—to a narrow edge only about half a mile to two miles wide, which—especially towards the west—slopes away steeply. In the north, where it widens out again, the water flowing towards the Mediterranean has cut a deep ravine in the valley of *Bittir*, which of necessity formed a natural frontier. In the east the lower course of the Kidron valley coming from Jerusalem had a similar effect.[2] Between the northern end of the ridge and that natural, diagonally running frontier lies Bethlehem, at all times the most important locality in this district.

Anyone going from Jerusalem to Bethlehem to-day, as

[1] The maps, with their reduced reliefs, give for the most part a wrong conception.
[2] The application of the name Kidron to the lower course itself is not correct. The ancient name must have been " Valley of Acacias," *cf*. Joel iv. 18 (Heb. Shittim).

did once the Magi who came from the east—*i.e.*, from Arabia[1]
—with their treasures, takes, as they did, his starting-point
from the gate by the old palace of Herod, the tower of which
has borne, since the fourth century, not his name, but
David's.   Should he desire to continue following their route
he would not cross the valley below Jerusalem by the present
thoroughfare on the dam of the Sultan's Pool, but earlier,
at the upper part.   He could then, in the neighbourhood of
the village—mentioned by Josephus as Ἐρεβίνθων οἶκος[2]—
below the present thoroughfare, take the old road which
passes alongside it through the plain of Rephaim, near its
high eastern edge.   This unassuming and scarcely practicable
route, which, however, has the advantage over the modern
high-road of not being dusty, can claim a considerable amount
of historic importance ; for it helps one to visualise the old
form of the most important traffic-artery of southern Palestine,
which, running along the watershed, was the scene of the
intercourse between its most important cities.   King David
took this road from Hebron in order to make Jerusalem his
capital (2 Sam. v. 6) ; Absalom also came by this route to
dethrone his father (2 Sam. xvi. 15).

The plain of Rephaim, sloping towards the west, now
called simply *el-Baḳ'a*, "the Plain,"[3] is unique in the
upland south of Jerusalem.   Hydrographically it is of importance as the head of the deep valley of *Bittir*, which runs
down from here to the coastal plain, and, finally, together
with a little stream called *Nhar Rubin*, breaks through the
dunes.   The railway now uses this incline as a means of
ascent to Jerusalem.   In former times the tortuous narrow
valley was not a route such as the Philistines, for instance,
might have used in their invasions of the highlands (neither
was it of any importance for the taking of Jerusalem during
the last war), but a boundary between the north and the east
(*cf.* above, p. 17), and, even in Saul's time, between the land
of Judah and the environs of Jerusalem, which were still
occupied by the Canaanites.[4]   The taking of this route prevents

---

[1] So Justin, *Dial.* lxxviii.   Later it was taken to be Mesopotamia (according
to Num. xxviii. 7, LXX), which, however, the Palestinian does not consider
" east " ; and besides it does not fit in with the presents brought by the Magi ;
cf. Nestle, *Z.N.W.*, 1907, p. 73.   [2] *Bell. Jud.* v. 12, 2.
[3] Schick has, after the English map, *El-Bukei'a*, but it is not usual.
[4] The frontier between Benjamin and Judah, as drawn in Josh. xv. and xvii.,
could have corresponded to the actual conditions only in later times.   See
Dalman, " Die Stammeszugehörigkeit der Stadt Jerusalem und des Tempels,"
in *Baudissin-Festschrift*, p. 107 *f.*

us from having a view over the watershed, with which on the left (*i.e.*, in the east) the plain terminates. But if we ascend it as far as the spur of *Ras-el-Mekabber*, we realise with surprise not only how steep the slope eastward is at this point, but also how deeply the *Wady en-Nar*, coming from Jerusalem, cuts into the mountains. This at times almost vertical canyon continues towards the Dead Sea, the natural frontier marked in the west by the railway-line. The road to Bethlehem leads up eventually to the southern edge of the plain, where, by the present monastery of Elijah, one can easily cross the bordering height; otherwise only the narrow pass of the valley of *Beit Sufafa* would be available. The watershed, which so far has run eastward alongside the highway, here crosses it, and then continues on its western side. This crossing-over at the monastery of Elijah, however, involves leaving not Jerusalem only but also the entire region to which it belongs beyond the horizon. The knowledge gained by taking the way through the valley of Rephaim is of no little importance for the understanding of the position of Bethlehem. This place is not, nor was it ever, a mere daughter town of the five miles distant Jerusalem. It was cut off from the latter by the natural dividing line between south and north which clove through the mountains almost midway between them. Jerusalem is the southernmost point of importance in the northern region; Bethlehem the most northern of importance in the south. Both were originally border cities, outposts: the former for the north, the latter for the south. The tribe of Judah had in Bethlehem its " thousands " who had penetrated farthest into Canaan. It was " small," according to Micah v. 1, and yet of particular significance. It was not merely an accident that David had his home here. Here, at the frontier of the Canaanite enclave, after which the Philistines hankered, it must have been realised how desirable was its removal, and the welding together of Israel and Judah.

The eminence on which the monastery of Elijah stands may possibly have been the " Baal Perazim " of 2 Sam. v. 20, the scene of one of David's victories over the Philistines, alluded to by Isaiah in the apocalyptic passage (xxviii. 21) as the " Mount Perizim." " The Lord hath *broken forth* upon the Philistines as the *breach of waters*," like a flood breaking through the dams, inundating the land and carrying everything with it. When the Philistines encamped in the plain of Rephaim, naturally with their front towards the east and with their outposts set on the heights of the roads at the watershed, it was David's first concern, when he came from Adullam in the hill-country, to mount the height on the great road from the Shephela towards *el-Khudr*, and from thence to take the way by a road (only partly marked on the maps) which runs into the main road through *Bejala*, directly in front of what is now the monastery of Elijah, in order to surprise the Philistines with a sudden attack at that spot, and then to break in from above, through the Philistine encampment, to the plain,[1] in a manner actually like water breaking through all its barriers. At no other place at the edge of the plain could such an action be so appropriate as here ; to no other eminence could such a peculiar name as " Baal of the breaches," or " Mountain of the breaches," have been given. There must have been an ancient heathen shrine upon it which was designated thus, because the end of the Judæan land was here broken through by the road.[2] Before the Redeemer of the world was born in Bethlehem, God manifested His redeeming activity in Israel when David triumphed here over the Philistines.

This same eminence, the summit of which is an isolated height away from the road,[3] has been associated with the Nativity, and at a short distance before crossing it by the road, at the left-hand side, a rock was shown which St. Mary blessed when she used it as a resting-place on the way to Bethlehem. " Now there is a place three miles from the city of Jerusalem, where St. Mary, the Mother of the Lord, got off her ass as she was going to Bethlehem, and sat down on a rock and blessed it. This stone did the governor Urbicius cut and fashion it like an altar. . . . It was brought back to the Sepulchre of the Lord and there an altar was made out of the rock, and at that altar men communicate."[4] Possibly it was the same great rock which was later considered to have been the one that closed Christ's tomb, and which is now on

---

[1] The second battle in the plain of Rephaim (2 Sam. v. 22) belongs, according to Isa. xxviii. 21 and 2 Sam. v. 25, to the plain of Gibeon, namely, the plain of Bekaim. The original reading in 2 Sam. v. 22 was probably not *Rephaim* but *Bekaim*. See also Procksch, *PJB*, 1909, p. 20.

[2] Vincent, *Jérusalem*, i., p. 119, thinks of Perazim—which he locates on the height of the Jaffa road, west of Jerusalem—as being the watershed of the land. But no native would ever think of this.

[3] The top looks like an ancient site and hence might have been the actual Baal Perizim. But one sees there natural soil and rocks.

[4] Theodosius (Geyer, *Itinera Hierosolymitana*, p. 148).

the altar of the "Church of Caiaphas" in Jerusalem.[1] On the site of the rock a church dedicated to St. Mary was erected in the year 450, in the proximity of which St. Theodosius lived before he founded the monastery called after him in the desert.[2] Near this church Antoninus (in 570) saw "water come out of the rock in the midst of the rock from which all men drink their fill, and yet the water is never more or less ; and it is sweet to drink. It is said that this water sprang up because the Blessed Mary, when fleeing into Egypt, sat down in that place and thirsted."[3] The church, to which a still existing small pond away from the road may have belonged, has long since disappeared, yet the old name "seat" (κάθωμα) still clings to a well near the highway on the northern slope of the eminence near an old nettle-tree (Celtis australis). This is the bir Kathisma,[4] of which it is related since the fourteenth century that here the Magi saw again the star which had led them to Palestine "till it came and stood over where the young child was" (Mt. ii. 9). It would certainly have been a confirmation of what they had been told in Jerusalem if they saw the significant star in the south. But it had nothing to do with that cistern on the road. To us it is only a reminder that Mary and Joseph, as well as the Magi, must have taken this route according to the Gospel narrative. It is the road itself which is important, and not any special spot on it, though in this particular case there was perhaps a very ancient resting-place, as is pre-eminently the well at the summit before the monastery of Elijah at the present time.

The view to the south which opens out at almost 800 metres above sea-level reveals quite a different kind of landscape. On a peak only 20 metres lower we see three-towered white Bethlehem stretched out. Behind, and above it, appears, rising somewhat to the west, the highest elevation of north Judæa, reaching a height of almost 1,000 metres, projecting in the east into the outpost of ancient Tekoa (849 metres). This, however, leads into the great slope of the mountains towards the Dead Sea, the deep-lying blue mirror of which can, however, only be seen at two points along the Bethlehem road—namely, in front and behind the height of the monastery of Elijah, because of the depression in the ground there. On

[1] PJB, 1913, p. 109.   [2] Vita Theodosii, Migne, P.G. cxiv., col. 476.
[3] Geyer, Itinera, pp. 178, 208. The place is there confused with Rachel's Tomb.
[4] Tobler, Topographie von Jerusalem, ii., p. 530 ; Klameth, Die neutestamentlichen Localtraditionen Palästinas, i., p. 60 ; Vincent and Abel, Bethléem, p. 2.

the other side of the Dead Sea, the east is closed to us by the
vast wall of the highlands of Moab, attaining towards the
south a height of 700 to 1,000 metres ; the part which lies
opposite here was called the " mountain of Makhwar," or
" Mekhawer " (Greek Μαχαιροῦς, now *Mukaur*),[1] after the city
and mountain-castle restored by Herod.[2] The scent of the
incense from the Temple in Jerusalem was, according to legend,
so strong in these mountains that the goats who browsed
there sneezed ![3] The high towers of the stronghold must
have been clearly visible from here, and the Baptist's disciples,
as they gazed on it, must have thought of their master who
was imprisoned and eventually foully murdered there.[4] On
the downward slopes of the range of hills on this side of the
watershed there arises in the south the old—and still, alas !
unexplored—*Herodeion*, the desert watch-tower of Herod the
Great, where he wished to be buried,[5] and which now, like
a gigantic tumulus, keeps green the memory of the last
eminent king of the Jews. It was then the official centre
of that district, the chief town of which must have been
Bethlehem.[6] One can observe here how these heights, on
whose loftiest summit stands Bethlehem, join the general
slope of the land eastward, on the farthest decline of which
the little village of *Bet Saḥur* lies, and how they finally terminate
in a small plain in the midst of which the olive-garden of the
so-called " Shepherds' Field " is set, a dark spot in the midst
of the surrounding fields. In the middle and foreground,
precipices and valleys, more or less thickly clothed with olive-
trees, stretch towards the main valley which drops down from
Bethlehem and in a south-eastern direction drains the highlands into the Dead Sea. The uncultivated desert cannot be
seen from here, but one cannot help noticing how cultivation
diminishes towards the south-east, and how the trees, which
in the foreground lend charm to the rocky landscape, disappear at even a short distance.

The city of Bethlehem, most of which from here is seen
clearly spread out, was evidently not merely a boundary city
of mid-Palestine which begins with Jerusalem, but was,
together with the watershed, above all an outpost looking
out towards the desert. Its vineyards, olive-plantations, and

---

[1] p. R. h. Shana, p. 58a.   [2] Jos., *Bell. Jud.* vii. 6, 2.
[3] Tamid iii. 8 ; b. Yoma 39b.   [4] *Ant.* xviii. 5, 2.
[5] *Ant.* xvii. 8, 3 ; *Bell. Jud.* i. 33, 9.
[6] *Bell. Jud.* iii. 3, 5 ; Pliny, *Hist. nat.* v. 14, 17.

fields descend in this direction with the slope of the land, until desert-nomads and drought set a limit to their cultivation. All that is unsuitable for this is used as pasture-land, which extends right into the desert as far as the shepherd is able to protect his sheep and goats with his club and gun (formerly with club and sling [1 Sam. xvii. 40]) against wild animals and cattle thieves. Bethlehem was a place of herds, but, nevertheless, deserved the name " House of Bread," in so far as it also possessed on the little plain below its mountain range, level and deep-earthed arable land, unusual in this region.[1] The story of Boaz and Ruth in the family annals of the house of David is fitly laid in Bethlehem, but there would never have been any lack of young men who, like the shepherd David, could fearlessly stand up against lions and bears (1 Sam. xvii. 34), and knew also how to sling a stone with good effect against an enemy (*ibid.*, 49) ; who were at home in the desert, and could find a shelter in its ravines and the caves when danger threatened at home.

Moreover, the obvious fact that the environs of Bethlehem are open towards the desert also implies the possibility of a thoroughfare running from here eastward, traversing the Kidron valley above the monastery of Saba, and terminating at the southernmost ford of the Jordan above the Dead Sea. This route may have been " the other way " which the Magi took on their return journey to the east (Mt. ii. 12). In fact, Greek tradition took this first route for granted and regarded a cave below the monastery of Theodosius,[2] which its founder originally inhabited, as having been the lodging place of the Magi on the first night of their return journey.[3] As can be seen from the *Vita Theodosii*, it was a generally used route at that time. Its importance increased owing to the fact that in the west (which cannot be seen from here), south from the *Bittir* valley, nature supplies a descent to the coast which abandons the watershed at *el-Khudr*, quite near to Bethlehem. David went this way with bread and cheese towards the " laager " (barricade of wagons), in order to fight against Goliath (1 Sam. xvii. 20). Bethlehem stood at the place where, south of that transverse frontier of the land, and north of the Dead Sea, the traffic had to cross the water-

[1] The threshing-floor of Boaz lay, according to Ruth iii. 3, 6, outside Bethlehem, thus probably in a field some distance from the city.
[2] According to Moschus, *Pratus spirit.* (Migne, *P.G.* lxxxvii. 3, col. 487), a staircase of 108 steps was erected there.
[3] *Vita Theodosii* (Migne, *P.G.* cxiv., col. 478).

shed. But in addition to the eastern desert road there was a second desert route, which directed the traffic from the narrow pass of Engedi and also from the south end of the Dead Sea towards Bethlehem. Saul took this route when he looked out for David in Engedi (1 Sam. xxiv. 3). The natural advantages of this road cannot be detected from here because of the hills behind Bethlehem. But the defiant fortress of Herodeion would not have been erected had not a military road led that way. Herod in his flight from Jerusalem to Masada had defeated the Jews there.[1] Besides, Tekoa in the south, the nearest Judæan town, was, like Bethlehem, an outpost towards the desert. The road thereto, with its continuation towards the south, was an important parallel road to the chief thoroughfare of the country along the watershed.[2]

The position of Bethlehem, as we have envisaged it so far, made it a good school for the warlike David and his commander-in-chief, Joab, without whom the history of Israel, after the tragic end of Saul, would have gone downhill. In David this experience produced, with much else, trust in God ; in Joab, his nephew—a semi-Bedouin—ferocity.

However, only one who has traversed the further environs of Bethlehem ; has ridden like the members of our Institute[3] along all the important thoroughfares in every direction ; and having viewed the town both from the summit of the highest neighbouring peak in the south-west (the *Sherifet en-Neby Danian*, 2,994 metres), and from the depth of the valleys in the east, has realised the importance of its position on the high land near Jerusalem—only such an observer can have a complete perspective view of all the possibilities of this city on a hill. Having perceived them, the traveller may well be surprised that Bethlehem, apart from being the "mother" of an important family, did not play any very prominent rôle in the great history of Palestine.[4] Still, the contribution which obscure cities make to the history of their land must not be under-estimated. That a community like that of

---

[1] *Ant.* xv. 9, 4 ; *cf.* xiv. 13, 9.
[2] If the Idumæan *Thresa*, on the farther route of Herod towards Masada, is to be read *Oresa* (so Schlatter, *Die hebräischen Namen bei Josephus*, p. 51), he started from here through Tekoa and *Beni-ne'em*. For Oresa could scarcely be identified with the unfortified *Khirbet Choresa*, but rather with the nearer *Khirbet Ranaim* or *Khirbet Istabul*.
[3] [The German Archæological Institute in Jerusalem, of which Dalman was for many years director.—TRANSLATOR.]
[4] It is uncertain whether judge Ibzan (Judges xii. 8 *f.*) was a native of this Bethlehem.

Bethlehem could withstand at this spot the attacks of the nomads of the desert, as well as those of the neighbours beyond the near-by northern frontier was, after all, of great importance for the whole of the Judæan land. Judæa would not have been the independent power it always was over against Israel had it not been for Bethlehem. The Philistines would not have had a garrison there in David's time (2 Sam. xxiii. 14), and Rehoboam would not have fortified it (2 Chr. xi. 6), if it had not been a strong strategical point. Nevertheless, its nearness to Jerusalem was fatal for Bethlehem. The Bethlehemite family which established Jerusalem's greatness made Bethlehem insignificant. By the side of royal Jerusalem and its troops, Bethlehem's little hill and its small band of capable fighting men ceased to be of importance. To Jerusalem's market streamed buyers and sellers from far afield; Bethlehem sent olives, oil, and sheep to the capital, and she herself could only maintain a small part of her own desert customers.

Bethlehem appeared on the stage of Jewish history for the last time when Hadrian posted there one of the garrisons charged with the capture of the rebellious Jews who fled from Jerusalem.[1] After that its only noteworthy Jewish appearance is in the legend concerning the birth of the Messiah, which is to take place in the royal (or Araba[2]) citadel of Bethlehem.

That the "city"[3] of Bethlehem, having scarcely 10,000 inhabitants, is at present of greater importance than it ever was in ancient times is due to the splendour which has been spread over the little place by the Saviour's birth. The late war showed how the "House of Bread," whose fields cannot supply enough grain for the increased population, must suffer great distress when cut off from the rest of the country, especially if, in addition, the locust plague has destroyed her olive and oil harvest for one year.

Anyone who looks now on Bethlehem from the beautifully situated Maltese settlement *et-Ṭanṭur*, for instance, on the right side of the Hebron road, from the outside and from a distance, notices nothing of the devastation caused by the war and the plague, which together have swept away a quarter

[1] Midrash Lam. i. 6 (Buber's reading). See Klein, *MGWJ*, 1910, p. 25.

[2] *Ibid.*, and p. Ber. 5a. For the var. lect. *cf.* Dalman, *Aram. Dialektproben*, p. 16, and Ginzberg, *Jerush. Fragments*, i., p. 9.

[3] Bethlehem has a city constitution and belongs thus to the few cities of the west-Jordan land.

of her inhabitants. Peaceful and pleasant, her houses, con-
vents, and churches still shimmer on her heights. Clouds of
dust from automobiles often cover the foreground of the
charming picture, entirely concealing the green of the olive-
trees and the plants on the slopes. In ancient times this evil
product of modern civilisation in limestone country did not
exist, and even now the evil is not so great in the Christmas
season, since the first heavy rains of the winter wash the dust
completely away. A sunny day at this season corresponds
to a mild day in our late autumn, only that the gay colouring
of our autumn foliage is scarcely to be found on these hill-
slopes. The blue fruits of the ever-green olives have ripened
and gone, the leaves have curled themselves up, so that their
bright under-side is hardly visible. Their pale dull green
now gives the impression of being paler than in spring and
summer. The fig-trees, which spring up among the creeping
vines, are already bare, and stretch out their naked, light-grey
branches in a spectral fashion. And their fading foliage,
which is more tawny than yellow, does not give them any
added beauty. The vines, which are not cultivated on stocks,
but allowed to creep on the ground, are completely bare, and
look as though they had been thrown away. Somewhere,
perhaps, a rare pomegranate-bush may show a few yellow
leaves, but the dark-green and glossy foliage of the carob-
bean trees is the only thing that stands out against the
red-brown soil or the whitish-grey limestone. That late
autumn in the Holy Land does not signify Death, but rather
a resurrection of Nature, the tender green sprouting everywhere is a proof. The fresh leaves and buds of the Alpine
violets are to be found in protected spots. Wild daffodils,
sea-leeks, and even mandrakes, push up their large exuberant
leaves. Small yellow and mauve crocus blossoms gently
proclaim the purple glory of spring, which, in the olive-
gardens and on the stony hillocks of the limestone mountains,
will unfold from the end of January onwards.

Continuing along this pleasant highway we are able to
get views, to the left, of the valleys which begin high up,
while on the right the view is limited by the top of the watershed on that side. But over this height is the valley of *Bejala*,
which drains into the Mediterranean. The sides of this
valley cannot fail to charm the eye with their unbroken vista
of olive-plantations. On the right-hand side of the road is
a small, domed building, similar in style to the innumerable

Muslim *welies* : the " Tomb of Rachel,"[1] which was revered already in the time of Christ, and over which Arculf in the seventh century saw an unadorned " Pyramid."[2] The " tomb " was erroneously transferred to this spot from the neighbourhood of Rama, north of Jerusalem.[3] One can understand that when the original place of Rachel's grave, the Benjaminite Ephrat, disappeared, the Ephrata of Judah could not refrain from appropriating to herself the grave of Jacob's favourite wife, especially since all the other wives of the Patriarchs rested in Judah. As patron saint, Rachel, even to this day, watches over the graves of the *Ta'amire* Bedouins, and the Jews come here on certain days to ask her intercessions. That according to Mt. ii. 17 *f.* she weeps over her children who had to suffer death on account of the new-born King, is not to be taken merely as a poetic expression ; from the grave, it is believed, her mother-heart continually follows the destinies of her people.

Apocryphal gospels have assumed the place of the Nativity to be in the neighbourhood of the tomb of Rachel. Here, that is to say, about a mile before the journey's real goal is reached, the Virgin is said to have been surprised by the birth of her Son, so that a cave had to be found, and here the shepherds, and later the Magi, hailed the Child. At one time I used to connect this cave with the " Seat of Mary " on the road.[4] But in the *Protevangelium* of James, xvii. 2 *f.*, the cave is " in the midst of the way," after Mary had had a vision three miles away from Bethlehem ; and the narrator is certain, according to xxi. 2 *f.*, that the prophecy of the birth of the Messiah in Bethlehem was fulfilled. The Magi also find the Child, according to xxi. 3, in this cave, over which the star stands. The narrator thus considers the cave as a part of Bethlehem, but this would be impossible in a position near what is now the monastery of Elijah. The same applies to the visit of the shepherds to the cave lying before Bethlehem, according to the account in Pseudo-Matthew xiii. 1 *f.* The *Historia Josephi* mentions expressly in chapter vii. the nearness of Rachel's grave. According to Abbot Daniel

---

[1] Gen. xxxv. 19 ; *cf.* Mt. ii. 18. The first witness is the gloss of the present text of Gen. xxxvi. 19 ; xlviii. 7, which identifies Ephrat with Bethlehem.

[2] Geyer, *Itinera*, p. 228. The " pyramid " must have been an erected baldachin. The present construction dates only from 1841.

[3] *Cf.* 1 Sam. x. 2 ; Jer. xxi. 15. Already Tos. Sot. xi. 11 ; Gen. R. lxxxii. (176a) endeavour in vain to reconcile Gen. xxxv. 19 with 1 Sam. x. 2.

[4] *Cf.* Clameth, *Lokal-Traditionen*, i., p. 61.

(1106) the Virgin was supposed to have descended from the ass at this place when her time had come.[1]   A cave in this neighbourhood which could have served as a place of the Nativity was not known at that time, and so Mary was made to wander as far as the grotto of the church of the Nativity. There is, however, no likelihood that there was ever a cave with such traditions.   The gospels of the infancy in contrast to the local tradition of the seat of Mary, which was probably suggested by a great flat rock, were legends originating outside Palestine, designed to explain the story emanating from Palestine of the Saviour's birth in a cave by assuming it to have been premature.

Behind the " Tomb of Rachel," where in the time of Jerome the grave of king Archelaus[2] who died in exile was shown, the way to Bethlehem forks off from the main road (which turns a little westward, in a direct southerly direction) and it is almost three-quarters of a mile from here to where the closely massed houses of the present city begin to cluster.

The ridge towards Bethlehem rises into a long hill almost north by south, but soon turns off to continue in a somewhat lower broad saddle along the Hebron road in a south-western direction.   The first-mentioned hill turns at first towards the south-east and then bends to the east.   The ridge runs in a wave-line with three elevations, the middle one of which is the lowest.   Then in the east comes a little slope which ends in a plain about 200 metres below, situated between two valleys, but itself having a depression in the centre ; and the river running through it finally empties itself towards the more southern of the two.   These two valleys, *Wady es-Samur* and *Wady umm el-Ḳala*, between whose heads, at the top of the ridges, lies Bethlehem, ultimately unite and terminate, after a long and almost straight course, in the steep *Wady ed-Derajeh*, which soon after breaks through the precipitous mountains at the Dead Sea into which its river runs. South of it runs the already mentioned road to the Dead Sea. In an eastern direction the road towards the Jordan crosses its northern edge and the northern branch-valley, not far from the summit of *Umm eṭ-Ṭala*, which is 671 metres high.

On the mountain-ridge just described, which branches off from the watershed and which looks, from the south-east,

[1] *ZDPV*, 1884, p. 39.   [2] *Onomastica Sacra* 101, 12.

like a high mountain, lies Bethlehem ; but the exact spot occupied by the old city has not yet been ascertained. It was without doubt a smaller city than that of to-day. If we disregarded all traces of the past, we should place it either at the top of the watershed to the west, or on its eastern spur, outside of what is now considered to be old Bethlehem. Our decision in the matter is not without importance in connection with the traditional site of the Nativity. In the first case it was far from the old city ; in the other case it was at its western end, that is to say, at its most important approach. The present Bethlehem occupies almost the whole of the long ridge which branches off from the summit, and in the south it stretches even beyond it. Its real ancient site, however, lies undoubtedly in the centre, *i.e.* on the lowest of the three elevations, and extends from west to east 500 metres long and half as broad, on a plain about equal in extent to that of ancient Etam and Mizpah. Bethlehem in olden times was, as now, situated not on a spur but on a saddle. We can also understand why this site on the bend of the saddle seemed suitable. Here the steep slopes of the valleys, which at this point draw nearer together on both sides along the length of the saddle, offered the best protection, and besides there was, in any case, only room for a small collection of houses. What Nature did not supply by the lie of the land, or supplied but grudgingly, had to be supplemented by building round along the continuation of the hill to the north and the east. The result was naturally not a stronghold. A city in this place did not command any of the high roads, and had therefore only a limited significance in the history of the land. But it sufficed to assert the independence of a small commonwealth which wished primarily to guard and maintain its own possessions.

The position of the gates of the ancient city, which can be seen best from the south, is shown by their natural approaches. Through the north-western gate the traffic issued northwards— towards Jerusalem : a second gate in the west, near which the Evangelical church now stands, led towards the south, in the direction of Hebron. The old road which turns off from here in a south-westerly direction towards the high road, although little used and not shown on any map, still exists. In the south and east a third and fourth gate must have opened towards the desert. It is of no use to look for evidence of springs at any of these gates, for Bethlehem is one of the innumerable examples of old localities in Palestine lacking springs. The nearest spring of importance was that of the village of *Arṭas*, below the ancient Etam, at a distance of about a mile and two-thirds. It would have been possible to get there from the west gate, and, doubtless, water was often fetched from there and even perhaps also from the conduit *Bir 'One*, below *Bejala*, only about a mile and a half distant. The water could not be conveyed to Bethlehem from these springs because they lay too low. It was otherwise with the spring *'En Saliḥ*, which lies higher and drains the basin of *el-Khudr*. As it originates at a height of 798 metres, the water could be easily brought down to Bethlehem (20 metres lower) by a conduit running along the watershed. But it is questionable whether Etam, the possessor of this spring, would have permitted this. Probably a central authority was the first to overcome this obstacle. When Pilate, regardless of opposition, provided Jerusalem with water,[1] the altitude was such that it was necessary for the conduit running along the eastern side of the watershed to cross the hill at the eastern end of old Bethlehem, through a short tunnel. We do not know when it was that Bethlehem managed to acquire some of the precious moisture which passed by, as it still does, not far from the church of the Nativity in the deep conduit *Bir el-Ḳana*. Jerome[2] at any rate emphasises the fact that Bethlehem was altogether dependent upon rain, which shows that in Roman times no consideration was shown to the little town in this respect. We can see that in ancient Israel there was one well only which supplied the best water in Bethlehem, since David's desire when in Adullam (where it was not difficult to get spring-water) was " to drink of the water of the well of Bethlehem, which is by the gate " (2 Sam. xxiii. 15). Since the thirteenth century,[3] a group of three fairly deep cisterns has been pointed out as being the " well of David." They are to be found sunk deep in the rock of a northern spur of the mountain-ridge, on which, farther south, Bethlehem lies to the left of the road when coming from the north, at about a quarter of a mile from the place where it may be conjectured the old city gate probably stood. This would fit in quite well with the statement in the Book of Samuel that the cistern with the best water was " by the gate of Bethlehem." Yet

---

[1] *Ant.* xviii. 3, 2 ; *Bell. Jud.* ii. 9, 4.
[2] In his commentary on Amos, ch. iv.
[3] For the first time, it seems, by the pilgrim Burchard (1280). See also Tobler, *Bethlehem*, p. 10.

it may be but a gratuitous attempt of a later generation to supply the spot.[1]

Even in the fourth century another memento of David, the graves of Jesse and David (Eusebius, Jerome[2]), was found to the north of Bethlehem in the valley,[3] probably in the neighbourhood of David's well. The pilgrim of Bordeaux read even at that time on the wall of the sepulchral chamber the Hebrew names of Asahel, Joab, and Abishai, the nephews of David, as well as those of Jesse, David, and Solomon,[4] so even Jewish pilgrims must have visited these graves. In the sixth century a church " To St. David " was built there.[5] It was evidently thought that, after the destruction of the royal graves in Jerusalem, David and Solomon were reinterred here in the graves of their forefathers, and the grave of the unknown father of Asahel (2 Sam. ii. 32) was also presumed to have been here. In the year 1795 it was thought that this Bethlehemite grave of David might be rediscovered just below the well of David, to the south, somewhat deeper in the valley. Examination, however, showed that sixty-one graves in a burying-place with niches here more probably belonged to the monastery which was erected by St. Paula.[6] In the past, various old graves in Bethlehem were taken to have been that of Jesse. To us they are only later memorials of that ancestor of the royal family of Jerusalem, and also of Joseph, who travelled, according to Lk, ii. 4, from Galilee to Bethlehem in order that he might be entered on the Roman tax register in the ancient home of his family ; probably also for the purpose of establishing his citizen and property rights on a firm basis. We may take it for granted that Joseph still possessed a small portion of the family estate there, as even to-day it happens that such portions as are too small for cultivation remain in the family as a tribal possession, whilst their owners try to find a living elsewhere and simply receive a small revenue either in kind or in cash from their ancestral home.

The place where Samuel once prepared that sacrificial meal at which he anointed Jesse's youngest son to be king over Israel (1 Sam. xvi. 13) must be assumed to be in the immediate neighbourhood of Bethlehem. Where exactly could it have

---

[1] In the twelfth century the cistern was seen, according to Petrus Diaconus, near the church of the Nativity (Geyer, *Itinera*, p. 109).
[2] *Cf.* also the Mausoleum of David in the letter to Marcella (Migne, *P. L.*xxii., col. 208).
[3] Arculf in Geyer, p. 257.   [4] Geyer, *Itinera*, p. 26.
[5] Antoninus (*ibid.*, p. 178).   [6] Séjourné, *RB*, 1895, p. 430, with plan.

been ? Where was Jesse's family accustomed to make its
annual sacrifice (1 Sam. xx. 6) ? The spot where the church
of the Nativity now stands, just in front of what was the
eastern gate of the old city, must always have been a suitable
spot, for there was there a wide flat space and an open view
towards the desert. Apart from this, it must have been a
spot where the inhabitants of Bethlehem liked to foregather.
There would have been no temple, no altar there, but one
might expect a rock, on which, from ancient days, the blood
of the sacrificial animals was shed ; perhaps also one or more
sacred trees were there, providing shade at the sacrificial meals.
It is not mere fantasy thus to suggest that the sacrificial height
of Bethlehem was in the vicinity of the church of the Nativity ;
for Cyril of Jerusalem[1] in 350 mentions that " until lately "—
which would mean before the erection of the church of the
Nativity—the district of Bethlehem was wooded, so that the
" fields of the wood " in Ps. cxxxii. 6 (LXX) refer to it ; and
Jerome states :[2] " The Bethlehem belonging now to us . . .
was once shadowed by the grove of Thamuz, that is to say,
Adonis ; and in the grotto where once upon a time the Christ-
Child cried, the beloved of Venus used to be lamented."
Yew-trees (*Taxus baccata*), which were dedicated to Venus,
were not native to Palestine, so probably oak-trees are meant,
for they occur, even to-day, south of Arṭas and at *Wady 'Arrub*,
and, in the year 1613, even covered the mountains west of
'*en Saliḥ*.[3] They were removed when the church of the
Nativity was built.

The church which now rises south of old Bethlehem is one
of the oldest in the world ; it has been robbed of its porch,
its façade is disfigured by later patch-work, and it is so built
in by monasteries that one can survey it only from neighbouring roofs or towers. Of the original three entrance-
doors, only a small wicket-gate in the middle one remains,
which prevents the horses of the Moslems from entering, and
one has to stoop in order to enter. A vestibule, only recently
feebly lighted by a window, leads into the wide nave and
double aisles of the Basilica, which is curious in that it gets
its cruciform shape from the transept with apses at the end.
A further peculiarity consists in this, that the main nave is
prolonged beyond the transept, accompanied by the inner

[1] *Cat.* xii. (Migne, *P.G.* xxxiii., col. 173).
[2] *Ep.* lviii. (Migne, *P.L.* xxii., col. 321).
[3] Amman (*Reis ins Globte Land*, p. 71) saw there " a high and wooded
mountain."

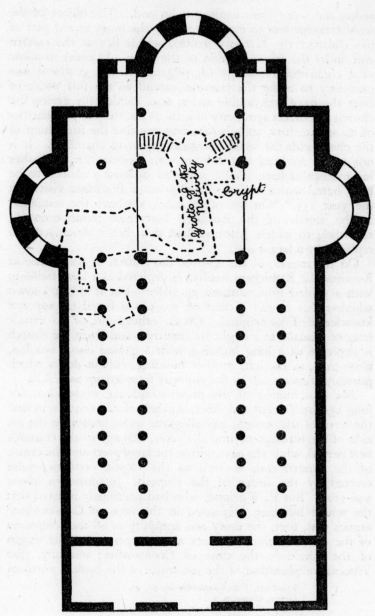

Plan of the Church of the Nativity, Bethlehem.

aisles, the outer ones coming to an end. The object of the wide transept was to expose to view the most sacred part of the church : the Nativity grotto, which lies at the eastern end under the raised portion of the nave. In order to allow of a comfortable passage for pilgrims to the grotto it was necessary to make the transept extend to the full width of both the nave and double aisles, thus incidentally giving the church its correct symmetry in spite of the various peculiarities of its architecture, and also making possible the furnishing of the choir with the usual liturgical adjoining chambers. It is not to be doubted that the emperor Constantine, or rather his mother Helena, in the year 326 ordered a church to be built here,[1] which church the pilgrim of Bordeaux visited in the year 333.[2] On the other hand, we have the statement in the annals of the Patriarch Eutychius (tenth century), according to which Justinian had this church destroyed and replaced by a larger one.

On the mosaic in the apse of the church of San Vitale at Ravenna the Bethlehem basilica is depicted as a long building with a gabled roof, without an aisle.[3] But it is not known whether this mosaic picture of 530-540 is based on any real knowledge of the original. On the other hand, of the mosaic map of Madaba this might be expected, and there the church is depicted as a long building with a gabled door, but has, close to it, to the left, another building without doors which possibly corresponds to the convent founded by St. Paula.

The examination of the present building, undertaken not long ago by Vincent and Abel, led them to the conviction that the nave of the church, including the outer angles on the far side of the transept beyond the nave, belongs to the church's first period, while the nave within the large piers and the centre of the eastern end, as well as the closed vestibule, were erected by the order of the emperor Justinian, in about 540-550.[4] But E. Weigand, who had previously insisted that the whole building originated in the time of Constantine,[5] argues that, first, the unity and antiquity of all the sculptures of the church, which Vincent also accepts, attest the origin of the whole in the time of Constantine ; secondly, that Vincent's explanation of the use made of the broken portions

---

[1] Eusebius, *Vita Constantini* iii. 41, 43.
[2] Geyer, *Itinera*, p. 25.
[3] Kraus, *Geschichte der christlichen Kunst* i., Fig. 336.
[4] Vincent and Abel, *Bethléem* (1914), p. 73.
[5] *Die Geburtskirche von Bethlehem* (1911).

of the original atrium in the altered building of Justinian
cannot be accepted ; and, lastly, that the supposed traces of
the reconstruction are not at all certain.[1] Hasak[2] finds a still
simpler solution of the riddle, namely that the building has
always had the present style of eastern end, for which parallels
can be found in *es-Suveda* and *Jerash*. According to him,
Justinian only built the transept, and added the apses as
vestibules.

The unity of the whole eastern end is a fact of which I
convinced myself afresh on November 26, 1921, and June 1,
1925. The same kind of walls of large stones, with layers
running through, continues from the apse over the projecting inner aisle to the furthest corner of the outer aisle. The
remnant supposed by Vincent to be a part of the east wall of
Constantine is as little discernible as is the supposed moulding-
wall of Justinian on the north-east corner, as can also be seen
in Vincent's illustration 26. The apses of the transept show
the same sort of wall as the eastern apses, so that even Hasak
could not have hit upon the right solution. In Weigand's
theory consideration of the missing connection between the
long nave and the narthex on the south side is omitted.
Perhaps the narthex was built as a substitute for the atrium,
after the latter had been destroyed. Only an examination of
the base of the building could lead to further progress. That
a still more exact survey of details than that carried out by
Vincent is necessary, is shown by the plan of the grotto of
the Holy Innocents by Mauritius Gisler, reproduced by
Weigand.[3] In any case, the Anakreontikon of Sophronius,
which dates from the year 610, refers to the building in its
present form :

> Subduing the excessive fervour of sacred love which
> would burn in my heart, I would straightway go to that
> little village of Bethlehem, wherein the Lord of all was
> born, and passing through a noble portico of four
> columns[4] into the midst of that most splendid triple
> vaulted building, I would dance for very joy. May
> Christ, who was born there, grant me the bliss of seeing
> the beauties of Bethlehem. As I viewed the close array
> of columns gleaming with gold, a delicately wrought
> work of art, I should escape the cloud of woe (which

[1] *ZDPV*, 1915, p. 89 ; 1923, p. 183.   [2] *Das heilige Land*, 1916, p. 19.
[3] *ZDPV*, 1923, p. 211.   [4] *I.e.* the Atrium.

now besets me) and, gazing up, view above me the
panelled roof which glitters like the stars of heaven,
for a grace as of the firmament shines forth from that
beauteous work.   I would visit the grotto wherein the
Virgin Queen of all brought forth the Saviour for all
mortal men, who was indeed both God and Man.   Upon
the famous floor whereon the Child God was placed, I
would press my eyes, my mouth, and my forehead, that
I might bear away from thence a blessing in my very
face, and in my heart the perpetual glory of His presence.
I would approach and adore the renowned manger, by
whose operation I, that was by nature weak and of no
account or worth, was granted the privilege of God's
Kingdom and His Word.   And thereafter would I enter
into the cave of the babes that were slain by the frantic
Herod's jealousy, when the Word became Flesh.[1]

According to this, the inner adornment of the church was
very similar to that of the Martyrion basilica of Constantine
in Jerusalem.   A gilded, panelled ceiling covered the now
ugly denuded rafters ; mosaics enlivened the wall-surface
below the windows ; the capitals of the pillars glittered with
golden radiance.   The adoration of the Magi was depicted
on the façade of the church—on the gable, it seems.   One of
the Magi is depicted as wearing Persian dress, and this fact
saved the church from destruction by the Persians in 614.[2]
The inner decoration, which in all probability goes back only
to the time of Justinian,[3] was renewed in Byzantine style
about 1169, in the time of the Crusaders.   The still existing
remnants and old inscriptions reveal its grandiose but peculiar
plan.   Upon the mosaics of the central nave both the Old
Testament and the Church pointed to Him who was born
in Bethlehem.   On the entrance-wall was a tree which grew
out of the sleeping Jesse.   From its branches the most
famous ancestors of Christ, as well as the prophets who
foretold of Him, looked out.   On the side-walls above the
pillars shone representations of our Lord's ancestors, those on
the right as according to St. Matthew, on the left as according
to St. Luke : above these were represented the most important

---

[1] Migne, *P.G.* lxxxvii. 3, p. 3812.
[2] See Vincent and Abel, *Bethléem*, p. 127.
[3] A document from the year 836 states, however, that Constantine demanded
for the basilica of Bethlehem a pictorial presentation of sacred events from the
Nativity to the Ascension, and of the miracles of the Apostles.   See Reil, *Die
altchristlichen Bildzyklen des Lebens Jesu,* p. 44.

Church councils with their resolutions, especially those apper-
taining to the Divine Nature of Christ and the dignity of His
Mother ; right above, between the windows, Angels soared.
Below, from the pillars, the saints of the Church—among them
king Canute of Denmark and king Olaf of Norway, their
stern countenances surrounded by halos—looked out upon
the faithful. To this accompaniment and after this preparation one entered the choir, where, on the walls, the development of the life of the God-man, promised in the Old Testament and believed in by the Church, was represented, from
the Birth to the Ascension.

All this splendour, now grown pale or entirely disappeared,
was, however, only of secondary importance compared with
the most sacred place of the Nativity, above which the choir
was built. It is reached by one of the two stairs which go
down under it from the north and the south. Costly lamps
give light here to a vaulted room, 42 feet long and 12 feet
broad, where at first we seek in vain the rock which should
form the manger. The walls, which are completely covered
by asbestos and marble, do not allow us to see what lies
behind. The ceiling is evidently of masonry. But a somewhat deeper side-room to the south, the so-called place of the
crib, is supposed to be recognisable in the rock,[1] and behind
the brick west wall is a narrow passage whose west and south
walls likewise are built of rock. One sees rock, certainly, in
this passage, and in an adjoining room further on also, to the
north of the grotto. It is therefore reasonable to assume
that it was originally a cave in the rock. Also its slope
towards the church gives colour to the assumption that there
was, if not an altogether natural cave, at least a room hewn
in rock. Willibald says that through the excavation of the
surrounding portion the ancient subterranean cave became
a " four-cornered house." Thus, as in the church of the
Annunciation in Nazareth, the hewn rock must have projected
over the floor of the church. An altar has been erected at
the east end, in a probably artificially built niche, under which
a star on the floor below was meant to indicate the exact
place of the Nativity. In the west and east other subterranean rooms are said to exist, of which, however, nothing
certain is known.[2] It is, above all, uncertain how the manger
was formed and where the original place was which led to it.

[1] Vincent and Abel, *Bethléem*, p. 79, denied by Tobler, *Bethlehem*, p. 151.
[2] Vincent and Abel, *ibid.*; Tobler, p. 151.

4

The so-called "Milk-grotto" which lies not far off in an eastern direction, the white chalk-stone of which is supposed to have miraculous properties, is entered from above. Usually one reaches such caves by a slope to the level; if the grotto had served as a stable, this would be a natural presupposition. Now, the church of the Nativity is situated on the upper edge of a northern slope, upon which the Franciscan monastery has been erected. Mounting a steep flight of steps from the vestibule of the church and taking the road downward to the east, the village Bet Saḥur is reached. Possibly this path, which now passes through the Franciscan grounds, originally ran up higher. The grotto which can be reached on the level, or by an easy climb from the north, has now many subterranean ramifications northward, which were perhaps laid out by the monks, for it is questionable whether it had them originally. If so, then there must have been here a simple, perhaps natural but artificially extended, grotto, of about the same size as the present one, before ever the church was built.

No one could discern in this former rocky chamber the place of the Nativity. The altar at the east end was perhaps not erected originally to designate the exact spot, although the background of the grotto would make it probable. Here also is the only remarkable feature in it, namely a small adjoining room which contains in the right wall a low niche resembling a manger. Now, according to the angelic message to the shepherds recorded in Lk. ii. 12, the manger was one of the signs of the Birthplace of the Christ-Child. Even before the erection of the church on this spot, Origen wrote, in the year 248 : "Should anyone desire still other proofs for the birth of Jesus in Bethlehem according to Micah's prophecy and the history described by the disciples in the Gospels, let him consider that, in harmony with the Gospel story of His Birth, a cave is shown in Bethlehem, where He was born, and the manger in the cave where He lay wrapped in swaddling clothes. And this is well known in those parts even by strangers to the Faith, namely that the Jesus who is revered and adored by Christians was born in this cave."[1] There were probably several caves near Bethlehem, but that just this particular one contained a manger was certainly considered significant. Even in the time of Jerome[2] the manger seemed

---

[1] *Contra Celsum* i. 51, following Justin.
[2] *Ep.* 46, 108, 147. See also Cyril of Jerusalem, *Cat.* x., and Antoninus Geyer, *Itinera*, pp. 127, 178.

to have been the proper place of veneration in the grotto. The first person to differentiate between the Birth-spot and the manger was Sophronius in the seventh century (*cf.* above, p. 35). He was followed in this by Arculf, in the same century.[1] The situation of the manger and the actual Birth-spot therefore require special attention.

Down two steps to the southward, through an opening supported by a pillar, is reached a low room, only about ten feet wide. On its east side an altar is erected, at the place where the adoration of the Magi was imagined to have taken place. A projection in the background is perhaps taken for the table at which the Virgin sat and ate with the Magi.[2] On the west side in a niche is a step covered with marble, in the centre of which a depression scarcely three feet wide and one foot broad, and almost open at the front, represents the place of the manger. According to the Latin Church, a wooden box stood within this space, the little boards of which are now kept in Rome as the actual manger of the Christ-Child.[3] But in a picture made in 1519[4] the step lacked the erection which encloses the apparent depression, and still earlier it was believed that the rock which actually forms the low step was the real manger, and pieces of it were taken to Constantinople and Rome. Jerome lamented that in his time a gold and silver manger had been substituted for the original one of clay, which he would have liked so much to have seen.[5] Thus even at that time the real manger could no longer be seen, but only a rocky step, of which it was thought that it had been made into a manger with clay to form the edges. This was removed at the erection of the church and a costly box of gold and silver substituted,[6] which, however, probably left the rocky floor of the manger visible. It was in its opening that Sabinianus put love-letters which his sweetheart was to find while she knelt there, for which Jerome reproaches him (*Ep.* 14). About 1172 the rocky step was covered with marble, but three holes in this covering made it still possible to kiss the rock of the manger.[7] At

[1] Geyer, *Itinera*, p. 256.   [2] Petrus Diaconus (Geyer, *Itinera*, p. 111).
[3] In the church Beata Maria ad Præsepe. Acknowledged as genuine by Dusterwald, *Der Jerusalems-pilger*, p. 329. Rejected by Vincent and Abel, *Bethléem*, p. 135.
[4] RB, 1913, in front of p. 261. But *cf.* Bernardino Amico, *Trattato delle Piante ed Immagini de sacri Edifizi di Terra santa* (1620), p. 10.
[5] Dom Morin, *Anecdota Maredsolana* iii. 2, p. 393.
[6] Still mentioned by Antoninus.   [7] Theoderich, ed. Tobler, p. 79.

present even this is not any longer possible. To us, a niche in the wall of a cave would not appear to be the manger, but in Palestine the manger (Aram. *orya*, Arab. *medwad*) is never a wooden box on feet, as depicted so often in Nativity pictures. Horses and donkeys are fed in the open air from a bag (Arab. *michlaye*) on the head, or simply by throwing the food before them on the ground. In stables for donkeys, cows, etc., the food is put into a flat trough, made of clay mixed with straw, or sometimes of stones cemented with mud. More rarely a niche with a deepened floor is built into the wall for the purpose. Old mangers built in this fashion in the rocky walls are found in Palestine in *'Arak el-Emir*,[1] *Der'a*,[2] *en-Neby Samwel*,[3] and *Khirbet Dustrey*.[4] Of these the last-mentioned date only from the Middle Ages. But that in *'Arak el-Emir*, on the rock of which is the name Tobia, probably the one mentioned in 2 Macc. iii. 11 (200 B.C.),[5] undoubtedly dates from pre-Christian times. Together with the manger fastened to the ground there is another manger known to Jewish Law, which is a moveable vessel, for which a bag can be used and which is occasionally fastened to the wall.[6] When we read of a splinter taken from a manger being used for cleaning teeth,[7] it does not refer to the material of which the manger is made, but to its contents. A stiff bit of straw would serve as a tooth-pick. Large cattle were fastened to the wall of the stables where the manger was on the floor.[8] So there is nothing unusual in the rocky niche with the simple manger in the grotto at Bethlehem, and one can also consider the deeper level of the adjoining room as being archæologically correct if the grotto itself was intended to be used as a dwelling-place and the adjoining room meant to be the stable for animals, especially for donkeys.

St. Paula was thinking of this place when she wrote in about 400 to Marcella : " With what words, with what voice, can we describe the Saviour's cave ? And that manger where the Babe cried is to be honoured more by deep silence than by feeble speech. Behold, in this small hole in the earth the Founder of the heavens was born, here was He wrapped in swaddling clothes, here seen by the shepherds, here shown by the star, here worshipped by the wise men, and this place, I

[1] *PJB*, 1908, p. 128.   [2] See plan in Guthe's *Bibelwörterbuch*, p. 141.

[3] *ZDPV*, 1918, p. 127.   [4] *PJB*, 1908, p. 17.

[5] *Cf.* Dalman, *PJB*, 1920, p. 33.   [6] Kel. xx. 4 ; Sab. 140b.

[7] Tos. Yomtob iii. 18.   [8] Gen. R. xx. (43b).

think, is holier than the Tarpeian rock, where the traces of its having been frequently struck by lightning show that it displeases the Lord."[1]

However, emotions are not of any value in deciding the question whether this grotto was actually the place of the Nativity. The Gospel of St. Luke says (ii. 7) that Mary laid her firstborn in a manger "because they had no room in the inn." This is not to be understood to mean merely that there was no room for the child; but that the inn in which they could have found lodging lacked a suitable room for the birth, as well as a suitable bed for the Babe, so that they had to leave the inn and find refuge in a crib in a stable. In the sign given to the shepherds in verse 12 this is hinted at, but is not expressed clearly. The narrative would have been clearer if it had run: "She brought forth her first-born son in a stable (or a cave), since they had no suitable place in the inn." But it must be admitted that in the East, where mangers are built into the floor or into the wall, manger and stable may mean the same thing. In the East to-day the dwelling-place of man and beast is often in one and the same room. It is quite the usual thing among the peasants for the family to live, eat, and sleep on a kind of raised terrace (Arab. *mastaba*) in the one room of the house, while the cattle, particularly donkeys and oxen, have their place below on the actual floor (*Ka' el-Bet*) near the door; this part sometimes is continued along under the terrace as a kind of low vault.[2] On this floor the mangers are fixed, either to the floor, or to the wall, or at the edge of the terrace. But this is not how the Evangelist conceived it to have been; he imagines that the manger was outside the inn, that is to say, in some particular stable, such as are used to-day for camels, sometimes, but more rarely for sheep. He takes it for granted that the stable was empty, as would be natural during the time when sheep spent the night in the open. In it must be imagined a manger up on the wall, which was to do duty as a crib for the Babe. It must be remembered that the Palestinian country folk know nothing of bedsteads, but their nightly couch is spread every evening anew upon the terrace of the house. It would hardly do to lay sucklings in this same fashion on the floor, where they would be in danger of being trodden on by men and beasts, and where it would be difficult to keep them clean.

[1] Jerome, Ep. XLVI; Migne, *P.L.* xxii., col. 207.
[2] *Cf.* K. Jaeger, *Das Bauernhaus in Palästina* (1912), p. 24.

They are wrapped firmly in swaddling-clothes so that they cannot move, in order that their limbs should grow straight[1] —as described in Lk. ii. 7, 12—then the child is laid in the only bed the house contains—a small wooden cradle (Arab. *serir*). A frequent changing of the baby is considered to be neither necessary nor useful. That the cradle should be rocked was customary even at that time.[2] According to a Jewish legend this rocking originated in the family of Abraham.[3] The construction of the cradle with high curved sides gives protection to the child from flies as well as from light and sun. Even " on the cradle of a royal baby flies would settle," and the nurse's duty was to drive them away.[4] The cradle is made light in weight, and so is portable, in order that the mother can carry it about with her to her work, even to the fields. The antiquity of this piece of furniture (its frame is that which is really referred to in rabbinic literature)[5] can be seen from the already mentioned legend that it was invented in the house of Abraham, and its popularity from Mishna Nidda iv. 1, where " from the cradle up " was then a common phrase as it is among us.

When we are told that Mary's Babe lay in a manger, it is as much as to say that He did not enjoy the advantages or comforts usual to babies, because it is evident that His birth did not take place in a human habitation, but in a stable. The peculiar couch of the new-born Child was due to the circumstance that his parents were on a journey and had no home in the strange place. When we have realised the position it is easy to understand that the real difficulty consisted not so much in the finding of a place for the Child, as of finding an undisturbed place for the Birth. The inn (κατάλυμα, *bet mashreja*) was for the narrator merely a place at which the parents had arrived. If the inn was a private house, it would be impossible to drive the family of the owner out. Anyone who has lodged with Palestinian peasants knows that notwithstanding their hospitality the lack of privacy is unspeakably painful. One cannot have a room to oneself, and one is never alone by day or by night. I myself often fled into the open simply in order to be able to think. At a birth alone is it customary to empty the house of its inhabitants. This

---

[1] J. Preuss, *Bibl. talmud. Medizin*, p. 468. The " wrapping in swaddling clothes " is referred to already in Ezek. xvi. 4.

[2] The Arabic cradles are made for rocking, but neither the Arabic designation (*serir, mahd*) nor the Hebrew (*'arisa*) means more than simply " bed."

[3] Gen. R. liii. (113b).   [4] Gen. R. lxix. (148b).   [5] Tos. Sab. xiii. 15.

consideration Mary could not expect, even at a proper inn. To judge by present-day conditions such an inn in a small place would be the spot in which the villagers and their kith and kin practise hospitality in common, or even themselves meet in the evenings. Such a guest-house (Arab. *medafe*) is a public place, where one has no right to be alone. A caravansary (*khan*), as is used on the great roads for night-lodgings, is scarcely to be taken into consideration in this case. In these the rooms for persons and animals surround an enclosed court, and nowadays, when they are well arranged, there are, apart from the stables on the ground floor, on the upper floor little empty rooms which can be hired; but often, again, only big common rooms with which all travellers have to be content.[1] Even if in the Gospel such a *khan* is meant, there would not have been a special room for the Birth. But just in such a case the stable would have been inside the inn premises. If the manger in Lk. ii. 7 is to be taken as having been outside the inn, the question as to its situation would be solved, if it were in a cave. The possibility cannot entirely be excluded that St. Luke harmonised a narrative concerning the Child in the manger with an account of His having been born in a cave, adding the interpolated remark concerning the inn which had no room for His Mother. A more distinct harmonisation of the various accounts is made by Pseudo-Matthew, when in xiii. 1 *f.* it records the Birth in the cave in Bethlehem, and in chapter xiv. makes Mary on the third day move into a stable, where the Child is put in a manger; and again in chapter xv. 1 makes her move on the sixth day into the city of Bethlehem. In this way we gain from Luke's narrative a reasonable support for the manger as the Child's bed, or, at most, a suggestion of the cave which, as a characteristic of the place of the Nativity, might have been explicitly mentioned. It is the Palestinian Justin who first, like the apocryphal Gospels, speaks of a grotto; but he, most likely, thought of the cave, east of Bethlehem, which is still shown, if, as according to him, Joseph had to be content with a cave lying outside Bethlehem because he could not find a lodging in the village.[2] Justin saw in this a fulfilment of the prophecy concerning the righteous King who should dwell in the high cave of a mighty rock (Isa. xxxiii. 16, LXX). This

---

[1] There would have been a reference to an inn by Bethlehem in Jer. xli. 17, if *gerut* did not originally refer to a threshing-floor.

[2] *Dial. c. Tryph.* lxxviii. 5.

was the cave then which in the time of Origen (248) was considered with certainty to have been the place of the Nativity.

We have therefore to accept it as an established fact that
in about the year 100 the two accounts were current in the
Church concerning the place of the Nativity. According to
the one it took place in a stable ; according to the other this
stable was a cave, which the local tradition located east of the
old city, thus being in harmony with the Lukan narrative, as
it seemed natural that Joseph, after searching in vain for a
lodging at the other end of the town, had to turn to a cave.
In the Western reading where " cave " is substituted for
" manger," the cave tradition also finally found a place in
the Gospel of St. Luke.

Now, in such a land as Palestine, rich in caves, where, outside the villages, easily accessible caves are used regularly for
animals, the two accounts are not far apart. Hence there
can be no real question of a contradiction between the old cave
tradition of Bethlehem and the Lukan account.

In the fourth century, however, it was said that the venerated
cave of Bethlehem had once been disgracefully desecrated ;
for Jerome (cf. above) and Paulinus of Nola mention in their
letters in the year 400 that the emperor Hadrian had established the worship of Adonis there. This must have happened
in the year 137. Some scholars think that the worship
of the god of annually dying vegetation was the original
worship in this spot, and that the Christians had substituted
Christ for Adonis. From what has been said on page 32,
it is possible that the place on the eastern hill may actually
have been an ancient sanctuary, but knowing primitive
Palestinian Christianity as we do, we can be sure that the fact
of ancient Tammuz-worship being associated with the spot
would have made them avoid designating that cave as the
Birthplace of the Saviour. The accounts of Origen and Cyril
(cf. above, pp. 32, 38) do not sound as though the place of
the Nativity had once been the abode of a pagan cult. Justin
Martyr,[1] at any rate, was convinced that the Nativity grotto
in Bethlehem was the proper fulfilment of the prophetic
description of the righteous King dwelling in a rocky cave,
while the caves of the Mithras mysteries and the supposed
birth of Mithras from a rock were a caricature of truth. It is
also possible that St. Luke intentionally refrained from mentioning the cave, in order that the Birth of the Saviour in a

[1] *Dial. c. Tryph.* lxxviii. ; *cf.* LXX.

cave should not seem to the heathen to be merely another
myth.

The most ancient local tradition out of which the church
of Bethlehem grew is, after all, not necessarily authentic, but
yet it may quite well have hit upon the truth. The grotto
under the church, which, with its manger, originally stood
outside Bethlehem, is not necessarily the exact spot where
Christ was born. But, at any rate, a hundred years after the
Crucifixion, it is with the city of David that the mystery of
His Birth was connected and, at the same time, it is the oldest
firmly established place of His veneration, out of which
veneration the Feast of the Nativity as such originated. There
is evidence that the ancient Church festival of the Nativity
was celebrated here on January 6 by the Christian community of Jerusalem in the fourth century, the feast being
solemnly observed at night on the evening of January 5,
and followed by a procession, with the Bishop at its head,
to the church of the Nativity, which was richly furnished
with gold-embroidered silk curtains and numerous candles.
And during the night the worshippers returned again to
Jerusalem, in order to continue the festivities for a whole
week in the church of the Resurrection and the Martyrion,
while in Bethlehem the local monks had to celebrate the feast
alone.[1] In the ninth century there was also a Christmas
celebration in the church of the Nativity on December 25,
while on January 5, in the afternoon, the festival took place
at the " Shepherds' Field," and then, on the 6th, early in the
morning, was brought to a close in the church of the Nativity.[2]

The Lukan narrative of the shepherds (ii. 8 f.) " abiding
in the open[3] and keeping watch over their flocks by night "
had its settled location, at the latest, soon after the erection
of the church in Bethlehem. St. Paula broke her journey to
Bethlehem, about the year 400, in order to go down to the
tower of Ader, not far from Bethlehem, where " the shepherds
were found worthy to hear the *Gloria in excelsis Deo*."[4] In
the year 670 Arculf found, in the East, a church with the
graves of " the three shepherds who, just in this neighbour-

[1] Etheria in Geyer, *Itinera*, p. 75 f.; *cf.* Pseudo-Chrysostom (Migne lxiv.,
p. 43 f.), and Hall, *Sitzungsberichte der K. pr. Ak. d. W.*, 1917, p. 405.
[2] Baumstark, *Nichtevangel. syr. Perikopen* (1921), pp. 119, 148. That on the
second day of Christmas the Jews from all Palestine gathered together at the
grave of Jacob and David, is stated by Antoninus (Geyer, *Itinera*, pp. 119, 148).
[3] Greek: ἀγραυλοῦντες, Pal. Syriac *mebitin betura* (*turaya*).
[4] Jerome, *Peregrinatio Paulæ*.

hood, were surrounded with the Glory of the Lord."[1] From
an unknown source Petrus Diaconus makes mention of a
big garden, surrounded by walls, containing a cave in which
was an altar purporting to commemorate the spot where the
Angel appeared to the shepherds.[2] The hegumenos Daniel,
in the year 1106, describes the position more precisely : " A
verst from the place of the Nativity towards the east, at the
foot of the mountain, in the midst of the plain," he saw, above
a grotto, the ruins of a church of St. Joseph ; the plain with
fertile fields and olive-groves was called ἄγια ποίμνα (ποίμνια),
i.e. " Shepherds' Fields."[3] The shrine of the Shepherds'
Grave had become a church of St. Joseph. Guarmani, in
1859, believed that he had found the shrine of the Shepherds
on a hill about a mile and a half below Bethlehem in an easterly
direction, in Khirbet el-Esjar. H. Zschokke[4] in 1867 (without
personal examination), the Franciscan Meistermann,[5] and also
Klameth,[6] all considered this a proved fact, but I seriously
doubt it.[7] We certainly do find ruins of old buildings there,
also a cave which was perhaps used as a stable, and cisterns
and ditches ; but nothing which could be said to match, in
any striking manner, the pilgrims' descriptions of the church
of the Shepherds. The supposed foundation of a " Tower
of Flocks " is a wine press ; the supposed grave of the three
shepherds is a cistern with steps into it ; the three-aisled
church discovered is probably but a part of the monastery
itself. It is possible that Khirbet el-Esjar is the monastery in
which Posidonius lodged in the year 400—" beyond the
Shepherds' monastery."[8] But the monastery of the Shepherds
must have been, according to the description of Daniel, whose
knowledge of Greek tradition must be taken for granted,
" Eastward of the place of the Nativity, at the foot of the
mountain, in the midst of the plain," that is to say, that which
the Greeks and Latins at present show as the Keniset er-
Ra'wat, the " church of the Shepherds."

It is possible to get there from Bethlehem in half an hour,

---

[1] Geyer, Itinera, p. 258.   [2] Ibid., p. 109 f.
[3] Khitrovo, Itinéraires Russes, p. 41.
[4] Österr. Vierteljahrschrift für kath. Theologie 1867, p. 617 f.
[5] New Guide to the Holy Land, p. 330.
[6] Neutestamentliche Lokaltraditionen Palästinas.
[7] PJB, 1911, p. 10 ; 1913, p. 11.
[8] Klameth, p. 55, note 2. Probably it was the monastery mentioned by
Cyrill Scythop—namely, that of Marcianus. Otherwise, according to Joh.
Moschus, there was also, two miles from Bethlehem, the monastery of St. George
with the designation ξηροπόταμος, which does not fit in with this, however.

taking an eastern direction, below the hill of *Khirbet el-Esjar*, in the middle of the afore-mentioned little cultivated plain. Now *Wady el-Khirbeh* is a considerable olive-grove which is divided off from the fields by tumbledown walls. In it is a low hill of rubbish, which may well conceal the remains of a little church and monastery. Under the *débris* is a sub-terranean vault arranged as if for Greek worship, which, according to Tobler,[1] measures from 20 to 30 ft.

The objection that the shepherds would scarcely have lain on that or any night in the midst of a plain of cultivated fields with their flocks is certainly justified, especially if the olive-grove sprang up only after the monastery was built, so that originally there were only such fields here.[2] Above, on the height of *el-Esjar*, the position seems to be more feasible. Yet it must not be forgotten that Palestinian fields are always used by the flocks in the summer as pasturage, because the sheep are made to graze the stubble bare the while they manure the land. In the winter this could only be the case while the fields are still unploughed. But the reference is not to pasture-land, but to a place where shepherds could spend the night in the open with their flocks ; such a place often lies far from the grazing-places. With us it is natural to think of the herds being only so far from home that at night they can easily return. But in Palestine grazing ground is not thus limited. The rule is that sheep and goats are taken for pasture- and sleeping-place far from the village, while just a cow or so is kept at home to yield milk for the family. Jewish law distinguishes between " pasture cattle " and " domestic cattle," and the question is asked whether animals left out the whole year, or only between Easter and the first rain, are entitled to the first designation ; or whether it is necessary, in order to acquire the second designation, to stay in the stable at night, or whether only staying within the Sabbath boundary is needful ; and, finally, whether staying out at night, but being driven into the township as twilight falls, is meant.[3] This passing of the night in the open takes place especially when several shepherds with their flocks unite for the purpose, without any arrangements for protection. The

---

[1] *Bethlehem*, p. 253.
[2] Meistermann asserts that here stood a Ruth monastery, *Der er-Raut* (more correctly *Der Ra'ut*), the ruins of which were erroneously turned into *Der-er-Ra'wat*, "shepherds' convent." But there is no tradition concerning a Ruth convent. The ancestress of David was no example for nuns.
[3] Beza v. 7 ; Tos. Bez. iv. 11.

shepherds then sleep in their clothes in the midst of their flocks. This way of spending the night is called in Arabic *haddsham* ; the place thereof *mehdsham*. Individual shepherds prefer to use a rough, round, stone rampart for their flocks, protected at the top edge with thorns, and for themselves a sleeping-place with a small semicircular wall for protection against the west wind. But in the rainy season they do not mind going a long way in order to reach a cave, or at least a semi-grotto (*shkaf*), the wide entrance of which they bar by means of a dry clay wall. Such a place is called *me'zab*, and the verb is *'azzab*. Occasionally the watch-tower of a fruit-garden also has an enclosure round it, into which the sheep are driven at night. Movable wooden hurdles, such as Luther uses in his translation of the Bible, are unknown in Palestine, which is poor in wood. In any case it is imperative to give the sheep, and still more the goats, who are more affected by the cold, the best possible protection against the chilly night wind ; sometimes a resting-place for the night may be found, although not without much trouble, on the mountain-heights. The time of the year is not without importance in regard to the choice of a place. From the beginning of October the nightly cold and the dew increase and it is not desirable to sleep in the open. The proverb says " *aiyid u-itla'salib u-a'ber*," " celebrate Easter and move (to sleep) out !—Celebrate the Feast of the Cross (14th September) and move in (do not sleep in the open) !"—and : " *ba'd 'id es-salib-la tamin es-shib*," " after the Feast of the Cross—do not trust the dew (because it begins to be heavy) !" Also : " *fi kanun-kinn 'and ahlak ya madshnun*," " In Kanun (December-January) remain at home, thou madman !" But the shepherd is able to find places which afford a certain amount of protection, until, about December, the torrential winter rains begin, when he is obliged either to return to the village, or to move into a warmer neighbourhood where green pasture grows more quickly than above on the mountains, where cold, and occasionally even snow, retard the growth of vegetation. A district such as this Bethlehem had in the neighbouring Judæan desert. The low-lying shepherds' plain must be taken as the place nearest to Bethlehem where scarcely any snow falls in winter,[1] and where in the case of need flocks can

---

[1] Richen, *Das heilige Land*, 1910, p. 23 *f.*, states that in Bethlehem snow is rare on December 24, but less than an hour east from there no snow falls at all. This agrees with my own experience : In Wady el Far'a, about six miles north-east of Jerusalem, snow never falls.

remain at night in the open ; for the great drop in temperature which sometimes occurs in the winter generally makes itself felt only after Christmas. St. Luke did not think of winter in his narrative, but it is clear that the place chosen by tradition corresponds to his purpose.

There were, however, no such general considerations for the choice of the "Shepherds' Field." At the Tower of the Flock (Migdal Eder) the "Shepherds' Field " was found. Of it Jerome says in the *Onomasticum* : " About a thousand paces away (from Bethlehem) is the tower Ader, which, being interpreted, means 'The Tower of the Flock,' which, through a certain prophecy predicted in advance, pointed to the fact that the shepherds should receive the knowledge of the Birth of the Lord." Jerome, in fact, held that this locality was the Migdal Eder beyond which Jacob, according to Gen. xxxv. 21, pitched his tent.[1] Later it was believed that the foundations of Jacob's house could be discerned nearby.[2] But Jerome thought above all of Micah iv. 8, according to which the old kingdom of the daughter of Zion should come to the " Flock-tower." This, he thought, was fulfilled when the Birth of the new King was proclaimed for the first time at the " Tower of the Flock." A Jewish tradition also designates the Migdal Eder as " the place from which the Messiah will be revealed at the end of the days."[3] The " Tower of the Flock " was therefore the appropriate place for the shepherds on that night. There was a locality which was known by that name at that time in the plain below Bethlehem. The Mishna (Shekalim vii. 4) refers to Migdal Eder as a boundary place in connection with an unclaimed animal fit for sacrificial purposes. "An animal found between Jerusalem and Migdal Eder, if it be a male must be brought as a burnt-offering ; if a female, as a peace-offering." Evidently, this Migdal Eder, which, according to Gen. xxxv. 21, must be sought in the south, was considered to be the point where the environs of Jerusalem definitely ceased and the pasture-land began. Within this point it is generally held that such an animal must have run away from the Temple precincts, where it was intended for sacrifice. Beyond this limit normal conditions obtain. At the same time it is pointed out in the same Mishna that Migdal Eder is only mentioned as an example,

[1] *Quæst. hebr.* on *Gen.* xxxv. 21.
[2] Petrus Diaconus, according to Geyer, *Itinera*, p. 111, where *Cades* is corrected to *Gader*.
[3] Targum J. i ; Gen. xxxv. 21. This is certainly founded on Micah iv. 8, but the Targum refers Migdal Eder to the Messiah as the Hidden one.

" according to the measure thereof—the same law pertains to all
points (*i.e.* of distance from Jerusalem)." Perhaps Migdal
Eder is specially mentioned as an example because even its
name suggests that the pasture-land for the flocks began just
here.[1] According to Jewish law, however, the desert is
exclusively the pasture-land for small cattle.[2] Large cattle
only are allowed to graze on cultivated land; the smaller cattle
are only permitted to do so for a limited time for the requirements of the slaughterers, and for weddings and pilgrimage
festivals.[3] It is not at all improbable that the ploughed land
of the little plain, bordering on the territory of the nomads, on
which, maybe, Ruth gleaned corn (Ruth ii. 2 *f.*), was protected
by a tower, around which a village eventually grew.

No conclusion can be drawn from all this as to the Migdal
Eder of Gen. xxxv. 21. That Jacob had his tents beyond it,
and not in it, looks as if a district had then begun to grow up
which was suitable to house the many flocks of the Patriarch,
while the place itself could not be used for this purpose. One
would be inclined to seek it, preferably, on the Hebron road,
where also the Migdal Eder of Jewish tradition could be placed.
But it would hardly do to disagree with the testimony of Jerome.
It is only from the fifteenth century onward that we find, in
literature, Jacob's house placed on the Bethlehem road, probably at *eṭ-Ṭanṭur*.[4]

This affixing of the " Shepherds' Field " to Migdal Eder has
thus a background in fact. But it does not follow that
the shepherds' experience of Lk. ii. took place just on this
spot. The interpretation of Micah iv. 8, according to which
the remote flock-tower east of Bethlehem was to be enwrapt
with the Messianic glory, can have no evidential value for us.
The shepherds' vision may have taken place in any of the other
valleys round about Bethlehem. But as we have no clue to
guide us, fellowship is not to be despised with the thousands
of Christians who, since the fourth century, have listened in
spirit with contemplation and longing to the Christmas hymn
of the Angels here among the olive-groves of the church of
the Shepherds.

[1] This does not exclude the possibility that originally the place was called
after a man with the name of " Eder " (1 Chr. xxiii. 23).
[2] Bab. K. vii. 7; Tos. Bab. K. viii. 10.
[3] Tos. Bab. K. viii. 11, 12; b. Bab. K, 79b.
[4] Tobler, *Topographie von Jerusalem* 11, p. 637. Johannes Poloner (1421) in
Tobler, *Descriptiones Terræ Sanctæ*, p. 247, is probably the earliest witness. But
he places there Jacob's struggle with the Angel.

On Christmas Eve in the year 1912, a silent little company of people set off in procession from Bethlehem to the " Shepherds' Field." It was the German Evangelical Community of Jerusalem. We had first visited the Nativity-grotto, which we did not find thronged for the festival. We did not dare to break the reverent silence which seemed to fill the grotto with a joyous Christmas song. Then we descended the hill in the twilight. The way which leads past outside the village *Bet Sahur* was not always easy to recognise, but at last we reached the plain which was carpeted by the bright green of the young seed, and we turned in at the tumbledown gate of the olive-garden of the church of the Shepherds. We halted at its ruin-crowned hill. Round about us stood the silent olive-trees ; in the glades between their deep, dark masses, a few small lights twinkled from afar on the height in the west. There were stars in the sky, but in the east clouds covered the horizon. A piece of candle which I discovered in my pocket was put in a niche of the old church wall and there made a vain effort to dispel the darkness. No bright light of a Christmas tree, and no divine brightness of heaven opened, spread around this small assemblage of Christians. The proclamation of the Gospel and the joyous hymn of praise alone broke the prevailing silence. These also presently faded away. The festive sounds of a lonely bugle recalled the " still, holy night," as we made our way home. Above, on the road to Jerusalem, we looked back. The moon rose above the clouds in the east. Its full light lay upon the city of the Nativity and the " fields of the Shepherds."

Peace on earth ! And yet, the second Christmas after this, the Bethlehem road became a military road. He who then blew the bugle was killed in the war. As so often since the murder of the Innocents, shrill discords drown the song of Bethlehem. Yet it rings on. . . .

Bethlehem, the city of the northern frontier of Judah, and the western boundary of the desert pasture-land, gave Israel, in the time of the Philistine wars, a powerful and yet humane leader, whose outstanding characteristic was that he considered himself to have been the servant of God. His actions seem insignificant in the history of antiquity. But from the narratives concerning him who was anointed in Bethlehem grew the expectation of a Prince, whose counsel was to be wonderful, whose power heroic, whose fatherly goodness has no end, and whose rule means peace (Isa. ix. 5). Within the compass of

such an expectation the last great Bethlehemite appeared indeed
as the rightful successor to David, but yet as merely a Babe in
the manger, not inheriting his earthly dominion or accepting
his conception of kingship.   Yet the cause of peace on earth
is hopeless unless this powerless Child becomes Lord.

That the foster-father of Jesus sprang, as a descendant of
David, from the Judæan Bethlehem, is taken for granted in
Mt. (i. 1, 16) and Lk. (i. 32 ; iii. 23).   The Mother of Jesus is
designated as a relation of an Aaronite woman (Lk. i. 36,
cf. verse 5).   If Mary was not also the daughter of a priest, it
is to be assumed that her mother was an Aaronite, and in that
case she herself also sprang from a respected Judæan family.
Also the Baraita concerning the Galilæan seats of all the priestly
orders shows, although it probably refers to the time after the
destruction of Jerusalem,[1] in what close relationship with
priestly families Galilee was thought to have stood.   The
priestly order Abia, to which Zacharias belonged, had its seat,
according to this account, in Kephar Uzziel, which S. Klein
is inclined to look for in *Khirbet Lueziyeh*,[2] but is rather to be
found in *Umm el-'Amad*, east of the *Battof* plain.[3]   But Nazareth
was also considered to be a priestly seat (see Chapter III).
Thus there are various possibilities for Mary's priestly
relationships.
In any case, Mary stood in such a close personal connection
with the priestly daughter and wife, Elisabeth, that she was
moved to entrust her with the mystery of the predicted birth.
Thus she came, in passing, to Judæa before she brought forth
her First-born in Bethlehem.   In Lk. i. 39, it is stated that she
went into a " hill-country " ($\epsilon i \varsigma \ \tau \grave{\eta} \nu \ \dot{o} \rho \epsilon \iota \nu \acute{\eta} \nu$[4]) into a city of
Judah, in order to visit Elisabeth, the wife of the priest Zacha-
rias.   No Galilæan would have spoken in such a general
way of a " hill-country," living as he did in a mountainous
country himself.   Writing for readers unfamiliar with the
land, St. Luke would have had to say " into the hill-land of
Judah."   If the text is not corrupt, it can only be justified
from the point of view of a Jerusalemite.   Such an one could
speak generally of " the mountainous country," as, in Neh.
viii. 15, the people from the Judæan cities and from Jerusalem

---

[1] See *PJB*, 1922-23, pp. 81, 89 ; Klein, *Palästina-Studien*, i., p. 52.
[2] *Beiträge*, p. 52.   [3] *PJB*, 1913, p. 49.
[4] Ev. Hier., AC, has in literal translation *turayta*, B simply *tura*, " the mountain."

go forth "into the mount" (*hahar*), and as in the Protevangelium of James, Mary and Joseph go for a little while
"into the mount" (ἡ ὀρεινή, xvi. 2), and Elisabeth and her
child also go forth there, where a cleaving rock protects them
from the machinations of Herod (xxii. 3 *f.*). The usage appears
also in the flight of the Judæans into "the mountains"
(Mt. xxiv. 16; Mk. xiii. 14; Lk. xxi. 21), and probably presupposes that the district of Jerusalem was called instead of
ἡ ὀρεινὴ Ἱερουσαλήμ, simply ἡ ὀρεινή, as Pliny has it.[1]   Among
the Jews this district was called in Hebrew *Har ha-Melekh*,[2]
in Aramaic *Tur Malka*,[3]—*i.e.*, Royal Mount.   In Judæa the
division was between "Mount" (*har*) and "hill-land" (*shephela*)
and "deep plain" (*'emek*).[4]   Perhaps in Jerusalem there was
also a distinction between the "mountain-land" and the
"desert" in the east, at the slope of the mountains, so that it
designated only the country west of the watershed, which is
cut asunder by both great northern side-branches of the *Bittir*
valley into three cross-running mountain-chains.   It is therefore a hinterland, poor in great lines of intercommunication,
through which the present thoroughfare to Jaffa makes a way
for itself only with difficulty.   In olden times this district,
which belonged to Kirjath Jearim, was, according to Neh.
viii. 15, well wooded, which was also the case in the Middle
Ages,[5] and even to-day it exhibits some remnants of forest.[6]
Such a region was well suited to serve as a hiding-place for
Elisabeth (Lk. i. 24), but also as a place of concealment for
those who fled from Herod (see above).   In this way it can be
understood why the Church tradition since the sixth century
pointed to *'Ain Karim*, about three and a half miles west from
Jerusalem, as the place where Elisabeth hid,[7] for it lies hidden
in a basin-like hollow.   Elisabeth's lodging and the birthplace of John the Baptist were placed, in the time of the pilgrim
Daniel (1106), in a cave near the village which is shown now in
the church of St. John; the hiding-place from Herod in a
grotto west of it, the other side of the valley, now in the crypt
of the so-called "church of the Visitation."   "The Hermits'

[1] *Hist. Nat.* v. 14, 70; *cf.* Jos., *Bell. Jud.* iii, 3, 5.
[2] p. Shebi 38d; Tos. Sheb. vii. 10, it is expressly said: "What is the mountainous country of Judah?   It is the mountain of the King."
[3] b. Gittin 55b, 57a.   [4] Shebi. ix. 2.
[5] Daniel (Khitrovo), p. 51; Theoderich (Tobler), p. 86.   Mukaddasi testifies
of abundance of oaks in *Nebi Samwel*.   See Schwarz ZDPV, 1918, p. 157 *f.*
[6] *PJB*, 1921, p. 97 *f.*
[7] Theodosius (Geyer, p. 140); *Commemor. de casis Dei*, Tobler, p. 79; and
Epiphanius Hagiopolita, Migne, *P.G.* cxx., col. 264.

Spring," lying about one and a half miles farther west, would
have been a suitable place for the upbringing of the child,[1] who,
according to Lk. i. 80, seemed to have grown up in the desert.
Beyond the mountain, which covered '*Ain Karim* farther west,
it was thought that John would be safe from the plots of the
suspicious king.

After all this there is no need to consider with Reland and
Zahn the priestly city Jutta (Josh. xxi. 16), now *Jatta*, as being
" the city of Judah " referred to in Lk. i. 39, especially as the
priestly towns of the Book of Joshua had (in spite of the
doubtful record of Neh. xi. 20) hardly any practical importance in the time of our Lord, and Jutta then lay in Edomitic
territory. Late Church tradition has mentioned apart from
'*Ain Karim*, Jerusalem, Hebron, and Bethlehem as the birthplace of the Baptist.[2] Hebron (and Bethlehem) were probably
taken into consideration because the place was thought to have
been one which, more than any other, deserved the designation
" city of Judah," and in comparison Nazareth stood on higher
ground. Hebron, being a priestly city, had a first claim. Among
the places in which priestly families lived, and which are known
through rabbinic literature, is Beth Zebaim (Zeboim),[3] which
Klein identifies with Ṣuba, west of '*Ain Karim*.[4] The hiding-
place of Elisabeth could be distinguished in this case from the
birthplace of John. Epiphanius Hagiopolita places the latter
in Bethlehem, but speaks at the same time of the patrimony of
the Baptist on the Carmelion mountain, west from Jerusalem,
by which he certainly means '*Ain Karim*.[5] There the matter
must rest : by ἡ ὀρεινή is meant the mountainous district near
Jerusalem, just as also the nurse who meets Joseph on the road
to Bethlehem comes, according to the Protevangelium of
James, ch. xix, from the " mountain-land " (ὀρεινή). And
the Biblical style predominating in Lk. i. and ii. is the reason
why the unknown city is not called " a city of *Judæa*," but,
in accordance with Jer. ix. 10 ; xi. 6 ; xxxi, 22, a " city of
Judah " (πόλις Ἰούδα). What Luke was not informed about,
we shall not be able to define with precision. The legend of

---

[1] This tradition is probably only authenticated since the fourteenth century.
See Tobler, *Topographie*, ii., p. 381.
[2] Mader, *Altchristliche Basiliken und Lokaltraditionen in Südjudäa*, p. 190 *f*.
Winer stated erroneously that the rabbis believed that John the Baptist came
from Hebron.
[3] Tos. Jeb. i. 10.
[4] *MGWDJ*, 61, p. 136.
[5] Migne, *P.G.* cxxi., col. 364.

the Protevangelium, for which a suitable locality was later found, cannot be considered by us as being based on actual knowledge. Yet the "mountain-country" west of Jerusalem, with its valleys rich in olive-trees, and its charming *'Ain Karim* in a side-ravine of the great valley of Kalonyeh, remains within the sphere which begins and ends in Judæa.

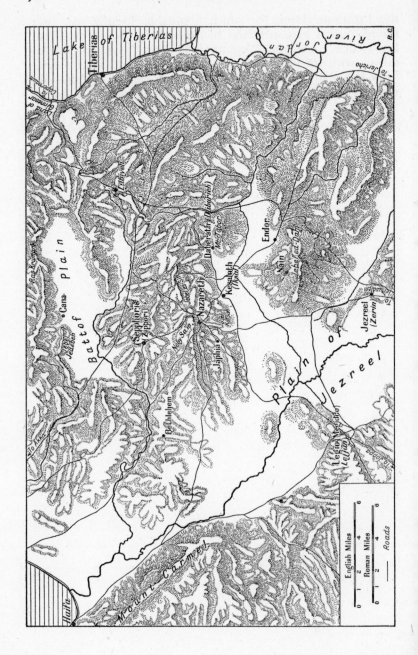

III

NAZARETH

BETHLEHEM as the birthplace of Jesus has been assigned by
not a few writers to the domain of legend. Others assume
that He was indeed born in a Bethlehem, but not in that of
Judæa. There is a Bethlehem in Zebulon, about twelve
miles north of Nazareth, at the edge of the oak-woods, on the
hills which form a frontier between the plain of Jezreel and
the coast, and where, at present, a German colony flourishes.[1]
Nazareth on the other hand had, according to some writers,
the singular fate of never having existed at all at that time.

According to Cheyne,[2] the name " Nazareans " was transferred to the Christians from a pre-Christian sect which venerated a certain Jesus as " saviour." Another hypothesis is that a
messianic name *Neser* or *Noser*, derived from Isa. xi. 1, was the
origin of this designation of Christians.[3] This is supposed to
be the origin of the place-name Nazareth, which was applied
to a Galilæan locality (according to Burrage, originally the
whole district occupied by the Christians on both sides of the
Jordan), or, perhaps, even called it into being. How it came
about that a merely " derived " name should have been affixed
to a definite place is indeed a puzzle, as Nazareth was not a
Christian place in early times. From another angle Burkitt[4]
has raised a doubt concerning the relationship of Jesus to
Nazareth. He argues that, as Jerome had already remarked,
the Galilæan locality was pronounced with *Tsade*, not with
Zayin, and so the designation of Jesus as Ναζωραῖος (Mt. ii. 23 ;
cf. Acts xxiv. 5), or Ναζαρηνός (Mk. xvi. 6), with a spirantic ζ,
does not fit it, but is more likely to have been derived from
" Nasirean " (ναζιραῖος). Accordingly, Jesus is supposed to
have been a Nasirean, and possibly the earliest Christian

---

[1] So Réville, *Jésus de Nazareth*, i., 2nd ed., p. 330, as quoted by Klausner,
Jesus of Nazareth, p. 232, who rejects it.

[2] *Enc. Bibl.* art. " Nazaret " ; W. B. Smith, *The Prechristian Jesus*, 1906.

[3] Burrage, *Nazareth and the Beginning of Christianity*, 1914.

[4] *Proceedings of the British Academy*, 1911-12, p. 391.

tradition did not designate Nazareth, but Chorazin, near Capernaum (mentioned in Mt. xi. 21) as His home. J. Halévy's assertion[1] that the native place of Jesus was called *Nesareth*, "ledge, plank," and that *Nesar* gave the name of the plain Genesar (=*ge nesar*) by the lake of Tiberias is equally untenable. All the Gospels, however, explain this title of Jesus as being a reference to His connection with the Galilæan Nazareth, evidently known at that time (Mt. ii. 23 ; Mk. i. 9 ; Lk. ii. 39 ; Jn. i. 46). And all Palestinians must have known that the Greek pronunciation of the name of Nazareth as Ναζαρέτ (Ναζαρέθ), or Ναζαρά (Mt. iv. 13 ; Lk. iv. 16) did not agree with the native one, although the Palestinian Lectionary writes, in agreement with the Greek form, *Nazarat* or *Nazorat*, and renders "Nazarene" with *Nazeraya* or *Nazoraya*. But, since in this Christian Aramaic work even Jesus is reproduced in its Greek form, one must suppose that the Palestinian Church wished to emphasise its connection with the Greek primitive Church and to move away from the Jews, while the East-Syrian Church, which called Jesus *Jeshu'*, found no reason to do so. That the name of the place was pronounced not with *Zayin*, but with *Tsade*, can be seen in the *Naserat* and *Naseraya* of the Peshita ; it is the direct witness of Jerome in his *Liber interpret. hebr. nom. de Ev. Matth.*, in the relation which he establishes to the Hebrew *neser* (*Ep.* 46 ad Marcellam), in the *Nasrat* of the elegy of the Jewish poet Kalir (see below), in the Jewish hebraised form *nosri* for "Nazarean,"[2] and in the Arabic *En-nasi-ra* (*en-nasiratu*) of modern Palestine. As a parallel to the Greek substitution of ζ for *ts* can be mentioned the Hebrew place-name *Tso'r*, which was pronounced by the Greeks Ζοάρα,[3] as also in Palestinian Arabic *zerir* is said for *tserir*, "small." Apart from this there was another factor which probably led to the connecting of the name of the place with *nezar*, viz., the fact that the Hebrew root *natsar* had in the Aramaic idiom *t* for *ts*, so that it was natural to derive a place-name which preserved the old form, unintelligible to the Aramaic-speaking persons, from a word which is also found in Aramaic. At the same time the Greek-speaking people were influenced by Ναζιραῖος, which was familiar to

---

[1] *Mémoire sur quelques noms géographiques de la Palestine*, 1890, p. 45.

[2] Ber. 17b ; Ab. z. 17a ; Sanh. 43a, 103a ; Taan. 27b (acc. to the Munich MS.) ; Sopher. xvii. 5 ; the Palestinian form of the eighteen Benedictions, see Dalman, *Die Worte Jesu*, p. 300.

[3] *Ant.* xiii. 15, 4 ; *Bell. Jud.* iv. 8, 4. So also Eusebius and Jerome, see Thomsen, *Loca Sancta* i., *sub voce*.

them. They must have certainly derived the name of the place from *neẓer*, "consecration," as is also presupposed by the translation καθαρότης in Eusebius. In what strange embarrassments the Hellenists found themselves where linguistic matters were concerned, may be deduced from Mt. ii. 23, where a prophetic passage which predicts the name of the Messiah is referred to Ναζωραῖος. This can only refer to a Midrash based on Isa. xi. 1, in the style of the Jewish proofs of Messiah's name by scriptural texts.[1] Originally it must have been formulated somewhat as follows : "Messiah is called *Neser*, because it says, 'And there shall come forth a rod out of the stem of Jesse and a *branch* (*neser*) shall grow out of his roots.' "[2] This could not be reproduced in Greek and therefore appears in our Gospel in a rather strange form, but this again proves that the reference is to a name with *ts*, not with *ẓ*.

The Hebrew formation of Nazareth is the same as the place-name *Daberath* in Josh. xix. 12; xxi. 28; 1 Chr. vi. 57; *Tsarephath* in Obad. 20, *cf.* 1 Kings xvii. 9; the names of women *Basemath* (Gen. xxxvi. 3; 1 Kings iv. 15) and *Asenath* (Gen. xli. 45); and the designation of the precious stone as *barekath*, Ezek. xxvii. 13 (*bareketh* in Ex. xxviii. 17; xxxix. 10). All these probably belong to the unusual verbal form *aẓelath* (Dt. xxxii. 36) for *aẓela*—i.e., to the antiquated *katalat*. Of a different nature are the place-names *Boskath* (Josh. xv. 39; 2 Kings xxii. 1), *Joṭebah* (2 Kings xxi. 19), and the Mishnaic *Borechath* (confirmed by inscriptions),[3] and *Jodephath* (*Jodfath*),[4] and *Joḳadt* (*Joḳart*).[5] For Boskath, Joṭebah and Borechath, the nominal forms *ḳuṭlath* and *ḳuṭilath* could be taken into consideration; Jodephat and Joḳadt are of a dubious nature. Samuel Klein[6] assumes for all place-names of this kind the pronunciation with *o* in the first syllable, and demands therefore the pronunciation *Notsrath* for Nazareth, which would be the elder form for *Notsra*. But this cannot possibly be harmonised with the Greek, Syriac and Arabic traditions of the name. This common tradition demands a clear *a* for the first syllable. The same is true of *Daberath*, which lies about four miles from Nazareth, and which Baer has changed, according to a MS. brought from Jerusalem, into *Dobrath*, against the Rabbinic Bible of 1518 and the edition of J. H. Michaelis of 1720. The transcription of LXX is here

---

[1] *Cf.* Sanh. 98b.
[2] Jewish antipathy against the Nazarine has pointed in contrast to Isa. xiv. 19 ; *neser nitab* ; Sanh. 43a.
[3] Thomsen, *Loca Sancta* i., p. 44.
[4] Arach. ix. 6 ; Taan. 23b.
[5] Taan. 23b.
[6] *MGWDJ*, 1923, p. 202.

uncertain, but Josephus with his *Dabaritta (Debaritta)*,[1] and the present *Deburieh, Dabura,* testify against the *o.* If *Natserath* was the right pronunciation, the meaning " it (she) guards " would be the most probable ; unless it is derived from *netser,* " bud," in which case the name would mean " it (she) buds." As a subject, the locality itself would be understood : " the town guards." The later form of *Natserath* with the same significance is *Natsera,* which is reproduced in the Greek Ναζαρά. The " Nazarene " was certainly in accordance with the Syriac form *natseraya.* The Jews used the Hebrew *notsri,* perhaps under the assumption that the place was called in Hebrew *Notseret,* or even more probably because *notsri* corresponded to the Aramaic *natserai.* That *notsri* was then also used is not to be wondered at. What is strange is that, in Greek, together with the more rare Ναζαρηνός, it was not, as might be expected, Ναζαραῖος that was used, but Ναζωρῖος. Was it perhaps that the Aramaic *natsora,* having the same significance as *natsera,* influenced it ? Jerome, in his *Onomasticum,* says, doubtless purposely, *Nazaraus,* and when he records that the village was in his time called *Nazara,* it also shows that the outstanding vowel of the place was an *a.*

That there was no mention of Nazareth before the Gospels has seemed strange to some, but would surprise no Palestinian. There are hundreds of old Palestinian sites, the names of which are not found in the early literature. Accidentally some of these are mentioned once or twice in the Bible. Even such an important city as Sepphoris in Galilee is never referred to there, but appears in Josephus and in rabbinic literature ; this latter contains many Galilæan place-names which are not mentioned in the Bible. Among these is Nazareth, occurring in fact in an old list now lost to us, which enumerated the Galilæan places where the twenty-four priestly divisions resided after the destruction of Jerusalem. This list the synagogal poet, Eleasar Kalir, used in the seventh century for two hymns for the ninth of Ab.[2]

That until the fourth century Nazareth was a purely Jewish locality is attested by Epiphanius.[3] Jewish Nazareth has also left us an important document in an ossuarium with an Aramaic inscription, now in the museum of the Franciscans in Nazareth. The inscription runs : " Soem, the son of Menachem, may his

---

[1] *Vita* 61 ; *cf. Bell. Jud.* xi. 213.
[2] An attempt of reconstruction is made by Klein, *Beiträge zur Geschichte und Geographie Galiläas,* p. 95.　　　　[3] *Adv. Hæreses* xxx.

soul find rest."[1] It is later than the time of Jesus, yet it confirms the reference of Epiphanius to the Jewish Nazareth, and we have no ground to doubt that the Nazareth which Eusebius found, fifteen Roman miles east[2] toward Legio (now *Lejjun*), was really the place after which Jesus was called.

After this preparation, we can now take a look at the place where Jesus grew into manhood, which was thus His actual home, and after which He was rightly named. To explain its position, we must make clear that the vast rift of the soil to which the Jordan valley belongs was connected with a western cross-rift, which split Palestine into two parts. This becomes particularly clear when one goes by sea for some distance along the Palestinian coast. There I once realised with astonishment how the southern mountainous district with Carmel suddenly breaks off and sinks apparently into the sea, out of which *Tabor* and *Jebel Daḥi* emerge like islands, and how, as suddenly, first the lower and then the upper Galilæan mountains rise up from the sea. In reality the situation is not quite what it appears at first sight. The cross-rift running from northwest to south-east is a deep ravine, which, however, itself rises to 100 metres, and, in the east and the west, is hedged about in different directions by the encroaching heights, so that one can speak of a wide basin which is, as it were, interposed between the chain of mountains. To-day it is named after a Bedouin chief, *Merj ibn ʿAmir* ; but in ancient times its eastern part was called after the city on its ridge : " the plain of Jezreel."[3] Over its northern ridge lies Nazareth, only 349 metres above the sea-level, and yet, especially since its buildings on the mountain behind the town have risen as high as 400 metres, it is visible from afar, and commands a wide view. Once one has ascended to the top of the pass of *Ferdes*, north of ancient Samaria, it appears, at a distance of about twenty-four miles, as a white glimmer upon the mountains of Galilee. Nazareth is by no means an out-of-the-way little place in a hidden corner of northern Palestine, but a frontier-town looking southward, over against mid-Palestine. This statement must, however, be qualified ; for *Kesaloth*,[4]

---

[1] See *PJB*, 1913, p. 45 ; 1914, p. vii ; *Yellin*, 1918, p. 58 ; Klein, *Jüdischpalästinisches Corpus Inscriptionum*, 1920, i. 166.

[2] More exactly, north-east.

[3] So Josh. xvii. 16 ; Judg. vi. 33 ; Hos. i. 5. There is no proof that the whole plain bore this name. In Ber. R. 98 (212b) it is evidently limited to the district south of *Jebel Duhy*.

[4] The Kesulloth of Josh. xix. 18 ; perhaps also the *Kisloth Tabor* of Josh. xix. 12, After it, the plain north of *Jebel Duhy* was called "the plain of Kesalu," Gen. R. xcviii. (212b) ; *cf.* Klein, *Jeshurun*, 1922, p. 449.

lying below it, at the foot of the mountain-chain, now called *Iksal*, and *Japha*,[1] on the road leading across the plain in a south-western direction, were frontier-places in a still fuller sense of the word. The former, lying on the plain only about a mile and a half south-east of Nazareth, is mentioned by Josephus as the southern frontier of lower Galilee (*Bell. Jud.* iii. 3, 1). The latter, one of the largest towns of Galilee at that time, was provided with a double wall and, in the Jewish war of independence, was one of the strongholds of the country which the Romans managed to take only after a fierce struggle.[2] It still stands prominently on a hill above its well-watered shady gardens in the valley. Josephus stayed there once, in order to occupy and guard from there the roads from Galilee towards the south.[3] Remnants of a synagogue found there[4] testify to its Jewish inhabitants during the Roman period. As it lay only about a mile and a half west of Nazareth, on the same road and still on the mountain, it dominated the district and, in comparison with it, Nazareth had only a subordinate significance. This Nazareth, indeed, although a frontier-place and, to judge by its name and position, perhaps a frontier outpost, was in no sense a mistress of the frontier; it was simply a Jewish village without independent political importance. But it does not follow that its position on the frontier was of no consequence. In any case, it meant a widening of the horizon to its inhabitants, who necessarily had relations, friendly or otherwise, not only with the inhabitants of the mountains, but also with those in the valley below and in the land beyond.

The great highways are places of far-reaching relationships and means of connection with distant centres of culture. To-day one would have to enumerate as such the road from Tiberias, through Nazareth, to Haifa, and that from Nazareth, through Nablus, to Jerusalem, as well as the Damascus-Haifa railroad, nearly six miles distant from that road, with its southern branch which reaches Nablus, and its continuation—which was constructed during the war—to Egypt. Formerly the conditions were not quite like this. The caravan-road from Damascus to Egypt, which crossed the plain of Jezreel south of Nazareth in the direction of *Lejjun*, reaching at this point the coastal plain by the pass of '*Ara*, corresponded to what is

---

[1] It was the Japhia of Josh. xix. 12, though the order of the places is confused there.
[2] *Bell. Jud.* ii. 20, 6 ; iii. 7, 31 ; *Vita* 45.   [3] *Vita* 52.
[4] Vincent, *Revue Biblique*, 1921, p. 434.

now the railway. From it, at *Lubiyeh*, a connection branched
off towards the seaport of 'Akka, and passed at the same distance north of Nazareth as that of the main road to the south.
Thus the most important of the great traffic routes did not
touch Nazareth directly, and the way from Tiberias through
Nazareth to Haifa, which must have existed even in the time
of Christ, could not then have had the importance which it has
to-day, because Haifa was at that time not an important harbour,
but only a small place. But it gained another connection,
which at the present day is due to Nazareth's own importance,
through its near relationship to Zippori, now *Sepphoris*, the
centre of the chief part of Galilee at that time. This town,
only three miles north of Nazareth, naturally needed above all
things a good connection in the south which should keep it in
touch with Jerusalem. The chief road of Palestine, which in
Judæa often follows the watershed, but farther on cannot do
this so easily, had to cross the plain of Jezreel from *Jenin* and
ascend the Galilæan mountains just at Nazareth, in order to
terminate in Sepphoris on the other side of the first of the four
spurs of those mountains. When Josephus guarded the roads
to the south in the neighbourhood of Japha, he concentrated his
attention chiefly on this direct road to Jerusalem, without, however, neglecting the cross-road which, starting from Sepphoris
and passing Nazareth and Japha, joined the great Damascus-
Egypt road via Lejjun, which road could also be used for the
journey to Jerusalem. There was, however, still a third way,
via Endor, which joins an important continuation *via* Jericho
to Jerusalem. In this way Nazareth was a radiating point of
important roads and a thoroughfare for an extensive traffic.

When on June 3, 1899, I rode up for the first time from
Jerusalem to Nazareth, the wheat was for the most part still
standing in the plain of Jezreel, and a great heat brooded over
the wide fields. The wheat was fully ripe, bleached white,
with heavy, bearded ears. The crickets, which in Hebrew are
rightly called *zarzur*, because of their strident noises, filled
the air with their shrill chirps of the deafening effect of which
one can have no idea in Europe. When the hot current of wind
passed through the wheat and bent it into waves, there was no
rustling sound like that of trees in a wood, but a sharp hissing
noise, which seemed to jeer at the pilgrim rider, suffering from
the heat : " Behold the Northerner ! Away with him !" A
genuine Palestinian would have interpreted the noise differently;
" Put ye in the sickle, for the harvest is ripe," says Joel (iv. 13).

More fully the Angel in the Book of Revelation (xiv. 15) calls
to the royal Son of Man that sits upon the cloud: "Thrust in
thy sickle, and reap; for the time is come for thee to reap; for
the harvest of the earth is ripe." Jesus Himself saw in the ripe
harvest-field the consummated growth of the Kingdom of God,
which exists first as the green seed, then brings forth the blade,
then the ear, after that the full corn in the ear (Mk. iv. 29).
"When the fruit is ripe, immediately he putteth in the sickle,
because the harvest is come." The ripened harvest-field proclaims not only judgment, but the achieved final aim of a
development which has salvation as its purpose.

Above the plain in the north there rises, to a height of about
250 metres, the threatening pile of the "Mountain of the
leap" (*Jebel el-Kafsah*), from which, according to tradition, the
Nazarenes attempted to push Jesus.

It is probable that in ancient times one could ascend to
Nazareth from the ravine on the western foot of the "Mount
of the leap." A steep path leads up to it; a better bridle-path
with some turnings has been made farther west; the new high-
road has had to make a still greater detour in the same direction.
For the explorer, however, the most important ascent is the
first-mentioned, for the valley of the "Mount of the leap" is
the valley of Nazareth. After climbing up the height, the way
turns to the north-east, and here becomes a part of the basin,
imbedded between the higher hills, over which Nazareth rises
335-380 metres above the sea-level. A large threshing-floor
and, farther to the north, vineyards, which the Fountain of Mary
supplies with water, fill this basin, and form the foreground of
the town, which with its tiled roofs has now a far too European-
ised appearance. Of late it has become a flourishing town,
providing a market for a wide neighbourhood reaching as far as
the other side of the Jordan. Here, as in Bethlehem, the
memory of the only great Nazarene has raised the insignificant
village more and more into prominence to such an extent that
Japha has had to take a secondary place and the high-roads
have become dominated by Nazareth. In place of Sepphoris,
Nazareth, despised by Nathanael, has become the seat of the
government. The background of the basin in which Nazareth
lies is formed by an important range of heights, running in a
west-easterly direction and called *Jebel el-Sih* at the eastern end,
which, just above Nazareth, at the tomb of *Neby Sa'in*, reaches
its highest point, 448 metres. It is only here, properly speaking,
that the first ascent of the land of Galilee from the plain ends.

But the bottom of the valley on which Nazareth is built—on the slopes of this height—does not run parallel to it, but south-west by north-east, and so gives the town more space to the south than to the north where, on a steeply sloping height, it has lately begun to curve eastward. Just at this curve springs up the most important well of the basin which, since 1100, can be proved to have borne the name of the Mother of Jesus.

In the neighbourhood of this well one would like to seek for ancient Nazareth, but there are no traces of old buildings just here. The churches of Nazareth which were built in the Byzantine period to mark the dwelling-places of Mary and Joseph lie at a great distance from it to the south, where the market-street, and in it the church—once synagogue—also indicate the centre of the town, where the most important ways of communication converge. Doubtless here stood Byzantine Nazareth ; and, if Byzantine tradition conjectured rightly, the town of Jesus also. It stood there in the angle formed by a low projection of the *Neby Sa'in* range, an almost insecure, even unfavourable position. A possible reason for this situation, disregarding the fact of the three roads to the south which radiate from here, is the well, which, though scanty in volume, at that spot, springs up to a considerable height.[1] Already in ancient times it was called *'En ed-Jedide*, " new well," probably because for some time it was blocked up. Later it was generally differentiated from *El-'En*, the chief well of the place, by being called *En-Neba'*. During the war the German military authorities set about to restore it,[2] but in 1921 it was again in ruins. It is strange that early tradition has no reference to it, perhaps because the stronger-flowing, though more distant, well in the valley was always considered to be the proper supplier of water for the town. Anyone knowing ancient Palestinian sites would prefer to think of Nazareth on the peak of the hill-projection, under which the smaller well springs. The hill slopes east, its perpendicular rocky walls being in close proximity to the well, and it is also, in the south and west, steep enough to give a small town, lying above, natural protection. In late years, a monastery was erected on the height, but nothing was made known concerning any archæological finds during the building of it.[3]

[1] It is illustrated in Serimgour's *Nazareth of To-day* (1913), Plate 8.
[2] P. Range, *Nazareth*, p. 12.
[3] At the upper part of the present town of Nazareth Klausner (*Jesus of Nazareth*, p. 230) claims to have seen the ruins of the old town. To me and to others they were always untraceable.

On the edge of the site, which goes back at least to the Byzantine period, the church of the Annunciation stands. A rocky grotto under its high altar contains a second altar, under the *mensa* of which the inscription *Verbum caro hic factum est* is intended to define the deepest meaning of the event. The grotto of Nazareth should rank as equal with that of Bethlehem.

Arculf (670) is the first writer to mention a second church in Nazareth.[1] It was erected in the centre of the town above two vaults connected by arches, between which there was a well from which all the inhabitants of the town drew water. From what Arculf says of the well it must be inferred that the church stood over Mary's Well. Daniel, in the year 1106, visited a round church of Gabriel over this well outside the town. Even now the Well of Mary has its first drawing-place in the Greek church of Gabriel; the present building, however, is of late date. Since early times a conduit has carried its water to a public cistern, where, from out of a covered trough, it discharges itself in many places. The fact that the well-church, situated near the town, was dedicated to Gabriel, shows that it was taken for granted that the angel appeared to Mary at the well. In fact, early tradition has it that the first salutation of Mary by the angel took place on the way to the well, or at the well, this being followed by the Annunciation proper, in the house, after her return with the pitcher.[2] But Arculf's reference to the church as being in the centre of the town and built over the site of the house where Jesus was brought up does not harmonise with this. Probably Arculf erroneously thought the cistern which was made under the " church of the Upbringing " to be a well. In that case it was the predecessor of the church built in the time of the Crusaders, the remnants of which Viaud dug out, some years before 1908, north of the church of the Annunciation,[3] and which has been rebuilt. This double-aisled church is much smaller (98 feet long) than the church of the Annunciation (250 feet long) of the same period, the arrangement of which it resembles. What is peculiar to it is the great subterranean grotto (33 feet long by 17 feet broad) to which a long, narrow, winding path leads, partly by steps. Besides this, a bottle-shaped cavern leads down to it from the centre of the church, and under the grotto at the same spot are two small cisterns, one upon the other, in the form of bottles. All looks

---

[1] Geyer, *Itinera*, p. 274. The description is not clear.
[2] *Protevangelium Jacobi* xi. 1, 2 ; Pseudo-Mt. ix. 1, 2.
[3] Viaud, *Nazareth*, p. 133.

as if it was meant for the storage of large corn-supplies ; these subterranean rooms could naturally also be used as water reservoirs. Two smaller basins, one of which is supplied with steps, show that water was kept in readiness above in a considerable quantity. Tradition, which can here be traced back with certainty only to 1620, assumed this site to have been the place where Jesus was brought up—*i.e.*, the house of Joseph. If the " church of the Upbringing," visited by Arculf, was situated here, it may have followed the direction of that path and basin, diverging from the church of the Crusaders. No traces are to be found of it. Probably the great cistern, approachable through the rocky path, was taken to have been the place where Joseph lived. The small cisterns were its water reservoirs. We are thus reminded of the water-drawing by the boy Jesus which the Infancy-gospels record[1] and which pilgrims, in any case, connected with the town cisterns[2] or even with the church of the Annunciation,[3] conceived of as the dwelling-place of Joseph.

A local legend, which can be traced only to the time when the Franciscans settled in Nazareth in about 1620, designates a colossal rocky block in the form of a table, near the " new spring," as a table at which Jesus ate with His disciples, or at which He sat with them ; He would then have drunk with them from that spring.[4] This " Mensa Christi,"[5] which is supposed to have slipped down, because of an earthquake, from the mountain height, was a counterpart of the stone table which was formerly shown at the lake of Tiberias at the place of the miraculous feeding of the 5,000. The peculiar formation of the rock naturally led to the origin of this legend. It is possible, of course, to assume that all localisations of events in our Lord's life in connection with Nazareth were similar in origin. Perhaps, even before churches were built at the Annunciation grotto (which might have been under an old house), and at the cistern of the " church of the Upbringing," the minds of the faithful dwelt on Mary and Jesus. Because of the famous grottoes of Jerusalem, of the Mount of Olives, and of Bethlehem, it may have been that here also grottoes were desired in memorial churches. The belief, much spread in the pagan world, that in subterranean places one comes nearer to the Deity, might have influenced the search after holy sites here as elsewhere.

[1] Pseudo-Mt., ch. xxii. ; the Gospel of Thomas, ch. ix. (Latin), ch. xii. (Greek).
[2] So Theoderich, ed. Tobler, p. 105, and Sæwulf.   [3] So Arculf.
[4] So in Slisanski (1660), *Reisebeschreibung*, p. 115.   [5] Tobler, p. 83.

We only know that in Nazareth, until then solely Jewish, the first church was built in the time of the emperor Constantine by a Jewish Christian, Joseph, who was raised to the dignity of a Comes[1] ; and that although Jerome (*Ep. Paulæ*) narrates that Paula visited the place, he is silent concerning any particular memorial-sites there. A fixed tradition in a place inhabited by Jews is not probable. Only if we are content to look upon the churches as monuments which mark the dwelling-places of Mary and Joseph, and to consider the grottoes and the spring by the town as relics of the Nazareth of Jesus' time, can we stand on firm ground.

If the old synagogue of the little place were still standing— the synagogue where Jesus proclaimed Himself as the Fulfiller of Isa. lxi. 1, 2 (Lk. iv. 16 *f.*)[2]—we should find ourselves on an historical site of first importance. Indeed, on the present market-road there stands a building, which has been used by the Greek Uniats as a church since 1741, and whose area, covered over with a barrel-vault, is shown as the " School of the Messiah."[3] It may be the same room, if not the same building, in which Jesus, according to Antoninus (about 570), learnt the ABC, and where there was a beam which is supposed to have once been a school-bench which no Jew was able to lift.[4] Four rectangular blocks with Hebrew letters, which were found near by, may have belonged to it.[5] This was at that time the synagogue of the place, and Antoninus praises the beauty of the Nazareth Jewesses who distinguished themselves by their kindness towards Christians. A church was built there[6] much later. It is not impossible that in the time of Christ the synagogue stood on the same spot. Hence the synagogue-church is for us the most important of the memorial sites of Nazareth.

In the small market of the town, which serves a large district, there is to-day no special lane of *Carpenters* or *Joiners*. Only the forging of sickles and winnowing-knives can be considered a trade characteristic of Nazareth. From Mk. vi. 3, Mt. xiii. 55, we know that Joseph and Jesus belonged to a class of artisans in Nazareth. The Greek τέκτων, used of our Lord, does not

---

[1] Epiphanius, *Adv. Hæres.* xxx., where he only refers to the permission to build, but it is taken for granted that it was accomplished.
[2] See *Jesus-Jeshua* (English tr., pp. 44-55).
[3] Tobler, p. 226 ; Horn, *Ichnographiæ*, p. 179.
[4] Geyer, *Itinera*, pp. 161, 197.
[5] Meistermann, *Capharnaüm et Bethsaïde*, p. 242.
[6] First mentioned by Petrus Diaconus ; see Geyer, *Itinera*, p. 112.

specify the trade.   Ludwig Schneller,[1] under the assumption
that it referred to the building trade, urges that Jesus could
only have been a bricklayer, since house-building in Palestine
did not require any other kind of workmanship.   But as early
as in the *Protevangelium Jacobi* (ch. ix. 1), we find Joseph with a
builder's hatchet.   Also the vaulted houses of which Schneller
is thinking here are even nowadays of a type generally found
in south Palestine only, while everywhere else in the country,
including Nazareth, the wooden props of the flat roof are as a
rule supported by stone arches.   Instead of these arches one
finds sometimes, in the north, beams resting on posts made of
wood or stone.   This must be considered as having been the
ancient manner of building in Palestine, as Jewish literature
assumes even for the Temple of the last period a roof resting
only on beams (Midd. iv. 6).   Jerome also states that in
Palestine as well as in Egypt the roofs were flat, resting on
beams.[2]   Such a roof can be partly uncovered, without causing
much damage to it, as can be gathered from Mk. ii. 4.   Thus,
according to Lev. R. 19 (50b), king Jehoiachin's wife was once
let down through the opened plastering (*maʿzeba*) of the roof
to visit him in prison.   When such a roof had to be opened
it was necessary to pierce through the plastering and remove
from under it some of the smaller pieces of wood.   Naturally,
no house owner would be ready to allow this without some
special necessity.   The putting up of such a roof did not
require the construction of a scaffolding, but merely the pre-
paration of somewhat large beams, as well as of shorter pieces
of wood which were laid across the beams, and supported a
roof which consisted simply of a layer of thorns and clay.
Sycamores, which from earliest times had supplied the beams
(Isa. ix. 9 ; Tos. Bab. mez. viii. 36), were formerly also planted
in lower Galilee for this purpose,[3] but at present there are few
of these to be seen and poplars are more used.   The shorter
pieces of wood could also be taken from oak and terebinth
trees, and there were certainly woods on the north-western
slope of the mountain-range of Nazareth.   In any case there
were wood-cutters, whose duty it was to supply building
material, and traders who sold the wood in the town.   Jerusalem had a special market for beams,[4] which could not have
been expected in smaller Nazareth.   It was the part of the
builders to put up the walls of new houses.   Nazareth must

[1] *Kennst du das Land?*, 1920, p. 58.   [2] *Epist.* 106.
[3] Shebi. 14, 2.   [4] *Bell. Jud.* ii.

have had its builders or masons ; but together with them, there must have been one or more workers in wood, who put up the roof-beams of the house and also supplied the modest requirements of a village, as, for instance, ploughs and yokes, and spare parts of these ; also doors, trunks, and bedsteads in particular. The post-Christian Jewish literature knows of no special carpenters, but together with the mason (*bannay*), the *naggar*, who was both mason and maker of the above-mentioned articles. And Jesus (as well as Joseph) was considered in rabbinic as well as in Christian-Palestinian writings to have been a *naggar*.[1] According to the *Protevangelium* of James (ix. 2 ; xiii. 1), he had to do with buildings, evidently as a carpenter, as in ix. 1, where He throws away a hatchet. On the other hand, according to Justin,[2] He made ploughs and yokes, and the apocryphal Gospels give a similar description.[3] It was accordingly something unusual for Joseph to make bedsteads. Only the Arabic Infancy-gospel, ch. xxxvii, mentions doors, milk-pails, boxes, and bedsteads. His trade sometimes even caused Joseph to stay away from home for certain periods in " Capernaum by the sea," where he eventually moved with his family.[4] Thus if Jesus was a worker in wood it is remarkable that, according to Mt. vii. 24, He speaks of the laying of the foundation of a house ; according to Lk. xiv. 28, of the erection of a tower ; according to Jn. ii. 19, of the building of the destroyed Temple ; but never of His own handicraft, not even when it had to do with building. His spirit was never enclosed in the narrow horizon of an artisan.

Together with agriculture, the cultivation of fruit—especially olives, figs, and vines—must have been the chief occupation of the inhabitants of Nazareth. An old proverb says : " It is easier to raise a legion of olives in Galilee than *one* child in the land of Judah."[5] Evidently the cultivation of olives was particularly extensive there. To-day this cannot be said especially of Nazareth. But the surrounding district is everywhere mountainous and abounding in rocky places, suitable for the cultivation of olive-trees. The " fourfold ground "

[1] In reference to our Lord, a *naggar* appears as among the descendants of Haman, Sopherim xiii. 6 ; Targum sheni on Est. iii. 1. The son of a *naggar* Jesus is in Pal. Evan. and in the Syriac Bible, Mt. xiii. 55.

[2] *Dial. c. Tryph.* 88.

[3] Pseudo-Mt. xxxvii.; *Historia Josephi* ix. ; *Evangelium Thomæ*, Greek xiii. 1, Latin ch. xi.

[4] Pseudo-Mt. x. 1 ; xl.

[5] Gen. R. xx (42b). The abbreviation *ay* is not of *eretz Yisrael*, but of *eretz Yehuda*.

(Mt. xiii. 3 *f*.) fits in with the nature of the landscape of Nazareth. In the valley below, the spring watered a little ground well fitted for the raising of vegetables—turnips, onions, and mustard. The rabbis once claimed that for sixteen miles round about Sepphoris, near Nazareth, the land literally flowed with milk and honey.[1] Rabbi Jose's son being sent to fetch olives from the upper room, found it overflowing with honey because even the bitter olives of this land trickle honey.[2] Turnip-rooted cabbages are said to have been seen there which weighed 30 pounds, and mustard shrubs the one branch of which could cover a potter's hut[3] (*cf*. Mt. xiii. 3 *f*.; Mk. iv. 31 *f*.; Lk. xiii. 19). Yet the example of the mustard-seed is used also in rabbinic literature, as in Mt. xvii. 20 ; Lk. xvii. 6, to express the smallest of things.[4] Even in the sixth century A.D. Antoninus[5] considered the neighbourhood of Nazareth a paradise. In the matter of wheat and field produce, according to him, it resembled Egypt ; but in wine, oil, fruit, and honey, it surpassed it. As to millet, it grows even against its own nature taller than a man.[6] These descriptions are affectionate exaggerations, but they show that in Nazareth there was no abject poverty, and that Jesus had ample opportunity to observe the work in the vineyards—which also produced, usually at the same time, figs (Lk. xiii. 6)—and the work in the olive-gardens.

The threshing-place, which is usually for preference on the heights, may have been already in the time of Jesus in the valley, as it is to-day. Here, as a boy, He could see the threshing oxen with uncovered mouths (Dt. xxv. 4), going in a circle. But this did not appear to Him so applicable to the Kingdom of Heaven as the fanning, which followed it, when the ground corn was cast in the air with the seven-pronged fork, in order that the different parts should be divided and then used according to their value. In a Jewish parable, the argument between chaff (*motz*), chopped straw (*teben*), straw (*kash*), and wheat (*hitta*), for whose sake the field was sown was settled by the master of the field, who was fanning. The chaff was scattered by the wind, the chopped straw he threw upon the field, the straw into the fire, but the wheat he gathered into a

---

[1] b. Meg. 6a ; Keth. 111b.   [2] p. Pea 20b.
[3] Sifre Dt. 317 ; p. Pea 20b ; b. Keth. 111b.
[4] Nidda v. 2 ; p. Ber. 8d ; b. Ber. 8d.
[5] Geyer, *Itinera*, pp. 162, 197.
[6] By *millium* Antoninus could not have thought of the common millet, *Panicum miliaceum*, but of *Sorghum annuum* ; perhaps Antoninus knew only the former one and considered *Sorghum annuum* as being the same.

grain-heap, which the passers-by kissed.[1] An Arab would
understand why the *teben*, *i.e.* the pieces of the softer upper
part of the grain-stalk (Arab. *tibn*),[2] are distinguished from
straw, *i.e.* the pieces of the harder lower part of the stalk
(Arab. *ḳaswal*). For this separation actually occurs at the
fanning. It is strange that in the parable the *teben*, which is
such an important article of food for cattle (Gen. xxiv. 25, 32 ;
Judg. xix. 19 ; 1 Kings v. 8 ; Isa. xi. 7 ; lxv. 25), is thrown away
as valueless. In reality it is put into a chamber specially
allotted to it (Arab. *matban*). The idea in the parable, however, was to make the wheat the real object of the sowing ;
so the importance of all the other parts had to be minimised.
In a different way and from a different cause the Baptist does
the same, when he differentiates only between wheat and
ἄχυρον (LXX for *teben*), rendered in Peshito and Pal. Ev. with
tebna (Mt. iii. 12 ; Lk. iii. 17). He must have thus relegated
all the parts of the straw to the fire, with the exception of the
finest chaff which would fly about in the wind. Jesus, in the
parable (Mt. xiii. 24-30), mentions tares (*i.e.* the darnel-
bundles) instead of straw, because the simultaneous growth
of the two kindred seeds is of special significance in the parable.
In fact, botanically darnel is closely related to wheat ; among
the various kinds of wheat, the spelt (*Triticum spelta*) with its
loose ears is most similar to darnel.[3]

The present inhabitants of Nazareth are not descendants
of the ancient stock of Jewish Nazareth. They do not differ
essentially in dress, looks, and language from those of other
north-Palestinian towns. At one time the Galilæans were
known as having long hair.[4] This has probably nothing to
do with the four pigtails of the present-day men living east of
the Jordan. The Aramaic of the Jews of ancient Nazareth
often lacked the pure Semitic sounds, probably owing to
Greek influence. It was said of them that in their pronunciation of the words for lamb (*immar*), wool (*'amar*), wine (*chamar*),
and ass (*ḥamar*), one could not distinguish one from another.[5]

---

[1] Cant. R. vii, 3 (69b) ; Gen. 4. 83 (177b) ; *cf.* Midr. Teh. ii. 14, where straw
and thorns wander into the fire.

[2] *Teben* is good when the field is harvested at the right time, but not when
in the wrong season, Cant. R. 8 (79b).

[3] Mt. xiii. 30 ; *cf.* vi. 26 ; Lk. xii. 24 ; *cf.* for these " garns," *i.e.* the chests
in the farmer's house for that purpose (Vogelstein, *Die Landwirtschaft in Palästina
zur Zeit der Mischna*, p. 71).

[4] Nonnus Panopolitanus (Migne, *P.G.* xliii., col. 760).

[5] Erub. 53b, but *cf. Gramm. des pal. Aram.*, 2nd ed., p. 57 *f.*, and *Jesus-Jeshua*,
p. 7 *f.*

It was characteristic of the position of the women of Galilee that the income from the weaving of linen belonged to them, not to their husbands.[1] Thus, the weaving of linen must have been the women's work, and, apart from the sleeves, Jesus' coat without seam (" woven from the top throughout," Jn. xix. 23), which could be made on a chain running round two staves, was most likely the work of Galilæan women. In our days, in the towns weaving is done by men ; only in the country and among the Bedouin is it done by women. In Galilee, as in the whole of Palestine, flax-growing has died out, and linen is displaced by cotton.

To get a view of the fields of Nazareth, one must climb the mountains. Going southwards, it is with surprise that one finds oneself standing on a steep precipice sloping towards the plain of Jezreel. Here tradition places the projecting " brow of the hill whereon their city was built," from which the Nazarenes desired to cast down one who dared to suggest that a Phœnician woman and a Syrian man might be of greater importance in the sight of God than a Jew (Lk. iv. 23-30).[2] The unbiased reader of St. Luke's Gospel thinks of Nazareth as standing on the summit of a height which at some point has a steep slope. The settlement on the slope of Nazareth to-day and in Byzantine times contradicts this notion. If the Nazareth of the time of Christ, or at least its synagogue, may be envisaged as lying on the height described on page 65, above the " new well," the " casting down " would be possible just near by, although the steep slope is not above 20 metres. But local tradition has a different conception. Already about the year 800 a church dedicated to St. Mary stood a mile distant from Nazareth at the spot supposed to be that of the intended " casting down."[3] That the spot lay to the south was later frequently stated.[4] The story was told that Jesus was suddenly transported to the slope of the mountain opposite,[5] which explains the Arabic designation *Jebel el-Ḳafsah*, " Mountain of the leap." At the present day also a spot to the south is pointed

---

[1] Bab. k. x. 9. In Judæa it was the case with wool. The Mishna takes it for granted that in Judæa there were many sheep, in Galilee much flax-growing, and that therefore wool occupied the same position in Judæa as linen did in Galilee.

[2] That according to Jewish legal tradition the one about to be stoned had to be first cast down from a height may be mentioned in this connection, because it shows how much the " casting down " was in keeping with the custom of the period.

[3] *Commemoratorium de casis Dei*, in Tobler, *Descriptiones Terræ Sanctæ*, p. 81.

[4] Theoderich, ed. Tobler, p. 106.

[5] After Burchard (1283), Laurent, *Peregrinatores*, p. 47.

out, about one and a half miles from Nazareth, at the highest
projection of the actual slope towards the plain, which, being
392 metres above sea-level, lies about 60 metres above the valley
of Nazareth. This can well be harmonised with the Lukan
expression, if by " the *hill* (mountain) whereon their city was
built " a range of hills is to be understood (which is quite
permissible).[1] Indeed the steepest and deepest precipice of
this highland was to be found here. But if this long and
difficult way makes one doubt this possibility, there is nothing
to hinder one from thinking with Klameth[2] of a more accessible
part of this slope. K. L. Schmidt[3] speaks of unsurmountable
topographical difficulties, and comes to the conclusion that
it was Luke who first provided a place for this synagogue-
speech of Jesus, which came to him attached to no locality—
though it is in point of fact associated with Nazareth by
the saying concerning the prophet in his own country (Lk. iv.
24; Mt. xiii. 57; Mk. vi. 4). But the fact that Nazareth lies
above a great slope cannot be denied. The present narrative
makes the Nazarenes lead Jesus there, but it may well have
been based on another form of the account, according to
which the purpose was to do away with Jesus for good, but
before they were able to attain this end He took His way eastwards, without their venturing to hinder Him. The ἔως,
" unto," in Lk. iv. 29 is rendered in Pal. Ev. by *'adma le,*
The same preposition is also found in Lk. xxiv. 50 for πρός,
whereby a direction is given to the aim which is not reached.
The Jewish-Aramaic *'ad* would have had in Lk. iv. 29 the
same meaning.

Another of the heights near Nazareth gives rise to considerations of greater significance. During some of my visits to
Nazareth I purposely avoided all the sites assigned by tradition,
in order not to be disturbed by considerations which concern
the history of the Church in Palestine rather than that of Jesus.
Instead, I ascended the plateau of *Neby Sa'in,*[4] above the town.
Up here one is free from the noise of its market-street and the
friendly pointing of the monks to definite, and yet so uncertain and often improbable, spots in the great reality which
is Nazareth. The village, which has developed into a town,
lies under the broad back of the mountain, and is to a great
extent obscured thereby. The eye turns chiefly to the distance,

---

[1] See p. 155.　　[2] *Die neutestamentlichen Lokaltraditionen,* i., p. 23.
[3] *Der Rahmen der Geschichte Jesu,* p. 41 *f.*
[4] The name is already known by de Bruyn, 1681.

and naturally first to the north, to a district which anyone coming from the south sees here for the first time. Behind rise two mountain-chains, ascending one behind the other like immense ramparts, first the wooded chain of the *Jebel Jedebeh* (543 metres) and the *Ras Kruman* (554 metres) (probably the mountain Asamon [Chashmon] to which the rebellious Zipporeans fled from the Romans)[1]; above it the 500 metres higher bluish wall of the *Jebel Ḥeder,* which encloses Galilee to the north. In the north-east the snow-speckled ridge of Hermon joins it. In the centre foreground of this magnificent picture appears quite close, *Sepphoris* (once *Zippori,* in Galilæan Aramaic *Zipporin*[2]), still imposing from its position on a broad hill in the midst of spacious olive-gardens, yet only a village, overlooked by an ancient tower. In the time of Christ it was the fortified city for the whole of Lower Galilee, and above it rose the royal citadel, which Herod had already established[3] and which undoubtedly received new splendour under his son, Antipas, at the restoration of the town[4] (after having been destroyed in the year 4 B.C.) as the capital of Galilee, called by the name (never used by the Jews) *Diocæsarea.*[5] As the residence of the jovial Tetrarch from about the year 2 B.C. until, at least, A.D. 18,[6] Zippori offered ample opportunities for observing feasts and displays in a grand style. At any rate, Jesus might have seen there a king who " made a marriage for his son " (Mt. xxii. 2). That a life of plenty prevailed there is evident from the statement[7] that in Zippori an impoverished man, once belonging to a wealthy family, was supplied daily with a pound of meat from the community, since it was in accordance with his former habits. At the seat of the government there could not have been any lack of moneyed people who had business relationships with both the upper and the lower classes. Together with arsenals for the troops, there was also a royal bank,[8] and the lending and investing of money was a common thing

---

[1] *Bell. Jud.* ii. 18, 11. *Cf.* for the name, *Asamonaios-Chashmonay, Ant.* xii. 6, 1 ; Midd. i. 6, and *Heshmon,* Josh. xv. 27, for which Lukian has *Asimon,* Eusebius, *Asemona.*

[2] This is hardly a plural (as perhaps Jerome has already thought), but the kind of ending favoured in Galilee. See my *Grammatik des Jud.-Pal. Aramäisch,* 2nd ed., p. 102.

[3] *Ant.* xvii. 10, 5.   [4] *Ibid.,* xvii. 2, 1.

[5] This name, however, is not known to have been used before the time of Antoninus Pius. Concerning the reading in *Ant.* xviii. 2, 1, according to which the name given to it by Antipas was Autokrateris, see Schürer, *G. d. jüd. V.,* ii., p. 214.

[6] Otto, *Herodes,* col. 182.   [7] Tos. Pea iv. 10 ; b. Keth. 67b.

[8] *Vita* 9 ; *Bell. Jud.* ii. 4, 1.

there. When Jesus showed familiarity with such things (Mt. xxv. 27), it was most probable that He made His first acquaintance with them in Zippori. To its market, which consisted of an upper and a lower street,[1] the Nazarenes went to buy and to sell, and to Zippori also they went to borrow money and pay taxes; to the court of justice, and to prison.

Above all, Jewish Zippori was also the religious centre of the district. At a later time it possessed eighteen synagogues and a number of greatly revered religious teachers.[2] Probably the church built by Joseph in the year 330 was erected on the site of one of these synagogues. At least, close to the ruin of a church dating from the time of the Crusaders (which later was considered to have been dedicated to Anna, the mother of Mary[3]) a remnant of an Aramaic inscription was found in 1909, on a mosaic floor under it, which, according to Clermont-Ganneau's and to my own examinations, should be read: " Remembered (for good) Rabbi Judan, son of Tanchum, (son of——) who gave this (tablet)."[4] Later Zippori was also considered to have been the seat of the priestly order of Jedaya and the priestly family of Amok.[5] From among its priestly families Jose ben Illem had the honour of representing the high priest in Jerusalem on the Day of Atonement.[6] It is reported that it was Arsela of Zippori who once led the scape-goat, on the Day of Atonement, into the desert.[7] The Eth-narch himself did not fail to appear in Jerusalem for the festivals.[8] All this meant that there was a lively intercourse between the town and the centre of legal learning and of worship. Nazareth, through which it had to pass, could not have been untouched by it. Judah, the son of Hiskia, after the death of Herod, kindled a rebellion in Zippori and its neighbourhood, the punishment for which was the burning of the town and the enslavement of its inhabitants.[9] From this height, the Nazareans probably watched their chief city going up in flames. It would have frightened them, as it did the later inhabitants of Zippori, from any attempt to participate in such rebellions, apart from the fact that Nazareth itself could not in any case have played much of a rôle. In every

---

[1] Erub. 54b. [2] Klein, *Beiträge*, pp. 32, 42.
[3] John of Würzburg (1170); Tobler, *Descriptiones*, p. 111.
[4] Viaud, *Nazareth*, p. 182 f.; *PJB*, 1912, p. 38; Klein, *Jüd.-Pal.-Corp. Inscr.* ii. 5. Concerning the lintel of the door of this synagogue with Greek inscription, see Lommens, *Le Musée Belge*, 1902, p. 55; Klein, *ibid.*, p. 100.
[5] Klein, *ibid.*, p. 10. [6] p. Yoma 38d; Tos. Jom. i. 4; *Ant.* xvii. 6, 4.
[7] Yoma vi. 3 (p. Talm.). [8] *Ant.* xviii. 5, 3; *cf.* Lk. xxiii. 7.
[9] *Ant.* xvii. 10, 5, 9; *Bell. Jud.* ii. 4, 1; 5, 1.

respect it was but an insignificant place. When Nathanael, a native of Cana, was of the opinion that no good could come out of Nazareth (Jn. i. 47), he probably meant nothing more than that this place had neither a present nor a past which could give rise to any expectations. Yet this insignificant place, just because it stood out neither politically nor religiously, had qualifications which made it pre-eminently suitable for the education of Him who called Himself " the Son of man."

Towards the south no larger town is to be seen from the heights above Nazareth, and while northward the land would seem to an Israelite to have no historical associations, he would have a succession of memories as his eye moved towards this direction. There, to the east, in the forest-districts, important for the Carpenter of Nazareth, stood out the round buckle of Tabor, from which Barak rushed down to the plain (Judg. iv. 6, 12); almost as high in the south-east, above the little town of Nain, could be seen the peaked summit of the *Jebel Dahi*, which concealed the battle-field of Gideon (*cf*. Judg. vii. 1). Joined to these, in the further distance, were the mountains of Gilboa, on which Israel's first king came to a tragic end (1 Sam. xxxi. 4), and the mountainous land of Samaria, as far as Ebal and Gerizim, on the northern frontier of which the fortified place Megiddo brought to memory the death of the last God-fearing king of Judah, Josiah (2 Kings xxiii. 29). To the west, the mountain-panorama ends in the far distance with the mountain-range of the Carmel, the summit of which (perhaps called after the Elijah-sacrifice) rises opposite, only about eleven miles distant from here, whilst its northern promontory, in the further distance, dips its foot into the Mediterranean. According to a Jewish legend this mountain, together with Tabor, claimed to be the site of the giving of the Law.[1] No Israelite could look upon it without remembering Elijah who fought there for the God of Israel (1 Kings xviii. 21 *f*.), and his disciple Elisha who from here was called to Shunem (2 Kings iv. 25). Elijah and Elisha must have been heroes as well known in Nazareth as Barak and Gideon. It was not mere accident that Jesus referred to the former two. The latter two would have been of greater significance to the above-mentioned rebel, Judah the son of Hiskia, in Zippori. Here—the *spirit* of God; there—the *sword* of God.

But also the south on the opposite side gave cause for reflection. The land of the Samaritans, interposed in the direc-

[1] Ber. R. 99 (215a); *cf*. Targum Jerushalmi (ed. de Lagarde) on Judg. v. 5.

tion of Jerusalem, with its Gerizim, and its claim to be the proper place of worship, puts even before one who has never come into personal contact with the Samaritans the question : "Which is the place of true worship ? Where does God manifest His presence ?" Jesus liked to retire to the mountains for prayer. Even in Jerusalem the Mount of Olives was perhaps more to Him for this purpose than the Temple. The lonely height of *Neby Sa'in*, with its purple anemones and its thorny heath (*Poterium spinosum*), must have been to Him the earliest of these places of worship.

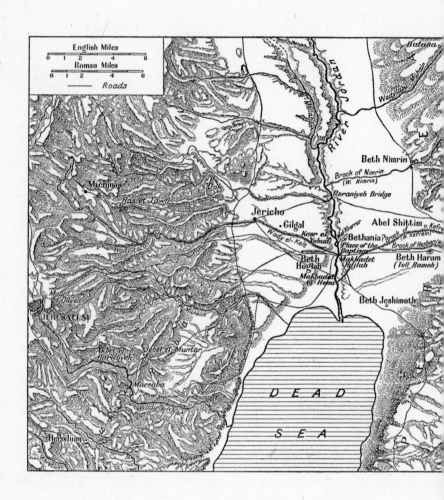

IV

AT THE JORDAN AND IN THE DESERT

THE Jordan is not the main outlet for the surface water of
Palestine; rather it carries off the water that comes from
Hermon and Transjordania. It rushes down a steep incline
with many windings along the broad bed which it has cut 50 to
60 metres deep in the marly soil of the long valley that cuts
Palestine into two halves, forming a little world of its own.
This valley again, because of the depth of the bed that the
Jordan has made for itself, is not watered by it. At the
southern end the height of the upland on the west cuts off the
rainfall, and the warmth of the climate causes so much evap-
oration that it can only be called a desert, which is suitable
for cultivation only where human skill, with the help of water
from springs or brooks, has formed watered patches, which
are little oases in its otherwise desert region. Nevertheless, it
must not be imagined that the Jordan valley is without its plants.
It possesses its own flora suitable to its dry climate. The
" pseudo-balm " tree (*Balanites ægyptica*)—which has nothing
in common with the genuine balsam-shrub—rears up its
small-leaved *corona* above the arid earth, but without supplying
any shade. The barren *Zizyphus lotus*, which requires a more
moist soil, forms, with its thorny branches, thick briers; a
proper tree, with small eatable fruits, and related to the former,
is the equally thorny *Zizyphus spina Christi*. The *Atriplex
Halimus*, with its pale green leaves, belongs to the *orach* species,
and offers, in the lowest parts of the plain, food more welcome
to camels than to men. The *Solanum sanctum*, which is related
to our potato, bears an uneatable yellow fruit with a bitter juice,
dangerous to the eyes. Fruits much like very large citrons,
but having only a woolly interior, hang upon the large-leaved
Calotropis procera. Legend (taken seriously by Josephus)[1]
makes these fruits of Sodom, which when plucked dissolve
into dust and ashes. On the ground creeps the coloquintida

[1] *Bell. Jud.* iv. 8, 4.

(*Citrullus colocyntis*) with its little leaves and yellow apples, resembling melons, which Elisha's disciples, who were evidently not natives of the district, wanted to cook as food (2 Kings iv. 39), but which are only of value as an aperient.   Milk is poured into the squeezed-out fruit and drunk.   The juice itself is too strong for this purpose.

The valley is on the whole a flat plain, dipping somewhat towards the middle, or else broken up into steps.   It is separated from the Jordan basin proper by a peculiar transition-region, in Arabic *el-Ketar*, " the hump," which is formed by the flow of the water into numerous ravines and fantastic table-shaped hills, reminding one of castellated mountains, but which, because of the softness and malleability of their material, cannot be used as strongholds.   To the pilgrim Theodosius[1] they seemed like the mountains " skipping like rams " of Ps. cxiv.,[2] " and when Jesus went down to Baptism, the very mountains walked or as it were skipped before Him, and look to this day as if they were leaping."   Only when, following a winding path, one has managed to find one's way among these " skipping hills," does one finally arrive at the real basin of this famous river.

One cannot see the water-course of the Jordan even when one is not far from it ; one is, however, aware of its presence because of the stretch of rich growth which encompasses it, and which the Palestinian Arab calls *zor*, " thicket."[3]   In comparison with the semi-desert above it, it gives the impression of lush fertility,[4] but is really only comparable with the alder-woods by the riversides of Germany.   The orach shrubs (*Chenolea arabica*) grow taller here and combine with the *Nitraria tridentata*—which bears reddish berries—to form a thick undergrowth.   Out of this, up to the banks of the river, rise Euphrates-poplars, the foliage of which suggests that of both our poplars and our willows ; and tamarisks with their slender, scaly branches and reddish blossom-panicles.   In the winter both these trees are bare and not at all attractive.   Only from April onwards is one charmed by their fresh green, in the midst of which doves coo and the nightingale of the East sings,

---

[1] Geyer, *Itinera*, p. 146.

[2] [The text is worth noting for comparison with the Vulgate : *Mare quare conturbatum es et tu Jordanes quare conuersus est retrorsum ? et uos montes, quare gestitis sicut arietes et uos colles sicut agni ouium.*—TRANSLATOR.]

[3] This is not applied to the whole of the Jordan valley, as it is usually stated, but only to its wooded parts.

[4] It was therefore called " the pride of the Jordan " (Jer. xii. 5 ; Zech. xi. 3)

and in October also one is delighted with the autumnal yellow, otherwise rare in Palestine, with which the winter announces its approach. The great masses of reed (*Phragmites communis*)[1] which grow to a height of 5 metres, and among whose brown panicles the wind plays, were also reckoned by Jesus as characteristic of the Jordan desert (Mt. xi. 7; Lk. vii. 24). The reed was praised as having better qualities than the cedar, for even when the strongest storm beats upon it, it only moves to and fro with the wind, while the cedar is torn out of the ground and broken down.[2] It is used for the building of huts as well as for other purposes as far away as Jerusalem. The reed which was put in our Lord's right hand at the Crucifixion (Mt. xxvii. 29) and the one on which the sponge was put (*v.* 48) must have come from the Jordan. Apart from the high-sprouting castor-oil plant (*Ricinus communis*) and the low-growing sweet-weed liquorice (*Glycyrrhiza glabra*) nothing else worthy of mention or offering anything of use to men grows here.

In the spring, the rising of the river to overflow its banks, together with the streaming of the rain-water down from the plains, often turns the ground near the bank into a swamp and drives away the visitor. In high summer again the intense heat makes sojourn here difficult. There are, however, periods in the spring and the autumn when the Palestinian lingers here with delight, and bathes in the river. And if he does not care to remain entirely in the open he can take up his abode in a hut, quickly constructed of boughs and reeds, although even in the winter it seldom rains here.

How often have I spent the night in this part! But one experience particularly impressed itself upon my mind. On November 8, 1910, I spent the night in the open air, with only three companions, near the bridge of the Jordan. The full moon which shone into our faces made sleep difficult. We listened to the sounds of the desert. Together with the soft murmuring of the stream and the play of the wind in the branches of the tamarisks, the howling of the jackals sounded through the night like the crying of children. A distant alarm-shot and the long-drawn-out anxious "Ho-ho-ho-ho," which the shepherds from the other side of the river gave out in high tones in order to call to their fellow-shepherds for help, brought to mind the

---

[1] *Arundo donax* does not seem to occur here, in spite of Killermann, *Die Blumen des Heiligen Landes*, ii., p. 14. Nor does papyrus grow here, although Josephus (*Ant.* xiv. 2, 3; *Bell. Jud.* i. 6, 3) uses this designation for the thicket by the Jordan.

[2] Taan. 20b.

serious business which lies behind this idyl, of the solitariness
of the Jordan, where, until the Middle Ages, lions and panthers
still lurked in the bushes.[1]

A hermit would be able to keep himself alive here by fishing and the hunting of wild pigs and snaring of wild doves,
especially if he managed to provide himself with bread and
had no lack of camel's milk or that of other grazing animals.
Locusts, which the Baptist ate, together with wild honey
(Mt. iii. 4), are, as a matter of fact, found more frequently in
uncultivated districts than in cultivated. Even to-day they are
used for food by the Bedouins, either cooked in salt-water, or
roasted on coals, then dried, reduced to powder, and eaten with
salt. But it is clear that from the uncertainty of the coming
of the locusts they cannot be considered as a regular article of
food. The Gospel of the Hebrews had good reason to suppress
the mention of the locusts. The same is true of the wild
honey even though in a time of less extensive bee-keeping wild
swarms occurred more frequently than at the present day.
Josephus refers to the Jordan region as being rich in honey.[2]
But at a later date "wild honey" was looked upon with
suspicion. In the seventh century Sophronius identified it
with the roots of a plant *meleagrion*[3] which can only be liquorice
and was found exclusively by the Jordan. With its stalks
water could be sweetened. Arculf, at about the same period,
had the round milk-coloured leaves of a tree pointed out to
him which, when dried and powdered, tasted like honey, and
which he calls " wild (or wood) honey."[4] This can only refer
to the afore-mentioned *Atriplex halimus*, which belongs to the
same neighbourhood and is still used for food by the Bedouins.
The leaves are cooked, then squeezed and eaten with curdled
milk. The Baptist would naturally have had to depend on other
things which the desert offered, besides locusts and honey.
To judge from his manner of life as described in the Gospels,
he must have avoided as much as possible all artificial things.
According to Lk. vii. 33, he neither ate bread nor did he drink
wine, and in his garments he avoided, according to Mt. iii. 4 ;
Mk. i. 6, linen, cotton, and sheep's wool, and his raiment was of
camel's hair with a leathern girdle, or, according to Codex D,
of camel's skin. As the girdle is mentioned separately, it

[1] See Jer. xlix. 19, and the lion running after a gazelle on the Madaba map.
[2] *Bell. Jud.* iv. 8, 3.
[3] Migne, *P. G.* lxxxvii. 3, col. 3756. The same in the Ebionite Gospel,
where μέλι ἄγριον with the taste of manna cannot mean honey.
[4] Geyer, *Itinera*, p. 272.

could not have been a leathern apron, or the strap (Arab. *berim*) of the Bedouins, which, in order to avoid delay in case of an attack,[1] is often wrapped round the naked body, and frequently not taken off even at night.

The Arab calls the Jordan *esh-Sheri'a*, and in order to differentiate it from its greatest tributary, it is also called—but only in the neighbourhood of the latter—*esh-Sheri'a el-kebire*. The usual translation is "the great drinking-place," but the Palestinian thinks—at least now—of *sheri'a* not in connection with the watering of herds—of which the banks of the Jordan do not permit anywhere—but rather of its swiftly downward-flowing (*shari'*) water. The soft substance of a former sea-floor through which it hastens towards the Dead Sea is the cause of its bed's not having an absolutely straight path. Now to the left, now to the right, the current pushes against the marl-heights of the *Ketar*, burrows under them, and breaks off pieces from them, so that we find perpendicular precipices arising. Occasionally also the river-bed is dried up for a time, as was experienced by the children of Israel (Josh. iii. 16), and as has also happened in later times.[2] The strong current and the crumbling nature of the steep banks make the otherwise unimportant river (which at the place of the Baptism is 50 metres broad and in February about 6 metres deep) at times, and especially at this point, a usually difficult and often impassable frontier. When its water is low in the autumn and flows more slowly, it is possible to swim across it and even to wade through its fords, with the clothes carried on the head; sheep being borne across on the shoulders. An old photograph shows this, and the persons carrying sheep are only up to the hips in water. Rabbi Ze'ira once waded through the Jordan in his clothes, in order to honour it as a part of the land of Israel.[3] In the spring, to swim it is an adventure; to wade across, impossible. The Dead Sea has risen since 1892 to the amount of 3 metres,[4] and made the fords of the lower course of the Jordan undercurrent, *Makhadet el-Henu* and *Makhadet Hajlah*, altogether impassable. If it were not for the bridge higher up, all crossing here would entirely have ceased.[5]

---

[1] I was told this by a Bedouin.

[2] *Cf.* the Arabic historian Nuwari's account of the Jordan being dammed by a landslip in this neighbourhood, so that the river-bed was dry, in 1267. *PEFQ*, 1895, p. 253. Also in October, 1914, a twenty-four-hour stoppage was observed near the Jordan bridge.

[3] p. Shebi. 35c.

[4] So deep the island (which disappeared in 1892) was found to be in 1917.

[5] The boats which are maintained by the Greeks are not used for public traffic.

7

Apart from it, the bridge at the *Roraniyeh* ford, which notwithstanding its steep ascent on both sides, was used during the
war even for automobiles, would have attracted all the traffic.
Transports of corn and charcoal, conveyed by donkeys, and
also sheep for the shambles, cross and often make a halt here
under the protection of the revenue officer in charge of the
bridge. He collects a toll for every animal crossing (men go
free), and, as the lessee of the customs, is naturally watchful
that no one should evade the bridge. In olden times there
was a ferry here which was used even by David (2 Sam. xix. 19),
and is represented in the Madaba map. But the traffic was then
doubtless distributed—unlike to-day—between the existing
fords, towards which, therefore, the only passable ways run.
The fact that the population of the southern Jordan valley,
now composed mainly of Bedouins, was formerly greater than
it is now, was also conducive to this. On this side, beside the
Sultan spring, lay the fortified town of Jericho with its grove
of palm-trees. Then, west of the Jordan, at *'En el-Rarabeh*—
rising to *Wady el-Kelt*—was Gilgal; beside the *Ḥajlah* spring
lay Beth Hoglah; farther west, at a spot now uncertain, was
Beth Haaraba; on the other side of the Jordan, on the steppes
of Moab, Beth Nimin flourished by the brook of *Nimrin*;
by the brook of *Kefrein* was Abel Shittim;[1] by the brook of
Hesban, Beth Haram (*Tell Rameh*), which became in the time
of Christ a Hellenistic city bearing the name of Livias (Julias),[2]
and by its spring was Beth Jeshimoth. The irrigated plains
about the brooks—in which at present the *Zizyphus spina
Christi* grows luxuriantly in an almost forest-like manner and
in which the genuine acacia (*Acacia tortilis orsejal*) also occurs,
probably as a remnant of a larger stock—were at that time
certainly cultivated. The widely extended grove of palm-
trees at Jericho had its counterpart here, as the Madaba map
shows, and people came here to see—as a venerable and
amazing relic, perhaps in the shape of stone ramparts—the
presumed remnants of the camps of the Israelites, reaching
from Beth Jeshimoth to Abel Shittim, twelve miles long.[3] So

[1] Abel once had the name Shittim attached to it because of the *acacias*
(Num. xxv. 1; Josh. ii. 1; iii. 1); the whole plain at the brooks of *Kefrein* and
Hesban was perhaps designated Shittim. It is also possible that both Christ-
thorns and acacias, in spite of their different fruits, were called Shittim.

[2] Jos., *Ant.* xvii. 2, 1; p. Shebi. 38d.

[3] Num. xxxiii. 49. *Cf.* Ætheria in Geyer, *Itinera*, p. 51. In Lev. R. xx. (52b),
p. Sheb. 36e; b. Yom. 75b, the extension of the Israelites' camp is deduced from
the distance between Beth ha-Jeshimoth and Abel ha-Shittim, namely, 12 miles
or 3 parasangs; *cf.* Sota 34a.

the present wilderness was then occupied by a settled population, and the traffic over the Jordan must have been brisk, in spite of the customs barrier (Lk. xix. 2).

Notwithstanding all its oases, the Jordan valley remained a barren desert, as Josephus also testifies, after his description of the glorious gardens of Jericho.[1] The work of the Baptist—the centre of which was the Jordan (Mt. iii. 1-6; Mk. i. 5-9; Lk. iii. 2-20), thus showing that from Judæa and Jerusalem the spot was easy of access—must have taken place here, at the lower course of the Jordan close to Jericho. The Fourth Gospel (i. 19) also takes this relationship with Jerusalem for granted, but gives the more precise information that the Baptist's abode, the place where Jesus also was baptised, was Bethania beyond Jordan (Jn. i. 28; iii. 26). According to this Gospel, Jesus took up His abode there once again before He died (x. 40). But it seems that even before that He developed an independent activity in that neighbourhood (Jn. iii. 22; iv. 1), for the reference in iii. 23 to John baptising somewhere else seems to suggest that Jesus was baptising at the place where the Baptist had formerly exercised his activity, although the Judæan place of baptism might possibly have been on the western bank of the Jordan.

The old reading *Bethabara* for Bethania—which Origen (on Jn. i. 28) favours because, as he thinks, Bethania did not lie at the Jordan—does not at any rate refer to the district of Scythopolis,[2] where there is at present a ford of 'Abara. According to Judg. vii. 24—where Beth Bara stands probably for Beth 'Abara—there was a " ford-house " or " ferry-house " to the east of the territory of Ephraim. The name might occur in different places on this and the other side of the river. Perhaps Bethabara is intended to substitute a known locality for an unknown, indicating more exactly that the place of the Baptism was at the well-known crossing of that name. It is, moreover, to be observed that the Aramaic *Bethania' ibreh dejardena* (Bethany beyond Jordan[3]) and *Bet 'abera dejardena* (Beth 'Abara of the Jordan[4]) are very similar to one another in the matter of their consonants.

It is not likely that it was a proper village, but probably there were a few huts there for the people manipulating the ferry, the frontier- and toll-guards, and the customs officer, and a lodging-house or caravansary. The Madaba map has at

[1] *Bell. Jud.* iv. 8, 3.   [2] Schmidt, *Der Rahmen der Geschichte Jesu*, p. 206.
[3] Pal. Evang. AC Jn. i. 28.   [4] *Ibid.*, Codex B.

the ferry, above the place of Baptism, a house standing on piles,
and a ladder, evidently designed with a view to floods. Jesus
and the disciples might have lodged in any of the already
existing houses (*cf.* Jn. i. 38), but it is more probable that He
and they dwelt in one of those easily erected bowers, made
from reeds and branches of the Euphrates-poplar, like many
of the huts which were probably put up by those who remained
with the Baptist for any length of time, and similar to those
which can be seen even to-day on the banks of the Jordan.
Nathanael, according to Jn. i. 49, was satisfied with the shade
of a cultivated, or wild, fig-tree, like a certain Rabbi who
also was fond of teaching under a fig-tree[1] or another who
was in the habit of sitting under its shade for health's sake.[2]
That Nathanael wished to see Jesus but not be seen by Him,
seems the most important deduction from what Jesus said to
him.[3]

Church tradition—referred to for the first time by Origen
in his commentary on St. John, then by Eusebius and the
Madaba map, and also in Pseudo-Matthew[4]—has always
represented the place where Jesus was baptised by John in the
Jordan as being in just the spot shown to-day, namely, the ford
of *Ḥajlah*. He who is not inclined to follow this tradition
should not mention such an unlikely place as that which Zahn
suggests.[5] According to him John dwelt on the mountain,
in *Baṭana*=Botnia (Eusebius) and Betonim (Josh. xiii. 26), and
baptised about five miles away from there, at the estuary of
Wady abu Muhair, while Jesus lodged on this side of the Jordan,
in *Wady el-Mellaḥah*. More local knowledge is shown by
Féderlin,[6] who suggests *Tell el-Medeshsh*, near the *Roraniyeh* ford,
as the place of Baptism. Its position at the *Ḥajlah* ford would
fix it at that important high-road of traffic which connects first
Jerusalem with *Beth Haram* (*Livias*), then Judæa with southern
Peræa. The direct route thereto already branched off up in
the heights from the Jericho road, running south from *Wady
el-Ḳelt*, and thus passed the *Ḥajlah* spring towards the ford.
One could, however, also descend from Jericho by the road
into the Jordan valley and reach the same spot by going north
from *Wady el-Ḳelt* over Gilgal. This latter road had historical

---

[1] p. Ber. 5c ; Gen. R. lxii. (130b) and parallels. [2] Yoma 83b.
[3] *Cf.* my article " Under the Fig Tree," in *Expository Times*, 1921, p. 252.
[4] According to ch. iv., the eight-year-old Jesus goes from Jericho to the place
on the Jordan where the Israelites passed over.
[5] *Neue kirchl. Zeit.*, 1907, p. 290. [6] *Rev. Bibl.*, 1910, p. 542.

significance, since the children of Israel must have travelled it
(Josh. iii. 4), and according to 2 Kings ii. the scene of Elijah's
last wandering can best be imagined here.   When the Baptist
wished to gather people around him by the Jordan, it was
imperative for him to go to a place where there was much
traffic, to a ford, say, which, at that time, was naturally connected with a thoroughfare, and this from ancient times was a
thoroughfare of the first order.   In its neighbourhood, by the
Jordan, it was possible to be alone and also to have human
intercourse.   Its historical memories gave the spot also a
consecration which could not have been without significance
to the Baptist, for, although he was not Elijah (Jn. i. 21), he
took up the work of Elijah (Mt. xi. 14; Mk. ix. 11 f.), in order to
raise a new Israel from the Jordan.   Mt. iii. 1; Mk. i. 3 f.;
Lk. iii. 2 f., as well as Josh. xv. 61 f., make no distinction between the desert and the Jordan district.   In fact, the southern
Arabah is "desert" in the sense in which the Bible usually
employs this expression, and is not essentially different from
the Judæan desert in the highlands, which also has its oases.

That John the Baptist dwelt in a place beyond the Jordan
might have been due to his desire to avoid staying within the
domain of the Jerusalem authorities.   But it can also be explained by the local conditions.   From the west the *Wady el-
Ḳelt* here empties itself into the Jordan.   But in winter its
stream only rarely reaches the Jordan and in summer never.
On the other hand, on the far side, and but a little above, a small
brook rising from a spring, the *Wady el-Kharrar*, does empty
itself into the Jordan.   This spring has its origin in five or six
partly sweet, partly salt, wells, which spring up at about one
and three-quarter miles from the river, in a valley close to a
grove of old Euphrates-poplars.   On the south side of the
basin a hill stands out with the remains of what is most likely
a church.   This was a place easily approached from the ford,
and was yet away from the road, close to which there might
have also been a little hamlet : an ideal place for the Baptist,
who could gather disciples here and lead them to the nearby
river to be baptised.   Here one must look for the Transjordanian Bethania.   The Madaba map has, in fact, correctly
indicated the well the other side of Βεθαβρά with the marginal
remark Αἰνὼν ἔνθα νῦν ὁ Σαπσαφᾶς, which is to differentiate
this spot from its Αἰνὼν ἡ ἐγγὺς τοῦ Σαλή(μ) (Jn. iii. 23).
The note is probably meant to indicate that the place was once
called *Ainon*, *i.e.* "Place of a Spring," but now in Aramaic

Ṣaphṣapha, that is to say, " The Willow " (also in Arabic *Ṣafṣaf*) which, according to b. Sukka 34a, may be " The Euphrates-poplar " (Arab. *rarab*). Then, as now, such poplars must have stood in that spot. The tract of country below the wells might even have been used, as it is to-day, as a fig-plantation, and in it Nathanael probably found the tree under which he sat (see above). John Moschus[1] undoubtedly means the same spot by his Σάψας to the left of which is the brook Χωράθ (reminiscent of the present name *el-Kharrar*), where, in a small cave, John the Baptist is supposed to have been visited often by Jesus.[2] The LXX mentions in Josh. xv. 61 among the Judæan places of the " desert " a small place *Ainon*. This would not have been correct if it referred to this Transjordanian Ainon. But it is conceivable that the Ainon by the Jordan, so important to Christian tradition, had at this time come into the Bible text. Also at that time no Bethania was known in this neighbourhood, but there was known to have been an Ainon on the other side of the Jordan. *Beth Ainon*[3] or *Beth Enayim* (Beth Enaya) may have been its proper name, which in the Fourth Gospel was confused with Bethania.

The Greek tradition concerning the place where Jesus was baptised—that is, near the wells of the *Wady el-Kharrar*—had as its starting-point the story of Elijah. The pilgrim of Bordeaux was shown a hill in this direction as the place of Elijah's ascension.[4] There Antoninus, perhaps rightly, found also the brook Kerith, where the prophet was fed by the ravens (1 Kings xvii. 3), as well as the well where John baptised, and even Mount Hermon of Ps. cxxxiii. 3, the dew from which was supposed to have come as a cloud over Jerusalem and there been gathered outside the churches and used for miraculous cures.[5] Near this outlet of *Wady el-Kharrar*, in 1902, the remnants of two small buildings dating from Byzantine times were discovered.[6] One had been erected directly on a back-water of the Jordan and stood on a foundation of 9 by 10 metres, consisting of a quadruple square of arches, evidently in order to let the water have a free course. Whatever stood upon it no longer exists. Farther away from the Jordan is the foundation of a square chapel, 5 by 5 metres, where four Corinthian capitals were found. The statement that Jesus—at His Bap-

---

[1] Migne, *P.G.* lxxxvii. 3, col. 2854.
[2] Also Epiphanius Hagiop. speaks of this cave.
[3] *Cf.* Bet 'Enun, north of Hebron ; in Eusebius, Βεθανίν, Βηθενίμ.
[4] Geyer, *Itinera*, p. 24.   [5] Geyer, pp. 165, 199.
[5] *PJB*, 1913, p. 22 *f.* ; 1914, p. 13 *f.* *Cf.* Mommert, *Ænon and Bethania*, p. 53.

tism and before His Death—stayed beyond the Jordan (Jn. i. 28 ; x. 40) has naturally led to the erection of chapels there. So the pilgrim Theodosius, who came in the year 530 from Livias to the place of the Baptism, seems to have found there, on the east bank, a church of St. John the Baptist, erected by the emperor Anastasius (about 500), which, because of the floods of the Jordan, rested on arches.[1] Near it, a cross on a marble pillar stood in the Jordan to mark the Baptismal spot. Antoninus[2] (570), who also mentions Livias in connection with the place of the Baptism, found only a pillar there surrounded by a fence,[3] from which steps probably led up to a wooden cross erected in the water. At that time the church of St. John the Baptist, built by Anastasius, must have already fallen into ruin ; floods may have destroyed its foundations. Then probably the second and smaller building was erected, the four capitals of which belonged formerly to the larger one. The Persian devastation and the Arab penetration soon made an end to all Christian sanctuaries on the east bank. On the west bank, where the Madaba map already locates Betaraba (Euse-bius fixes it on the east bank), was a monastery of St. John with a church, erected even before this time, which undoubtedly existed in the time of Justinian,[4] and is also shown on the Madaba map with the designation : " τὸ τοῦ ἁγίου Ἰωάννου τοῦ Βαπτίσματος." This was situated above the river, on the height of the, at this point, narrow strip of land called Ketar, and was meant to be an important centre for the pilgrims who visited the Jordan from Jerusalem. The new building erected on this site in 1882 contains, under the church, undubitable remains from Byzantine times. Arculf, in 670, found under this monastery a small chapel resting on vaults on the bank, at the spot where Jesus was supposed to have taken off His clothes.[5] A stone bridge led over the water to a wooden cross at the place of Baptism, which in time of flood disappeared entirely under water. In this way at that time they tried to reach the old place. Later, even this was given up, and

---

[1] Geyer, *Itinera*, p. 145. The pilgrim in a later passage mentions things which were found on the east side, and the sentence : " Ubi Dominus baptizatus est trans Jordanem, ubi est mons modicus," would thus scarcely have been formulated if the author had not thought that the place of Baptism was near the eastern bank.

[2] Geyer, pp. 165, 199. [3] Geyer, p. 166 *obeliscus*, p. 200 *tumulus*.

[4] See Procopius, *De aedificiis* ; Antoninus (Geyer, *Itinera*, pp. 168, 201) ; Arculf (*ibid.*, 266).

[5] Geyer, p. 265 *f.* ; mentioned also by Phocas (1177) ; Migne, *P.G.* cxxxiii., col. 952.

instead, a stone was shown on the west bank to which point
the water was supposed to have risen at the time of the Baptism
of Jesus.[1]   A chapel also stood there once.   This place of the
Baptism on the west bank was originally, as it would seem,
directly opposite the place to the east, just below the monastery
of St. John (*Kaṣr el-Yehudi*), where the ford must also once have
been.   Here the *Wady el-Kharrar* provided a natural and easy
ascent towards the opposite valley.   Now the place of Baptism,
though without any precise indication of the actual situation,
is shown about a mile below this, where the Jordan, after a
bend to the east, again turns to the west, and there, in the
neighbourhood of the mouth of the *Wady el-Kelt*, is easy of
access from the plain.   The present ford (which has recently
become useless) lies to the east of this place of Baptism, near the
twist of the river from east to west, below a marl-bank, which
is washed away underneath, making the ascent to the eastern
plain difficult.   The river-bed at this point must often have
shifted since the time of Jesus.   Yet the water (which is grey
in the spring and reminded Arculf of milk) flowing strongly
between Euphrates-poplars in this region (about 380 metres
below sea-level) brings to mind events connected with the
history of the Old as well as of the New Testament Israel,
though no one can say with certainty where exactly the ford
was when Israel passed over the Jordan, or where the Baptist
went down with Jesus into its waters.   In the seventh century,
as also to-day, Epiphany was celebrated here by a consecration
of the water by night, after which the multitude plunged into
the cold floods, in order to participate in their beneficial power.[2]
The shirt worn at this time was believed to ease the hour of
death, and the water that was drawn and carried home was
supposed to be of great value in troubles of all kinds.   This
superstition originated probably in an Egyptian Nile-custom,[3]
for which the Feast of Epiphany was intended to be a substitute.
However, it does not alter the fact that the water with which
our foreheads are sprinkled at baptism has an inseparable
historical connection with the Jordan water.   At the same time
it must be observed that, according to Jewish legal tradition,[4]
the water of the Jordan is unsuitable as a water of purification
from defilement in connection with dead bodies, since, according to Num. xix. 17, this must always be " living water," *i.e.*

---

[1] Theoderich, ed. Tobler, p. 73 *f.*   [2] Antoninus (Geyer, p. 167).
[3] Holl, *Sitzungsberichte d. K. Pr. A. d. W.*, 1917, p. 435.
[4] Para viii. 10.

spring water,[1] while the Jordan water is a mixture of spring water and such as is unsuitable for the uses of purification, *e.g.* swamp-water or water of hot wells. What the Baptist and Jesus carried out in the Jordan has no connection with the system of Jewish legal purifications.

When the deep ditch of the Jordan valley was formed, the western side did not remain stationary, but sank by two grades between this deeply rent fissure and Jerusalem. In this way a slope of the land was formed which, because of the warmer air rising here, has less rainfall the deeper it is. While at a greater height the ridge has, in its wild flora, still the character of the upland, and exhibits similar possibilities of cultivation, about midway the desert flora begins, and scanty pasturage is the only thing that the soil offers. The German translation of the Hebrew *midbar* by " Steppe," introduced by Kautzsch in his translation of the Bible, gives, neither in the higher nor in the lower levels, a proper conception of the nature of this *desert*, which lacks at all seasons the exuberant growth of a steppe. In fact, it is not a steppe because it is not a plain but has been cut up all over by torrents into mountains and valleys, with bold precipitous walls where the depth of the fall gave the water a greater cutting power, but elsewhere exhibiting softer forms because of the nature of the Senon (chalk). The few springs rising here lie so deep that in their valleys narrow strips of a richer vegetation are discoverable, it is true, but these cannot be made use of for the watering of a larger area. Hence oases with wide irrigated districts, such as are found in the Jordan valley, are out of the question in the desert uplands. The transition from the flat wilderness of the Jordan valley to the upland wilderness is so marked by the slope of the fissure, which reaches a height of 300 metres, and is often almost perpendicular, that the " leading up " of Mt. iv. 1 needs no explanation to a Palestinian, and to describe it as a " transference through the air "[2] seems unjustifiable. The contrast between these two areas is heightened by the irrigated district near Jericho, with its palm-grove lying towards the Jordan, which was admired even as late as the seventh century A.D.[3] Josephus[4] ascribes to this area an extension of seven by two miles, which is impossible even when the water of the three

[1] It is thus translated in Targum Jer. 1, without further explanation.
[2] So Spitta, *Die synoptische Grundschrift*, p. 37.
[3] Arculf, in Geyer, p. 268.
[4] *Ant.* xv. 4, 2 ; *Bell. Jud.* iv. 8, 3. What Bede (Geyer, p. 314) says of it is taken from Josephus and is not found in Adamnanus, *ibid.*, p. 263.

springs in the upper current of the *Wady el-Ḳelt* and the springs
of *Doḳ* and *Naaran* are included. At present, the water of the
Sultan spring does not travel above two and three-quarter
miles, but Treidel[1] thinks that were the water of the *Wady el-
Ḳelt*—which now flows uselessly away—utilised, a larger portion
of the land could be brought under cultivation. But even if
Josephus' estimate were lessened by half, what is left is considerable, when compared with the present conditions of the
parts round Jericho.[2] The estimate given by Jewish tradition
of the "fat area" (*doshna shele-Jericho*)[3] is far below the actual
fact. According to this, it consisted of 500 square ells only
(*i.e.* 4·25 hectares). That estimate is not based on an observation of the actual spot, but is deduced from the measurement
of the Sanctuary in Jerusalem.[4] When, that is to say, the
tribe of Benjamin relinquished this area, it received an equivalent in the "fat area of Jericho" which had belonged till
then to the Kenites.[5] Antoninus exaggerates when he writes
in connection with Jericho of dates a pound in weight,
citrons weighing 40 pounds, and beans two feet long.[6] According to Josephus, apart from palms (instead of which now
bananas are grown), the genuine balsam-shrub, the aromatic
henna (*Lawsonia alba*) and the myrobalanus (probably *Balanites
ægyptica*)—which is the only wild tree left—were grown there
in the time of Christ. But the oleander-bushes of Jericho, the
many-petalled (*i.e.* filled) blossoms of which were admired so
much in later times,[7] were already famous in those far-off days.[8]
Anyone coming to the highlands from the Jordan ascended,
indeed, from a gloriously situated oasis to a desolate mountain
desert.

In the lower part of the desert Senon-chalk is exposed to
view and, in the absence of shade, blinds the eyes of the traveller.
That he can occasionally catch a glimpse of the brook in the
depths of the *Wady el-Ḳelt*, coursing through its tall reeds, is no
consolation to him, because of the desolate and arid landscape
which surrounds him. On the hills around, black bands of

---

[1] In Blankenhorn, *Naturwissenschaftliche Studien am Toten Meer*, p. 71.
[2] The account given by Theoderich (ed. Tobler, pp. 69, 7) of the *hortus Abraham* is not quite clear. It was supposed to have begun half a mile from the
Jordan and have been a mile in extent.
[3] Sifre on Num. lxxxi. (English translation by P. P. Levertoff, S.P.C.K.).
[4] Midd. ii. 1 ; *cf.* Ezek. xlii. 16.
[5] *Cf.* my article, "Die Stammeszugehörigkeit der Stadt Jerusalem und des
Tempels," *Graf Baudissin-Festschrift*, p. 116.
[6] Geyer, pp. 169, 202.   [7] Theoderich, ed. Tobler, p. 74.
[8] Sirach xxiv. 14.

flint show how the upper layers of the Senon folded themselves at their sinking. On the slopes, where sheep and goats find a little pasture in the winter even here, parallel paths pass diagonally. Here and there a miserable-looking shrub of broom (*Retama rœtam*) reminds one of the fleeing Elijah resting in the desert (1 Kings xix. 4).[1] It is vain to look for shade here. I remember how on April 22, 1900, I wandered here alone in the intense heat. A robust Bedouin girl came towards me carrying on her head a large bundle of thorns which she had collected. Crying loudly, she threw the burden to the ground. When I asked her : " What is the matter with you ?" she only said : " *Atshane* " (" thirsty "). I gave her to drink from a little flask which I had fastened to my horse's saddle, and was then glad to discover in this hot, blinding world, in which it was impossible to sit still in the sun, a little shade beneath a bridge. So one can understand the rabbinic admonition to empty out a jug containing honey, when in the desert, to save the water from another which has cracked. For " it is water, not honey, that saves life in the desert."[2]

How helpless one is in the desert ! Every lonely traveller is looked upon with suspicion, and at any sign of foul play it is the custom quickly to disappear (Lk. x. 31 *f.*). Bedouins would then, as now, have tended their flocks and pitched their tents here and there in this desert. In the time of Jesus the Essenes often lived here, in such places as contained wells to supply them with water ; probably in the very ravines of the *Wady el-Ḳelt, Wady Mukelik, Wady Far'a, Wady er-Rawabi, Wady en-Nar, Wady Khreṭun*, where, later, Christian hermits settled. John the Baptist might also have lived somewhere about here, before he started on his public activities at the ford of Jordan. In later times the deserts Kutila, Ruba, and Suka were differentiated ; the last is in the neighbourhood of *Wady Khreṭun*,[3] whilst Ruba must be sought in the *Ibḳe'a*[4] and Kutila lay farther south near the Dead Sea.[5] Suka reminds one of the desert *Ṣuḳ*, where in the time of Christ the scapegoat was sent down from the Temple on the Day of Atonement.[6] A distance of twelve miles is estimated for this, which would take it almost as far

[1] [The Hebrew *rothem* is incorrectly translated in the A.V. *juniper* (after Jerome). —TRANSLATOR.]
[2] Tos. Bab. K. x. 28 ; p. Bab. K. 7e.
[3] *Vita Charitonos*, Migne, *P.G.* cxiv., col. 914.
[4] *Vita Euthymii*, P.G. cxiv., cols. 662, 676.
[5] Joh. Moschus, *Prat. spir. P.G.* lxxxvii. 3, cols. 2908, 2958 ; *Vita Euthymii,* cxiv., cols. 606, 676.
[6] Yom. vi. 4-6 ; Sifra 80a.

as the Dead Sea. A place called *Beth Hadudu*[1] is mentioned as the beginning of the desert, and this is only three miles from Jerusalem. This fits neither the *Herodium*[2] nor the mountain-peak *Ṭantur Ḥdedun*,[3] with which it had been identified, but the locality *Khirbet Ḥaredan*,[4] after which, on the way to Marsaba, the '*Akbet el-Harediyeh* is named. This lies in the *Wady en-Nar*, three miles from Jerusalem, and is, in fact, the real beginning of the desert from the direction of Jerusalem. In this direction, then, was the scapegoat led to the neighbour-hood of the Dead Sea, and the name *Suk* would have comprised the desert between *Wady en-Nar* and *Wady Khreṭun*. North of *Wady en-Nar* the desert of Ruba began.

Jesus stayed only a short time in the desert; He found temptation in it, and soon returned to inhabited country. Stones, which are frequently enclosed in softer lime, and appear to take the form of loaves, remind one even to-day of those stones which the Tempter desired our Lord to turn into bread (Mt. iv. 3 ; Lk. iv. 3). Up the ascent towards the west there is also no lack of places in the desert from which one can get good long-distance views, even though the view of " all the kingdoms " is not possible from any mountain on earth. On the edge of the Jordan valley the mountain which was called " the stronghold of *Dok* " in the time of Christ, rising to about 250 metres,[5] best fits the episode. Already in the year 340 its caves tempted Chariton to found a hermitage there.[6] Since the time of the Crusaders it has been looked upon as the place where Jesus fasted for the forty days, and was given the name *Quarantana*. Theoderich[7] mentions the zigzag way which led up the steep side of this mountain, first to a chapel dedicated to Mary, then to an altar in the form of a cross, near to which, halfway up the mountain, was the spot which was (and is still) shown as the rocky seat of Jesus. On the peak, near one of the Templars' citadels, the Tempter's seat was indicated on a rock. The extensive view from here to the east over the Jordan valley and the Dead Sea, and from Hermon to the southern frontier of Moab—as well as to the west, as far as the watershed of the highland—took in at that time only the small

[1] Yom. vi. 8 ; *cf.* Targ. Jer. i.; Lev. xvi. 10. Variants : Haduru, Haduri, Harudu, Charuru, Choron.

[2] See Klein, *ZDPV*, 1910, p. 33 ; *Erez Israel*, pp. 38, 118.

[3] Schick, *ZDPV*, 1880, p. 218 *f*.

[4] Thus according to my enquiries; the English map has *Haradan*.

[5] 1 Macc. xvi. 15 ; *Ant.* xiii. 8, 1.

[6] *Vita Charitonos*, P.G. xcv., col. 912.   [7] Ed. Tobler, p. 70 *f*.

domains on both sides of the Jordan ; yet in spite of its diminu-
tiveness it could well have been a glance into the wide world
and the glory thereof (Mt. iv. 8 ; *cf.* Lk. iv. 5), within which
the Tempter carried on his work. But the same would be
true of the 599 metres high *Ras et-Tawil*, east of Michmas,
which, according to 1 Sam. xiii. 18, looked towards the " valley
of the hyænas " (Zeboim), in the direction of the desert ; this
may have been, and in the thirteenth century was considered
to have been, the Mountain of the Temptation.[1] The *Jebel
el-Muntar* (523 metres high) by Marsaba, from which the whole
of Palestine, from Hermon to the south of the desert of Judah,
can be viewed, would also be eligible ; but, above all, the
Mount of Olives (2,723 feet above sea-level), on the high
land at the edge of the desert, with its magnificent view over
the eastern regions. The synoptic narrative mentions no
particular spot, but it has local colour when it speaks of a wide
perspective. The desolation and the distant views are characteristic of the desert of Judah, sloping towards the east.
The transition from the " high mountain " to Jerusalem and
her Temple (Lk. iv. 9), which lie behind the height just here, is
then natural. The purpose of the reversed order in Mt. iv. 5
would in that case have been an intensifying of the Temptation,
i.e. from the Temple-pinnacle to the Mountain.

The Essenes in the time of Christ lived in the desert in order
to avoid coming into contact with the ritual uncleanness of
humanity. The Baptist stayed in the wilderness only in order
to judge the sinful life of the people. Jesus left the desert,
the scene of His Temptation, in order to spread the seed of the
Kingdom of God throughout the whole world.

The opinion of Grätz (*Geschichte der Juden* iii. 3, pp. 294, 660)
that the name of the Essenes is to be derived from the Aramaic
ashae, as meaning *tobelim*, " baptisers," has been used by
Raschke (*Werkstatt des Markus-evangelisten*, p. 123 *f.*) as a proof
that John, by his designation as " Baptist," was thought of as
being an Essene. But the Aramaic *seha* is the usual word for
" bathing," not " plunging." Should a never-occurring *Aphel*
be formed from it, it is only the participle *mashe* which could
be brought into consideration here, which, however, does not
lead to Ἐσσαῖος, and in any case would designate a " bather,"
not a " baptiser," *i.e.* one who causes others to plunge into
the water. Also the *tobele shaharit*, " the morning bathers " of
Tos. Jad. ii. 20, p. Ber. 6c, b. Ber. 22a, are not such as make

[1] *PJB*, 1913, p. 27.

others dive but persons who do it themselves. John's epithet is unique : it can be translated into Hebrew only with *ha-maṭbil*; in Aramaic the same root as *maṭbela* or *maṭbelana* could be used. The Palestinian *Evangeliarium* has *aṣba'* for "baptising," *maṣhe'ana* for " the Baptist "; the Peshita has *a'ḥmed* and *ma'medana*. The root *'amad*, for " plunging," is east-Aramaic ; *ṣeba'* stands in Jewish west-Aramaic specially for " colouring." As *ṭebal* is the word for ritual baths, *maṭbelana* must be considered as the most probable Jewish form of the epithet. Thus the epithet does not make John an Essene. But, apart from this, he could not have been one from all we know of his activity. He lived as a hermit, while it was characteristic of the Essenes that they realised their religious ideal in community life. Above all, the daily bathings of the Essenes were of a ritual nature, and had nothing in common with the solitary Baptism of John as a sign of the moral turning to God and the desire for purification from sin (Mt. iii. 11 ; Mk. 1. 4 ; Lk. iii. 3).[1] That the Jordan water, being of a mixed nature, was not considered legally admissible for purposes of purification has been mentioned before. It is remarkable that Josephus (*Ant.* xviii. 5, 2)—differing from the Evangelists—records that John taught that the Baptism, the purpose of which was bodily purification, was only pleasing to God when the soul had already been purified. That would mean that John, in fact, *warned men off baptism* and in that case could not be considered as the " Baptist." If the passage is authentic, then Josephus did not grasp the real attitude of the Baptist. But even if Josephus' characterisation be right, it would not make John an Essene. If he originally belonged to them, he must have come to the conviction that their baths could not save the people from the divine judgment and that something greater and better was needed. Even if their name is connected with the east-Aramaic *ḥasya*=ὅσιος[2]—which, however, cannot be documented from Palestinian literature—even then there is no connection between them and St. John the *Baptist*.

---

[1] [For the significance of the Baptism of John, *cf.* Levertoff, in the *New Commentary* (Mt.), p. 133 *f.*]

[2] Thus Schürer, *Geschichte* ii. 4, p. 654 *f.* ; Klausner, *Historia yisraelith* ii. 2 (Jerusalem, 1924), p. 92 *f.*

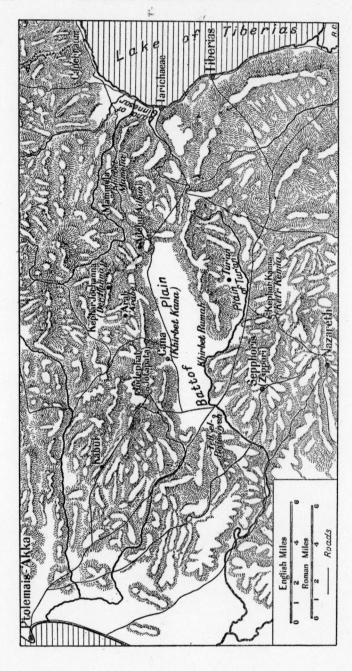

V

CANA IN GALILEE

THE miracle at the marriage-festival in Cana (Jn. ii. 1 f.) leads us from the desert to the north, towards fertile Galilee. It is, moreover, noteworthy that, according to this Gospel, the way of Jesus from Judæa to Galilee led Him twice to this Cana (i. 43 ; cf. ii. 2 ; iv. 43, cf. ver. 46). If the expression " Cana of Galilee " in ii. 1, 11 ; iv. 46 ; xxi. 2 is accurate, this Cana must be sought in *Khirbet Ḳana*, about seven and a half miles north of Nazareth. This is the only place where the name Cana is preserved in Galilee proper, and the constant specification τῆς Γαλιλαίας was meant most probably to distinguish it from the Tyrian Cana, proving that Galilee had but *one* Cana, which in all likelihood was *Khirbet Ḳana*.[1] Josephus' stay in Galilæan Cana[2] fits in with this also ; on a certain night he marched with 200 men from there to Tiberias. For the fortified place which dominates the *Baṭṭof* valley, four and a half miles to the north of the old Galilæan capital, Sepphoris, lay on the straight road from Tarichææ to Ptolemais-'Akka, which at this spot enters the uplands, in order to reach its destination through Jotapata and Kabul, while from here also a more convenient southern by-road branches off towards the same place.[3] Thus Cana was suitable as a centre for anyone who wished to organise rebellion in Galilee, but had powerful enemies in its larger towns, and therefore could not make any of them his permanent abode.

That this is the Cana of the New Testament was well known

---

[1] The Peshita rendering of Cana with *Katne*, which might also be read *Katna*, is as puzzling as is its rendering of Cana in Josh. xix. 28 with *Kaa*. One is inclined to think that the real name was, for one reason or another, offensive to the Syrian translators. Ravanelli, *Bibliotheca sacra* (1660), suggested that the Galilæan Cana was thus designated " small " (*katne*) in contradistinction to the Tyrian Cana, as it is by Jerome in his *Onomasticum*. But this topographical combination (also applied by Lightfoot, *Horæ hebr. et talm.*, p. 973) is improbable.

[2] *Vita* 16 f.   [3] *Cf.* Masterman, *PEFQ*, 1914, p. 179 f.

even from the time of the Crusaders to the sixteenth century.
Witnesses to this are Sæwulf in 1103, Burchard in 1283,[1]
Marino Sanuto in 1321, Johannes Poloner in 1421.[2] Daniel,
1106, could also not have meant anything else, when he arrived
there *via* the village Isavovo (read *Isavoro=Sephoro*),[3] and John
of Würzburg also is to be thus understood, although his
assertion that the direction of Cana from Sepphoris is eastwards
is as wrong as his saying that Mount Hermon lay in an eastern
direction from Tabor.[4] Indubitable witnesses also are two
Florentine maps of the twelfth and thirteenth centuries respectively, which set Sepphoris between Cana and Nazareth.[5]
The reference is always to *one* Cana only, which the Archbishop
of Nazareth made over to the Johannites in the thirteenth
century.[6] This Cana was probably visited also by Willibald
in 726,[7] by Antoninus in 560,[8] by Theodosius in 530,[9] and by
St. Paula in 400,[10] although one cannot come to any certain
conclusions from their statements.   Only from the seventeenth
century on do we find other statements.   Quaresmius in 1620
still mentions that in Nazareth and its neighbourhood Cana of
Galilee is pointed out as being in the north, but adds that north-
east of Nazareth there is a " Sepher Cana " (read Cepher Cana)
where the ruins of a church are recognisable.[11] From this
time onward the pilgrims Roger (1631), Neitschitz (1636),
Surius (1644-47), and Doubdan (1652) only describe a Cana
lying to the north-east of Nazareth, on the road to Tiberias,
and are evidently thinking of the present *Kefr Kenna*, which
will be dealt with in Chapter VI.   There is no doubt that after
a century-long break in the Christian tradition this change was
brought about by the Franciscans,[12] who came as strangers to
Nazareth in 1620.   The convenient position of the new Cana
on the way to the lake of Tiberias was doubtless an effective
motive for this change.   Robinson[13] in 1841 was the first
to draw attention to *Khirbet Kana*, which at the time he saw

[1] Laurent, *Peregrinatores medii ævi quatuor*, p. 44.   From Burchard, Bernhard
of Beydenbach (1483) copied.   Latin ed. 1502, Germ. ed., *Reyszbuch desz heyligen
Lands* (1584), pp. 67b, 68b.
[2] Tobler, *Descriptiones Terræ Sanctæ*, p. 271 f.
[3] Leskien, *ZDPV*, 1884, p. 55.
[4] Tobler, p. 112.   [5] *ZDPV*, 1891, Plate I.; 1895, Plate V.
[6] Rohricht, *ZDPV*, 1887, p. 253.   [7] Tobler, p. 25.
[8] Geyer, *Itinera*, p. 161.   [9] *Ibid.*, p. 139.
[10] Tobler, *Palæstinæ descriptiones*, p. 24.
[11] *Elucidatio Terræ Sanctæ*, ii., p. 852.
[12] The story of the Franciscans suffering in Nazareth is described by Meistermann, *New Guide*, p. 482.
[13] *Palästina*, iii., p. 445.

only from a distance, and Sepp[1] in 1846 was one of the first to examine it more fully.

The Jewish liturgical poet, Eleasar ha-Kalir, is undoubtedly thinking of the Galilæan Cana when, in his elegy *Echa yasheba chabazzeleth*, he refers to the priestly order of Elyashib as " the priestly order of Kana."

Coming, according to Jn. i. 44 ; iv. 46, from Judæa, Jesus' easiest route to Cana would have been by way of Nazareth. The nearest way led at that time through the hilly district of Zippori and through this place. At *Khirbet Rumah*, which Josephus[2] and rabbinic literature[3] refer to as Ruma—inhabited by Jews—the traveller enters into the wide plain of *Baṭṭof*, which was then called after a place, at its eastern end, which has now disappeared, " The plain of Beth Netopha."[4] It is not so suitable for cultivation as one might expect, because it slopes not towards the west where it has its natural outlet, but towards the east. In the winter, therefore, the water gathers there, forming a swamp, which even in April often looks like a lake. The edges of the plain, however, are higher, and are therefore able even to-day to supply the needs of three villages at the southern edge as well as of one on the north-west. Quite high mountain-chains (about 500 metres high) bound the plain on the north and south, and make it, together with a barrier across east and west, a world in itself. It has a natural approach on the south side, by its connection with the plain of *Ṭur'an*, through which its chief thoroughfare connects it with east and west. Opposite the junction of this route with the plain lies *Khirbet Ḳana*, in a commanding position on a hill which rises on its northern edge, isolated on the west by a long valley opening out here on the east to a little plain, and on the north by a low watershed between the two, so that one can call it detached. Round about, higher mountains rise on three sides, partially wooded, where the bushes of broom (*Spartium junceum*) and *Calycotome villosa*, with the richness of their yellow blossoms among the dark scarlet-oaks, terebinths, carob-beans and arbutus-trees, make a delightful picture. A gentle slope southward now shows the remains of a village on a terrace, probably dating from Arab times. In it Burchard and Poloner visited a subterranean vault, shown as the hall of the marriage-feast, and also the place where stood the six water-pots of stone of Jn. ii. 6. The marriage-couch seen by

[1] *Jerusalem und das Heilige Land*, ii., p. 101.   [2] *Bell. Jud.* iii. 7, 21.
[3] p. Erub. 22a.   [4] Shebi. ix. 5.

Antoninus in 570, on which he laid himself down and wrote the names of his parents, may have been in this same place; also two water-pots, one of which he filled with wine and carried on his shoulders to the altar. A cistern was there also, in the hallowed water of which he bathed. But the original and oldest town of the ancient locality must have stood on the still higher rocky summit of the hill (165 metres long and 60 metres wide) as the ruins and cisterns also suggest.[1] The six pots of purification-water could not have been filled from a well, as there is no water bubbling from any depth in the neighbourhood. But on the height above, water was gathered in cisterns, as it is still in the middle of the southern slope of the town's hill. The locality had its special importance because it held the key of access to the fortified place *Jodephat* (Jotapata),[2] approachable by the valley on its western side; as well as to the roads towards the coast which passed near by and to the more northerly Galilee. These two places, Jodephat and Cana, only about a mile and a half distant from one another, were also, it would seem, closely linked by the fact that in both priestly families resided (in Jodephat the order of *Miyamin*).[3] Another reason must have been that the inhabitants of Jodephat possessed landed property in the plain, for the name of "Plain of Jotebath," or Jodephat,[4] can hardly be otherwise understood, since the town, enclosed as it was by the mountains, had no plain in its immediate neighbourhood.

Opposite Cana, in the south, lay Ruma, where at one time wealthy Jews used to distribute figs to the poor.[5] It was situated on the western end of the plain of Shichin[6] (now *Tell el-Bedewiyeh*).[7] To the east, the nearest neighbours were *Arab* (now *'Arrabeh*), on the other side of the mountainous northern edge of the plain; and, on its steep mountain-ridge, *Kephar Jochanna*, now *Der Ḥanna*.[8] The three latter places were in later times, like Cana and Jodephat, considered as seats of the priestly orders.[9] Among them, *Kephar Jochanna* had an ancient history, for it is most probably the *Channaton* of Zebulon

[1] Albright, *Bulletin of the American School of Oriental Research*, xi., p. 11, found here Hellenistic and Roman pottery.
[2] *Bell. Jud.* iii. 7; *Erach.* vi. 6.   [3] Klein, *Beiträge*, p. 50.
[4] Tos. Nidda iii. 11; b. Nidd. 20a.   [5] Tos. Er. iv. 17.
[6] *Cf.* Klein, *Palästina-Studien* i., p. 5 *f.*
[7] Albright found here traces of an ancient habitation, *Bulletin of the American School* (October, 1923), p. 11.
[8] *PJB*, 1913, p. 48 *f.*
[9] Klein, *Beiträge*, pp. 63 *f.*, 75 *f.*, 84 *f.* Windfuhr, *PJB*, 1922-23, p. 87 *f.* Kephar Jochanna, Klein identifies with Kefr 'Anan.

(Josh. xix. 14), and the *Hinatuni* of the Amarna letters, where a Babylonian caravan was once attacked on the way to 'Akka.[1]

Nathanael, whose home was in the fortified and important Cana (Jn. xxi. 2), had reason to look down with disdain on insignificant Nazareth (Jn. i. 47). Hesychius[2] had also understood the surname of the Apostle Simon (" the Canaanite," Mt. x. 4 ; Mk. iii. 18)—in spite of the rendering ζηλωτής, " the zealot," in Lk. vi. 15—in the sense of being "from Cana." This, however, would only be possible if one may assume the doubling of the last syllable in the name of Cana, according to the *nunation* popular in Galilee. One could then for this interpretation of Κανavaîoς refer to Nonnus Panopolitanus,[3] who renders Cana of Galilee (Jn. ii. 1 ; iv. 46) with πέδον Κανavaîον Γαλιλαíης (Γαλιλαíων), as if it were " Cana-plain in Galilee."

To reach this Cana the nobleman from Capernaum (Jn. iv. 46-54) had a rather troublesome journey of fifteen miles, which meant practically a day's travelling, even if he took the most direct route. On the way he would pass *Mammela*, now *Khirbet Mamelia*, the later seat of the priestly order Chezir, and *Ailebu*, now *Ailbun*, where the priestly order Hakkoz lived.[4] Had he started at sunrise, he could have reached his destination at noon, and at the seventh hour (Jn. iv. 52) have heard the soothing words of Jesus, but would have been able to do only half of his return journey, as far as *Mammela*, on the same day, so that his servants would have met him at the plain of Gennesaret on the following day.[5]

The miracle of the healing from a distance, the locality of which is irrelevant, is connected with the marriage-miracle in Cana. If there was already a settlement of priests there at that time, it would be conceivable that it became our Lord's home for a time, and that Mary was present at the marriage

---

[1] Karge, *Rephaim*, p. 299, looks for it in Kefr 'Anan, which, however, does not fit it phonetically. A convenient road leads from Akka, through Der Hanna, to the Via Maris.

[2] Migne, *P.G.* xciii., col. 1405.

[3] Migne, *P.G.* xliii., col. 760 *f.*

[4] Klein, pp. 50, 73 *f. Cf. PJB*, 1913, p. 49 ; 1922-23, p. 84 *f.*

[5] It cannot be proved that the past day was called " yesterday " in the evening, so that the nobleman might have returned the same day. On the contrary, in Ruth ii. 19, for instance, it is referred to as " to-day." In p. Pea 21b, we read of one who asks in the evening to be pardoned for not having come to eat " to-day." Although the day was reckoned from evening to evening, the use of " to-day " and " to-morrow " was the same as with us.

(Jn. ii. 1) because it was connected with her priestly relations (see above, p. 52).   It is not without cause that the Fourth Gospel's record of this event is found in the context in which the other Gospels relate the temptations of the desert.   " The Baptist came, neither eating bread nor drinking wine. . . . The Son of Man is come, eating and drinking. . . ."

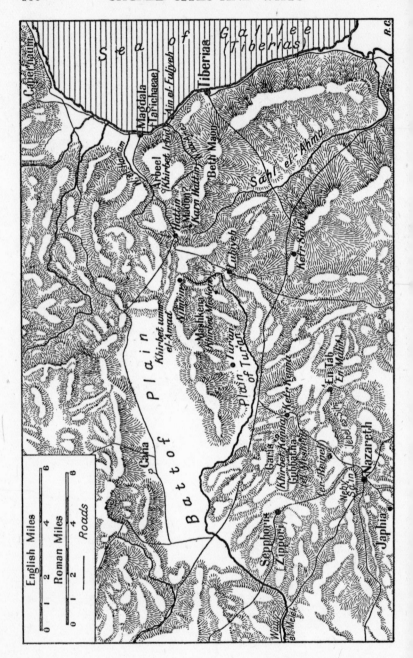

VI

FROM NAZARETH TO THE SEA OF GALILEE

St. Mark speaks of our Lord's teaching activities in the synagogues of " all Galilee " in one passage (i. 39), where St. Luke (iv. 44) substitutes " Judæa " for " Galilee,"[1] although the context points to Galilee only. His purpose was probably to emphasise by the general expression " the Jewish land " ('Ιουδαία) the great extent of Jesus' activity.[2] Similar statements are found in other places also, in Lk. (iv. 15 ; viii. 1) and Mt. (iv. 23 ; ix. 35). Out of Galilee, therefore, the fame of Jesus spreads over the whole of Palestine and draws from all parts listeners to His words and sick persons seeking help. Lk. mentions (vi. 17) Judæa, Jerusalem, and the coast of Tyre and Sidon ; Mt. (iv. 25)—Galilee, Decapolis, Jerusalem, Judæa, and Peræa ; Mk. (iii. 8 f.) leaves out the Decapolis, but mentions Idumæa (bordering on Judæa in the south) and the districts of Tyre and Sidon. It is taken for granted that Galilee has close connection with all parts of Palestine, so that information concerning Jesus quickly reached all the corners of the land. Even if the Gospel statements are merely intended to emphasise how generally Jesus became known, and the expressions, exaggerated in oriental fashion, need not be taken too literally, yet it is true that Galilee afforded an opportunity for broadcasting the news about Jesus. The Galilæan pilgrims, as well as wandering scribes, brought news about Him to the south, and the trade-route to the coast did the same westwards. The Decapolis as a neighbouring land, Peræa as the second part of the domain of Herod Antipas, were both connected with Galilee. Unfortunately, it is not stated exactly what points in Galilee the activity of Jesus reached ; but if we take Nazareth as a starting-point, this, with the inclusion of

---

[1] [*I.e.*, in the best MSS.—Translator.]

[2] Spitta uses it in support of his theory that an extended ministry in Judæa was described in this source. *Cf. Streitfragen*, p. 32 ; *Die synoptische Grundschrift*, pp. 67, 114.

Japha, can be considered its approximate western,[1] and Cana its northerly, limit.

Capernaum must certainly be considered the eastern limit; consequently the way to it from Nazareth must necessarily be reckoned among the ways that Jesus traversed, and considered as a field of His activity. According to Mt. xiii. 54; Mk. vi. 1; Lk. iv. 23, He returned again from the lake to His native town. The way which He would have to take from Nazareth is clearly defined by the local conditions. In the north-east the wide plain of Ṭur'an had to be crossed, then, somewhere, the descent towards the lake of Tiberias had to be made, the coast of which would be followed as far as Capernaum. It is worth while to study the way carefully and in detail.

To begin with, by the well of Nazareth, it passes the chain of hills of the *Neby Sa'in* on the far side of which it crosses the two heads of a valley which carries off the drainage of the *Baṭṭof* plain, that is, the *Wady el-Melekh*.[2] The first of these valley-heads—abounding in springs and laid out with fruit orchards— is now dominated by the conspicuous village *er-Reineh*, which Guthe[3] identified with Cana, because the English map of Palestine erroneously calls one of its wells *'En Ḳana*, instead of *'En el-Ḳana* ("main-spring"). According to Klein, this village— with its present name (*Reineh*)—was the place where grew one of the three famous *asheras* of Palestine mentioned in Jewish literature,[4] a sycamore, worshipped by the heathen. This sycamore, however, belongs to the Carmel promontory.[5] More likely *er-Reineh* was the *Abel* where the water conduit of Zippori started,[6] although it has so far been proven only in regard to the village *el-Meshhed*, with which we shall now deal.

---

[1] As a place of a Jewish community, apart from Japha, Simomias—about four miles distant — was known. See p. Jeb. 13a; Gen. R. lxxxi. (173b). But farther away lay Bethlehem, Bethsharay, Ardiscos, Tabaon. See *PJB*, 1922-23, pp. 27, 34, 38.

[2] Probably the one-time "Valley of Iphtah-el" (Josh. xix. 14, 17), which had this name because God opened a brook there; cf. Ps. cv. 41; Isa. xli. 18; *PJB*, 1922-23, p. 35.

[3] See *PJB*, 1912, p. 39; 1914, p. 39.   [4] Tos. Ab. z. vi. 8.

[5] Namely the place Shikma or Shikmona (Sykaminon) in proximity to the present Haifa. The text—which would have mentioned four *asheras* instead of three—must have originally run: *shikma she-barashe shel-lakarmel* ("The sycamore of the Carmel promontory").

[6] Erub. viii. 7; Tos. Erub. ix. 26. The map of Marino Sanuto and one of the two Florentine maps (*ZDPV*, 1891, Plate I.) mark an Abelina east of Sephorum (Sepphoris), near the grave of Jonah, but they probably mean only the 'Abellin lying farther away in the west, from which Sepphoris did not get its water.

On the heights of Nazareth, behind *er-Reineh*, may be seen a conspicuous hill, 382 metres above sea-level, to the foot of which a little village now clings. This is *el-Meshhed*—a name which really refers only to the grave of *Neby Junis*, *i.e.* the prophet Jonah, venerated there. This tradition is old, for Jerome also knew[1] that the Jews of his time had identified this spot as *Gath Hepher*, the native place of the prophet Jonah according to 2 Kings xiv. 25[2]; although the place at that time was not called Gath, but Gubebatha, or Gubbatha,[3] and generally " Gubbatha of Zipporin," to distinguish it from the Gabatha—now *Jebata*—on the plain of Jezreel.[4] A schoolmaster named Jonathan, belonging to this place, was known, and there was talk of a miracle-worker who amazed people there by his jugglery : for instance, he threw a ball into the air which came down as a calf.[5] Near it, probably, lay Hepher, which is referred to as the place where a certain Rabbi Tanchum taught.[6] Thus both were localities which had Jewish populations. Perhaps *Gubbatha* had two parts, one corresponding to the present little village *el-Meshhed*, containing the prophet's grave; the other being the older locality which stands on the top of the hill above it, and was called by the special name of *Hepher*.[7] Both would have been proud to be the guardians of the famous prophet's grave, since he had been their countryman, and therefore of the tribe of Zebulon (as Rabbi Jochanan deduced from his birthplace, according to Josh. xix. 13[8]), and in addition probably the only prophet from Galilee. One can well imagine that this prophet's grave was of great importance to all Jewish Galilæans. Jesus might even as a boy have noticed it from the mountains around His native place, and no doubt had it in mind when He promised to the scribes no other sign but that of the prophet Jonah (Lk. xi. 29*f.*; Mt. xii. 39*f.*).[9] Jesus was thinking of the call to repentance which would end in His death, but the preacher of repentance to

[1] *Comm. in Jon. præf.* In the *Onomasticon* it cannot be discerned whether he means the prophet or the Book of Jonah.

[2] Yet, according to Pseudo-Epiphanius (Nestle, *Marginalien und Materialien*, p. 242), Jonah was buried in the land Sur (Saar, Sarar), in the grave of the judge Kenez (probably=Othniel), *i.e.* in south Palestine.

[3] Gen. R. xcviii. (212) ; *cf.* Klein, *Beiträge*, p. 28.

[4] See Eusebius, *Onomasticon* 246.

[5] p. Meg. 74b.   [6] p. Sanh. 25d.

[7] In the above-mentioned passage where Gubebatha, or Gubbatha, occurs, it is designated as a plural (Gen. R. 212b ; *cf.* p. Sanh. 25d).

[8] p. Sukk. 55a. According to Pseudo-Epiphanius (ed. Nestle, p. 24), Jonah was born in Kariathmau by Asdod.

[9] *Cf.* Levertoff's suggestion in Bishop Gore's *Commentary*, p. 159.

Nineveh also awakened in Him the thought that heathen, not rarely, put Israelites to shame. It is also likely that the faith in the universal mercy of God came to the disciples as a legacy from the book of the Galilæan prophet, who was indignant when he realised it.

On the other side of the mountains, which rise on the right of the road, lies the village of *'En Maḥil*, which one is justified in identifying with *'En Tab*,[1] a neighbour to Gubbatha, where it was customary to fix the position of the new moon in connection with the Jewish year,[2] which presupposes a place with an open view. And close to *'En Maḥil* is the highest peak of the *Jebel es-Siḥ*, scarcely 2 metres lower than Tabor.

The height of Gath Hepher leads the traveller into the wide plain of *Ṭur'an*, the name of which is perhaps derived from the Aramaic *tur'an*, " sheep mountain." A considerable mountain-chain separates it in the north from the greater *Baṭṭof* plain, with which it is connected by a wide opening. On one of the slopes, which sink gradually from the south towards the plain, lies—only about half a mile from *el-Meshhed*, close to a deep spring—the good-sized village of *Kefr Kenna*, with its three churches towering above it, a place which owes its present prosperity to the old assumption that it is the Cana of St. John's Gospel. Its name, however, is decisively against this theory ; for that it has to be pronounced Kenna, not *Ḳenna*, can be seen from the fact that the natives pronounce it *Tshenna*. As a place-name, combined with *kefr* (village), it will have originated at the time when Aramaic was the vernacular, and is not to be traced back to *Kana*, but to *Kephar Kanna*.[3] The older rabbinic literature knows no place with such a name, and yet it is evident that it was Jewish from an Aramaic mosaic inscription which was found there under the Latin church, on a lower floor. It runs :

> *Dekir le-tob Josa bar Tanḥum bar Buta u-banoi de-abdu hadda tabla tehi lehon birketa amen.*

May Jose, son of Tanchum, son of Buta, and his sons, be remembered for good, who have made this plate. May blessing be theirs. Amen.[4]

---

[1] p. Sukka, 53a.

[2] p. Ber. 7e ; Taan. 66a ; Pesikta Rabb. 41.

[3] Also Gershom ben Asher (about 1550) in Yichus ha-Zaddikim (ed. Jerusalem), p. 82, and Chayyim Horowitz (1850) in Chibbath Jerushalayim (ed. Wilna), p. 3t, write it thus. They mention it because of the proximity of Jonah's grave.

[4] *Cf.* Klein, *Jüd.-pal. Corpus Inscriptionum* ii. 4.

A step leads down behind into a still lower chamber with a cistern.   It is more likely that it was a synagogue with a ritual bath belonging to it, than a church built perhaps by the " Comes " Joseph of Tiberias.[1]   The vaulted building of 20 by 40 feet, with a row of pillars in the centre, seen there by Doubdan in 1654 as a mosque, was in any case not originally erected as a church.   This does not exclude the possibility that the synagogue was turned into a church in comparatively early days.

One can bring only with great hesitation *Kefr Kenna* into relationship with the *Ḳaṭṭat* of Zebulon mentioned in Josh. xix. 15.   Later this place was called, according to p. Megilla 70a, *Ḳeṭonit*, and Ḳatna became Ḳanna, and in Arabic through the influence of *kenna*, " daughter-in-law," it was turned into *Kenna*.   But, according to Judg. i. 30, *Ḳaṭṭat* stands perhaps for *Ḳiṭron*, which, according to b. Megilla 6a, was the old name for Zippori.[2]

On a high hill in the north-west stands *Kefr Kenna*, opposite the ruin of *Khirbet Kenna*, which is evidently identical with *Garis* (two and a half miles from Zippori), where Josephus entrenched himself in order to attack Zippori from there at night,[3] and where he made an unsuccessful attack on the Romans.[4]   This *Garis* does not occur in rabbinic literature. Less than a mile north of it there runs the important high-road 'Akka to Tiberias, which must have served to connect Zippori with the new residence of Herod Antipas.   This road, behind *Kefr Kenna*, is presently joined by the road from Nazareth to Capernaum.   It would be interesting to know the ancient name for *Ṭur'an*, which lies charmingly between gardens below the mountains at the northern edge of the plain and occupies a large share of it.   Klein identifies it with *Tir'an*.[5]   But the women of *Tir'an* who " did not offer their rings for the pre-paration of the golden calf "[6] can only be connected with a Galilæan locality, if it can be proved that the place-name was in some way related to a name of a tribe whose women played this rôle on Sinai.   In the Bible there is no such name, for the Kenitic Tiratim of 1 Chr. ii. 55 still belong to Judæa, and in later literature are never mentioned in any connection with Galilee.[7]

[1] Meistermann, *Guide to the Holy Land*, p. 522.   [2] *Cf.* p. 103.
[3] *Vita* 71.   [4] *Bell. Jud.* iii. 6, 3 ; *Vita* 74.
[5] *Erez Jisrael*, p. 62.   [6] Cant. R. vi. 4 ; *cf.* Lev. R. ii. (4b).
[7] See Mech. on Ex. xviii. 27 (60b) ; Sifre on Num. lxxviii. ; Sanh. 104b.

The road to Tiberias south of the village of *Ṭurʿan* divides
into two.   One way at first goes almost directly eastward,
then, curving towards the south, passes by *Kefr Sabt* (the old
Kephar Shubtay) and *Beth Maon*[1] towards Tiberias.   This ancient
road is still put down in the English map of Palestine as a main
road.   It is now, however, entirely superseded by a more
northerly second road, running through *Lubieh*, which, oddly
enough, is not marked on the English map at all, doubtless
because its significance has not been realised.   It crosses the
height over a saddleback between *Lubieh* (280 metres high)
and *Khirbet Meskene* (333 metres).   That it was also of importance in antiquity may be realised from the fact that the
Palestinian Talmud knows *Mashkena* as a meeting-point
exactly between Tiberias and Zipporin.[2]   There the traveller
left behind him the ascent to the highland and henceforth had
an easy journey on the plain.   This spot was at the same time
the place where anyone going towards the northern shore of
the lake would have to turn off in a north-easterly direction.
Here also is the spot where basalt, so important in the environment of the lake, appears for the first time.   Only a few steps
from *Mashkena* a volcano at one time covered the neighbourhood with this mineral, out of which a powerful circular rampart
was erected on the height, apparently as a cattle-yard or place
of refuge.

Another and much more important volcano was that lying
farther east, at a height of 316 metres, namely *Karn Haṭṭin*,
whose top, partly enclosed by Cyclopean walls, was once a city
which is still recognisable from its ruins, and which probably
bore the name Madon (Josh. ii. 1).   It is possible that in the
time of Christ it was already a ruin.   If so, its top, which has a
splendid view of the northern part of the lake, 524 metres below,
would have been an appropriate place for the Matthæan
" Sermon on the Mount."[3]   The actual crest would have been
suitable for the choice of the disciples, and the adjoining slope on
the south, at the foot of the hill, towards the plain *Sahl el-Aḥma*,
for the gathering of the crowd to whom Jesus afterwards
descended (Lk. vi. 17).   But according to Mt. viii. 5, as well
as Lk. vii. 1, He came to Capernaum after He had finished
His discourse.   This necessitates a search for the " Mount "
of the Beatitudes above the northern bank of the lake.

---

[1] Gen. R. lxxxv. (183b).   [2] p. Ber. 14d ; Sanh. 21a.
[3] The Franciscans, however, who fixed Cana also on the road to Tiberias,
have only located it there since the seventeenth century.

Only about two miles south-east from the projecting peak of *Ḥaṭṭin*, at the edge of the plain towards the lake, there are boulders scattered about, which the people now call *ḥajar en-Naṣara*, " Christ-stones," or *el-khamse khubzat*, " the five breads." A stone which stands in their midst is considered to be the " Seat of the Messiah " from which He ordered the hungry people to be fed. During processions of pilgrims, when this stone is passed, the priests of the Greek Church cover it with a cloth and put on it little cakes, which they sell to the pilgrims as mementoes of the miraculous feeding. Meistermann[1] endeavours to prove that this indeed was the place where the 4,000 were fed (Mt. xv. 32), and that ancient tradition also placed it there. But even as late as the thirteenth century it was shown on the northern bank of the lake. Here, it seems, the Bethulia of the Book of Judith was found,[2] but the attribution of the miraculous feeding (*i.e.* of the 5,000) to this place can only be traced as far back as 1596. The Franciscans, at a time when the lake bank could not be visited, linked up the Sermon on the Mount and the feeding of the 5,000 and attributed both to this spot, where possibly they had long been pointed out from a distance to the pilgrims.[3] Quite independently of all tradition Merx[4] considered the Markan narrative of the feeding of the 5,000 conceivable only on the western bank of the lake, north or south of Tiberias. In that case this point—which could be reached through the *Wady el-'Ames*, between Tiberias and Magdala—would be justified. But later it will be shown that both feedings belong to the eastern bank of the lake, and so it follows that no known event in the Life of Jesus can be placed anywhere on the way from Nazareth to the lake.

So we leave the height with the wide horizon, and turn back to the way from Nazareth which we left behind *Mashkena* and there we soon reach *Nimrin*—which stands high up and is probably identical with the priestly place *Kephar Nimra*, once noted for its tapestry[5]—and farther away *Khirbet umm el-'Amad*

---

[1] *Durchs Heilige Land*, p. 490 ; *Guide*, p. 527.

[2] John of Würzburg. Tobler, *Descriptiones Terræ Sanctæ*, p. 189 ; John Poloner, *ibid.*, p. 272 ; Theoderich, ed. Tobler, p. 192. The exact position of Bethulia is nowhere made clear by these writers ; but on the map of Marino Sanuto and in Daffer's *Asia* Bethulia is undoubtedly Ḳarn Ḥaṭṭin, Dothan Ḥaṭṭin.

[3] Occasionally the Tabor was used for such perspective views ; see Phocas (Migne, *P.G.* cxxxiii., col. 937) ; Slisansky, *Neue Reisebeschreibung*, p. 115.

[4] *Die vier kanonischen Evangelien*, on Mt. vi. 45.

[5] K. Klein, *Beiträge*, p. 70. The priestly order Bilya had here its seat.

with its synagogue-ruin[1]—possibly the ancient *Kephar Uzziel*,[2] where the priestly order of Abia lived and to which John the Baptist belonged.[3]   Then, at the edge of the *Karn Ḥaṭṭin*, the road goes steeply down and touches at its foot first the well of *Ḥaṭṭin*, then, 113 metres above sea-level, the village itself, which must be traversed.   Although we know nothing of a Jewish settlement in *Mashkena*, there is proof of a Jewish population in *Ḥaṭṭin*.[4]   The locality bears the name of *Kephar Chattiya* in Jewish literature, which an old interpretation explains as "Sinners' Village," because frivolous folk ate and drank there on Sabbath nights in the synagogue and ended up by throwing bones at the beadle.[5]   The rabbis were convinced that it was to be identified with the place *Ha-Ziddim* in Naphtali of Josh. xix. 35.[6]   At one time the locality—besides having extensive olive-gardens on its western side, beyond the valley with its brook which rose in a well—had its most valuable possession in the upper part of the flat plain which stretches eastward from the steep foot of the *Karn Ḥaṭṭin* and the precipice, towards the deep *Wady el-Ḥamam*, and sinks at last gently towards the *Wady ʿAmes*, through which it issues in the lake.   The plain of *Ḥaṭṭin*, in olden times called the " Plain of Arbeel " (*Irbid*) after a place in its centre, was a famous wheat district.   It was said of it that one *sea*[7] of wheat produced a *sea* each of five different kinds of flour, from the finest wheat to the coarsest bran ; later, however, this fertility departed.[8]   It is also recorded[9] that the valley once revealed the peculiarity of Palestinian soil when ploughed deeply by throwing up glowing sand which burned the seed.   Evidently dead dry soil was reached, which did not stimulate the germinal vitality of the seed.   The plain became a battle-field when Herod, in the winter of 38 B.C., coming from Zippori by the road just described, routed the followers of the last legitimate ruler of the Jews, Antigonus, and then apparently pursued them past Capernaum as far as the Jordan.[10]   Redemption from foreign domination was the hope of the two rabbis who once observed from here the light of the dawn before sunrise and saw in it a symbol of the gradual progress of Redemption :

[1] Kohl and Watzinger, *Antike Synagogen in Galiläa*, p. 71.

[2] *Cf. PJB*, 1913, p. 49 ; 1922-23, p. 84.

[3] Lk. i. 5.   [4] Klein, *Beitrage*, p. 82.

[5] Gen. R. lxv. (139a).   [6] p. Meg. 70a.

[7] [A particular measure of grain, the σάτον of LXX and the N.T.—TRANSLATOR.]

[8] p. Pea 20a.   [9] p. Taan. 69b ; Lam. R. Pet. (17a).

[10] *Ant.* xiv. 15, 4 ; *Bell. Jud.* i. 16, 2.

Thus will be the Redemption of Israel : first little by little ; then more and more.[1]   But the real beginning of Redemption connected with this plain is expressed in a Midrash which Eleasar ha-Kalir[2] made use of in his Redemption-hymn " *Baya-mim bahem* " (" In those days ").[3]   The first verse of this hymn[4] runs :

> In those days and in that time,
> In the first month, in the month of Nisan,[5]
> On the fourteenth day, indeed,[6]
> Menachem, Ammiel's son, cometh.[7]
> In Arbeel's valley his beauty blossoms,
> When in beauty he decketh himself,
> Adorned with garments of vengeance.

The war which this Messiah carries on against Israel's enemies, and for which Michael and Gabriel come down from heaven, is not fixed by the poet in any definite locality.   But the Zerubbabel-Apocalypse, on which he depends, describes how the Messiah, whom the wise men of Israel do not at first wish to recognise, defeats the hostile armies, led by Armilos,[8] on the plain of Arbeel, so that it is covered with their dead. A remnant which finds refuge in a rock (most likely below the plain at the *Wady el-Ḥamam*) is also killed there.   There is no direct evidence that such messianic ideas clung to this plain in the time of Christ, but they were essentially native to Galilæan Jewry.

According to the Roman manuscript of the Palestine Talmud,[9] it was on this plain that the Jew was ploughing, to whom an Arab interpreted the roaring of his ploughing beast as

---

[1] p. Ber. 2e.

[2] Accepted as the author of this hymn by Zunz, *Literaturgeschichte*, p. 50 ; Landshut, *Ammude ha-Aboda*, p. 44.

[3] Similarly in Sepher Zerubabel, Jellinek, *Beth ha-Midrash*, ii., p. 54 *f.* ; *cf. PJB*, 1922-23, p. 50.

[4] According to Machzor Romania, Constantinople, 1510, p. 143b ; *cf.* Machzor Romi, Bologna, 1540.

[5] In this month comes Redemption according to b. Rosh h. S. 11a ; Mech. Bo. xiv.; Cant. R. ii. 8 (30a *f.*) ; Ex. R. xv. (33a) ; Pes. 47b ; Sopher. 21, 2 ; Midr. Tanchuma and Midr. Agada on Ex. xii. 2.

[6] Redemption is expected on Passover night, Ex. R. xviii. (48b) ; Pesik. zutra on Ex. xii. 42 ; Targ. Jer. i. 11 on Ex. xii. 42.

[7] This name of the Messiah is based on Lam. i. 16 ; see Dalman, *Messianische Texte*, p. 28 ; *cf. Der leidende und der sterbende Messias*, p. 14.

[8] Concerning this Armilos, which occurs also in Targ. Jer. i., Dt. xxxiv. 3 ; see *Der leidende und der sterbende Messias*, p. 14.

[9] p. Ber. 5a ; Ginzberg, *Jerushalmi Fragments*, i., p. 348 ; Luncz, *Talmud Jerushalmi* (Jerusalem, 1907), i., p. 20a.

signifying that the Messiah Menachem was born in Bethlehem.
The child was soon snatched away from his mother by whirl-
winds, but (it goes on to say) here, at the place of the annunciation concerning him, would the vanished one appear in his
glory in order to begin his work of Redemption.

The township of *Arbeel* which lay on the edge of the ravine
of *Wady Ḥaman*, 35 metres above the sea-level, but 243 metres
above the lake, must have been of greater importance in the
time of Christ than *Kephar Chattiya*. It certainly occupied the
larger portion of the plain with its slope towards the *Wady
'Ames*. At present it lies in ruins, which are called *Khirbet
Irbid*. Once it was a flourishing Jewish place, as the remains
of the fine synagogue—facing south, with a double-floored
colonnade—bear witness.[1] Priests of the order of Joshua
dwelled there.[2] Josephus once summoned the representatives
of Galilee to an important conference in this place, a meeting
which he evidently did not wish to hold either in Tarichææ,
where he himself at that time had been staying, or in Tiberias,
but in some locality which it would be easy to reach from both
these places.[3] From Jewish literature we know that this was
the native place of the pre-Christian scribe Nittay, who urged
men not to have any fellowship with the wicked, and not to
forget divine punishment.[4] The economic importance of
Arbeel consisted in the production of durable thick linen.[5] The
flax for it must have been grown on the plain ; water for the
bleaching was found below, in the brook of the *Wady el-Ḥamam*,
or in the lake close to 'En el-Fuliyeh.

This Jewish Arbeel was not touched directly by the road
from Nazareth to the lake ; for, after crossing the plain, the
road dipped downward just before reaching Arbeel, in steep
and serpentine windings through a ravine, into the *Wady el-
Ḥamam*—which was once undoubtedly called after Arbeel—
and followed it as far as the lake. The traveller notes with
amazement the high perpendicular rocky walls which here
enclose the valley on both sides, above vast rubble-slopes.
There is no real bottom to the valley. Laboriously, an often
dry brook-bed breaks through the boulders, thorny shrubbery,
and magnificent, high, dark-red mallows (*Althæa lavateræflora*).
And beside it runs the path which once was an important road.

---

[1] Kohl and Watzinger, *Antike Synagogen in Galiläa*, p. 59 *f.*
[2] Klein, *Beiträge*, p. 52 *f.*   [3] *Vita* 60.
[4] Abot i. 7 (where the *var. lect.* has also Mattay for Nittay).
[5] Gen. R. xix. (38b) ; Eccl. R. i. 18 (75b).

Until, finally, the valley widens and descends towards the lake. This wild valley has its history, for " the caves of Arbela," once natural, were, later, artificially extended with grottoes in two places in the southern wall of the valley ; one below *Irbid*, and the other in the opening of the valley towards the plain. And in the Maccabæan period these were already places of refuge for the strict Jews who adhered faithfully to the law and against whom the Syrians fought with such success.[1] In the year 38 B.C. the place was used, as Josephus[2] puts it, by " robbers," whom Herod caused to be " smoked out " with fire-brands, by soldiers who were let down in boxes. This seems to have been more possible in the grottoes below Irbid, where the rocky wall is not as high as it is in the other groups of caves, which, through the walling up, have become an Arab stronghold. The so-called " robbers," who here occupied the important road towards the lake, were certainly the remnant of the armies of the last Hasmonean prince, Antigonus. They fought, trusting in the God of Israel, against the dominion given by Rome to Herod. The king by the grace of Rome, who built Cæsar's temples as zealously as God's temple, did not scruple to build up the caves to support his own power.[3] In this state did Jesus see them when He passed this way. What had taken place sixty years before, and the consequences of it, could not have been forgotten so soon. Since then things had gone from bad to worse. It seemed as if the Romans and their gods ruled absolutely. As at the sight of Zippori, He would here too be thinking of the struggle to establish the rule of God which was the duty now imposed on Him, and of the final triumph of the Kingdom of God.

Below the mighty gate of the valley of Arbeel, the road from Nazareth to the lake of Tiberias ended at the town of Magdala, which will be dealt with later. Ten places with Jewish populations have been proved to have existed on and near the road. None of them, except Cana, is mentioned in the Gospels, but they all undoubtedly belonged to the domain of our Lord's activity, and they prove how very Jewish the land was wherein He wandered and worked.

[1] 1 Macc. ix. 2 (read Μεσαδωθ) ; *Ant.* xii. 11, 1.
[2] *Ant.* xiv. 15, 5 ; *Bell. Jud.* i. 16, 4.   [3] *Bell. Jud.* ii. 20, 6 ; *Vita* 37.

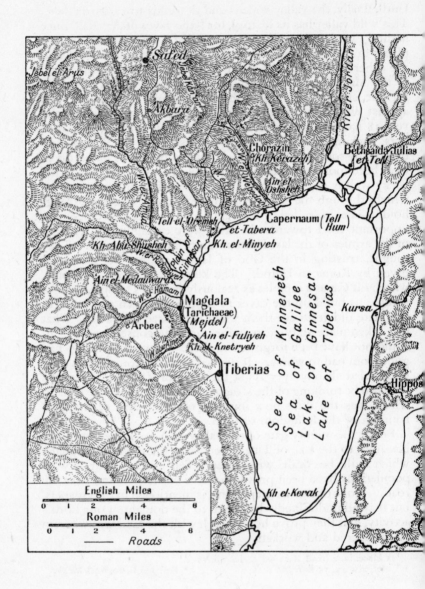

VII

MAGDALA AND GINNESAR

WHEN Jesus left Nazareth (according to Mt. iv. 13) and took up His abode in Capernaum, it meant for Him a separation from His family, which endeavoured in vain to call Him back (Mk. iii. 31 f.), and from its modest property (Mt. viii. 20), and from the paternal trade. But it also meant a great change of scene and climate. The son of the highlands became a dweller on the banks of a deep-lying lake. Nazareth lies about 350 metres above the sea-level; the Lake of Tiberias, 208 metres below the sea-level. In olden times the lake was called "The Sea of Galilee" (Mt. iv. 18; xv. 29; Mk. i. 16; vii. 31; Jn. vi. 1, with the addition " of Tiberias "); "The Sea of Tiberias" (Jn. xxi. 1; Tos. Sukk. iii. 3; p. Kil. 32c; Keth. 35b; Shek. 50a; Gen. R. 98 [214a]; Tg. Jer. 1 on Dt. xxx. 23); "The Lake of Gennesaret" (Lk. v. 1 f, however, has Gennesar); "The Lake of Gennesar"[1] (Jos., *Bell. Jud.* iii. 10, 7[2]); "The Sea of Ginnesar" (Targ. Onk. Jer. ii. 5 on Dt. xxxiii. 23; Onk. Jer. 1 on Num. xxxiv. 11); or "The Water of Gennesar" (1 Macc. xi. 67). The lengthened form of Gennesar, *Gennesaret*, which also occurs in Mt. xiv. 34; Mk. vi. 53, and which is not imitated in the Palestinian *Evangeliarium* with its *Yamma de-Gennesar*, is foreign to Aramaic-speaking people, and is most probably a wrong formation, on the model of Nazareth, which presupposes a determinative *Ginnesera*.[3] It must also be borne in mind that in Hebrew and in Aramaic *yam* can mean both sea and lake, and that the Greek of the LXX, *e.g.* Num. xxxiv. 11, imitates this by using θάλασσα also when a "lake" is meant. Thus the

---

[1] The *e* of the first syllable corresponds in Greek transcriptions of Hebrew words to the *i* of Biblical vocalisation (see my *Gramm. des jüd. Aram.*, 2nd ed., p. 84), so that we can pronounce it Ginnesar.

[2] Where Josephus has also simply ἡ Γεννησάρ, although he himself says that the lake was called after the district of the same name. For the inhabitants it was surely the Lake *of* Gennesar.

[3] Buhl explains it as *ge Nesar*, although a plain is not a " valley."

Gospels always speak of the Sea (of Galilee), with the exception of Luke, who introduced the Greek word for lake, λίμνη. The native designation in the time of Jesus was doubtless *Yam Ginnesar* or *Yamma de-Ginnesar*. The interpretation of *Ginnesar* as *ganne sarim*, "Princes' gardens,"[1] and as *hortus principis* by Jerome, shows how impossible a feminine ending was to the linguistic sense of the people.[2]

Fertile plateaus on the east and west slope steeply from a height of about 500 metres towards the shore and stand around about the lake like high walls of regular altitude. In the north the lake is bounded by mountains, whose summits rise 1,058 metres above its level. In the south there is a more open vista, but only at the point where the Jordan breaks through. So the lake has a rather monotonous, though peculiar, aspect. When looking down on it from a great height, one is charmed in spring by its blue surface set in a green frame. While in autumn it often appears as green framed in yellow, and from the south the double-peaked *Jebel Kan'an*, round about which the town of Safed is situated, offers an unforgettable view. On the left of it is the broad bulk of the *Jebel el-'Arus*, and on the right, over the Jordan breach, the ridge of Hermon, snow-capped in winter, which, because of its great distance, does not look high.

Jesus, who, from the mountain over His native place, had seen the sun sink into the sea at the foot of Carmel, and surveyed Palestine from Ebal to Hermon, now found Himself in a hollow, from whence He could greet the snowy Hermon alone as an old acquaintance, and even when He ascended the heights round about, it was always the blue lake alone which increasingly filled the view. The lake can, if necessary, be ridden round in a day. Its waves are easily agitated, owing to the winds which eddy fitfully over it. White and rosy pelicans, in compact throngs, move on its surface like swimming islands ; black cormorants stand on stones at its margin and thrust down to share the fishes caught by the pelicans. Fishermen ply busily in, and on, the water, steering and sailing with ready skill. Many different kinds of edible fish are found in the lake.

Such was the world into which Jesus now had entered.

---

[1] Gen. R. xcviii. (214a).

[2] *Ginnosar* in some Jewish texts must be considered as a scribal error, and ought not to have been entered by Sappir and Krause in their Palestine Map (1913). In Tos. Kel. v. 6, for instance, it is *Ginnoser*, whilst in Tos. Teh. vii. 7 it is written *Ginnesar*.

Here the mountain-dweller of Nazareth misses the evergreen
olive-trees, locust-bean trees, and oaks which grow between
the light-grey layers of chalky rocks ; the rose-coloured Alpine
flowers (*Cyclamen latifolium*), and the glorious beauty of the
Iris Nazarena with its lilac-coloured outer and violet inner
petals. Instead of these, one is struck by the black, rounded,
basaltic, shiny blocks, which cover whole slopes, making
difficult walking for man and beast and hindering the growth
of the young blades (Mt. xiii. 5) in the little fields. These
rocks supply building material for houses, which therefore
look dark and gloomy. Nevertheless, here plants shoot up
more exuberantly than in the limestone district. Where
there are fields, they yield a produce greater than one has any
notion of in the highlands (Mt. xiii. 8). Thistle, wild fennel,
and wild mustard[1] grow to such a height that a rider can
scarce see over them. Yellow chrysanthemum (*Chrysanthemum coronarium*), rose-coloured mallows, and the white
umbels of *Ammi majus*, are found in such masses that it is
difficult to make a pathway through them. Instead of leafy
trees we find the Christ-thorn, which gives very little shade,
and whose almost ineradicable shoots spread about the fields
and, in conjunction with the annually seeding thistles, threaten
the grain (Mt. xiii. 7).[2] Down by the brooks and on the
shore, which is covered with small shells, oleander-bushes and
the chaste-tree shrubs (*Vitex agnus-castus*)—which can grow to
the height of trees, and are not found on the mountains—
please the eye with their red and blue blossoms. All this is
to-day as it was in the time of Jesus. But the fruit-trees
praised by Josephus,[3] the palms, the fig-trees, the walnut-
trees, the olives, the vine, and the citron, have shrivelled to
miserable remnants of their old selves. The Bedouins, who
occupy the most fertile plains by the lake (to the north-
west and north-east), have allowed the district to become
bare and barren, because they are uninterested in the
cultivation of trees. The eucalyptus, banana, and willow
plantations of the German monks on the north bank, and the
groves of the Jewish colonies on the west and south, appear
like oases in a landscape which everywhere might be well

[1] Plants as high as 2·60 metres were measured by E. Schmitz, *Heiliges Land*,
1916, p. 189.
[2] The seed falls among thorns in so far as the seed of the thistles or the roots
of the Christ-thorn are found in this place ; *cf.* Dalman, *PJB*, 1926, p. 126 *f.*
[3] *Bell. Jud.* iii. 10, 8. The olive-trees were certainly planted only on the
slopes of the mountain-edges, which is also seen in the remnants of ancient
olive mills in *Khirbet Minieh*, *PJB*, 1922-23, p. 58.

shaded, and of which Arculf,[1] as late as A.D. 680, says that it possessed great forests.

In winter time, which does not here entail cold weather,[2] the hills and the shores everywhere are green; but in the long summer, which begins in May, a desert-like aridity spreads over everything that has no deep roots.   It is a delight to pluck roses in March on the lake shores ; but when, in May and June, the thermometer rises as high as 104° Fahrenheit in the shade, and there is no real coolness even at night, and when in August the fowls often die of heat, it is difficult for anyone who has been used to living in the mountains to work by day and sleep at night.   During a trip on the lake one can almost die of heat, and some have tried to sleep at night in the water, which is sometimes 84°.   Even the stone houses, with their closed windows, are little cooler.   Out of doors one misses the refreshing breeze, which the mountains cut off, especially on the western side.   When, in addition, malaria (Mt. viii. 14 ; Mk. i. 30 ; Lk. iv. 38 ; Jn. iv. 52) hammers on the temples, and the sting of the sand-flies tortures the body, one is tempted to think that Jesus, who had settled here, must often have made occasion to escape from this pitiless climate to His beloved mountains.   The sons of Herod, Antipas and Philip, built themselves capitals on the lake, in Tiberias and Julias ; but in summer they certainly exchanged their castles on the lake for residences in the mountains. When Jesus transferred His abode from Nazareth to Capernaum it must have been because He hoped to find a more suitable place for His activity there, and He was not disappointed.   Peter and Andrew, James and John, the first who attached themselves permanently to Him (Mk. i. 16 f.), together with Philip (Jn. i. 44) and Levi (Mt. ix. 9 ; Mk. ii. 14 ; Lk. v. 27), were natives of the lake district.   According to the Fourth Gospel (i. 46), Jesus made the acquaintance of three of them, by the Jordan with John the Baptist.[3]   The acquaintance made there drew Him to their native place.

[1] Geyer, p. 269.

[2] The lowest temperature was in the winter of 1913-14, 84·42° Fahr. (ZDPV, 1915, p. 152).

[3] Peter, Andrew, and Philip came, according to John i. 44 f., from Bethsaida ; James and John, according to Petrus Diaconus (Geyer, p. 112), from Tiberias, which, however, as it was only founded in A.D. 18, must have been the *forerunner* of Tiberias, a place which was later called " village " (*kiphra*) of Tiberias (p. Meg. 70a).   In what an arbitrary way the easily accessible Tiberias was later provided with holy sites can be seen from Daniel (Khistrovo, *Itinéraires Russes*, p. 62 f.). H. Raschke, *Die Werkstatt des Markusevangeliums*, 1924, p. 137,

Owing to the position of the lake, deep in the Palestinian basin, only narrow strips of land suitable for cultivation encompass it. On the eastern bank this strip is a real plain, but in the west it is much less even. There are places where it ceases to exist entirely; and the mountains come down practically to the edge of the lake. This is especially the case at *Tell el-'Oremeh* in the north-west; and south from Magdala, where the shore road wends its way along a steep mountain-slope. In the north it is different; there the glebe does not break in, but, with a curve, slowly slopes towards the lake. In the south the southern barrier of the lake forms a low transition to the wide and here very fertile Jordan valley.

The cultivated plain at the southern end of the lake had no direct significance in connection with our Lord's life and work. On the northern end of the western bank, however, the alluvial soil brought down by the three brooks issuing here (the *Wady el-Ḥamam*, with an inconsiderable quantity of water, farther north the *Wady er-Rabaḍiyeh*, with a plentiful supply of water, and *Wady el-'Amud*) filled up a former bay, and thus created a shore-plain of considerable extent, now known as *el-Ṛuwer*, but in the time of Jesus called " The Plain of Ginnesar " (Hebrew *bik'at ginnesar*). Josephus speaks of the land of this name.[1] In rabbinic literature once we find it extended to include the whole western shore of the lake.[2] At the present day this plain is chiefly used for the cultivation of grain, which, in the south, the Jewish colony Migdal (founded in 1910, and situated above its western edge), and, on the northern side, the diligence of the German Lazarists of *et-Tabera*, have intensified. The water of the *Wady er-Rabaḍiyeh* and of the vigorous spring *'Ain el-Medauwara* in the south-west is made use of for the irrigation of the plain. A whole grove of eucalyptus trees, plantations of bananas and oranges, and alleys of palms and cypresses, have grown up there. Thus the fruit-orchards are again revived, the fresh dates of Naphtali, for instance, which were much praised in early times,[3] and also palm-trees so

---

concludes from the name Ζεβεδαῖυς, which is connected with Zebadya, that James and John came from Bethsaida, which, according to him, was also called Beth Zebadya. But Gen. R., on which he bases his assumption, adduces the extension of Zebulun as far as Sidon (Gen. xlix. 13), *Zebud digelila*, which must thus lie near the Mediterranean Sea, where it can be identified as *Khirbet Zebed*. R. would have done better to quote Epiphanius Hagiopolita, who, in *Vita B. Virginis*, makes John come from Sebede, which Jesus visited, but which is differentiated from Bethsaida. He might have had in mind *Khirbet Zebud* near Meron.
[1] *Bell. Jud.*, iii. 10, 8.
[2] The same as the old designation *kinnereth*, according to Gen. R. xcviii. (214a).
[3] Sibre Dt. ccclv. (147b); *cf.* Onk. Gen. xlix. 21; Targ. Jer. i. Dt. xxxiii. 23.

often referred to.[1]　It was said of the fruits of the plain that they ripened as quickly as the running of the hart,[2] and were as sweet as the sound of the Kinnor (harp).[3]　One could eat a hundred of them without being sated, and because of their sweetness it was necessary to take something salty afterwards, with or without bread.[4]　Because the fruit season was long there—according to Josephus, it lasted ten months for grapes and figs[5]—the watchmen's huts had to be constructed so as to permit of family life.　Millstones and fowls were not wanting there, but Jewish law could not consider these huts as houses in the matter of the paying of tithes.[6]　Alongside of the plantations of trees there must also have been fields, especially in south and the north, where the adjoining towns grew their supply of grain and vegetables.[7]

Of these towns the most important was *Magdala* (now *Mejdel*), at the southern end of the plain.　Its proper name, *Magdal Nunaiya*,[8] "Magdal of fish," shows that the town, which certainly held an important part of the plain, was at the same time a fishing town.　From its Greek name Tarichææ[9] one may conclude that the art, now extinct, of salting fish was practised there.　In that case it was not only a centre for fishing, but was also an important fish-market.　According to Josephus, it had a population of 40,000 souls and a fishing fleet of 230 (or 330) boats.[10]　A hippodrome[11] shows that the inhabitants also liked to enjoy themselves in the Greek fashion, and were probably non-Jews for the most part.　The city lay directly beside the lake where the important high-road—coming through the valley of Arbeel (now *Wady el-Ḥamam*;

---

[1] Tos. Sheb. vii. 11 ; p. Sheb. 38d.　　　　[2] Gen. R. xcix. (217b).

[3] b. Meg. 6a.　　　　[4] b. Ber. 44a ; Pesikta zut. on Dt. xxxiii. 23.

[5] *Bell. Jud.* iii. 10, 8 ; *cf.* PJB, 1922-23, p. 75.　　　　[6] Maaseroth iii. 7.

[7] That even cavalry could fight here (*Bell. Jud.* iii. 10, 3) shows that it did not consist entirely of orchards.

[8] b. Pes. 46a, but Magdala, for instance, p. Maaser 50c. ; Sanh. 19d.

[9] That the Tarichææ of Josephus lay north of Tiberias follows from the fact that Vespasian, coming from the south, advanced there from this town (*Bell. Jud.* iii. 10, 1).　His camp had a suitable place on the hill of *Khirbet el-Ḳneṭryeh*, close to '*Ain el-Fuliyeh*.　The *Khirbet el-Kerak*, lying far from the mountains, at the south end of the lake, which I and others (also Masterman, *Quart. Stat.*, 1910, p. 274 *ff.*) used until 1917 to identify with Tarichææ, has, notwithstanding Pliny, to be given up, because Tarochææ, "like Tiberias," lay under a mountain (Jos., *ibid.*).　The misunderstood "opposite" Tarichææ and Gamala (*Bell. Jud.* iv. 1, 1) only means to define the general position of both towns on this and the other side of the lake.　When John of Gishala passed unmolested the—to him hostile—town (*Vita* xx. 59), it took place either at night or in a round-about way, by land or by water.

[10] *Bell. Jud.* ii. 21, 4, 8.　　　　[11] *Bell. Jud.* ii. 21, 3.

see above, p. 118) from the western highlands—descended
to the shore.   A little south of Magdala another road came
down through the *Wady 'Ames* from the highlands (see
Chapter X.), which was used, at least at the end of the Middle
Ages, as a thoroughfare between Damascus and Egypt.
Both routes are of importance in connection with the "way
of the sea" of Isa. viii. 23 (Heb.) (which, according to the
Hebrew idiom, does not mean "the way *on* the sea"[1]—as
it is interpreted by LXX and the Palestinian Syriac translation); that, in the absence of further details, must be considered as referring not to the sea of Kinnereth but to the
Mediterranean, and, according to the context, must have led
through the Jordan valley and then across southern Galilee.
A third important route here was the shore road itself, which
conveyed the traffic far towards the north and the south.   It
avoided the town,[2] which was only walled on the land side,[3]
between it and the ascent of the mountain.   Here the passage
was so narrow that arches which were put up above, on the
slope (naturally not to the full height of the mountain), drove
away the protectors of the town from their wall and enabled
the passage of an army division.   But the narrowness of the
passage also made it possible under ordinary circumstances
for the town to blockade it.[4]   At any rate, its position on important roads was of consequence for the fishing trade.   Magdala
was, therefore, originally the most important city on the western
bank of the lake, contributing a wagon-load of taxes,[5] until
Herod Antipas raised up a rival on the lake by building
Tiberias.   Magdala probably had her scribes, like that schoolmaster Nakkai (second century) who had the audacity to
oppose the great Rabbi Simeon ben Jochai in connection with
the declaration by the latter of Tiberias' ritual purity.[6]   The
priestly order of Ezekiel is supposed to have had its seat there.[7]
But the reputation of the city was bad.   It is said eventually
to have gone to ruin because of its harlotry.

---

[1] *Derek* is always connected with the direction of the aim (Ex. xiii. 18; Num.
xxi. 4; Dt. i. 40; ii. 1; 1 Kings xviii. 43; Ezek. xli. 12).
[2] *Bell. Jud.* iii. 10, 3.
[3] Josephus claims to have erected this wall (*Bell. Jud.* iii. 10, 1), but surely this
cannot mean its erection for the first time.
[4] It should cause no surprise that Tarichææ, at Vespasian's entrance, did not
gather her forces here, but on the plain " before the city," which can only mean
in the north.   There alone was the most suitable place for it, and the one most
safe from disturbance by the Romans.
[5] Lam. R. ii. 2 (49a); *cf.* p. Taan. 69a; Klein, *Beiträge*, pp. 64, 84.
[6] Gen. R. lxxix. (1706).   [7] Kalir, *PJB*, 1922-23, p. 86.

Mary Magdalene (Aram. *Magdelayeta*)[1] was certainly a native of this place. It is not mentioned anywhere that Jesus visited this city. It is only of its environs that Mt. xv. 39 and Mk. viii. 10 speak, if *Magadan* in Mt. and *Dalmanutha* in Mk. are to be traced back to *Magdal* and *Magdal Nuna*, respectively.[2] In the undoubtedly parallel passages, Mt. xiv. 34; Mk. vi. 53, they refer, if not to the city of Ginnesar, at least to the district of this name, *i.e.* the plain north of Magdala. And according to Mk. viii. 11 (*cf.* Mt. xvi. 1) as well as Mt. xiv. 35, Mk. vi. 54, the people came from localities adjacent to where Jesus was, when He had landed on the shore. So it remains uncertain whether one is to count Magdala among the towns which Jesus, according to Mk. vi. 56, visited from the region of Ginnesar. The fact remains, however, that He did not make it a centre of His activity. Although coming from Nazareth it was the first place on the lake which He would strike. The restless, politically significant city, with its mixed population, evidently did not seem to Him suitable for His purpose.

The shore road of the Ginnesar plain in which the *Via Maris* continued does not follow the edge, but runs for the most part somewhat further inland; now through blackberry-bushes, chaste-trees and oleander-shrubs, and once, certainly, through palm-groves. In winter, it may happen that the *Wady er-Rabadiyeh*—although a part of its waters runs down through the mill-stream of Abu Shusheh—becomes for many days impassable even on horseback. I have heard of people who were drowned there. At such times one has to take the road along the western edge of the plain.

Shortly before one comes again from the alluvial soil of the plain to the limestone mountains, there lies on both sides of the road a low heap of earth and ruins, a little site, now called *Khirbet et-Tineh* or *Khirbet el-Minyeh*. No remains from pre-Islamic times have so far been found there. It would not be noticeable were it not for the fact that some have sought Capernaum,[3] others Bethsaida,[4] in its neighbourhood. The position of Capernaum on the northern shore of the lake by *Tell Ḥum* is, however, so firmly established by the evidence of pilgrims from the fourth century onwards, that to-day there

---

[1] Also in Syr. and Pal. Evang.

[2] *Cf.* B. Δαλμανουνθα ; Pal. Evang. *Magdal.* It may also be traced to (*ar'a*, land) Magdelayeta.

[3] So Schuster and Holzhammer, *Handbuch zur Biblischen Geschichte* ii. (1910), p. 176 *f.*

[4] So Meistermann, *Guide to the Holy Land*, p. 539 *f.*

is scarcely any doubt about it.   As to Bethsaida, there would
only be cause to place it in this neighbourhood, if " towards
Bethsaida " in Mk. vi. 45 signified the goal of the voyage on the
lake of Gennesaret.   We shall deal with this question in Chapter
IX.   Tradition also, up to the times of the Crusades, knew of
no Bethsaida between Tiberias and Capernaum, but rather
looked for it east of Capernaum.   According to Arculf[1] and
Petrus Diaconus[2] the pilgrims from Tiberias visited only the
place of the miraculous feeding and Capernaum.   The order :
Tiberias, Magdala, place of the feeding, Capernaum, Bethsaida, is quite clearly fixed, especially by Theodosius (530),[3] and
the distances from station to station are given.   But the route
is also given by Willibald (724-727),[4] by Theoderich (1172),[5]
and John of Würzburg (1170).[6]   Bethsaida appears for the first
time as being near the place of the feeding in Daniel's (1106)[7]
account, which is, however, not at all clear, but it seems later
to have become the ruling opinion, held also by Burchard
(1282)[8] and Poloner (1421).[9]

The name *Minyeh* has been derived from Minim, the Jewish
designation of the Jewish Christians, or was taken to be a
diminutive of the Arabic *mina*, "harbour."[10]   It is, however,
a frequently recurring Arabic place-name.[11]   If it is not the
Arabic *minya*, "wish," it is perhaps derived from μονή "dwelling," "convent,"[12] and this *Minyeh* was really called *Muniat
Hisham*, after the Caliph of that name (723-724).   That the
old name of the place was not *en ha-Teena*[13] (although the
spring near it is now called *en et-Tineh*) is clear from the fact
that this place had somehow a connection with the road from
Tiberias to Zippori,[14] and is therefore best looked for in the
neighbourhood of the latter.   The fine spring, now forming
a pond, at the north-west corner of the lake, must certainly
have always had some importance.   In the time of Jesus one
has rather to think of it as Ginnesar, from which the adjoining

---

[1] Geyer, *Itinera*, p. 273.   [2] *Ibid.*, p. 112 *f.*
[3] *Ibid.*, p. 137 *f.*, where, according to Thomsen, *Loca Sancta*, i., p. 79, *Khan
Minieh* is meant.
[4] Tobler, *Desc. T. S.*, pp. 23, 63.
[5] Ed. Tobler, p. 102.   See also Eugesippus, Migne, *P.G.* cxxxiii., col. 995.
[6] Tobler, p. 188.   [7] Khitrovo, *Itinéraires*, p. 64.
[8] Laurent, *Peregrinatores*, p. 40.   [9] Tobler, p. 271.
[10] So Meistermann, *Guide to the Holy Land*, p. 539 ; Christie, *Studia Semitica et
Orientalia* (1920), p. 28.
[11] A Judæan *Khirbet el-Minieh* lies near Tekoa.   For other occurrences of the
name, see *ZDMG*, 1916, p. 481.
[12] See Gildemeister, *ZDPV*, iv., p. 194 *f.*
[13] So Klein, *Beiträge*, pp. 30, 55.   [14] p. Taan. 68a ; Eccl. R. vii. 7 (193b).

plain in the south derived its name (see above).   The Pilgrim's Guide of the beginning of the twelfth century, which was used by Fretellus-Eugesippus,[1] John of Würzburg,[2] and Theoderich,[3] speaks of a village lying here on the left side of the lake in a " bend " of the mountain, having " special air " of which every visitor was aware even at a distance of two miles from Magdala.   There was also a place called Ginnesar, the native place of Jonathan ben Charsha,[4] from which a sick person was taken to the hot springs of Tiberias, and died on the way.[5] A question of law concerning private and public territory was discussed there.[6]   From here also the heretic Elisha ben Abuya must have come, who taught in the plain of Ginnesar. He noticed that once someone climbed up a palm-tree, where he found a bird's nest, and in accordance with the Deutero- nomic law (Dt. xxii. 6-8), he let the dam go and took the young, but then fell from the tree and was killed.   This caused the great teacher to become a sceptic; for is it not written (ibid.) : " that it may be well with thee, and that thou mayest prolong thy days "?[7]

The site of el-'Oremeh on the hill—called by that name and, according to Karge,[8] one of the oldest and most important settlements on the western shore of the lake of Tiberias, with a history going back to the neolithic period—must originally have dominated the Ginnesar region.   This tallies with Kinnereth which lay north from Tiberias (according to Josh. xix. 35), and at the northern end of the Jordan—a tract of low ground, according to Dt. iii. 17—and may perhaps best be located in the small hill-site at the western edge of the Ginnesar plain, Khirbet abu Shusheh.   Ginnesar—identified in Jewish tradition with Kinnereth[9]—would, in that case, have been the successor of this older place, and may also have been the Ginnesar where the boat of Jesus once anchored (Mk. vi. 53; Mt. xiv. 34).   Only the Palestinian Evangeliarium speaks (Mt. xiv. 34) of the " land Ginnesar."   In any case, it is un- thinkable that Jesus should not often have come into contact with this Ginnesar.   The northern terminus of the main road, at the western edge, and the harbour at the north-west

---

[1] Migne, P.L. clv., col. 995 (with complete text).   Meistermann, Capernaüm et Bethsaïde, p. 131 f., using the incomplete text of P.L. clv., thinks of the neigh- bourhood of Magdala, which is supposed to get its special " air " through the wind blowing from Wady Hamam.

[2] Tobler, Desc. T. S., p. 188.   [3] Ed. Tobler, p. 102.

[4] Maas. 48d ; Tos. Kel. B. b. v. 6.   [5] Tos. Tehar. vi. 7.

[6] Tos. Er. x. 13.   [7] p. Chag. 77b ; Ruth R. vi. 6 ; Eccl. R. vii. 7.

[8] Rephaim (1918), p. 172 f.   [9] p. Mag. 70a.

corner of the lake, so near Capernaum, could not have remained outside the sphere of His saving activities.

The well below the rocky wall of the hill of *el-'Oremeh*, and the spring-water which gushes up everywhere here in the strand, are really more attractive than the water-brooks of the *Heptapegon* (see p. 133 *f.*).   Chaste-trees with blue blossoms, with wild fig-trees and willows, offer their shade. High reeds and tall cypresses—but not papyrus[1]—hem in the spring-fed pond where once perhaps the harbour was.   The view extends far over the lake towards the neighbourhood of *el-Kursa* on the eastern shore. In this district Jesus encountered the scribes and Pharisees from Jerusalem, who saw (most likely on the shore) how the disciples ate without having washed their hands (Mt. xv. 1 *f.*; Mk. vii. 1 *f.*). And here the proclamation of the great principle which differentiates Christianity from Judaism, Islam, and all ancient religions was made:

> That which goes into the mouth defileth not a man, but what cometh out of the mouth, this defileth a man. (Mt. xv. 11 ; *cf.* Mk. vii. 18.)

[1] Erroneously ascribed to the whole region by Killermann, *Die Blumen des Heiligen Landes*, i., p. 37.

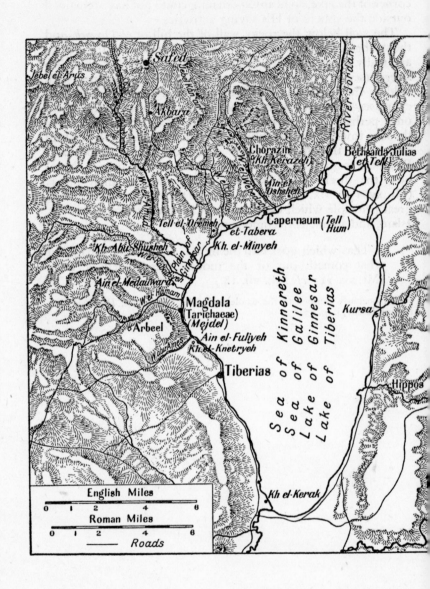

VIII

CAPERNAUM AND CHORAZIN

WE come nearer to the centre of the activity of Jesus when, after crossing, or going round, the hill of Kinnereth, we reach the northern side of the lake. Here we find first a very small plain[1] of alluvial soil, formed by the *Wady ed-Jamus*, which comes down from the north. It is bounded on the west by the *Tell el-'Oremeh*, on the east by the spur of a mountain, on which in recent years a little Italian colony has settled. The district is now called—after the region of the spring which belongs to it, at the foot of the eastern hill—*et-Tabera*, or in Bedouin pronunciation, *ed-Dabera*, a name which is rightly traced back to the Greek ἑπτάπηγον (*i.e.* χωρίον), " Seven springs." This designation (in Latin *Septem fontes*) can be traced as far back as Byzantine times,[2] but has, however, nothing to do with the Beersabe (seven springs) fortified by Josephus[3] on the northern border of Lower Galilee, which is to be looked for farther west. The plenteous tufa-forming water of the various springs is not uniform in temperature (which reaches 89·6° Fahr. in some cases) or ingredients.[4] None of the springs supplies drinking-water, but one of the colder ones (in *Tannur Aiyub*) is considered to possess special healing properties, perhaps because of its radium activity, which, however, have not yet been investigated. Thus the direct value of the abundant water which rises from the chalk formations near the lake, and slightly above its level, is limited. Yet from ancient times efforts were made to use it for irrigation and the working of mills. This was only made possible by catching the springs in tower-shaped basins—of which one eight-cornered and two round ones have been preserved—letting them flow away

---

[1] The first western branch of the valley is called *Khallet es-Sammak*.
[2] In the Greek form, Cyril Scythop.; *Vita Sabæ*, ch. xxiv.; *Commemor. de casis Dei*; Epiphanius. In Latin, Paulus Diaconus; Theodosius.
[3] *Vita* 37.
[4] The analysis of the two springs is given by Blankenhorn, *Naturwissenschaftliche Studien*, p. 344.

in lofty aqueducts.   In this way the water was drawn off towards
the district on the other side of *Tell el-'Oremeh*, and also made
to drive five mills, two of which are still in operation.   This
working of mills—which can be traced back to the year 1174
—does not seem to go back to the Byzantine period, for in
Arculf's time (670) the ground was unploughed and without
buildings.

It is possible that in earlier times the spring-water was simply
allowed to run into the lake without any use being made of
it.   But numerous palm-trees mentioned by Petrus Diaconus,[1]
of which a few insignificant remnants only exist, together with
a wild thicket of brambles and oleanders, must have testified
to the abundance which nature here displays.   Moreover, the
water renders to the shore-dwellers at least one important
service, in that, by its warmth and its flavour, it attracts the
fish, which, in this part of the lake, are caught on the flat
shore with rod, casting-net, and draw-net; but farther away,
especially at night, with the deep-sea net, trailing in the water.
The usual eatable fish found in the lake are, above all, the
Chromis niloticus (Arab. *musht abyad*) and *tiberiensis* (Arab.
musht labad); the narrower *Hemichromis sacer* (Arab. *kelb*),
together with the scale-less sheath-like (*siluris*) *Clarias macracanthus* (Arab. *barbut*)—prohibited to Jews, but not to be
classified among the " bad " fish of Mt. xiii. 48.[2]   In autumn
the *Barbus canis Valenciennes* (Arab. *kersin*) is caught chiefly.
Among the Jews it was once asserted that the lake of Tiberias
resembled, in this, flowing water, since pure and impure fish
do not swim together there.[3]   In fact, the Palestinian zoologist,
J. Aharoni, told me that the inedible fish of the lake—like the
Clarias macracanthus and all the species of the *Nemachilus*—always
stick to the slimy ground, while the *Chromides* and all other
pure fish prefer the higher levels of the water.   The Jordan
and the lake are said to be alike in this.   Nowadays fishermen
from Tiberias settle here in the spring for a longer period,
attend to their trade, and dry their nets on the shore.   It must
always have been the same here.   Jewish law prescribed that
the tribe of Naphtali should have the exclusive right of fishing
in the lake of Tiberias; the southern shore to the width of a
net-rope was also supposed to belong to them.[4]   Nevertheless

[1] Geyer, p. 113.
[2] For the different species of fish, *cf.* Masterman, *Studies in Galilee* (1909),
p. 43; E. Schmitz, *Das Heilige Land*, p. 18; Aaroni in Blankenhorn, *Naturwissenschaftliche Studien*, p. 434.
[3] p. Ab. z. 42a.
[4] Tos. Bab. k. viii. 18.

there was a traditional belief that an ordinance of Joshua enacted that members of other tribes could fish in the lake with hook and draw- or drag-net (*mikhmoreth*),[1] but were not allowed to set sail for fishing or to anchor a boat in the lake for that purpose.[2] This theory could scarcely have been put into practice in the time of Jesus owing to the mingling together of the shore-dwellers. It is likely, however, that the Jewish fishermen of Capernaum gained their living mostly round the " Seven Springs." With the hook[3] fastened to a line, without a rod, Peter, standing in the water, drew from the lake the fish which had in its mouth the tribute money (Mt. xvii. 27), and he either put the fish into a pouch attached to his hip, or fastened it to a cord attached to his foot in the water. Peter and Andrew—with clothes tucked up, or in short shirts—walked in the shallow water by the shore, and threw out, with a skilful swing, the 3 to 5 metres wide circular fishing-net,[4] so that it fell, out-spread, on the surface of the water. Then they drew it back again by the rope attached to the middle, when Jesus called them (Mt. iv. 18; Mk. i. 16). From the shore, the draw-net[5] cast with the help of a boat was dragged with long ropes to the beach, and there the fishes were sorted out (Mt. xiii. 47 *f*.). It might also naturally happen that the fishes were collected in a boat. Sitting in a boat, James and John, with their father Zebedee, prepared their deep-sea nets[6] for the next draught of fishes (Mt. iv. 21 *f*.; Mk. i. 19 *f*.). To fish in the deep water, which is best undertaken in two boats, Peter and the sons of Zebedee joined forces (Lk. v. 10). They started out together; laid out the nets—which were heavily weighted at the edge—in a great curve, so that they hung in the water like a 2 metres high wall; then drove the fishes into the meshes of the double or threefold net, in which, finally, they were dragged into the boat. Standing on the shore, they washed the nets which had become dirty from the last catch (Lk. v. 2), in order afterwards to spread them out on land, between poles, to dry. Peter was standing

---

[1] [σαγήνη, Mt. xiii. 47.—TRANSLATOR.]   [2] b. Bab. k. 81a.

[3] ἄγκιστρον, Jewish Aramaic *ḥakketa* (Targ. Hab. i. 15); Christian Pal. *ṣinnoreta*; Pal. Arab. *ṣunnar*.

[4] ἀμφίβληστρον, Pal. Arab. *meṣadeta*, as all species of nets, because of the lack of technical knowledge. Traditional Jewish law differentiates the following kinds of nets: *ḥerem*, supplied with a more tight part (*ẓuṭ*) for the taking in of the fish; *reshet*; *meṣuda*; *mikhmoreth* (Kel. xxiii. 5; Machsh. v. 7; Cant. R. iv. 8 (51b). It does not make it clear, however, what the different forms actually were. Also the Greek designations are given here only hypothetically. Greek archæology does not supply us with positive information.

[5] σαγήνη, Pal. Arab. *jarf*.   [6] δίκτυον, Pal. Arab. *mbaṭṭen*.

naked in the boat when he recognised the Risen Lord (Jn. xxi.
7), since he had to be ready to spring into the water and dive
to free the net—which had been dragging along the bed of the
lake—from stones and rocks.[1]   He quickly drew on his short
shirt [2]—such as was used by the drag-net fishers on landing—
in order not to stand unclothed before the Master.   It has
been thought strange that Peter should don what was probably
a wet garment.   Sven Hedin,[3] however, states that when
sailing on the lake in July, with an air temperature of 87·8° Fahr.
and the water at 84·1°, he found it very pleasant to pour water
over his clothes and let them dry in the wind.   Such scenes
as these could be witnessed at the Seven Wells by the lake
then as now.

In the days when the settlement on the hill in the west
flourished, it would doubtless have included the nearby district
of the wells; later the environs of Capernaum probably only
extended as far as this, without including them.   Josephus
must have assumed this when he makes the inhabitants call
the fertile well of the Ginnesar plain " Kepharnaum," *i.e.*
" Well of Capernaum."[4]   He, however, ascribes to the well
an importance which it did not possess at that time, assuming
that its water was even at that time conducted to the district of
the *Khan el-Minyeh*.   His personal reminiscence of this district
of the spring, with the rare Nile fishes, was probably so vivid
that he could not withhold it from his readers.   The brooks of
the plain he forgot—or did not find it necessary to refer to
them.

In the sixth century the place of the miraculous feeding of
the 5,000 was shown at the " Seven Wells."[5]   Arculf[6] in 670
saw here, at the edge of a well, pillars lying about—presumably
those of the church which, according to Petrus Diaconus,[7] had
as an altar the stone which Jesus used for a table when blessing
the bread.   And on the mosaic floor Karge found, to the west
near *Birket 'Ali eḍ-Daher*,[8] a remnant of the altar with a picture
of a basket with four loaves and a fish on each side.   How
this place came to be thought of is not quite clear.   That the
Fourth Gospel (vi. 10) lays stress on the abundance of wild

---

[1] See also Masterman, *Studies in Galilee*, pp. 41, 43.
[2] ἐπενδύτης, Christian Pal. *kolba* (κολόβιον).   *Cf.* also the description of the
Egyptian Nonnus Panopolitanus in his paraphrase of Jn. xxi. 7.
[3] *Till Jerusalem* (1917), p. 155.   [4] *Bell. Jud.* iii. 10, 8.
[5] Theodosius (Geyer, *Itinera*, p. 138).   [6] *Ibid.*, p. 273.
[7] *Ibid.*, p. 113.
[8] According to Petrus, the church lay at the open road.   That was the case
here.

plants (" grass ") in the place, and that Mt. xiv. 19 ; Mk. vi. 39, also mention " grass," on which the people sat, could not have been the only reason for the choice of this spot. It is more likely that the assumption was influenced by the fact that the Sermon on the Mount was thought to have taken place on the hill directly above the " Seven Wells " (see below, p. 155). It seemed natural to identify the mountain of the feeding (Mt. xv. 29) with the mountain of the Sermon, and, in this way, to have the place of instruction near to the place of the feeding. It is also possible that the localisation in this case, as often in other cases, did not rest upon real tradition, but on the wish to help the pilgrims to visualise, in an easily approachable place, the memory of an important event. But another event might also have attached the feeding of the 5,000 to this spot. The appearance of the Risen Lord at the lake, according to Jn. xxi., was located by tradition at the Seven Wells, although it is only in the year 800 that it is directly so mentioned, namely in the *Commemoratorium de casis Dei*.[1] A church of the Twelve Thrones then stood there, near the lake, and the table at which Jesus ate with the disciples was shown. Distinct from this was the monastery *Heptapegon* at the place of the feeding of the 5,000. Also Epiphanius of Hagiopolis differentiates between the place of the feeding, lying near the shore, and the church of the miraculous feeding.[2] From then on the two holy places on the Seven Wells are often referred to. Daniel mentions, after the place of the feeding, a church of the Apostles, at the spot of the Appearance.[3] Burchard in the year 1283 pointed to a stone, at ten steps distance from the shore, misplaced by the Bedouins, with three foot-impressions in it, on which Jesus was said to have stood when He appeared to the disciples, and right by the shore also, to the place where he ate with them, which place was called *tabula* or *mensa*.[4]

The Fourth Gospel records Peter's decision to go a-fishing in his native lake, and our Lord's call to him to tend His sheep (Jn. xxi. 2-17). It was natural to compare the call of Peter and Andrew at the lakeside to become fishers of men with this (Mk. i. 17 ; Mt. iv. 19 ; Lk. v. 10). Both narratives presuppose a place on the lake where it was usual to fish and to land. Thus it came about that both calls took place at the same spot, and that near Capernaum. Our Lord's saying that He would meet His disciples, after the Resurrection, in Galilee (Mk. xiv.

---

[1] Tobler, *Descr. T.S.*, p. 81.
[2] Migne, *P.G.* cxx., col. 269.
[3] Khitrovo, *Itinéraires*, p. 63 f.
[4] Laurent, *Peregrinatores*, p. 40.

28 ; xvi. 7), certainly pointed to the place well known to them
of old where He had been used to converse with them, and the
lost end of St. Mark must have contained a record of this
meeting. The five appearances of the Risen Lord which St.
Paul refers to in 1 Cor. xv. 5 *f.* were certainly each attached to
a definite place, mentioned in the narrative. One of them would
correspond to that mentioned in St. John. So it is permissible to assume that tradition had good cause to look for
the place of the appearance by the lake in the vicinity of
the Seven Wells. When I landed by boat not far from
there on April 9, 1913, from Bethsaida, our boatmen carried
with them two little fishes which they had caught there, in
the shallow lagoon, with their hands. While we went off
to Capernaum they made a fire on the stones on the shore,
let it burn down, then put the dressed and salted fishes on
the glowing coal. These they offered me on my return.
They tasted somewhat smoky, but otherwise quite palatable.
So there we made a picture similar to that which the disciples,
according to Jn. xxi. 9, witnessed : " a fire of coals and fish
laid thereon." How often our tents have stood beside the
Seven Wells—probably several times directly on the place
where tradition showed the *Mensa Christi*—while at night the
fishermen were busy on the lake plying their quiet trade and
supplying also for our table the tasty fish of the lake. If
anywhere, here by the lake we were in the very home of
Christianity. The feeding of the 5,000, however, does not
belong to this spot, because it is only $1\frac{1}{3}$ kilometres from here
to the Fig-spring, and only $2\frac{1}{3}$ kilometres to Capernaum, and
so the lack of sustenance, which was the cause of the miracle,
could not have arisen in such a spot.

The road on the north shore of the lake first cuts across
the projection of the chalk-hill which shuts in the region of
the well to the east—of which more will be said later. But
even afterwards it does not run along the shore, which curves
a great deal. For there is no beach, and the slopes of the
upland, which are covered with basalt-rubble, stretch down to
the lake. The road thus follows the shore, raised slightly
above it, for some distance. It touches the site of *Khirbet Tell
Ḥum*—which we consider to have been Capernaum—not at
the shore, but on its northern edge. On this road a stone
block with a cross marked in the ninth century the place
where the woman with an issue was healed,[1] which, however,

[1] Epiphanius Hagiopolita, Migne, *P.G.* cxx., col. 269.

it would seem more reasonable to place (from the accounts in Mk. v. 21, 25 ; Lk. viii. 40, 43) at the harbour of old Capernaum. *Tell Hum* opens to the view as soon as the hill-projections east of the Seven Wells are passed. On this side of the opening of a descending valley, the *Wady el-Webedani*, a fairly level—although not more than 300 metres wide—stretch of land separates the lake from the gradual upward slope of the highland. The promontory of *Ras Jirnis* gives protection to the shore from the west wind, so that boats can be moored there. And farther east a very small bay, at present choked up, which runs into the shore about 50 metres, could have been used as a harbour. Here, about halfway between the two best fishing places on the lake— the neighbourhood of the Seven Wells and the mouth of the Jordan—was an appropriate position for a fishing village. So far, however, no well has been discovered. The nearest supplier of water was *'Ain el-'Oshsheh*, 1½ kilometres to the east. The necessary grain could be cultivated on the shore, which is fairly level, although narrow, on both sides of the bay. Vine- and fig-plantations could also flourish on the slope. This unfortified place was unfitted to be a centre of political or martial activity, but a population gaining its livelihood chiefly by fishing could easily be sustained.

A field of ruins, found nowhere else on the north shore of the lake, shows that the locality was actually used for the purpose which called it into existence. Of town walls there is no trace. That the ruins consist mostly of unhewn stones may be due to the fact that *Tell Hum* was used as a quarry for Tiberias. A small erection, standing not far from the shore and probably of Arab origin, contains a basin about 2 metres high (5 metres square) belonging to an aqueduct— now lacking the connecting pipe—which brought water from the Seven Wells or from the lake (by means of a lifting apparatus). A whole collection of millstones, oil-presses, and other implements, betrays the one-time practice of a craft which made use of the basalt of the neighbourhood. A necropolis (with tombs from the Græco-Roman period, among which a notable subterranean construction of hewn stones, with the superstructure now destroyed, was perhaps once considered by the Jews to be the "tomb of Tanchum") and also simpler grave-hills and grave-circles, supplement the remains of the old town. In striking contrast to the mainly insignificant remains is the ruin of a considerable

building of limestone which, with its rich late-Roman ornamentation, is unequalled on the lake, indeed in the whole
of western Palestine. That it was intended for a synagogue
is evident from its similarity to other Galilæan buildings of
the same kind bearing Jewish inscriptions. According to the
careful examination of the remains by Kohl and Watzinger
in the year 1905[1] on behalf of the German Oriental Society,
the building was erected about A.D. 200, by order of the

Synagogue at Capernaum (Reconstruction).

emperor Antoninus Pius, so Watzinger suggests. But more
likely it was in consequence of the permission granted
then to the Jews to replace their dilapidated or destroyed
synagogues by new ones built in accordance with current
taste. Meistermann[2] and Orfali[3] endeavour to prove that
there is nothing against ascribing the synagogue of *Tell
Ḥum* to the Herodian period. They are certain that it
is the synagogue which the centurion built for the Jews
(Lk. vii. 5), probably as a substitute for an older, less stately,

[1] *Antike Synagogen in Galiläa* (1916), p. 4 *f.*
[2] *Capharnaüm et Bethsaïde* (1921), p. 163.
[3] *Capharnaüm et ses Ruines* (1922), p. 67.

building.   Orfali thinks that this noble officer was even
recognised by a Tannaitic *halakha* as the founder of this
synagogue.   He points to the Tosephta Megilla iii., quoted
by Bacher.   There, indeed, it speaks of bequests to synagogues

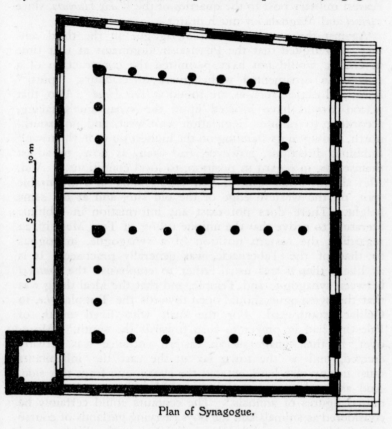

Plan of Synagogue.

made by Gentiles.   But in that passage,[1] as also in connection with bequests for the Temple,[2] it is shown plainly
with what hesitation such gifts were accepted from Gentiles.
Antoninus[3] provided a lamp for a synagogue.   Rabbi Jehuda I.
praised God for it, but it was later suggested by some rabbis
that Antoninus was probably a proselyte.[4]   There is no

[1] iii. 5; Arach. 6a.   [2] Tos. Shek. i. 7.   [3] p. Meg. 74a.
[4] The Antoninus frequently mentioned in connection with R. Jehuda I.
was certainly an emperor of this name, but it is uncertain which one is meant,
or how much of these accounts is merely legendary.

reference anywhere in rabbinic literature to the erection of
a synagogue by a Gentile. That this, nevertheless, actually
took place in Capernaum need not therefore be doubted;
although Orfali is wrong in assuming that this place was the
nearest military post to the quarries of the *Wady Ḥamam*, since
Arbeel and Magdala lay much nearer.

Against the erection of the synagogue in the third century, it is argued that the Pharisaism dominant at that time
in Galilee would not have permitted the construction of a
synagogue ornamented with figures of centaurs, " putti,"
lions, and eagles, such as are found at *Tell Ḥum*. Also, that
period would have insisted upon the synagogue's facing,
according to rabbinic legislation, east-west, and not south-
north, and upon its standing on the highest point in the town.[1]
Rabbinic directions, however, had then, as now, to adjust
themselves, in regard to position, to local conditions.[2] And,
after all, the synagogue of *Tell Ḥum* stands on a favourable
spot, on the western edge of the old site, and at the same
height. There does not exist any information in rabbinic
literature to prove that the unique ruling of Tos. Meg. iv. 22
regarding the eastern position of a synagogue, analogous
to that of the Tabernacle, was generally practised. It is
as likely that it was usual rather to emphasise the *contrast*
between synagogue and Temple, and that the ideal thing was
that the synagogue should open towards the Temple—*i.e.* in
Galilee, southward. For the man who lived north of
Palestine had in prayer to turn towards the south.[3] Moreover, in this synagogue an eastern entrance was actually
erected, and as the town lay in the east the inhabitants
must in any case have entered the synagogue from this side.
And as to the ornamentations, rabbinic law expressly permitted figures of animals.[4] The centaurs could certainly be
considered as animals and the boys carrying garlands of course
had nothing to do with heathen religion. In the third century
the Jews began to ornament the walls with figures, without
opposition from the Galilæan authority, Rabbi Jochanan.[5]
Finally, there was also a difference between the execution
of such pictures by Jews (which might have been prohibited),
and their use by Jews after having been made by Gentiles

---

[1] All this is emphasised by Orfali, p. 86 ; similarly Meistermann, p. 552.
[2] Tos. Meg. iv. 23 ; b. Sab. 11a.   [3] b. Bab. b. 25b, see below, p. 145.
[4] Tos. Ab. z. v. 2 ; p. Ab. z. 42c ; b. Ab. z. 42a.
[5] p. Ab. z. 42d.

for non-religious purposes. The above-mentioned Jochanan, for instance, did not even hesitate to make use of a vase on which there was a picture of a heathen deity. It is true, there had been times when Jews thought differently about such matters. In the year 4 B.C. the golden eagle erected by Herod in the Temple was pulled down,[1] and Josephus, who expressly declares all representations of living creatures to be prohibited, was directed by the Jewish authorities in the year 66 to destroy the palace of Herod Antipas in Tiberias, because of the pictures of animals on its walls.[2] Now Meistermann and Orfali attempt to make the iconoclasts of that time responsible for the systematic disfigurement of the pictorial representations of *Tell Ḥum*.[3] But it is very improbable that the Galilæan synagogues with their ornamentations were erected at a time when such ideas predominated. The final decision in this matter will be reached by further excavations and, above all, by examination of the foundations of the *Tell Ḥum* synagogue, with the help of pottery which may be found. Unfortunately, the excavations carried out by Frater Wendelin Hinterkeuser in 1905-14, and by Pater Dr. Orfali in 1921, have produced no further progress in this direction.

Of greater importance than the decoration of the synagogue is its interior construction, which certainly did not take this shape for the first time about the year 200. Three doors afforded convenient entrance on the gable-end looking south (*i.e.* towards the lake), which also contained the chief window of the building, a convenient mode of entrance from a platform running alongside it. The interior, 22·5 metres long and 16·4 metres broad, resembled a basilica without an apse, with a double-floored colonnade built round three sides, the upper floor of which must have been intended for women ; the colonnade ceased on the entrance side. The pillars of the lower colonnade, standing upon high plinths, have Corinthian capitals ; the smaller pillars of the upper colonnade belonged to the Doric order. A fragment of a pillar shows from its inscription[4] that individual ornamental parts of the synagogue were bestowed by certain persons. The benefactor mentioned in the inscription was called *Zebida bar Jochanan*, whose name reminds one of the Apostle John, the son of Zebedee (*Jochanan*

---

[1] *Ant.* xvii. 6 ; *Bell. Jud.* i. 33, 2.   [2] *Vita* 12.
[3] Meistermann, p. 552 ; Orfali, p. 100. Also in Petra all pictorial representations were destroyed, evidently by the Arabs. It is possible that also in *Tell Ḥum* the Islamic law played a rôle in the disfigurements.
[4] Dalman, *Aramäische Dialektproben*, 2nd ed., p. 38.

bar Zabday).   Double stone-benches run along both side-walls. Unfortunately we know nothing more about the interior arrangement.   One expects, according to the Palestinian Talmud,[1] wooden benches with or without backs (κλινήρ, συψέλλιον), but, above all, a dais (βῆμα) with a lectern (ἀναλόγειον) for the reading of the Law, and the chest (*aron, teba*) for the rolls of the Law and other sacred writings, with their wrappers.   This chest, which often took the form of a small cupboard with folding doors,[2] might be provided with a special cover (*killa*)[3] which was, perhaps, attached as a curtain or canopy.   Without any sure evidence, Watzinger takes it for granted that the dais in the Capernaum synagogue was placed quite near the entrance, and that an ornamental wall, of which certain parts were found,[4] covered up the middle door, in the background.   Even if this structure was once actually in existence here, the original style of the synagogue certainly does not presume it.   For the chief entrance would not have been constructed in order immediately afterwards to be blocked up.   Orfali[5] supposes that the richly ornamented ark of the Law originally stood before the northern colonnade, as in the Parthenon in Athens the cultus image stood in this position, which also would explain the reason why the north wall was left without seats.   Here, however, it was not an image to gaze upon, but a desk, from which the Law was to be read.   The shrine for the rolls of the Law, whether it had the form of a chest or a cupboard, was, in any case, not connected with the dais.   This follows from the different grades of sacredness attached to the two things,[6] and, still more, from the fact that the shrine had to be movable. It was brought, on fast-days for rain, into the open.[7]   Also for the service (the chief purpose of which was the reading of the Law[8]) the shrine, which evidently was otherwise kept in an alcove,[9] had to be "put up."[10]   It is possible that the

---

[1] p. Meg. 73d, with Greek designations for most of the structural objects of the synagogue.

[2] See Tos. iv. 21, according to which the ark had a front-side which had to be directed towards the congregation. *Cf.* also the representation on a head-piece of a door, found in Capernaum, with an ark of the Law, a palm branch, citron, and Mazzot dish in Watzinger, *Antike Synagogen in Gal.*, p. 39 *f.*, Ahb. 76 (misunderstood by the Author).   [3] p. Sab. 17e ; Meg. 73d.

[4] *Cf.*, however, plates 70-73 with plates 21-23 in Kohl-Watzinger.

[5] p. 69 *f.*   [6] p. Meg. 73d, *cf.* b. Meg. 32a.   [7] Taan. ii. 1 ; Tos. Taan. i. 8.

[8] Dalman, *Jesus-Jeshua* (English trans.), p. 38 *f.* ; *cf.* Levertoff, " Synagogue Worship in the First Century " (*Liturgy and Worship*, S.P.C.K.).

[9] A vaulted space, built at the north-west corner of the *Tell Ḥum* synagogue, would probably have been used for this purpose.   [10] Tos. Meg. iv. 21.

little temple on wheels which is delineated on a head-piece
of a door found in *Tell Ḥum*[1] represented this shrine and its
cover—for which the sculptor might have had in mind the
model of the festival chariot of Aphrodite. The structure
might have been similar to the five-aisled synagogue at Alex-
andria, which had its wooden dais in the centre.[2] The shrine
had to be placed in such a way that its front was directed
towards the people and its back towards the Sanctuary,
i.e. the Jerusalem Temple.[3] When turned towards the congregation the priests stood before the shrine as they pronounced
the blessing; the elders sat before the dais, facing the congregation, which looked towards the Temple.[4] In the synagogue
of *Tell Ḥum*, the southerly direction of the three aisles is in
itself a proof that it was meant for a congregation that should
turn primarily towards the south, *i.e.* the Jerusalem Temple.
The large window on the south side supplied the necessary
light for the reading in the middle of the nave. When the
doors were opened, the glance of the worshippers swept over
the glittering surface of the lake, and sought in the distance
the Temple—destroyed, or still in its glory—which to pray
towards was the custom from of old.[5] Even if the Capernaum
congregation in the time of Christ used another building as
a synagogue, they could not have faced differently at prayer.

We can thus understand why the Galilæan synagogues
hitherto explored always had their entrances on the south,[6]
like that of *Tell Ḥum*. There is no need to connect their
facing north with the old myth of the seat of the gods in the
north,[7] or to explain it by a mere thoughtless imitation of the
synagogues of Southern Judæa,[8] or even by the consideration
of the perspective of the building.[9] The ancient custom,
that all Israel turned in prayer towards *one* place, *i.e.* the

---

[1] Watzinger, p. 193 *f.*, suggests that it represented a chariot in honour of
the Jewish Patriarch. But neither would it have been an appropriate form for
the purpose, nor any motive for keeping it in the synagogue. A movable
ark (*cf.* 1 Sam. vi. 8; 2 Sam. vi. 3) is more likely than the divine chariot of
Ezek. i., which also had four wheels.

[2] p. Sukka 55a.   [3] Tos. Meg. iv. 21; *cf.* 26.   [4] *Ibid.*

[5] 1 Kings viii. 38, 44, 48; Dan. vi. 11; Ezra iv. 58, and in many rabbinic passages.
According to a later opinion, all directions are permissible, except the eastern,
"because of the Minim," *i.e.* Hebrew Christians, who turned to the east at
prayer (Bab. b. 25a).

[6] The synagogue of Irbid is also directed south-north, although the entrance
lies in the west.

[7] Mieses, in Bloch's *Wochenschrift* (1912), p. 549.

[8] Krauss, *Die Galiläischen Synagogenruinen*, p. 4. In his *Synogogale Altertümer*,
however, he gives up all attempts of explanation.

[9] Elbogen, *Der jüdische Gottesdienst*, p. 460.

Temple, was thus respected. It is quite certain that care was purposely taken to avoid arranging the synagogue like the Temple, the sanctuary proper towards which the prayers were to be directed. It was also practical to have the entrances and the chief window in the south, from whence there would be no disturbance from an unpleasant wind, and from which point plenty of light could be expected.

On the eastern side of the synagogue of *Tell Ḥum* was a court with a trilateral colonnade. It was connected with the synagogue by a door, but it could not have been intended merely as an ante-room or back-room, as it has on its three free sides—at least, according to the diagram of Orfali[1]—no less than eight entrances, three each in the north and the east, and two only in the south, because a staircase made a third impossible there. It is true, Orfali does not state how he recognised—especially on the east side—the number of these entrances. A stair leads up from the east to the platform before the south front of the court and the synagogue. Ten steps are preserved. Orfali, who does not say anything about the height of the steps, enumerates in his plan sixteen steps,[2] and thus presupposes on its east side a difference in height of about 3 metres between the ground of the court and the street. The eastern entrances must thus have had stairs, but none were found, and the account of the excavation does not even mention the necessity for them. It is natural to suppose that the number of the lintels determined the number of the entrances. Also the capitals are arbitrarily distributed. Three capitals of different height are supposed to belong to the arcade of the court, and their different heights are said to have been intended to correct the slope of the ground towards the east,[3] although the ground surface of the court is level! Quite new explorations of a different character must be made. The court, which seems to have been added later, was, in any case, an atrium, lying along the side, which was perhaps intended to make the eastern approach to the synagogue the principal one. According to Krauss[4] it was an open-air place of prayer where the Jews prayed, turning towards the "sanctuary," *i.e.* towards the synagogue (which was also supposed to have been roofless). It is more probable

---

[1] *Capharnaüm*, p. iii.
[2] According to Kohl-Watzinger, p. 2, there were thirteen steps of 22 centimetres height each.
[3] Orfali, p. 56.   [4] *Synagogale Altertümer*, pp. 329 *f.*, 439.

that it was the " parvar " (esplanade) of the synagogue, which
was not permitted to be used as a mere passage.[1] Possibly
the basin stood there[2] which in the synagogue of Beth Shean,
for instance, afforded an opportunity for the washing of the
hands and feet.[3] Orfali[4] calls attention to three stone vessels
about 70 centimetres high with 66 centimetres upper and
33 centimetres lower width, which were perhaps used for
purifications. They remind us of the six water-pots of stone
in Jn. ii. 6, and of the rabbinic ruling that vessels of stone,
earth, and cattle-dung are not included in the law concerning
the defilement of vessels (Lev. xi. 32-34).[5] There is no
rabbinic precept concerning cleanliness in entering a synagogue.[6] There was, however, the custom among Palestinian
rabbis of washing the hands before the daily recitation of the
Shem'a (Dt. vi. 4-9; xi. 13-21) and the prayers following it.[7]
The putting on of the phylacteries also required a clean body.[8]
Of a different character, of course, was actual defilement, when
the required bathing had, if possible, to be accomplished
before the recitation of the Shem'a.[9] The daily bath taken by
Judith before prayer (Judith xii. 6-9) goes beyond any rabbinic
" precept." There is no trace of a bath in the Tell Ḥum
synagogue[10]—the lake supplied all the requirements of this
kind. What Jesus thought of the washing of hands before
meals we know from Mt. xv. 2 f.; Mk. vii. 2 f.; Lk. xi. 38.
It is not likely that His attitude towards the washing before
prayer was different. On the other hand, St. Paul presupposes such a custom when he figuratively demands the lifting
up of pure hands for prayer (1 Tim. ii. 8).

Since 1894 Tell Ḥum has been in the possession of the
Franciscans, and is the residence of a Franciscan monk.
In the area of the ancient site of the town the Arabs now
begin to settle. One would prefer to see it in its old
wild condition which early photographs show, and which
even on my first visit on June 6, 1899, I no longer saw.
A detached lonely palm-tree; here and there a Christ's-
thorn; between high thistles, jut out from the ground, white

---

[1] p. Meg. 74a. [2] Aram. *gurna*; *cf.* Arab. *jurn*. [3] *Ibid.*
[4] *Ibid.*, p. 64. [5] Kel. x. 1; Bab. Mez. v. 1.
[6] According to Staerk, *Die jüdische Gemeinde des Neuen Bundes in Damascus*
(1922), p. 73, this community was prohibited from entering the synagogue in
an impure condition (xi. 22). But this refers, in spite of vi. 12, to the Temple;
cf. xi. 17-19; xii. 1; xvi. 13.
[7] Ber. 14b. [8] p. Ber. 3e; b. Sab. 130a. [9] Ber. iii. 4, 5.
[10] A papyrus refers to a great demand for water in an Egyptian synagogue;
cf. Schürer, *Geschichte der jüd. Volkes*, iii., p. 48.

limestone blocks with wonderful sculptures.   Unchecked by
the walls of the large Franciscan estate, the glance wanders
eastward, to the neighbourhood of Bethsaida and the highland
beyond it, and northward to the gradual ascent of the dark
mountain area, the highest tops of which are brought out in
strong relief by the bright colouring of their limestone
structure.   In the south-west, on the other side of the rocky
gate of Arbeel, the present *Wady el-Ḥamam* opens up, with the
descent towards Nazareth.   By the shore the waves of the
lake splash, moved by the south wind.   No village is seen
in the whole neighbourhood.   The shore road above is
desolate, used only occasionally by Bedouins and pilgrims.
But in other days it must have been different.   Not only did
the town's own commerce and its glorious synagogue enliven
it, but after Herod Philip had founded his capital Julias beyond
the Jordan estuary (4-2 B.C.), an important part of the trans-
port of the district had to use the northern road by the lake—
which meant a connection with the whole of Galilee and part
of the Mediterranean coast.   The land east of the northern
end is to-day primarily Bedouin domain.   In ancient times a
settled population lived there, which had relationships also
with the west.   From this the one town on the northern
shore gained increased importance.   The fishing village
became a marketing centre.   In the time of Christ the Jordan
here formed the frontier between the tetrarchy of Philip and
that of Antipas.   Since no considerable town lay on the
Jordan itself, the settlement on the north shore of the lake
became the border town.   It must have had a custom-house,
which naturally also looked after the lake traffic.[1]   It will also
have had a small garrison, which guarded the frontier and
assisted in the collection of the customs.

The Capernaum of the Gospels, which was the centre of
our Lord's activity round the lake, fits in with all these facts.
Its hellenised name goes back to *Kephar Nachum*, which is
also used by the Pal. Evangeliarium and the Peshita,
according to the Jewish usage.[2]   Among its inhabitants were
found fishermen, some of whom originally came from Bethsaida
(Jn. i. 44), but now lived here, owing, perhaps, to matri-

[1] Some think that Capernaum is to be sought at *Khan el-Minyeh*, because there
must have been a custom-house there on the Via Maris.   But 20 kilometres from
the frontier—on the Jordan ford, at " Jacob's Bridge "—there certainly was
no custom-house.
[2] Eccles R. i. 8 (70b) ; vii. 26 (129b).   About the name Capernaum, see Abel,
Journal Pal. Or. Soc., viii., p. 24 *ff.*

monial circumstances (Mk. i. 30 f.; Mt. viii. 14; Lk. iv. 38). The Jewish life of the place throbbed, above all, in its synagogue (Mt. xii. 9; Mk. i., 21 ; iii. 1 ; v. 22; Lk. iv. 31 ; vi. 6 ; viii. 41). There was a customs office, from which Jesus called to an official to follow Him (Mt. ix. 9; Mk. ii. 14; Lk. v. 27). A heathen centurion lived there with his men (Mt. viii. 5 ; Lk. vii. 2) ; perhaps the same who, in Jn. iv. 46, is called a " king's officer," although Herod Antipas never received the longed-for royal title. The centurion did not disturb the predominantly Jewish life of the town with its Pharisees and scribes, for he built them a synagogue (Lk. vii. 5). Furthermore, this Capernaum must have been identical with *Tell Ḥum*, because Josephus, having been injured near Julias, had himself brought to the village of the " Kepharnokers,"[1] evidently, because this was the nearest town on this side of the Jordan to offer him safety. Moreover, it is absolutely certain that Capernaum was shown here in the Byzantine period, between the Seven Springs and Bethsaida,[2] at a time when the Jewish life of Galilee was not yet extinct.

Orfali[3] gives a very gloomy picture of the supposed unutterable immorality of the inhabitants of the Jewish Kephar Naḥum. Closer examination of the sources, however, leads to something quite different. We read, for instance, that Chananya, the nephew of Rabbi Joshua, a famous scribe (about A.D. 120), was bewitched by the *minim* (*i.e.* Jewish Christians) and made to ride a donkey on a Sabbath.[4] His uncle, after anointing him with oil and healing him, advised him to go to Babylon, " since the ass (*ḥamara*) of that godless one has risen in thee, thou canst not any longer live in the land of Israel."[5] By the " godless " one *Jeshu* (Jesus), who has been twice mentioned already, must be meant. Obviously there must have been a tale told about Him of a ride upon an ass—probably also on the Sabbath—which may have ended with Jesus' reference to Zech. ix. 9. The application

---

[1] *Vita* 72. Niese accepted the reading Κεφαρνωκον into the text, but Κεφαρνωκωον or Κεφαρνωκον is most probably the more correct reading, in spite of Schlatter, *Die hebr. Namen bei Josephus*, p. 118.

[2] Theodosius, Geyer, p. 138. See also above, p. 128 f.

[3] *Capharnaüm*, p. 3 ; *cf.* Meistermann, *Capernaüm et Bethsaïde*, p. 31 f.

[4] Eccl. R. i. 8 (70b).

[5] It is unnecessary to read with Schlatter (*Die Kirche Jerusalems*, p. 11) *ḥamra* (wine) instead of *ḥamara* (ass), as if it referred to the wine of the Lord's Supper. For similar rabbinic legends *cf.* Huldreich, *Historia Jeschuæ Nazareni* (1705), p. 52 ; Krauss, *Das Leben Jesu nach jüdischen Quellen* ; Levertoff, *Die religiöse Denkweise*.

of the Cæsarean teacher Issi (probably fourth century) of the words in Eccl. vii. 26 ("whoso pleaseth God") to the above-mentioned Chananya, and the last words of the verse ("and the sinner shall be taken by her," *i.e.* by the woman = heresy) to the inhabitants of *Kephar Nahum*,[1] is based on the same story. This is a reflection on the conditions in Capernaum at the time, not of Issi, but of Chananya. The essential point in the characterisation is the supposed lawlessness of the inhabitants and their attitude to Jesus. They are represented as Christians, and the story told about the disciple whom Jonathan ben Eleazar (third century) brought back from the heretics (*minim*)[2] who practised immorality,[3] also refers to Christians. The narrator alludes to supposed orgies of the gatherings of the Christians. Hence one is not justified in drawing any conclusions concerning the moral conditions prevailing in Jewish Capernaum in the time of Jesus from such invectives against misunderstood Christianity. Our Lord's lament over Capernaum (Mt. xi. 23 ; Lk. x. 15) makes it improbable that it became a Christian place in early times. In the fourth century the Jews allowed neither Christians, nor Samaritans, nor Gentiles to settle there.[4] Perhaps the only historical kernel in these Jewish references to Capernaum is that it presupposes a connection with Jesus.

At the beginning of the fourth century Capernaum was still an exclusively Jewish place, when the *Comes* Joseph was allowed to build a church there.[5] According to Petrus Diaconus, pilgrims visited there the house of Peter which had been turned into a church, and went up by a staircase to the synagogue, which was built of squared stone. Arculf, who in the year 670 observed Capernaum from a neighbouring mountain, relates that "it has no walls and is confined in a narrow space between the mountain and the lake, extending along the sea-coast for a long distance ; having the mountain on the north and the lake on the south, it stretches from west to east." In later centuries the Jews went there on pilgrimages, and visited the grave of the prophet Nahum— or Rabbi Tanhum (Tanchuma)—from which perhaps the name *Tell Hum* originated. It is to Byzantine Capernaum that the remains of buildings, 35 metres south of the synagogue between it and the lake, discovered by Orfali in 1921, belong.

---

[1] Eccl. R. vii. 26 (109b).   [2] *Ibid.*, i. 8 (70b).
[3] Read *aphroniyot* (πορνεία) instead of *aphtoniyot*.
[4] Epiphanius, Migne, *P.G.* xli., col. 135.   [5] Epiphanius, *Adv. Hæres.* xxx.

A threefold octagon, about 25 metres in diameter, is recognisable there in the foundations. A threshold on each of the three western sides of the middle octagon proves the orientation of the building, and hence its ecclesiastical purpose. The floor consists not of small slabs as in the synagogue, but of mosaic. Simple geometrical patterns predominate in the outermost space, and plant *motifs* in the centre. The innermost space of 7½ metres diameter has a border of irises or lotus flowers, a pattern of scales, with flowers on its surface, and in the middle a circle of 1½ metres diameter with a representation of a peacock, the fully spread-out tail of which almost completely encompasses the body. Orfali supposes that the inner space, the floor of which rises a little at the edges, was meant to be the basin of a baptistery. But there are no analogies to this. The baptismal basin is always let into the floor of the centre of the nave, in the building specially erected for this purpose, and does not fill the centre space of the church, the dimensions of which would make it a size elsewhere unprecedented, and here uncalled for. Since it belongs to a comparatively late period, as is shown by the level of the floor, which is nearly that of the ground outside, the octagon is undoubtedly a Byzantine building which was intended as a memorial chapel rather than a parish church, and might well have been built by the *Comes* Joseph. The absence of any Christian symbol is intelligible enough in the case of a tesselated pavement. The altar may have been a stone table with feet, without any platform. The peacock is found elsewhere in Palestine in church mosaics : in Jerusalem, for instance, on a mosaic with an Armenian inscription ;[1] in the monastery of the Cross near Jerusalem ; in the church found near Hiram's Tomb ;[2] and also near *Umm Jerar* in the southern border,[3] as well as in a synagogue near '*Ain ed-Duk*.[4] To be sure, the house of St. Peter, turned into a basilica, which Antoninus saw here and of which Petrus Diaconus testifies that its walls still stood in his time as formerly, has nothing to do with the octagon. This perhaps fell into ruins at an early date, and a building, supposed to survive from ancient Capernaum, was considered to be the church on the historical spot. This draws attention to the cruder remains in the neighbourhood, between the octagon and the synagogue, where Orfali also

[1] *ZDPV*, 1895, p. i.
[2] Jacobi, *Das geogr. Mosaik von Madaba*, pp. 10, 17.
[3] *PEFQ*, 1918, p. 122. [4] *Ibid.*, 1920, p. 8.4

found mosaics, but which, since they were of late date and built out of old material, he did not consider worthy of closer examination. His plan gives no proper idea of them, and nothing is said about the relation of their level to the ground of the octagon. As far as I recollect, the long room, in which there were three column-bases, remnants of the old roof-supports, which Orfali describes, was on a lower level than the octagon. But of still greater importance, perhaps, are the two rough columns, formerly supporting a roof, which he found nearer the synagogue. One of these buildings might have been the house of the Apostle which the pilgrims saw. It is to be hoped that continued digging will finally establish the level of the soil in the time of Christ and thereby also disclose the remains of buildings of that period.

Taking all this into consideration, we are on safe ground when we regard the synagogue of *Tell Ḥum*, which we hope will never be rebuilt, as a reconstruction of that in which Jesus healed one possessed (Mk. i. 21 ; Lk. iv. 31) and restored the withered arm of another sufferer (Mt. xii. 9 ; Mk. iii. 1 ; Lk. vi. 6). In the perhaps not far off house of Peter He healed the mother-in-law of His disciple of malaria (Mt. viii. 14 ; Mk. i. 29 ; Lk. iv. 38), and probably also sent back home—with sin forgiven and body healed—the lame man who had been let down through the roof (Mt. ix. 2 ; Mk. ii. 3 ; Lk. v. 18). Within the area of the town stood the house of the centurion whose servant the word of Jesus healed (Mt. viii. 5 ; Lk. vii. 1 ; *cf.* Jn. iv. 46) ; and also that of the chief of the synagogue, Jairus, in which Jesus healed the dead damsel with His " *ṭalita ḳumi* " (Mk. v. 41 ; *cf.* Mt. ix. 25 ; Lk. viii. 54) ; and, besides, the private house of the publican Levi, where he honoured his new Master with a feast. On the other hand, the custom-house from which Levi had been called (Mt. ix. 9 ; Mk. ii. 14 ; Lk. v. 27) must have stood outside, by the harbour. There, on the shore, the people crowded when Jesus spoke from the boat in parables concerning the Kingdom of God (Mt. xiii. 1 ; Mk. iv. 1).

It is impossible to determine with certainty the exact sites of all these places. But there is no spot in the whole of Palestine where memories heap themselves up to such an extent as in Capernaum. And when we stand here on the shore, where the Franciscans now have their small harbour, and look with delight over the sparkling surface of the lake, we hear especially with the inner ear two sayings of our Lord :

the question to the scribes who were present in the house of
Peter : *Ma hu ḳallil denemor limerashshela shebiḳin laḳh ḥobakh,
o denemor ḳum sab arsak weṭayel* (" Which is easier, to say to the
sick of the palsy, Thy sins are forgiven, or, Arise, take thy
bed and walk ?" Mk. ii. 9) ; and the challenge to him who
hesitated to enter with the disciples into the boat where Jesus
was : *Etha laḳh batheray, ushebok mitaya ḳaberin mitehon* (" Follow
thou me, and leave the dead to bury their own dead," Mt.
viii. 22). It is this Jesus whom we meet when we visit
Capernaum.

Already Eusebius and Jerome refer to a deserted place
near Capernaum as *Chorazin* (Christian Palestinian *Korazin*).
The latter states that it was two miles distant from Capernaum.
Indeed, 3 kilometres above *Tell Ḥum*, 270 metres above the
level of the lake, is a place *Kerazeh*, which the ruins of a
synagogue, richly ornamented with sculptures,[1] show to have
been a Jewish town.   In contrast to Capernaum where, notwithstanding the basalt hard by, the synagogue, as we have
seen, was built of limestone, here the building material was
the native black stone.   Also here we have three doors in
the gable-side, looking south, and in the interior is a double-
floored colonnade.   Among the sculptures we are surprised
to see, apart from animal *motifs* (among them a sucking ass,
of apotropaic significance), representations especially of grape-
gathering and grape-pressing, and of centaurs fighting with
lions.   A certain Judan bar Ishmael dedicated the colonnade
and the stairs, and he is mentioned on one of the seats.   The
pilgrims were told that the Jews could not finish building the
synagogue, because the workers, when asked by Jesus what
they were doing, replied : " Nothing," and our Lord then
said : " If what ye do is nothing, nothing will it remain for
ever."[2]   It would have been more appropriate to point to
our Lord's dirge in Mt. xi. 21, 23 ; Lk. x. 13, 15.   This
Kerazeh is doubtless the *Kerazaim* which, together with *Kephar
Aḥum*, is mentioned, as a place where fields, because of their
southward slope, might have supplied the Omer-sheaf to the
Temple if they had not been so far away.[3]   The volcanic
soil near *Kerazeh* is indeed excellent for wheat growing,
although an extensive agriculture was out of the question here.
A close relationship to Capernaum, which lies below on the
shore, and to Bethsaida, was natural.   The traveller is sur-

---

[1] See Kohl und Watzinger, *Antike Synagogen*, p. 41.
[2] Petrus Diaconus (Geyer, p. 113).   [3] Tos. Men. ix. 2.

prised to come across this not insignificant place in a desolate
basalt wilderness. It lies on the spur of a hill projection
which stretches from a wide depression into the *Wady et-
Webedani*. The advantage of this position—together with an
abundant spring on the east side and a cistern on the north—
explains how the town, built on the site of a much older
settlement, came into being just here. It must have had
fields to a somewhat larger extent chiefly in the east, where
a more level ground permits of them, and orchards, probably
on the slope between it and the spring. A road from Capernaum passed by it northwards—probably also towards the
Jordan ford on the *Via Maris*. Thus *Khirbet Keraẓeh* intensifies
the impression that, in contrast to the present desolation, in
the time of Jesus an active population endeavoured, in defiance
of all the obstacles of nature, to extract profit from that fertile
ground which basalt produces. The synagogue of Chorazin
would not have been so richly provided with figures and
symbols taken from the growing of the vine, if the inhabitants
had not prospered by it and enjoyed it. One can well conceive that they were less accessible to spiritual influence than
the fishermen of Capernaum who, in the struggle with storms
and waves, learned more than others that human endeavour
alone does not guarantee prosperity.

The environs of Capernaum cannot be conceived of apart
from the desolate land, covered with basalt-blocks, above it.
Chorazin must have had its cultivated fields east of the deep
Wady et-Webedani. To the west, between it and the *Wady
ed-Jamus*,[1] lay the mountainous region and the pasture-land of
Capernaum. It is peculiar to the northern shore of Ginnesar
that, though there is no proper shore-plain, a fairly regular,
gradual ascent leads up to a hilly tract of country about
250 metres above the sea-level. Then only do the highest
portions join it, including the *Jebel Kanʿan* which is 842
metres high. From there a glorious view is obtained of the
Lebanon and Hermon and the small Simchu lake in its green
depression to the north, as far as the plain of Golan in the
east, framed by a row of extinct volcanoes, and over the wide
level of the lake of Ginnesar in the south. A wearisome
climb of three hours' duration is necessary to reach the top,
which therefore cannot be considered as belonging to the

---

[1] As I showed in 1914, its upper course encompasses on the east side the
Khan Jubb Jusif. The English map erroneously gives to the *Wady et-Webedani*
a non-existent side-branch.

environs of Capernaum. It is different with the lower,
preliminary stage. Here, especially towards the east, is found
a wild tract covered with basalt blocks, attempts to cultivate
which were often made in old days, as the still existent stone
circles and rough walls testify, but which, in the main, can only
have been used as pasture-land, and must always have been
a lonely spot. Anyone in Capernaum wishing for privacy
would find it up here—and not on this particular spot
alone.

From this it follows that the " desert place " to which Jesus
withdrew from Capernaum (Mk. i. 35; Lk. iv. 42) cannot be
identified with any particular hill-top. The whole mountain
region north of the lake is the " mountain " (Christian Palestinian *ṭura*) where Jesus "continued all night in prayer" before
choosing His disciples (Lk. vi. 12; *cf.* Mt. v. 1; Mk. iii. 13);
below which, on a level spot (Lk. vi. 17), He gathered the
people about Him; and from which He came to Capernaum.
Also the " mountain " in Galilee on which the Risen One
showed Himself for the last time (Mt. xxviii. 16) is best envisaged here near the lake. The Greek ὄρος must (not only in
Mt. v. 1; Mk. iii. 13; Lk. vi. 12, but also in Mt. xiv. 23;
xv. 29; Mk. v. 11; vi. 46; Lk. viii. 32; Jn. vi. 3, 15) be
translated " Mountain *range* " (" highland "). For in all these
passages it is not a definite single mountain—in contrast to
other mountains—that is meant, but—in contrast to the
shore and its flat-land—the more lonely heights, which, by the
lake, are never a mountain, but everywhere a more or less
furrowed highland. In fact, the Greek ὄρος, as well as the
Hebrew *har*, can have the meaning of " mountainous country,"
and in the Aramaic of the Palestinian Talmud[1] and of the
Palestinian *Evangeliarium*[2] *ṭur* is used for " mountain " as well
as for " field." The " desert place " in Mk. i. 35 and
Lk. iv. 42, and the " mountain " in Mt. v. 1, are essentially
the same : the sheep remain, according to Mt. xviii. 12, on the
" mountain," but according to Lk. xv. 4 in the " wilderness " ;
the shepherds on the night of the Nativity kept watch,
according to the Greek text of Lk. ii. 8, in " the field," but
according to the Christian Palestinian, *beṭura*.

It is not a matter of surprise that tradition has indicated
for the Sermon on the Mount a definite spot in the mountains round about Capernaum. The earliest pilgrims do not

[1] Sab. 3b; *cf. Jesus-Jeshua*, p. 101.
[2] See Schultness, *Lexicon Syropalæstinum*, under *tur*.

mention it, but Petrus Diaconus[1] speaks of a cave in a mountain near the Seven Springs, where Jesus uttered the Beatitudes. This is probably the same mountain which, according to Burchard (1283)—two bow shots long and one stone's throw wide—rose up on the road to the east, and had a spring surrounded by a wall,[2] and must therefore have existed on the spur of the hill, directly east of the Seven Springs. Also Fretellus and John of Würzburg[3] in the twelfth century could not have meant any other place when, about two miles from Capernaum and one mile from the "Feeding" place, they indicated the mountain-slope as that of the Mount of the Sermon, since no other hill is here in question. The close proximity of the flat land (Lk. vi. 17) to the mountain of the choosing of the Apostles must have been of decisive influence. The only real plain in the neighbourhood of Capernaum must have been meant. Our Lord was supposed to have stood on its edge when delivering the Sermon. Thus the low hill above the Seven Springs—which now bears the name *Sellajet esh-Shech*, from the tomb of *Shech Ali*—is the traditional place of the Sermon on the Mount in the immediate neighbourhood of the traditional place of the feeding of the 5,000 (see p. 136). A small grotto on the brow of the hill, looking towards the lake, is supposed to show traces of a chapel built upon it,[4] which, however, I could not discern. But the cave mentioned by Petrus Diaconus may actually be here. The district round about the well, together with the hill with its palm-grove, was certainly an attraction for the inhabitants of the neighbouring places. When Jesus wished to gather round Him a considerable multitude, He could easily accomplish it here. Also the notion of multitudes streaming in from the whole of Palestine, which occasioned the Sermon (Mt. iv. 25 ; v. 1), is in keeping with a place which was near to the great highways. Jesus, accompanied by His disciples, ascended a mountain, and was apparently alone with them, and yet at the conclusion of the Sermon we find that the multitude had heard Him and followed Him when He came down (Mt. vii. 28 ; viii. 1). This points to a greater distance, as is presupposed in Lk. vi. 12, for the place of the appointment of the Twelve. The privacy desired by Jesus was not

---

[1] Geyer, p. 113.   [2] Laurent, *Peregrinatores*, p. 35.
[3] Tobler, *Descr. T. S.*, p. 187.
[4] Heidet, *Das Heilige Land* (1917), p. 98 ; Karge, *Rephaim*, p. 321 ; Meistermann, *Guide to the Holy Land*, p. 546.

to be had on the hill by the lake, where the road to Capernaum runs along only to the west, in order then to pass over the southern slope.

At a great distance from the lake, on a ridge of hills between the *Wady ed-Jamus* and the *Wady ed-Jihash,* an eastern lateral branch of it, the Bedouins called three trees—*es-sadsharat el-mebarakat,* "the blessed trees." All three have now vanished; two were terebinths and a third was a jujube. It has been suggested that an old tradition made this the site of the Sermon on the Mount. Karge,[1] who found, near the trees, cyclopean masonry, and the name *Der Makir* (*cf. μακαρισμός*), is inclined to connect it with the account of Fretellus (see above), although the slope of the mountain where these trees stood does not reach the road from Capernaum in the direction of the place of the miraculous feeding. Heidet[2] suggests that this was the place of the appointment of the Apostles which, according to him, was other than that of the Sermon on the hill above the Seven Springs. Meistermann again is certain that the traditional place of the Beatitudes was here, but would rather look for the historic spot nearer to the lake.[3] Our view is that the Gospels do not give an exact spot at all, but only a general indication that the mountainous region above Capernaum was of importance in the life and activity of Jesus. The place where He habitually prayed and taught was really not the synagogue, although He visited it, but the "wilderness." The whole "wilderness" on the heights must be conceived as the region where He was wont to pray, and the whole slope as His habitual seat for instruction, in contrast to the custom of the scribes.

The fresher air on the heights above the lake would have reminded Him of His native mountains. Besides the basalt which crops up continually, limestone is found. There are whole fields of daffodils (*Asphodelus microcarpus*), reminding one of the daffodil-meadows of the Odyssey, which Lundgreen suggests are identical with the "lilies of the field."[4] Between them the yellow umbrellas of the ferulas wave on their high stalks: in these Prometheus brought fire to the earth! Crimson anemones (*Anemone coronaria*) gleam from among the green of the grass—out of which, in summer, thistles

---

[1] *Rephaim,* p. 321 f.   [2] *Das Heilige Land,* p. 105.
[3] *Capharnaüm et Bethsaïde,* p. 86 f., illust. 4 ; *Guide,* p. 546.
[4] *Neue kirchl. Zeit.* (1917), p. 829 f.   Cf. Dalman, *Arbeit und Sitte in Palastina,* i., p. 361 f.

shoot up a yard high and remind one of the "lilies of the
field" of Mt. vi. 28 ; Lk. xii. 27. There, κρίνον—which goes
back to the Hebrew and Aramaic *shoshana*[1]—although correctly
translated "lily" or "iris," has, like the "grass of the field"
in verse 30, a more general meaning, referring, as does the
Arabic *ḥannun*, to all the blossoms, distinguished by size and
colour, of the wild flora of the country. If by "field" is meant
the cornfields, then neither the cornflowers—the nearest of kin
to which, the *Centaurea cyanoides*, is, in Palestine, not a usual
field-weed—are possible, nor the corncockle (*Agrostemma
Githago*)—the red petals of which are quite stunted in Palestine
—but rather the glorious gladioli (*Gladiolus segetum* and *atro-
violaceus*) which, with their bright-red and dark-violet blooms,
might well suggest the purple of a king, and they are frequently found in the fields near the lake of Tiberias.[2] But it is
more probable that by "field" Jesus meant "desert place,"
in which these flowers are not so characteristic as the thickly
spread and beautiful anemones,[3] which at the end of the spring-
time are succeeded by their next of kin, the red ranunculus
(*Ranunculus asiaticus*).[4] The iris species which are found only
here and there are not probable, in spite of the beautiful
Iris Nazarena ; and the Palestinian lilies—a species to which
the daffodil belongs (see above), with its not very striking
colour—need not be seriously considered. The white lily
(*Lilium candidum*), foreign to Palestine as a wild flower, is
naturally quite out of the question.[5]

The chief feature, of the otherwise rather monotonous height,
is the view. Below, stretched out between green mountains,
is the wide surface of the blue lake, behind which the distance
dissolves in the mists of the Jordan lowland. On the right,
on the shore, below its citadel, gleams the Tiberias of the
Jewish tetrarch Antipas ; on the left, on a steep height, the
Hellenistic free city Hippos, as a "city on the hill which
cannot be hidden" (Mt. v. 14). All the strivings of the
Jewish adherents of Rome, the hellenizers, the political and
religious zealots, lay below the solitary worshipper. His soul
was lifted to His Father above. He came here not to luxuriate

---

[1] In Christian Palestinian it is translated with *shoshanne deṭura*.
[2] Seen by me between *es-Samra* and *Samakh*.   [3] *Arb. u. Sitte*, p. 351 *f*.
[4] That in Hebrew the word *shoshanna* can be applied to several flowers can
be seen from Lev. R. xxiii. (61a), where the rose is so designated.
[5] Also J. Löw, *Die Flora der Juden*, ii. (1924), p. 70, who otherwise considers
the white lily as the *shoshana*, finds that it does not suit Mt. vi. 28, but does
not suggest any flower instead.

idly on the beauty of the flowers and the landscape, but that He might bring the Father down to the people below.   They, in their struggle for existence, needed Him so much and understood Him so little—Him who clothes the flowers, feeds the sparrows, and commands the storm.   Above the semi-Jewish tetrarchies of Antipas and Philip, and the heathen Decapolis— the domains of which surround the lake—and above the Rome that ensnares them all, stands the Kingship of the Father above. He who introduces it into this torn world becomes the Redeemer of all.   But the Kingdom would not be what it is to be without a will which determines the action of the man made in God's image and supersedes all earthly legislation—even that given by God Himself through Moses—by a more excellent way.   Therefore, Jesus had to put His sixfold *we-ana amar lekhon* (" But I myself say unto you ") in opposition to the *shemʿatun de-itamar le-ḳadmaye,* " ye have heard what was said to the ancients."[1]   He was convinced that this was in accordance with the real purpose of the God who spoke from Sinai. It is clear, however, that in this mountainous region Israel's Mount Sinai was superseded by a Sinai for humanity.   The Jews once believed that the concealed vessels of the Tabernacle were hidden in a cave of the neighbouring *Wady el-Amud* by *ʿAkbara,*[2] and that some day they would once again be restored: Even to-day they point, high above the lake near Merom, to a peculiar rock as the " Seat of the Messiah " who is to come.   The Christians at one time considered Chorazin the home of the Antichrist.[3]   But the " Seat of the Messiah " who came to destroy the old Temple and to build a new one was the highland above Capernaum.

[1] Mt. v. 21 *f.   Cf. Jesus-Jeshua,* p. 67 *f.*
[2] *Chibbath Jerushalayim* (Wilna, 1875), p. 29a, 85a ; *Shaare Jerushalayim* (Lemberg, 1879), ch. v.   Cf. *PJB,* 1915, p. 54.
[3] Theoderich (Tobler, p. 101).

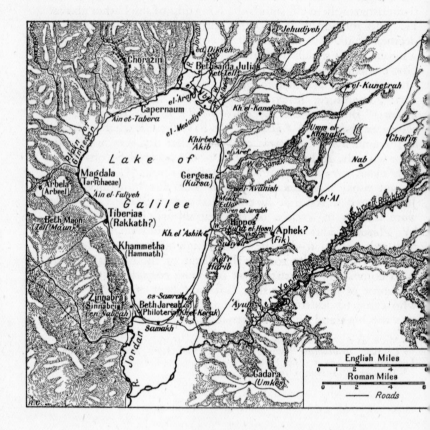

IX

BETHSAIDA AND THE EASTERN SHORE OF THE GALILEAN LAKE

WHERE the Jordan enters into the lake of Tiberias, probably along the line of a fissure, there was originally a great bay. It cut north-eastwards into the coast, which was gradually filled up by the alluvial deposits of five streams which flow in from the north and north-east, and was transformed into the marshy plain which is now called *el-Ibteḥa*. It is marshy chiefly because a shore-barrier, formed by the counter-current of the lake-water, hinders the regular outlet of the moisture. There are lagoons, remnants of the original bay, which give to the north-eastern shore of the lake its peculiar character. The conditions of the currents in the lake cause bars to form before the river-mouth.[1] On October 10, 1921, I saw that it was almost possible to cross over the Jordan dry-shod, just where it enters into the lake. An absolutely dry bar lay before the mouth. From the shore there was but a short space to wade through the water to reach the bar, at the centre of which there was a similar little opening through which the river ran out. Although these bars are mostly covered by shallow water, they can be used as fords for shore-traffic where it is interrupted by the mouths of the streams. The lagoons, on the other hand, could be used as natural harbours for sailing boats. The vegetable and animal matter deposited in the lake by the streams must have been an attraction to the fish; consequently, at all periods, an important fishing place must have existed at this north-eastern corner of the lake, where it is only natural to find a place with the name *Beth Tzaida*, " Fishery-home."[2]

This place one expects to find, particularly on the spot where the bar joins the mouth of the Jordan on the eastern side and reaches as far as a small lagoon which opens into the lake.

---

[1] Blankenhorn, *Naturwissenschaftliche Studien*, p. 342.
[2] See concerning this Bethsaida, Stave, *Sjön Gennesaret* (1892), p. 59 *f.*; Spitta, *Streitfragen der Geschichte Jesu* (1907), p. 101 *f.*

This gives us a strip about 850 metres long and 140 metres wide, the most easterly portion of which, somewhat higher than the rest, about 200 metres long, can indeed be recognised, from the stones and potsherds in its soil, as the site of an ancient settlement going back to the Roman period.   At present it is named, after a sacred zizyphus-tree, *Khirbet el-'Areje*, or *el-'Araj*.

The two-storied house and the workman's cottage of the present Damascene owner point to the fact that this neighbourhood might still be usefully cultivated.   And the remains of a modest conduit shows how the water of a spring on the landward side could be made available.   So the present *Khirbet el-'Areje* must be connected with ancient Bethsaida.   When Herod Philip, soon after his accession to power in 3 B.C., " raised the village Bethsaida on the lake of Ginnesar to a city, provided it with a multitude of inhabitants and other power, and named it Julias after the daughter of the emperor,"[1] the new city doubtless had an important military station on the shore of the lake.   But it is very probable that a rocky hill now nameless and known only as *et-Tell*, which rises to the east about 3 kilometres away and has a well at its foot, was the site of the citadel which also contained the palace of the tetrarch, and must have been reckoned the acropolis of Julias.   In that case it was here that Herod Philip died in A.D. 34.   The tomb he built for himself,[2] it may be assumed, was in the neighbourhood of this hill.   But this also must have been the site of the *original* Bethsaida, because the hill with its flat top, of considerable size, was exceptionally suitable for a stronghold, and the lake, or its lagoons, into which the *Wady es-Safa* issues, must in ancient times have reached here.   The spot attracted settlers also because the road, which comes from the north and is connected with the west by a ford over the Jordan, took the main traffic of the district, passing south of the hill. When Josephus erected an entrenchment on the Jordan, a stadium distance from Julias, in order to threaten from here the enemy which were encamped five stad. distance beyond Julias,[3] the road running southward from the ford is presupposed, and so, almost certainly, this hill was the site of Julias.   Near it, at that time, important roads descended to the lake from Seleucia in the north-east, and from Gamala in the south-east (the latter

---

[1] *Ant.* xvii. 2, 1 ; *cf. Bell. Jud.* ii. 9, 1.   On the other hand, the Julias mentioned in *Ant.* xx. 8, 4 ; *Bell. Jud.* ii. 13, 2, belongs to the southern Jordan valley.
[2] *Ant.* xviii. 4, 6.   [3] *Vita* 71.

certainly passed over *el-ʿAl*, and through the *Wady es-Samak*).
When Philip chose a place at the southern end of his domain
for his capital, he certainly was not merely thinking of the harbour on the lake which abounded with fish. He thought of the
fact that here was the natural place for the traffic with Palestine
and the coast to pass, so that the commerce of a town founded
here, and the tolls, promised him good revenue. In order to
avoid the swamp mentioned by Josephus, the town had to be
connected with the lake by means of an artificially made road,
running near the Jordan towards the bar. But a direct connection with the lake must have also been facilitated by the
fact that, at that time, the lagoons extended further inland than
they do now. There must have been a lively traffic, in spite
of the toll-frontier, between this place and the neighbouring
town of Capernaum, which was only 4 kilometres distant over
the lake. The fishermen from the two places met in connection with their trade. A ferry at the mouth of the Jordan
must have connected the districts on the two sides of the lake.
To-day the tents of the *Tellawiyeh* Bedouins in the marsh-land,
and their provision huts, together with two tombs of saints on
the hill, and the lonely house of the Damascene on the shore,
are the only evidence of human life in the whole district. By
the shore the buffaloes, standing in the water up to their necks,
lift up their heads to greet anyone who lands by boat. Their
quaint habits already astonished the pilgrim Willibald.[1]
Ancient Bethsaida together with its whole hinterland had
probably sunk back, as long ago as the Arab period, into a low
state of nomadic culture. But perhaps it no longer belonged
even to that culture, since the population now here disposed of
its dead, on the heights, on both sides of the Jordan, in strong
stone boxes above the earth.[2] The plain by the lake had an
importance of its own to the town built here by Philip, since,
like the Ginnesar plain in the west, it attracted an intensive
fruit cultivation, because of the abundance of its water-supply
and the warm climate. Nowadays, its marshy character is the
chief hindrance to the winter sowing of grain. Only for the
summer grain—*e.g.* millet or maize—does the soil become dry
enough. Wild figs near the wells, zizyphus-trees and shrubs
in the marsh-land, occasional terebinths and sycamores on the
edge of the hills, represent the world of trees. An isolated
citron-garden by the Jordan-mouth shows what could be

[1] Tobler, *Descr. T. S.*, p. 27.
[2] See Karge, *Das Heilige Land*, 1915, p. 125 *f.* ; *Rephaim*, p. 419.

grown here. When the marsh-land was drained by canals and by keeping open the mouths of the streams, all kinds of vegetables, rice, sugar-cane, cotton, together with dates, citrons, figs, and pomegranates must have flourished here, providing not only a means of maintenance but even *prosperity* for a town. Julias in this was similar to Magdala, while Tiberias, with her narrow shore, could in no way compare with it.

The old name of the place, *Bethsaida* (Christian Palestinian *Bet Sayda*, Mk. vi. 45 also *Bethsaidan*), had probably never become extinct among the native population by the lake, and is therefore exclusively used in the Gospels. In rabbinic literature it occurs in the form *Saydan* (with the *nunation*, popular in Galilee) as a town where there are wild fowls ;[1] as a place where three hundred different kinds of fish can be placed on one dish ;[2] and as the home of a number of scribes.[3] Christian tradition drew attention to it as the native place of three of the Apostles.[4] About 725 Willibald saw a church there, on the site of the house of Zebedee.[5] However, pilgrims, for the most part, gave up visiting it, though Theoderich (1172) knew[6] that the Jordan flows between Bethsaida and Capernaum. And a twelfth-century map has it correctly placed on the east of the lake.[7]

Lk. (ix. 10) and Jn. (i. 44) call the fishing place, which had become a capital and a residential district, a *city* ; Mk. calls it a village (Mk. viii. 23, 26). The latter term could be justified on the assumption that the old Bethsaida by the shore had always remained what it was. But the Evangelist might also have used the word because he was not aware of the different designations in use. In Aramaic *medina* and *karya* are differentiated as " city " and " village " (see Pal. Evang. Lk. viii. 1) ; the first denotes the centre of a judicial district, while the second is in itself quite indefinite. Rabbis were sent out to put in order (*i.e.* to appoint the necessary Bible and Mishna—teachers) " the places of the land of Israel." The words used are *karyata de-ar'a deyisrael*.[8] From place to place (*'alel karta wenaphek karta*) the trader goes who seeks the new-born Messiah, and finds him in Bethlehem, which is itself

---

[1] Eccl. R. ii. 8 (77a). By pheasants here mentioned, red partridges are probably meant.

[2] p. Shek. 50a. The *Editio princeps* and a Geniza MS. (according to Ginzberg, *Jerushalmi Fragments*, p. 135) read *Zaydan*.

[3] *Cf.* Klein, *MGWJ*, lix., p. 169 f.

[4] Theodosius (Geyer, *Itinera*, p. 138).

[5] Tobler, *Descr. T. S.*, p. 26.

[6] *Ibid.*, p. 101.

[7] *ZDPV*, 1895, illust. v.

[8] Lam. R. Intr. (1a) ; p. Chag. 76e.

called *ḳarta*, although in the narrative it is described as having a citadel (see above, p. 25). *Ḳarya* (determinative *ḳaryeta*, *ḳarta*) is the general designation ; *naṭore ḳarta* in p. Chag. 76c cannot be translated otherwise than " guardians of the city." But Mk. would certainly not have used the word κώμη if he had intended the capital city of Philip.

According to Jn. i. 44, three of our Lord's disciples, Philip, Andrew, and Peter, came from Bethsaida. Being Jews, they naturally were closely connected with the Jewish Capernaum. St. John (xii. 21) takes it for granted that Philip, being a native of the " Galilean Bethsaida," understood Greek, since Galilee had a mixed population and was therefore bilingual.[1] At the same time, he reckoned, if indeed the exact position of Bethsaida was known to him, the trans-Jordan Jewish land as a part of Galilee, as Ptolemy also reckons that Julias belonged to Galilee ;[2] as also " Judæa beyond Jordan " was a common phrase ;[3] and as even to-day the seashore of the *Ibteḥa*-plain with the site of Bethsaida is attached to western Palestine. Klausner,[4] in his *Jesus of Nazareth*, considers it simply as a careless error on the part of the Evangelist. He might, however, have mentioned that, according to Sukka 27b, Cæsarea Philippi was in Upper Galilee, unless, in accordance with manuscripts and the Tosephta parallel,[5] Galilee is to be omitted. Still, it was possible to think of this town as belonging to Galilee. Which is not surprising, since the plain lying below it was apportioned to Galilee at the division of the land into principalities.[6] That Josephus on one occasion calls Judas of Gamala a Gaulanite and at other times a Galilæan was probably because eastern Gamala was familiar to him (*cf.* above, p. 9). Anyone brought up in Bethsaida would not only have understood Greek, but would have been polished by intercourse with foreigners and have had some Greek culture. But wherever there were Jews there must also have been some place for the public reading of the Law and for prayer. Thus Bethsaida must have had a synagogue, although we find no traces of one. In *ed-Dikkeh*, however—only 1½ kilometres north-west of the citadel in the Jordan valley—were found the remains of a synagogue built in the simplest form, with an entrance from the west and six columns as ceiling-props.[7]

[1] *Cf. Jesus-Jeshua*, pp. 1-7.
[2] *Geogr.* v. 16, 4.
[3] Mt. xix. 1 ; Jos., *Ant.* xii. 4, 11.
[4] *Jesus of Nazareth*, p. 288.
[5] Tos. Sukk. i. 9.
[6] Georgius Cedrenus, *Hist. Comp.* i. 133 ; Migne, *P.G.* cxxi., col. 369.
[7] Kohl and Watzinger, *Antike Synagogen in Galiläa*, p. 112 *f.*

A considerably larger building was the synagogue of *Umm el-Ḳannaṭir*, with a double-storied colonnade and an entrance from the east. It stood on rising ground, 12 kilometres from Bethsaida, in the south-east, on a branch of the *Wady es-Samak*, with a distant view towards the lake.[1] West of it, on the other side of the valley, by *Khirbet el-Kanef*, and only 7 kilometres from Bethsaida, the lintel of a door with an Aramaic inscription[2] shows there must have been a third synagogue in the neighbourhood. The name *el-Jehudiyeh* for a high-lying, citadel-like site in the north-east speaks of a Jewish settlement in the district going back to the Arab period. These synagogue ruins may not go back beyond the third century A.D., but the Jews who prayed there were, after all, the descendants of Jews who had long been settled there. The Jews of Bethsaida were not shut off in isolation here in the east, but had fellow-countrymen in the neighbouring villages with whom they could foregather for religious practices and prayer.

That Jesus visited Bethsaida can be assumed from his woe over the town (Mt. xi. 21 ; Lk. x. 13). And it is expressly stated in Mk. viii. 22 that He healed a blind man who was brought to Him before the town. Because Codex D has, instead of Βηθσαιδαν, Βηθανιαν, Schmidt[3] thinks of the Bethany of the Baptist, which he wishes to place near Scythopolis ; but a place so far south does not fit the context. Perhaps Bethsaida was purposely omitted by someone from the text. The pericope is absent from the Christian-Palestinian Lectionary, where one also looks in vain for the woes over Capernaum, Chorazin, and Bethsaida.[4] The healing account in Mark makes it probable that Chorazin also had a healing narrative attached to it, which, perhaps, now appears in connection with another locality.

According to Luke (ix. 19), Jesus withdrew with the disciples, after their return, to Bethsaida, κατ᾽ ἰδίαν, *i.e.* apart, in seclusion, but the multitude followed Him. Accordingly, He was in a " desert place " (verse 12), even though there were villages round about, and so had to supply the crowd miraculously with

---

[1] *Ibid.*, p. 125.

[2] ZDPV, 1914, p. 135 *f.* ; Klein, *Jüd.-pal. Corp. inscr.* ii. 12. The inscription runs: " May Josa, the son of Chelbu, the son of Chanan, be remembered for good."

[3] Especially remarkable is the missing of Lk. x. 13-15, as x. 1-12 and x. 16-18 are given. But also Mk. vi. 45, with the mention of Bethsaida, is missing. For Lk. ix. 10, see Dunsing, *Texte und Fragmente*, p. 147.

[4] *Der Rahmen der Geschichte Jesu.*

food. One wonders why Luke in this connection could have mentioned the town of Bethsaida, in the immediate neighbourhood of which one could hardly expect a " desert " place to which anyone would go from Capernaum in order to find privacy. The insertion of εἰς τόπον ἐρημόν does not improve the matter, but rather makes it worse, for no one could thus confound town and " desert place "; although round about the plain of Bethsaida there was no lack of desert places on the heights. When one compares the Lukan account with the proximity of desert and mountainous places by the lake in the accounts of the other Evangelists, concerning the same miraculous feeding, one is inclined to think primarily of the district with which the plain of Bethsaida ends in the south. And thus one comes near *Khirbet ʿAḳib*, which lies on a projection of the eastern shore, where a bay of the lake would be suitable as a landing-place. But no one with a knowledge of the place would call the arrival there a " setting out " towards the town of Bethsaida. The rendering of the Syrus Sinaiticus, "towards a desert place of the city of Bethsaida," or, still better, an Aramaic *madbera debet ṣayda*, "the desert of Bethsaida," would be what should have been said. Merx[1] suggests that Mk. vi. 45, where a journey in the direction of Bethsaida leads away from the place of the miraculous feeding, has influenced the Lukan text; whilst Spitta,[2] on the contrary, explains the rather surprising mention of Bethsaida in Mk. by the influence of the Lukan text. As to the Lukan source, he says the journey to Bethsaida was to introduce not the miracle of the feeding, but the prediction of the Passion (ix. 18 *f.*). According to him, the Lukan account of the miraculous feeding has been inserted in an awkward place. The latter is probable. But it is hardly accidental that also according to Mk. viii. 22 Jesus was in Bethsaida before His prediction of the Passion, and that He arrived there after a journey in which the forgotten bread became the occasion of a reference to the miraculous feedings. This may have been taken as an allusion to the place of these feedings and have induced St. Luke to insert the account of the feeding here. He may have thought of the neighbourhood of Bethsaida as desolate, at the same time assuming that the Jews would find themselves in a foreign environment, so that

---

[1] *Die vier kanonischen Evangelien nach ihrem ältesten bekannten Texte*, on Lk. ix. 10.

[2] *Streitfragen der Geschichte Jesu*, p. 101 *f.*; *Die synoptische Grundschrift in ihrer Überlieferung durch das Lukasevangelium*, p. 219 *f.*

Jesus could be alone there with His disciples, but also where the lack of bread would present a difficulty. In this way the incomplete phrasing in Lk. could be explained, but the place of the feeding still remains to be fixed. This requires a survey of the whole district.

Apart from the *Ibṭeḥa* valley—which belongs partly to the eastern edge of the lake—this coast has all along it a narrow strip of shore, spreading out to a breadth of 1 kilometre in those places where the soft alluvial soil is washed out of the valleys into the lake. And from this there is a steep rise up to the high plain which lies at the edge of the plateau 525 metres above. The upward slope is divided into three parts by two important valleys, the brooks of which, however, do not even in the spring reach the lake. The more northerly one is the distant *Wady es-Samak*, which affords a convenient ascent to the plateau (*cf.* p. 163); the more southerly is the narrow and steep-sided *Wady en-Nḳeb*,[1] which can have no importance for traffic. Yet, on its south side, by a parallel-running gorge, the possibility of a steep ascent is afforded, which is of advantage to the town of Hippos enthroned above. Farther south, the lake, the shore of which takes on a south-westerly direction, recedes from the ascent to the plateau, and at this point there is, between it and the shore, a ridge of hills rising only 100 metres above the lake which includes the *Tulul eṭ-Ṭa-ʿalib*. The shore way, which runs generally without any hindrance along the coast, divides here. The one line curves round the southern end of the lake; the other runs directly south towards the valley of Yarmuk (which here enters the Jordan valley, which it crosses by a ford) in order to rise on the opposite side to *Umkes*, once the town *Gadara*, on the summit of a narrow spur of the highland. Before reaching the Yarmuk, however, the same road also crosses another important road here which starts from the southern shore of the lake to reach the plateau, but which really belongs to the road between Damascus and Palestine and, farther on, Egypt—connections of great importance in ancient times, and even in the Middle Ages. This is the only important traffic route with which the eastern shore of the lake had any frequent connection. The road on the eastern shore itself served the local traffic only, which, however, must have been brisker when the city, Julias, was here to keep up its connection with the south. The warm spring of *Ḥammet el-Meze-freh* wells up at *Moḳaʿ ʿEdlo*, where the heights approach the

---

[1] Concerning its name, see *PJB*, 1912, p. 50.

shore very closely, but it is so small that it could never have had any importance. The narrowness of the coastal land is reason enough why no important settlement ever developed here. Only very small older sites are recognisable on the alluvial land of the two valleys that open into the lake : *Kursa* at the mouth of *Wady es-Samak*, and *Khirbet el-'Ashik*, south of *Wady en-Nkeb*. The wider shore-land in the south is occupied by the little coastal village of *es-Samrah*, whose predecessor was perhaps a place on the hills of the *Tulul et-Ta'alib*.

Quite otherwise were, and are, the conditions on the high lands. Here, first of all, was the spot at which the afore-mentioned road to Damascus touched the head of the *Wady en-Nkeb*, the reason for an old settlement now called *Fik*, once perhaps, the *Aphek* mentioned in 1 Kings xx. 26 ; 2 Kings xiii. 17, as the scene of battles between the Syrians and the Israelites.[1] An Aramaic inscription[2] and pictures of the seven-branched candlestick show that the locality, which was known to Eusebius as a large village, was inhabited by Jews. Near it in the tenth century was shown the monastery *Der Fik*, hewn out of the rock, and possessing a stone upon which Christ was supposed to have sat. It was taken to be the place of the call of the Apostles,[3] but probably was originally meant to have been taken as the " mountain " on which Jesus sat with His disciples before the miraculous feeding (Jn. vi. 3). It was located at " a mountain which is connected with a steep path to Fik," *i.e.*, evidently, west of the rise of the road coming from Yarmuk, between *Kefr Harib* and *Fik*, at the edge of the valley.

Below *Fik*, in the valley—which later widens into a deep basin—erosion has created a long horseback-like ridge, on which a very small hamlet can be discerned. The name *Susiyeh* (which must go back to the ancient *Susitha*, " the Mare," the Aramaic name for Hippos) still clings to it and its neighbourhood. Perhaps the more ancient Susitha[4] was situated here. But the Hellenistic autonomous Hippos was certainly not here, but occupied the narrow, table-like summit which rises up arrogantly, south of *Wady en-Nkeb* towards the lake. Steep slopes encompass it there on three sides, and a narrow lower ridge only makes it possible to block easily the

---

[1] One usually thinks here of the Aphek by Endor, but which Eusebius mentions only in connection with 1 Sam. xxix. 1.

[2] Klein, *Jüd.-Pal. Corp. Inscr.* ii. 13.

[3] Sachau, *Vom Klosterbuch des Sabusti*, p. 14.

[4] The inhabitants of Hippos call themselves on coins " Antiochians by Hippos " ($\pi\rho\dot{o}\varsigma\,{}^{\prime\prime}I\pi\pi\omega$).

connection with the road leading up this way from the shore
to Aphek. A conduit, about 25 kilometres long, brought
down the spring-water from the upper course of the *Wady
es-Samak*. Extensive ruins, which are now called *Ḳul'at el-
Ḥosn*, show that a Hellenistic town of importance was once
situated here, which, according to all ancient records, could
only have been Hippos (and not Gamala for instance), which,
with its environs, abutted on the lake and lay opposite Tiberias.[1]
The Gospels never mention Hippos, although it also had a
Jewish population,[2] yet everywhere round about the lake, the
town, enthroned 370 metres above its level, must have seemed
its mistress. Along the lake its territory must have comprised
the stretch from *Wady es-Samak*—which forms a natural
frontier—to the valley of Yarmuk.[3] In the east the *Raḳḳad*
is a natural frontier. Gamala, on the other side of the river,
belonged to the domain of Philip, and was considered as a part
of Gilead.[4] It corresponded to the land of Tob, where
Jephthah once sought safety (Judg. xi. 3, 5)[5] and where, in the
time of the Maccabees, many Jews were killed.[6] It was considered by the rabbinic authorities to have been a "pure"
district, because it lay in the domain of the land of Israel. But
it was exempt from the duty of tithes and the observance of the
Sabbatic year; against which, however, it was argued that since
the region had been acquired by conquest it should have been
subjected to these duties.[7] Hippos itself was predominantly
a Gentile town,[8] but a number of districts belonging to it
were liable to pay tithes. Together with some places which
cannot now be identified, the following are mentioned:
Ayanish (now '*Avanish*), *Kephar Charib* (*Kefr Ḥarib*), *Iyon* ('*Ayun*),
Nob (*Nab*), *Chispiya* (*Chisfin*), *Kephar Zemach* (*Samach?*).[9] In
regard to the last-named, R. Jehuda ha-Nasi was of the opinion
that it was not liable, evidently considering that it had never
belonged to the land of Israel through conquest.

As the district of Hippos near by Yarmuk bordered upon
that of Gadara, and the latter, even north of this stream,

[1] *Bell. Jud.* iii. 3, 1 ; Pliny v. 71 ; Gen. R. 31 (62a).   [2] *Bell. Jud.* ii. 18, 5.

[3] See Th. Schlatter, *PJB*, 1918, p. 107.

[4] Thus according to the source of Georgius Tedrenus, *Hist. Comp.* i. 133 ;
Migne, *P.G.* cxxi., col. 369, where Γαλάθα can mean only Γαλαδα.

[5] p. Sheb. 36c.   [6] 1 Macc. v. 13.

[7] p. Shebi. 36c ; Tos. Ahil. xviii. 4.

[8] p. R. S. 57d.   The natives of Hippos killed many Jews in A.D. 66, *Bell. Jud.*
ii. 18, 5.

[9] Tos. Shebi. iv. 10 ; p. Dem. 22d, to be corrected after the Roman MS.,
see Ginzberg, *Jerushalmi Fragments*, p. 357 ; Lunz ed. (Jerusalem, 1914, *ad loc.*).

possessed hot springs, quarrels were natural. In fact, the
carrying off of women is said to have been frequent on both
sides, so that it once happened that a certain Bar Gaius of
Gadara killed Lukas of Susitha in combat, not being aware
that he was his own father.[1] Hippos must have attracted to
itself as much as it could of the traffic to Damascus, as is shown
by the four Roman milestones on the upper road near it. In
addition, there was a brisk cross-traffic over the lake with
Tiberias, on the other side,[2] whose market it supplied with
leather shoes,[3] but with which, however, it was in jealous feud,[4]
probably expressed especially in connection with the fishing
in the lake and with extortionate tariffs. So *Khirbet el-'Ashek*
(see above, p. 169) on the lake must have been the harbour of
Hippos.

Even now the eastern shore of the lake is far from being a
desert. It is cultivated land, worked by Bedouins and peasants ;
less fertile where marly soil is brought down by floods, but
with luxurious vegetation at the outlets of the valleys, the
brooks of which provide a certain amount of water. Wild
plants and cereals ripen here to such a height that the pedestrian
loses all sight of the surrounding country. Yet the strand is a
lonely district, where one rarely meets a soul, except when field-
work is going on. In the time of Christ the cultivation was
no doubt the same but the loneliness was not so great, because
the settled population was more numerous and the civilisation
of the three nearest towns, Julias, Hippos, and Gadara, much
greater, in comparison with that of the present villages on
the table-land. However, even then the large towns lay on the
top. How little the connection between the table-land and
the strand need be can be seen from the fact that the Turkish
judicial administration apportioned the strand, south of *Moka'
'Edlo*, to Tiberias, and the highland only to the Gaulanite
Kunetrah. The steep slopes and spurs of the table-land were
at all times lonely, and were only of importance as pasture-land
in winter and early spring for shepherds and their flocks. The
political division of the strand into districts under Jewish and
Gentile rule meant, to the northern third part of the territory,
the predominance of the Jewish element. In the south the
Jew felt himself a stranger and, as we have seen (p. 170), it was
questionable whether the land there was liable to tithes.

---

[1] Pes. Rabbati xxi. (107a), ed. princeps, must thus be understood.
[2] *Cf*. Gen. R. xxxii. (64a). [3] p. Sheb. 38a (? L.).
[4] Lev. R. xxiii. (61b).

The feeding miracle must have taken place on this strand, according to Jn. vi. 1 ; for the far side of the lake can, in this Gospel, refer only to the eastern shore.   What is said in *v.* 23 concerning the coming of the boats from Tiberias to the place of the feeding makes it evident that it is thought of as being opposite Tiberias (*cf.* p. 176).   According to *vv.* 3 and 15 Jesus was on a " mountain " both before and after the feeding ; and the miracle took place, according to v. 10, in a locality where, in the Passover season, there was " much grass."   In Matthew and Mark (Mt. xiv. 13 ; Mk. vi. 31) the place of feeding, reached by boat, is not expressly designated as being on the other side of the lake.   Yet the crossing of the lake leads from there to Ginnesar (Mt. xiv. 34 ; Mk. vi. 53), while in the Fourth Gospel the destination is Capernaum (Jn. vi. 17, 24). Also, in other respects, the situation is the same : there is a " mountain " near by (Mt. xiv. 23 ; Mk. vi. 46), and there was grass (Mt. xiv. 19 ; Mk. vi. 39).   Further, the fact that, according to Mt. xvi. 5 ; Mk. viii. 16, a journey to the further shore was again the cause of want of bread, is another argument in favour of the eastern shore.   Luke evidently set the narrative in a different connection, which excludes a journey across the lake towards the feeding-place.   His indications may therefore be disregarded.   The narrative of the feeding of the 4,000 also indicates the eastern shore, by its account of the return journey by boat towards the district of Magdala (Mt. xv. 39 ; Mk. viii. 10 ; *cf.* above, p. 177).   On the western shore, only the neighbourhood between Magdala and Tiberias could be taken into consideration, as the neighbouring " mountain " excludes the Ginnesar plain.   But in the middle of the 5 kilometres distance between the two towns, at the spring *'Ain el-Fuliyeh*, there is the old site which Albright suggested was one of the Magdalas,[1] and, only 4 kilometres above it, one reaches Arbela.   It is unthinkable that the feeding should have taken place on this cultivated spot.   And when one climbs up to the " Christ stones " (see above, p. 115), along the edge of the elevated plain, one finds oneself in close proximity to the only 2 kilometres distant Beth Maon (=*Tell Ma'un*).   There is, however, no justification for placing it farther south, past Tiberias and Khammetha, as there is no indication whatever of Jesus having any connection with that neighbourhood.

Coming back thus to the eastern shore, the " mountain " in the locality near where the feeding of the 5,000 took place

[1] *Annual,* ii.-iii., p. 43.

excludes from consideration the plain of Bethsaida. On the other hand, the mention in Mk. vii. 31 of the district of Decapolis before the feeding, speaks decidedly in favour of that part of the eastern shore which belonged to Hippos. One can well understand that Jesus and the disciples should have sought privacy in the heathen district; there also the embarrassment caused by the lack of bread was particularly great. The crowding of the Jews (Mt. xiv. 13; Mk. vi. 33), however, does not permit one to place it too far south. Hence the lonely neighbourhood between *Wady es-Samak* and *Wady-en-Nkeb*, where the table-land with its fore-heights approaches the lake very closely, may be taken with the greatest amount of certainty to have been the scene of the event. The miraculous feeding would then have taken place on the narrow strand, and above, at *Moka' 'Edlo*, would have been the "mountain" where Jesus sought privacy.

The Markan additional clause, " the people seeing the departure of Jesus, ran afoot thither . . . and outwent them, and came together unto Him," seemed even to early readers difficult to visualise. According to Syrus Sinaiticus, the crowd just followed for a while and saw the landing-place from a distance, so that they could later visit Jesus there.[1] Merx thinks that this could only be possible at the western shore of the lake, north and south of Tiberias—as, in the east, the Jordan would have prevented the crowd from following in the direction of the boat; but Mark's presentation would have, at any rate, been intelligible even there, if he thought of the boat as sailing. Then only the accident of a favourable wind would have made a direct journey possible. Otherwise, the aim would have to be reached by crossing, and with the assistance of rowing. The difficulty that the crowd had in crossing the Jordan, the mouth of the lagoon of Bethsaida, and the wide projection of the *Wady el-Dalieh* by *el-Mes'adiyeh*, was, even apart from the bars (see p. 162), not so great in the time of the old Julias as it is now, because special provision must have been made for the crossing. Be that as it may, the author, whose chief purpose was to describe the zeal of the crowd, was scarcely aware of the difficulty, and thus it is unnecessary to take his remark about their going on in front into consideration. One can, however, unhesitatingly agree

---

[1] See Merx on Mk. vi. 33, 45. Also K. L. Schmidt, *Der Rahmen der Geschichte Jesu*, thinks of the western shore, without considering the above-mentioned difficulties.

that the aim of Jesus' journey was soon observed, and that anyone wanting to meet Him on land could, by following the strand, keep an eye on the boat, and so make sure of the landing-place. On the way, others joined the crowd. Especially if at first they had no definite plan, it can be understood that those who were in search of Jesus rushed to the place, without making any provision for a longer absence from home. Moreover, when they were detained there till the evening, because of our Lord's healing and teaching, it became impossible for them to return. And, although there would have been no harm in spending the night in the open-air in the climate of the lake in March or April (Jn. vi. 4), the lack of food would be the more distressing, since the Oriental counts on the evening meal as the chief one of the day, and consumes little during the day. It can be taken for granted that the people felt very hungry after the exertion of the journey. Even to-day people prefer not to walk after sunset (*cf.* Jn. xii. 35). To buy bread at a late hour in strange villages, would not be easy, even if they were within reach, for there could have been no bakers' shops. At the present time the peasants consider it below their dignity to *sell* bread, and they have no great supply of it, as often they bake only sufficient for the day. The simplest thing under the circumstances would have been to remain there over night, and to return home at dawn. This is what would be done at the present day in such a case. Jesus, in His human pity, could not suffer the people to go hungry because of their eagerness to hear God's word, although the need was, as yet, not acute. Therefore food had to be provided (Mt. vi. 33). The " bread of the day,"[1] for which He taught them to pray (Mt. vi. 11), should be provided for them. And it should be a proper meal. The grass (Aram. *'isba*) which was found there (Mt. xiv. 19 ; Mk. vi. 39 ; Jn. vi. 10),[2] and which now would serve as a carpet, was, of course, not a grass-plot such as we know, but the exuberant wild growth of herbs which, in the spring and through the greatest portion of the rainy season,

---

[1] *Lahman deyoma* is the most probable original form of the phrase, as was pointed out already by Chase, *The Lord's Prayer in the Early Church* (1891), p. 45, according to the old Syrian text. In an evening prayer, the bread of the approaching day is naturally that of the morrow, as it is in the Gospel of the Hebrews.

[2] The grass receives in the three Gospels an ascending emphasis. In Mt. it is only the natural presupposition for the lying in the open air ; in Mk. it is a piece of realism, for which reason the colour is mentioned ; in Jn. it is exuberant, suggesting a providential provision for the occasion.

cover the whole uncultivated ground in the lake district,[1] and
even the mountains (Lev. R. xxvii. 72a). The people spread
themselves out as for an ordinary meal, at which there
is a group around each dish (Mk. vi. 39 ; Lk. ix. 14) ; or like
garden-beds (Mk. vi. 40)—a simile readily intelligible in the
East, where the irrigated garden is divided up into small
square plots (Arab. *meshakib, meshatib*),[2] with raised borders,
into which the water is brought in streamlets running between
the plots. Then Jesus, lifting up His eyes,[3] pronounced over
the bread the blessing of the heavenly Giver[4] (Mt. xi. 19 ;
Mk. vi. 41 ; Lk. ix. 16 ; Jn. vi. 11), according to the Jewish
table custom. In the East, silence is customary during a meal.
There, behind the Galilean mountains, where Tiberias lies
in their shade, the sun had set. The red glow of the sunset
spread over the wide surface of the lake, whose long waves
broke on the shore in soft splashes. Then what Moses said
concerning the Manna in the wilderness found its realisation :
*Man does not live by bread alone, but by every word that proceedeth
out of the mouth of God* (Dt. viii. 3).

Another peculiarity of the Markan account is that Bethsaida
is mentioned as the goal of the return journey (vi. 45), although
in such a way that the expression πρὸς (not εἰς) Βηθσαϊδάν
seems to mean that the landing-place was only in the neighbourhood of Bethsaida, not at the town itself. Perhaps the
one who inserted " Bethsaida " here thought that the " other
side " referred to the eastern shore, and mentioned the eastern
Bethsaida in order that the reader should conceive of this as
the destination that was originally intended. This was
reasonable, inasmuch as that Jesus originally intended to
return home by land. Then it might have been supposed
that the disciples awaited Him at Bethsaida in order that
He might continue the journey with them. The storm which
took place that night changed this plan. Jesus came to the
disciples " in the midst of the sea " (Mk. vi. 47) and continued
the crossing with them towards Ginnesar on the western
shore. On April 6, 1908, a journey over the lake by the staff

---

[1] According to Mt. it must have occurred in winter and spring ; according
to Jn., March and April are the months of rich growth.

[2] The dictionaries do not seem to mention either. The corresponding
Mishnaic Hebrew word is *malbenoth* (Pea iii. 1, 4).

[3] There was a difference of opinion among the rabbis whether, during a
prayer, the eyes should be raised or dropped (Jeb. 105b ; p. Ber. 8c).

[4] The Jewish benediction is : " Blessed art Thou, O Lord, King of the world,
who bringest forth bread from the earth." *Cf. Jesus-Jeshua*, pp. 133-139.

of the Institute resulted in a similar experience. Coming
from the eastern edge below Hippos, we wished to sail northward along the shore in order to land again in Bethsaida.
But a strong wind rising at noon from the east made it impossible to land, and drove us to Capernaum.[1]

If this explanation of the Markan mention of Bethsaida
is not acceptable, a way out of the difficulty would be the
supposition that the tradition attached to the Seven Springs
as the place of the feeding caused the insertion of " Bethsaida."
The description of the storm " in the midst of the sea " would
not be suitable to the short journey from the Seven Springs
to the plain of Ginnesar. It would suit a journey of some
distance, the goal of which was more likely to have been in
the east, but the storm drove the boat back to the west. However, Mk. seems to assume also in viii. 22 that Bethsaida was
in the east. For, according to *v.* 13 *f.*, a journey towards the
other side of the shore took place, for which no sufficient
provision of bread was made—the starting-point had evidently
been home—and, after the healing of the blind man, *v.* 27,
follows in the proper sequence : " And Jesus went out . . .
into the villages of Cæsarea Philippi." This fact of a Bethsaida lying in the east—a fact also confirmed by Josephus and
early Church tradition—from which the one in the west ought
to have been differentiated by a prefix or additional title, speaks
against the assumption of a Bethsaida in the Ginnesar district,
supposed to be attested to in Mk. vi. 45.

There need be no doubt whatever concerning the Johannine
account (vi. 23) of the conveying of the crowd by boats to
Capernaum from Tiberias. For not only has the cross-
route between Tiberias and the harbour of Hippos to be taken
into consideration, but also the fishery of Tiberias. This
probably had to use the eastern shore, because Magdala,
Capernaum, and Bethsaida requisitioned the northern portion
of the lake.

The story of the journey on a stormy night towards the
country over against Galilee, where Jesus suffered demons
to enter into a herd of swine (Lk. viii. 26), which resulted in
their wild rush down into the lake, undoubtedly points to
a heathen district on the eastern shore. According to
Mk. v. 11 ; Lk. viii. 32, the herd was feeding on, or by, a
" mountain," which must thus have been situated on the shore
of the lake. And, according to Mt. viii. 30, the herd was

[1] *PJB*, 1908, p. 13.

far from the place where Jesus came across the demoniac,
which, according to Mk. v. 2 (*cf.* Lk. viii. 27), He did immediately on landing. The scene of the event is, in Mt. (viii. 28),
" the country of the Gadarenes," in whose town—that is to
say, Gadara—the proprietors of the herd lived. Eusebius
(*Onomasticum*, ed. Klostermann, p. 47) had in mind a town on
the other side of the Jordan, east of Scythopolis and Tiberias,
on a mountain, below which there were hot springs, the
Umkes of the present. Mk. (v. 1) has "Gerasenes";
Lk. (viii. 26), "Gerasenes" or "Gergesenes." Pal. Evangelarium has exclusively "Gergesenes" (Aram. *Gergeshaye*) in
both Mt. and Lk. (the Markan parallel is missing). It seems
then that in Palestine the narrative was localised according
to this name. That Jesus came there for privacy's sake is
hinted in Mt. viii. 18, and can be inferred from the context
of Mk. iv. 35 and Lk. viii. 22. Thus far this narrative confirms
what was said above concerning the place of the feeding.
Origen (on Jn. vi. 41) knew of " an ancient city, Gergesa,
by the lake now called Tiberias, by which is a cliff overhanging
the lake, from which they show that the swine were cast down
by the devils." According to Eusebius, a village bearing that
name was shown " on the mountain." Yet he also mentions
that others connect the Girgashites of Dt. vii. 1 with the
Arabic Gerasa (*i.e. Jerash*) or with Gadara (=*Umkes*). To-day
the name *Kersa* is given to a small place on the shore, south of
the opening of the *Wady es-Samak*. And almost on the side of
a spur of the mountain there is a ruined tower which is called
Gurza. The little place is situated on a very small hill, probably formed by ruins. It is a large walled quadrangle, which
cannot be considered as a place of any importance, and a part
of it projects landwards. Only in the distance, far away from
the lake, there is a high precipice on the slope of the highland
north of the *Wady es-Samak*, which is called *el-'Aref*. Remains of a larger settlement have so far not been discovered
in this district; but the name *Kursa* or *Gurza* seems to have
been familiar in this neighbourhood for a long time. Theoderich (1172) places Chorazin here, four miles from Cedar
(=Gadara) (ed. Tobler, p. 101). We find the same on a map
of the twelfth century (*ZDPV*, 1905, pl. v.), which, however,
inserts a Gerasa between Chorazin and Cedar. It is also
peculiar that the Pal. Talmud (Sheb. 36c) connects Susitha
(=Hippos)—in the district in which Gergesa must have
been situated—with the Girgasites (Josh. iii. 10), who are said

to have been converted to the God of Israel and to have
voluntarily emigrated to Africa at the time of the Israelitish
invasion (the same is said of the Amorites, Tos. Sab. vii. 25).
An old place-name in this neighbourhood may have occasioned
this story.   Thus there should not be any hesitation in assuming the former existence of a place Gergesa by the lake,
although the details given by Origen and Eusebius do not
agree, and were influenced perhaps by the Biblical narrative.
The reading " Gerasenes " might have had its origin in the
Gospels through the substitution of a well-known name for
the obscure one " Gergesenes." This might have been changed
into " Gadarenes " by someone acquainted with Palestinian
geography.   He might have thought that it was unlikely that
the distant Gerasa in Gilead was meant, but that it could only
refer to Gadara, whose position near to the lake was well
known, and which, as an autonomous city, seemed to be more
in keeping with the narrative. The southern shore of the
lake suits the story in that there, as on no other part of the
shore, does water eat into the land, and has thereby formed
a steep shore 6-12 metres in height. A herd wildly rushing
over the shore-plain might easily be drowned here, coming
so suddenly to the precipice. Since Gadara, which was two
hours distant from the lake and separated from it by the
Yarmuk,[1] could not have been the town from which the inhabitants came to Jesus ; Zahn[2] considers the site of *Tulul
eṭ-Ṭaʿalib*, on the shore this side of the river, likely to have
been the town of Gerasa, supposed to have been situated in
the district of the Gadarenes. There is, however, no evidence
that the territory of Gadara in the Jordan valley crossed the
Yarmuk. According to Josephus,[3] the territories of Gadara
and Hippos adjoined those of Tiberias and Scythopolis, and
hence were exposed to the hostility of the inhabitants of
Tiberias. In that case, the frontier of Hippos must have
reached the Jordan. A coin acquired by me in *Umkes* shows
that the emblem of the triremes, hitherto taken as referring
to the lake of Tiberias, can only denote a naval battle fought
at the famous hot spring of Chammat Gader[4] on the Yarmuk.

[1] Yet a bridge is mentioned (Pal. Erub. 22d). The bridge was necessary,
as, according to Tos. Erub. vi. 13, it can be assumed that the traffic between
Gader and Chammeta with its hot springs (north of the Yarmuk) was considerable.

[2] *Comm. on St. Mt.* viii. 27.   [3] *Vita* ix.

[4] Eccl. R. v. 10 (95b) : " Hast thou ever been to Chammat Gader ?" According to p. Sab. 5d, one of the specialities of the place was very small eggs, as
small as hawthorn fruits, which were very tasty.

For here Gadara is designated as "the one which arranges
naval battles on the river."

The doubtful similarity in sound between Gerasa and the
steep mountain peak *Ḳren ed-Jeradeh* ("Locust-horn"), north
of *Wady en-Nḳeb*, caused Lagrange[1] to look for the scene of
our narrative here. But because of the great distance of this
mountain from the lake it seems very improbable. So it is
safest to think of the *Kursa*, or Gurza, on the *Wady es-Samak*,
although there is no town on the mountain. In that case
one has to visualise the landing of Jesus and the meeting
of the demoniac at some distance southward from there. It
is true that there are no graves there, out of which the demoniac could have come (Mt. viii. 28 ; Mk. v. 2) ; but according
to Lk. viii. 27 he dwelt among the graves but *came* from the
town. The episode of the herd of swine, especially as
described by Lk. (viii. 32), according to which they were
feeding on the mountain and from it ran violently down
a steep place into the lake, does not fit in with the shore-plain,
which is specially wide there. Yet, as Wilson first suggested,[2]
it might have taken place 2 kilometres further southward,
where, at *Moka'-'Edlo*, a fairly steep slope, 44 metres high, of
a projection of the highland reaches to within 40 metres of
the seashore. This would then be the same neighbourhood
as that in which, according to our conviction, the miracle of
feeding also must have taken place (*cf.* above, p. 172). Thus
Jesus again sought a spot familiar to Him, and solitude which
He loved, and, contrary to His purpose, it was just there that
His hidden glory was revealed.

Probably the Jews watched this drowning of the swine of
the Gergesenes with malicious satisfaction, those animals
being forbidden them for eating (Lev. xi. 7 ; Dt. xiv. 8), for
keeping (Bab. K. vii. 7), or trading (Shebi. vii. 3). Even
prayer in their proximity (p. Ber. 4e) was prohibited. Cursed
is he who rears them (b. Bab. K. 82b). But the Gospel
narrative suggests nothing of the kind. It directs the
attention entirely to Him whom the unclean spirits recognise
as "Son of God," and to whose power they give way, whereby
the habitation chosen by them is immediately lost to them.
Whatever one thinks of the unclean spirits, the eastern shore
of the lake in the district of Hippos must be considered as
the background of the episode, as well as of the miracle of

---

[1] *RB*, 1895, p. 521.
[2] *The Recovery of Jerusalem*, p. 368 *f*.

the feeding. Jesus was, on and by the lake, not only a teacher of the Reign of God, but also an administrator of its power on earth. A fact which, on one occasion, He made clear to the Baptist, adding however: "Blessed is he whosoever shall not be offended in me " (Mt. xi. 6).

No certain evidence points to the activity of Jesus on the southern and south-western shore of the lake. The former is now dominated by *Samakh* which, as a station of the Damascus-Haifa railroad and as starting-point for the steamboat service, has gained a new importance. It was, perhaps, once called *Kephar Zemach*.[1] The altar, with a dedication to a son of Zeus, dating probably from 30-31 B.C., which is to be found there, must have been brought from elsewhere. In the time of Christ, between the two forks of the Jordan which formerly flowed into the lake here, was situated the important Beth Jareah, or only Jareah.[2] This place, once provided with an excellently constructed spring-water aqueduct and now called *Khirbet el-Kerak*, is doubtless the ancient Philoteria which Antioch the Great conquered in 218 B.C. on this lake, and whose fertile environs were connected with those of Scythopolis.[3] It is not Tarichææ, as I once thought —being misdirected by Pliny. In its extent it considerably surpasses the usual settlements of ancient Palestine, and, among the places on the lake, is inferior only to Tiberias. Judging by the pottery found there, the city had its period of prosperity in pre-Israelitish times and only revived again in the Hellenistic period.[4] In the time of Josephus, however, it was no longer autonomous and must have belonged either to Hippos, or, more probably, to Scythopolis. Probably Alexander Jannæus had already destroyed its former glory.[5] Of more importance in the time of Jesus was Zinnabraj (Tennabris in Jos., *Bell. Jud.* iii. 9), now *Sinnabris* or *en-Nabrah*, situated west of the Jordan, quite near and opposite Beth Jareah, and dominating the road to Tiberias. Both places must have been inhabited by non-Jews : Philoteria was a Macedonian foundation. Beth Jareah lies, properly speaking, on the western shore of the lake. Only 5 kilometres north

---

[1] Thus Schlatter, *Zur Topographie und Geschichte*, p. 308, after p. Dem. 22d, Tos. Schebi. iv. 10, from which, however, it is only certain that it refers to a place in the district of Hippos.

[2] Often mentioned in rabbinic literature ; *cf.* Gen. R. xciv. (203b).

[3] Polybius, *Historiæ* v. 70.

[4] Albright, *Bulletin* No. 11 (October, 1923), p. 12 *f.*

[5] Georgius Cincellus, *Chronogr.*, ed. Dindorf, i., p. 558 *f.*

of it one comes upon Khammetha (Hammath),[1] Greek Ammathus,[2] the hot springs of which the Jews declared were heated by Gehenna![3] This ancient city (Josh. xix. 35) was not without its Jewish inhabitants. Their synagogue, facing south and north with an eastern antechamber, was excavated by Slousch in 1920.[4] It must have been the Chammath Ariah in which priests of the order of Ma'azia lived.[5] It may have received its " by-name "—to differentiate it from other places of the same name—from Beth Jareah,[6] by those who were unwilling to call it after the encroaching Tiberias, but took it for granted that it had once belonged to the domain of that city. Besides, the Masoretes of Tiberias did not wish to be called after this city, and substituted for it the name of the priestly order Ma'azia.

Close to Khammetha was Tiberias, only founded in the time of Christ (after A.D. 17), which participated in the rebellion against Rome, and was therefore predominantly Jewish. But the fact that it was built on a burial-place[7] (perhaps that of the ancient Rakkath, Josh. xix. 35) which continued its existence as " the village " (Kiphra)—possibly in the neighbourhood of the modern " castle of Tiberias "—would at first have frightened off the " Pharisees and scribes " from settling there. The citadel of Herod Antipas, which looked down from the height on to the city spread out along the lake front, in the palace of which, with its gilded roofs, the animal portraits caused offence, was certainly a centre of secular Hellenistic life. The stadium lay between the citadel and the city.[8] Jesus would hardly have avoided visiting this city because of "its impurity." The life of the city, with its intrigues and the machinations of the court, and the evil disposition of that " fox " Herod (Lk. xiii. 32), were certainly not to His liking, but that did not prevent the wife of Chuza, Herod's steward, from following and ministering unto Him (Lk. viii. 3). The Hellenistic world which impressed its character on the whole of the southern half of the lake was not the world of Jesus, although He, as well as His disciples, could not entirely avoid coming into contact with it.

---

[1] Tos. Erub. vii. 7.

[2] *Ant.* xviii. 2, 3 ; *Bell. Jud.* iv. 1, 3.

[3] Sab. 39a.

[4] See Kobez i. 1, pp. 5 *ff.*, 28 *ff.*

[5] After Kalir, see Klein, *Beiträge*, p. 89 *f.*

[6] *Jareah*-moon was perhaps changed into *Ariah*, because the moon can be an object of worship. Apart from this, the moon is so called because she is a " wanderer" (Aram. *areah, arah*). The district of Ariah is mentioned in Tos. Kil. i. 3 ; p. Kil. 27a ; the place Gupta (Guphta) de-Ariah in Sifre Numeri 47b (English translation, p. 139).

[7] *Ant.* xviii. 2, 3.

[8] p. Erub. 22b ; *Bell. Jud.* ii. 21, 6.

If we include the journeys on the lake—through which, by
the way, according to ancient belief the Jordan traverses
without mingling with the lake water[1]—in the sphere of His
activities, then the whole northern half of the lake becomes
the scene of a great part of His life.   Each journey on it renews
for us the memory of the Master.   Often the lake is as smooth
as a mirror, so that the movement of the boat and the oars
alone disturb the pale green surface into furrows and whirl-
pools.[2]   In the morning especially there is either complete
stillness or a little wind, which makes it a favourable time
for sailing.   But the sailors fear the west wind which may
suddenly descend upon the lake even at midday.   Ofttimes
they will rest on their oars, to hear whether it is not already
discernible above, on the heights, before it "comes down"
on to the surface of the water, as is written of the storm in
Lk. viii. 23.   At the present day triangular sails are used on
the boats, which are about 6 metres long.[3]   One side of the
sail is attached to a long pole which is drawn up high on
a short mast, and then one end is tied to the stem of the boat
so that the other end stands up sharply.   The helmsman
holds the free end of the sail in his hand by a rope, in order
that he may quickly relax and slacken it when the wind suddenly
rises.   When there is a strong wind blowing steadily, the pole
is let down and the sail rolled up on it.   The Arabs do not
like sailing boldly into the wind with the boat at an acute
angle.   They hasten to take up the oars and get as quickly
as possible out of the reach of the storm.   They row with
the 4 metres long oar, which moves freely before a peg, standing with one foot planted against the bench.   There is one
man to each oar.   By alternate singing, which the front
rower strikes up, rhythm and swing are sustained.

On the east the wind is strongest and the waves are highest,
"like mountains" in the imagination of the Oriental.   On
the western shore the high mountains offer protection, and it
is surprising how quickly one gets out of the storm-tossed
seas into perfect calm.   However, storm in the scientific
meaning of the word, with a velocity of wind at 7, is a rare
occurrence on the lake.   The meteorological station of 'Ain eṭ-
Ṭabeṛa reported only one day of storm (November 30) for 1915,
and for 1914 four storms during the period from February to

---

[1] Ber. R. iv (8a).   [2] About the colour of the lake, cf. above, p. 122.
[3] Yet the Madaba map shows on the Dead Sea a boat with a four-cornered
sail on a horizontal pole.

April. The months from March to July are generally the windiest, with the west wind predominating. Autumn and winter are quieter, which does not, however, exclude some stormy days. The members of the Archæological Institute experienced such a bad day on April 9, 1907. We ourselves rode in the morning to the Seven Springs, but saw boats on the lake struggling against wind and waves. One of them, which was to have brought one of our company over the lake, landed in the land of Ginnesar, far from its destination, because the majority of the sailors considered a further journey impossible.

Nearly always the wind is stronger at noon than in the morning or evening. The disciples of Jesus could take it for granted that on their night journeys there would usually be either calm or light wind. But when a storm did break, the position was the more serious. During such a storm Jesus slept in the hinder part of the boat, with His head upon a pillow, which probably was kept under the bench of the helmsman (Mk. iv. 38), to be used as a cushion for Him, as He did not take part in sailing the ship, or in fishing. In the meantime His disciples worked at the oars in order that the boat should not come side-on to the waves. They had cause to be anxious. They called: " *Maran shezeb, abadnan !*" ("Our Master, help, or we perish !"). But He answered: " *Ma attun dahelin, ze'ere hemanuta ?*" (" Why are ye so fearful, ye of little faith ?") (Mt. viii. 25 *ff.*). And to the storm He called: " *Ishtattak hashe,*" " Be silent and cease " (Mt. iv. 39). And there was a great calm. His trust in the Father made Him Lord over the elements. The faith which this awakened in the disciples was but the beginning, and would need much deepening. Yet the loveliest lake of Palestine remains the place where God's redeeming power appeared to men for the first time on earth in a new guise, like a light, and thus was the prophetic word (Isa. viii. 23 ; ix. 1) concerning the great light in the land of Zebulon and Naphtali abundantly fulfilled (*cf.* Mt. iv. 14 *ff.*). This came to pass when Jesus, by word and act, brought toiling, anxious, hungry, troubled men to a faith which does not consist in emotion and quietism but in the act of will of one who, when in distress, calls, and not in vain, to the Otherworldly.

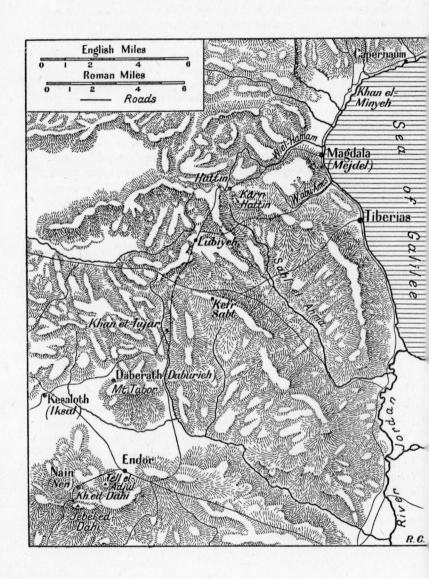

X

FROM CAPERNAUM TO NAIN

NAIN, mentioned only in Luke (vii. 11 *f.*), lies towards the southern frontier of Galilee. Jesus, according to Lk. vii. 1, set out for Nain apparently from Capernaum, and near the gate of the town met a funeral procession which halted in order that He might bid the dead man arise. The position of the little town is ascertainable from Eusebius' information as well as from actual discoveries. Hence the route taken by Jesus to reach it can be established with certainty. It must have been the *Via Maris* which He followed. The importance of this road from of old as the thoroughfare between Damascus and the coast, and even Egypt, is, in view of its geographical position, unquestionable (*cf.* above, p. 126 *f.*). The tradition (which can be traced back to the tenth century[1]) that the meeting of Abraham by Melchizedek (Gen. xiv. 18) took place at Mount Tabor, takes it for granted that the natural route from Dan to Hebron passed by this mountain. It is, however, only since the sixteenth century that we hear in greater detail of its use. We learn that then, at any rate, the way did not lead upwards via Hattin, but evidently south of *Mejdel* through the *Wady abu 'Ames*, near the stones of the Feeding (see above, pp. 115, 172), reached the heights below *Karn Hattin*. There, east of *Lubiyeh*, the now dilapidated Khan was reached, where 'Abd el-Rani must have rested in 1680, since he knows, as a station between *el-Miniyeh* and *'Uyun et Tujar*, only a green region with a cistern, but not Hattin or *Lubiyeh*. This also is the nameless station of Sultan Selim I. in his Egyptian campaign in 1516, who, in his march there and back again, did not touch Hattin. It can well be understood that the narrow pass of Wady el Hamam (see p. 118), which can so easily be blockaded by robbers, was avoided in this way. From *Lubiyeh* the way proceeded along a level track in a

---

[1] Epiphanius Hagiopolita, Eugesippus, Daniel, John of Würzburg, and Phocas, are the first witnesses.

southerly direction, which in the time of Jesus was already probably a well-cultivated district, until the springs near the present *Khan et-Tujjar*[1] invited the traveller to rest. A greater *détour* led through Tiberias and *Kefr Sabt*. Even as late as 1613 the company of Hans Jacob Ammann,[2] travelling in Palestine, used this route. He himself took a roundabout way through Tiberias and reached a little village (*Lubiyeh*), passing by the stones of the Feeding, and consumed the fishes caught in the lake near an " inn " facing Tabor, *i.e.* at the *Khan et-Tujjar*.

On the way, poppy-red, rose-red, purple and white anemones, in rare profusion and of great size, delight the eye in spring. In March and April, the traveller standing among the wide cornfields, rich in spite of the absence of manure, will observe the women weeding. They are bent almost double as they tear out the weeds from among the young corn. These weeds take the form particularly of thistles which, like the *'akkub* (*Gundelia Tournefortii*), grow into shrubs with wide leaves which choke the good seed (Mt. xiii. 7). *'Akkub* was taken to be the " thorns and thistles," which, according to the primæval curse, the earth was to bring forth (Gen. iii. 18), and which, according to rabbinic interpretation, were meant originally for human consumption.[3]

Nowadays, darnel (Arab. *zauwan, Lolium temulentum*) growing among the corn is generally left undisturbed, not because this narrow-leaved grass cannot be distinguished prior to the formation of the stalk and the ears of the wheat (although it would not be easy, *cf.* Mt. xiii. 26, 29), nor because it is left to the harvest-time (*cf.* Mt. xiii. 30), but rather, it would appear, because to take such trouble over the darnel would not be worth while since, in any case, the seed would be separated at the sifting of the wheat (*cf.* Lk. xxii. 31), as, indeed, we find in the Talmud.[4] The seed of the darnel is used as a food for fowls, as the Rabbis seem to assume when they speak of its being sown and taken from place to place.[5] Sometimes, however, the darnel is weeded out after it has reached the stage of having ears formed like wheat. It is then possible to walk among the standing corn which, although

---

[1] Two caravansaries are found here, one of which is perhaps that which Shams ed-Din built before the year 1444. The other was probably erected by Sinam, the governor of Damascus, in 1582. *Cf.* Porter, *Five Years in Damascus*, vol. i., p. 47.
[2] *Reiss ins Globte Land*, p. 59.
[3] Gen. R. xx (43a) ; Pes. 118a.
[4] Tos. Ter. vi. 10 ; p. Ter. 43d.
[5] Kil. i. 1 ; p. Kil. 26d.

high, is still green.   Since the seed is not sown closely in the
East, walking through the corn is not fraught with such
serious consequences as with us.   This custom of destroying
the weed when full grown is presupposed in Mt. xiii. 26, 30.
It may be that in the time of Christ the keeping of fowls was
not so general as in later times, and so the darnel would be
useless for the farmer.   Jesus used a popular idea, for the
purpose which the parable has in mind, when He attributed
the tares to an enemy who sowed them by night (Mt. xiii. 25,
28, 39).   Such malicious acts were not unknown, as appears
from a Palestinian folk-tale, where reeds were sown in a field.[1]
Jesus likened the tares to the " children of the wicked "
(Mt. xiii. 38), and the Arabs to-day consider the tares to be
bewitched wheat, while, according to a Jewish interpretation
of Gen. vi. 12, the deterioration of the earth before the Flood
was observable in the fact that it brought forth darnel (*zonin*)
when wheat had been sown, so tares went back to before the
Flood.[2]   But, apart from this historical background, there
was a firmly established conviction that among grain there is
an adulterous depravity,[3] as is observable in the nature of
darnel seed, which is really a species of wheat.[4]   That Jesus
specified darnel and not weeds in general was probably due
also to the peculiar damage caused by that particular weed,
but possibly still more to the close relationship between it
and wheat, the seeds of the two plants being, according to the
Mishna (Kil. i. 1), among the number of those the mixing of
which was not prohibited.[5]   Seeing the seldom absent darnel
in the cornfields, Jesus was reminded of the character and
destiny of the two kinds of men which exist side by side in
this world.

At the southern edge of the plain the road enters what was
formerly an extensively wooded district which, in the north,
joins Tabor.   If it was early summer when Jesus travelled
here, He must have enjoyed the fresh young foliage of the
two kinds of oak (*Quercus lusitanica* and *ægilops*), reminiscent
of our beech-trees, which abound here ; also the perfume of
the white clusters of the storax ; the strong aroma of the
briars of the mastic terebinth ; the dark lustrous leaves of the
carob-bean trees, and the exquisite pink and white of the
zistus blossoms.   All these must have attracted His notice,

---

[1] Schmidt and Kahle, *Volkserzählungen aus Palästina*, p. 32.
[2] Gen R. xxviii. (57b).   [3] Sifra on Lev. xix. 29 (90d).
[4] p. Kil. 26d.   [5] *Cf.* above, p. 72.

especially when coming from the hot lake-shore where quite
different kinds of trees and flowers grow. Mount Tabor
turns its steeper side to the north and, therefore, despite
its considerable height (562 metres) above the surrounding
country (less than 100 metres), it makes a less striking impression when viewed from this side than from either the east
or west, from either of which we understand why the Jews
represented it as vying with Mount Carmel for the honour of
being the mountain of the Law-giving.[1] Proudly it says to
Mount Hermon : " Shekinah must dwell upon me; she
belongs to me. When, in the beginning, in the days of Noah,
the Flood covered all the mountains of the earth, the water
did not come up to my head and shoulders ; therefore am I
higher than all the mountains, and God must needs descend
upon me."[2] Hyperbolically, the antediluvian wild bull is
compared with Tabor for size, that is 40 parasangs (220 kilometres) high.[3] Of course, it is only in Babylon that one could
talk like that. The dome-like outline of Tabor, which the
ancients were wont to liken to a mother's breast,[4] is, in fact,
quite unique in Palestine, and, together with Hermon, could
well be considered in that land as being among the wonders
of creation (Ps. lxxxix. 13). From its foot, in a north-westerly
direction, there stretches a low hill on which is a settlement
called *Khirbet Dabura*, to the south of which, as it slopes into
the plain, is the present-day village *Deburieh*. The former is
most probably the *Deberath* of Josh. xix. 12, and also the
Dabaritta, where Josephus ordered the guarding of the plain,
especially, that is, the roads from it to Jerusalem.[5] The
Jewish village, *Dabira*, mentioned in Eusebius, may have been
identical with the *Daburieh* of to-day.

A Palestinian tradition, possibly presupposed in 2 Pet. i. 18
and universally accepted in the fourth century, identified
Tabor with the mount of Transfiguration.[6] The reason for
this was probably Origen's quotation (on Jn. ii. 6) from the
" Gospel of the Hebrews," where Jesus says of Himself :
" My mother, the Holy Spirit, took hold of one of My hairs
and brought Me to the high mountain Tabor." This was
believed to refer to the Transfiguration. In any case it shows
a desire to fit this remarkable mountain into the history of our

[1] Mech. on Ex. xx. 2 (66b) ; Mid. Teh. lxviii. 9 ; Meg. 29a.
[2] Targ. Jer. on Judg. v. 5, ed. De Lagarde.   [3] Zeb. 113b.
[4] Polybius, *Hist.* v. 70.   [5] *Bell. Jud.* ii. 21, 31 ; *Vita* 26, 62.
[6] Origen ; Eusebius ; Cyril. Hieros., *Cat.* xii. 16 ; Jerome.

Lord. Attempts were evidently made then, as now, to harmonise this with the Gospel narrative of the Transfiguration (see under XI.). On the summit three churches were built in the sixth century in memory of the three tabernacles (booths) which Peter wished to set up for Jesus, Moses, and Elijah. They were visited by the pilgrims Antoninus and Arculf.[1] The remains of the church of the Transfiguration of the time of the Crusaders, visible in the newly completed restoration, shows a deep-lying apse, which perhaps was the crypt of the earlier building. There were probably two small chapels to the right and left of it, one of which is still recognisable, and these, together with the chief church, formed the three churches of the Byzantine period.[2] The eastern end of the long, narrow plateau was chosen as the site of the churches, thereby hitting on a delightful position, affording charming views over the plain of *Ahma* and a portion of the surface of the lake of Tiberias towards snow-clad Hermon. In the Canaanite period there was already a settlement here, according to the archæologists.[3] This does not mean that it has always been inhabited, since food conditions could never have been favourable. Mount Tabor is referred to in 1 Chr. vi. 62 as a Levite settlement, but not in the parallel passage Josh. xxi. 34 *f.* The original stronghold must have been a fortified town. In 218 B.C. Antioch the Great,[4] and later, in 100 B.C., Menander Jannæus conquered it.[5] In A.D. 66 Josephus surrounded the whole stretch of the mountain (1,300 metres by 300 metres) with a still recognisable encircling wall.[6] So it is impossible to locate the mount of Transfiguration here ; the Synoptic tradition excludes the identification. This mountain, rearing its mass beside a great high-road, is more conceivable as being the place where the Galilæan adherents of Jesus gathered after the Resurrection, *i.e.* the unspecified mountain of Mt. xxviii. 16 *f.* (*cf.* 1 Cor. xv. 6), and it may be that this assumption, as evidenced by Theodosius (about A.D. 530),[7] was the original nucleus of the Galilæan local tradition, which later was extended to the Transfiguration.

---

[1] Geyer, *Itinera*, pp. 162, 275. See also *Commemoratorium de casis Dei* ; Tobler, *Descr. T. S.*, p. 82.

[2] See plan in Meistermann, *Le Mont Tabor* (1900), fronting p. 137 ; Meistermann, *Guide*, p. 505.

[3] Schollmayer, *Theologie und Glaube*, 1913, p. 748 *f.*

[4] Polybius, *Hist.* v. 70.

[5] Georgius Syncellus, *Chronogr.* I., p. 559 ; *cf.* Jos., *Ant.* xiii. 15, 4.

[6] *Bell. Jud.* ii. 20, 6 ; iv. 1, 8 ; *Vita* 37.

[7] *Cf.* St. Barnabé (Meistermann), *La montagne de la Galilée*, p. 60 *f.*

Naturally, it was only after the summit of Mount Tabor was deserted that such an assumption became possible. The peculiarly shaped mountain, made more remarkable by the wealth of its timber and vegetation, must in any case have stirred the emotions of the pilgrim ; even to this day the sight is arresting. But he who is unwilling to let imagination run riot will prefer to dwell on the thought that Jesus had His home in Nazareth 9 kilometres away. The wood upon the mountain's slopes in this neighbourhood must have been of no small importance to the Carpenter of the little town, and it is scarcely possible that He who loved the mountain solitudes did not often visit the most remarkable mountain of the neighbourhood. But on His way to Nain, when crossing from *Daberath* southward over the narrow strip of the plain of Jezreel, His attention must have been particularly drawn to the dominating mass of Tabor.

A characteristic of the plain of Jezreel, which slopes and drains towards the north-west, is that in the east two valleys connect it with the valley of the Jordan. At first these are separated by the mighty range of the *Jebel ed-Daḥi*, which is 515 metres above sea-level and not much lower than Tabor. " Issachar is a strong ass crouching down between cattle pens " (Gen. xlix. 14) was referred by the Rabbis to this place, since in the centre is the mountain with the plains of Kesalu and Jezreel respectively on either side.[1] Thus the Kesalu plain containing the settlement Kesaloth, now called *Iksal*, lying north of this mountain, and the unnamed mountain can only be *Jebel ed-Daḥi*. It is distinguishable from Tabor by the lava which is found at its western foot, and by a crater on the north-east ; its summit, too, is peaked, an infrequent occurrence in Palestine. Passers-by are therefore impressed by it, and it is easy to understand why pilgrims have often mistaken it for Mount Hermon,[2] probably because of the words, " Tabor and Hermon rejoice in thy name " (Ps. lxxxix. 13).[3]

[1] Gen. R. xcviii. (212b). The present text, also ed. Constantinople 1512, Saloniki 1593, has *Paslan*, but Cod. Vat. *Aksalu* (*cf.* Klein, *Jeshurun*, 1922, p. 447). This fits in with the Χσαλοῦς of Eusebius. The Biblical *Kesaloth*, now *Iksal*, could have become, by way of *Kesaloth, Kesalu*.

[2] Origen on Ps. lxxxix. 13 ; Petrus Diaconus ; John of Würzburg ; Theoderich, ed. Tobler, p. 98.

[3] On the other hand, Antoninus found the " little Hermon " of Ps. xlii. 7 at the place of Baptism on the Jordan. Geyer (*Itinera*, pp. 165, 199) and Poloner (Tobler, *Descr. T. S.*, p. 273) differentiated between the Little Hermon, lying on the other side of the valley, south-east of Tabor, and another mount Hermon at the foot of which is Nain. Maybe he meant by the first the extinct volcano *Tell el-'Adjul*, which, in fact, lies like a small mountain beside a large one.

The view from this spot has with justice been extolled,
extending as it does over the whole of Galilee, from Hermon
to the Mediterranean Sea. Although the Gospel narrative
implies that the field where the disciples plucked the ears of
corn on a Sabbath (Mt. xii. 1 ; Mk. ii. 23 ; Lk. vi. 1)[1] was
in the neighbourhood of Capernaum, there are those who
have sought to place it in this neighbourhood, probably
near the little village of *ed-Dahi*, which is situated on the
mountain slope below the summit. There was also a stone
on which our Lord was supposed to have rested.[2] It may
be that in ancient times this mountain was the " hill of the
oracle-giver " (*Moreh*, Judg. vii. 1), but that may have been, on
the other hand, farther south, near *el-Mesarr*. The sanctuary
on its summit where counsel was sought had disappeared
long before the Christian era ; but it may have been succeeded
by the grave of some local hero, out of which Islam later made
its *Neby Dubaya*,[3] a companion of the Prophet.

North of the chief height in this group of mountains,
facing the foot of *Dahi*, on a terrace sloping towards the plain,
is *Nen*, the village which once was *Nain*. The name is derived
from *na'im*, " lovely " ; although even the Syriac translation,
as well as the Pal. Evangeliarium, has Nain. Midrash Gen. R.
(xcviii. 212b) has in the domain of Issachar a certain *Naim*
as well as *Tin'am*. That might well be *Nain*, for name and
position correspond. The hill slope upon which the village
is situated is of sufficient height to afford a certain security to
an ancient town. Below the village a spring, formerly credited
with curative powers bestowed by the blessing of Jesus,
makes possible a garden of olives and figs, which stands out
impressively from the wide corn-lands below. In the ancient
town which, according to Luke vii. 12, was walled, a western
gate leading to the spring is to be expected and also one
opening on to the great plain and the neighbourhood of
Nazareth, not to speak of an eastern or north-eastern gate by
which it would be possible to get not only to nearby Endor
in the east, but also to Daberath which lies opposite in a

---

[1] In later times this was not even forbidden by the Rabbis, as long as the ears,
being ripe, allowed of the husks being blown away and no implement need be
used to remove them : just what the disciples did, in fact, is frequently done
to-day.

[2] Petrus Diaconus *ad loc.* It is probably the same stone on the summit which
Christians still look upon with veneration. *Cf.* Paton, *Annual*, i. (1920), p. 64.

[3] Thus was the saint named to me on the mountain, emphasis being laid on
the fact that the mountain is called *Jebel ed-Dahi* and the village *Khirbet ed-Dahi*.

northerly direction. A straight flat road, from which the
Via Maris branches off in a south-westerly direction, passes
through the fields along here and ascends finally to the watershed between east and west, on which Nain lies. The rocks
projecting out of the hillside have been used for graves, and
it was to one of these that the widow's son was being carried
on a bier (not in a coffin). In the van of the mourning procession the young men-friends of the deceased would be walking, according to Galilæan custom,[1] eulogising in their dirges
their dead friend as the only stay and hope of his mother.
But Jesus passed by on the way from Daberath and called to
the dead: "*Talya kum*" ("Young man, arise!"), "And he
that was dead sat up and began to speak" (Lk. vii. 14). In
later times the grave that had been destined for the young
man, and the house of his mother, which had been turned
into a church,[2] were pointed out. We have no knowledge
of the circumstances which brought Jesus to Nain. He
might have turned off here, on His way to Jerusalem, from
the *Via Maris*. Nain was mentioned in the fourteenth century
as a station on the way from *Jenin* over *Ḥaṭṭin* to *Safed*.[3] In
any case, Jesus was here on the southern frontier of Galilee.
Josephus[4] sets this at Debaritta and Kesaloth, which, however,
only means that a great part of the plain between the Galilæan
mountains and the *Jebel ed-Daḥi*—the landmarks round about
these villages—belonged to Galilee, and therefore does not
exclude the insignificant town of Nain from Galilee. From
this we may conclude that the activities of Jesus in Galilee
extended beyond the limits suggested by the fact that Capernaum was chosen as a centre.

[1] Sabb. 153a. In Judæa the mourning singers followed *behind* the bier.
[2] Petrus Diaconus *ad loc.* According to Meistermann (*Guide*, p. 514) the
present church, erected by the Franciscans in 1880, stands on the site of the old
one, which had been turned into a mosque.
[3] Hatmann, *ZDMG*, 1916, p. 490.
[4] *Vita* 62; *Bell. Jud.* iii. 3, 1.

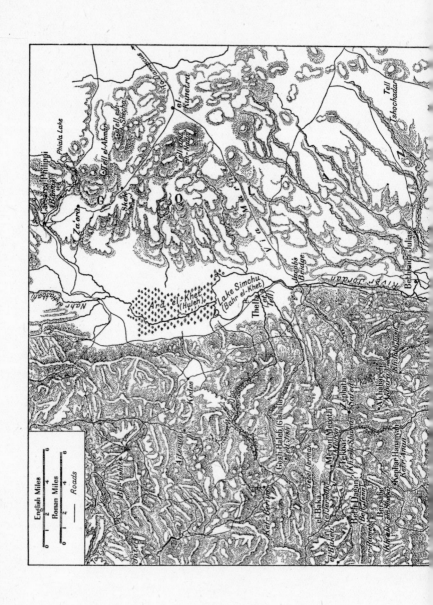

XI

THE DISTRICTS OF TYRE AND CÆSAREA
PHILIPPI

THE first natural frontier of Palestine to the north, which can
already be seen from the mountain above Nazareth (p. 75), lies
spread out clearly before one's eyes in the chain of mountains
round the lake of Tiberias, ending, in the east, with *Jebel
Kan'an*, 842 metres above sea-level. Here, too, one can see
that between this height and the lake is ground somewhat
lower, behind which, in the dip of Joseph's Pit (244 metres,
invisible to the observer), the *Via Maris* is enabled to find an
outlet from the upper Jordan district to the level of the lake.
In the western range this was accomplished by means of three
steep ladder-like descents. Over the plain of Jezreel (about
90 metres high), on the other side of the heights before
Nazareth, lies the Battof plain (p. 103), which forms the first
step and is about 150 metres high; above this is the plain of
'*Arrabeh*, about 250 metres high; then, at the foot of the
highest range (about 1,040 metres high), comes the valley of
er-Rameh, 380 metres.

These steps, separated from one another for the most part
by steep wooded heights, give Galilee its character, and are
also the reason for the distinction in the time of Jesus between
Lower and Upper Galilee. Dispatches from Rabban Gamaliel[1]
and Simeon ben Gamaliel (and Johanan ben Zakkai[2]), sent
in the period when the Temple still stood and had jurisdiction
over Palestinian Jewry outside as well as within Judæa, were
directed to "the sons of Upper and Lower Galilee." The
Aramaic designations in Gamaliel's dispatches for both the
regions are *Gelila Ar'a'a* and *Gelila 'Illa'a*, severally. Sycamores
are to be found only in Lower Galilee, which shows it to be the

---

[1] Tos. Sanh. ii. 6; p. Sanh. 18d; Maas. sh. 56e; b. Sanh. 11b. *Cf.* Dalman,
Aram-Dialektproben, p. 3.
[2] Midr. Tan. on Deut. xxvi. 13. *Cf.* Klein, *Tora wa-Erez*, i. 4, p. 1.

warmer region ;[1] while in Upper Galilee, as one would expect,
oaks abound.[2]   *Kephar Ḥananyah* is mentioned as being the
line of division between the districts.[3]   In Upper Galilee the
highest points are *Beth Dagan*,[4] *Tekoa, Meron*, and *Gosh Ḥalab*.[5]
Of these *Meron* and *Gosh Ḥalab*—the Gishala of Josephus—
are certainly identifiable with *Meiron* and *ed-Jish* in the neighbourhood of Safed.   The Galilæan Tekoa is possibly *Khirbet
sh-Shamaʿ* near *Meiron*, and *Beth Dagan* probably *Beit Jenn* to
the west of it ; all of which are situated at a height of from
760 to 915 metres on the other side of the height that shuts in
the third step, which is near.   *Kephar Ḥananyah*, Jewish tradition
has rightly identified with *Kefr ʿAnan*,[6] that is to say, about
360 metres above sea-level, in the mountain range which
separates the second step from the third.   Because of the
difference in their altitudes these two Galilæan districts had
different customs in regard to the removal of the field fruits
(the consumption of which was prohibited) of the Sabbatic
year, in which respect the district of Tiberias, as a third part,
also had a special position.[7]   But they were also administrative
districts, as Josephus, under whom both districts were placed
in the period of the revolt, testifies.[8]   According to his account,
the frontier line between them was at *Bersabe*, which can be
identified with *Khirbet abu-sh-Shebaʿ*, scarcely 1 kilometre distant
from *Kefr ʿAnan*.[9]   In the neighbourhood of the lake, *Akha-
bareh* (*ʿAkbara*) must have been to him the southernmost
point of Upper Galilee.[10]   That, in the west, Lower Galilee
reached the slope of the upland towards the coastal plain is
evident from the fact that *Ḥabulon* (=*Kabal*) is mentioned as
a frontier in this direction.   It is clear that Upper Galilee did
not stretch far in a westward direction.   For *Meroth* (=*Meiron*)
on the eastern slope of the *Jebel Jermak* appears, in Josephus,
as its most westerly point.[11]   This would still permit the inclusion of *Beit Jenn* (see above) on its western side, but hardly
of *Baka*—the northernmost point of Upper Galilee in Josephus
—and would continue westward as far as the otherwise not-

---

[1] Shebi. ix. 2.   [2] Tos. Shebi. vii. 11.
[3] Shebi. ix. 2.   [4] Tos. Shebi. vii. 13.
[5] p. Shebi. 38d ; b. Pes. 53a.
[6] *Yiḥus ha-Ṣaddikim* (Jerusalem 1898), p. 64; *Hibbath Jerushalaim*, p. 44b.
[7] Shebi ix. 2.   [8] *Bell. Jud.* ii. 20, 3.
[9] *Bell. Jud.* iii. 3, 1.   *Hepta-pegon*, which is usually suggested, is out of the
question, since it does not lie opposite Iskaloth=Iksal, the place mentioned
by Josephus before that, and, besides, it belongs to the sphere of the district of
Tiberias, which he refers to as the eastern point.
[10] See *Bell. Jud.* ii. 20, 6 ; *Vita* 37.   [11] *Bell. Jud.* iii. 3, 1.

quite-impossible *el-Buḳeaʿ*.[1] The village of *Jermaḳ*, the ancient name of which was, as I remember being told by the natives, *el-Baḳaʿ*, would deserve more serious consideration as a possibility. To this neighbourhood belongs the cave of Peka[2] or Bekaʿ,[3] where R. Shimʿon ben Jochai hid himself.

The eastern border reached as far as Lake Simchu (*Baḥr el-Khet*), for *Gelila ḳadmona* (Ezek. xlvii. 8) was taken to mean eastern Galilee and it was believed that the Temple spring in the time of Salvation would first cause the fish in this lake to increase abundantly, repeating the miracle in the lake of Tiberias, and then in the Dead Sea.[4] Thella " in the neighbourhood of Jordan," asserted by Josephus to be the easternmost point, corresponds to this natural frontier, and the ancient locality *et-Tell* on lake *Khet*, $1\frac{1}{5}$ kilometres from the mouth of the Jordan, fits in with this.[5] The Mesopotamian Tella, which Meistermann erroneously locates here,[6] merely proves the possibility of such a name without any further amplifications ; and Klein's[7] proposal to trace it back to 'Aithelu ('Aitahlu) and locate it in *ʿAiterun*, 11 kilometres west of the Jordan, in the upland of the Tyrian region, has nothing to recommend it. Thus, Upper Galilee undoubtedly found its natural northern frontier in the precipitously deep *Wady ʿOba*, and its southern frontier in a line running towards the Jordan from *Kefr ʿAnan* over *Jubb Jusif*. The Jordan itself formed the eastern frontier ; while the western frontier extended from *Kefr ʿAnan* over *Beit Jenn* to the opening of the *ʿOba* valley, including the mountain group of the *Jermaḳ* which contained the loftiest peak in Palestine (1,199 metres). From this it follows that all the Galilæan places, roads, and byways hitherto described in connection with the itinerary of Jesus belong to Lower Galilee. This was His own country, and the natural scene of His Galilæan activity.[8] The natural frontiers of this part of Palestine were also His frontiers, beyond which He went only on special occasions. When, for instance, His

---

[1] Klein, *Palästina-Studien*, i., p. 38, is inclined to identify it with *Ter Bicha*, lying far in a northerly direction, but this is geographically improbable and linguistically impossible.

[2] Koh. R. x. 8 (122a).   [3] Pesikta 88b.

[4] p. Shek. 50 a, *cf.* Tos. Sukk. iii. 8 (with changed text).

[5] *PJB*, 1911, p. 23.

[6] *Capernaüm et Bethsaïde*, p. 51. But see Martin, *Chronique de Josué le Stylite* p. lii. 50, where the position of this Thella in Mesopotamia is clearly located.

[7] *Pal. Studien*, i., p. 50 *f.*; ii. (Heb.), pp. 18, 29.

[8] Only later Jewish fables connect it with Upper Galilee, *cf.* Krauss, *Das Leben Jesu nach jüd. Quellen*, pp. 42, 72.

wanderings took Him beyond these frontiers to the further
shores of the Galilæan lake (p. 161 *ff.*), it was due to His desire
to escape notice, to avoid the domain of Herod Antipas, and
also, to be alone with His disciples, to woo them from other
distracting influences and to dedicate Himself entirely to them.
The account of His overland journeys to the regions beyond
Lower Galilee must be viewed in a like manner. It may be
imagined, however, by anyone who knows something of the
oppressive heat of the lake of Tiberias—which, it is true, is
modified somewhat in the north-east and east of the lake by
the west wind—that Jesus, in the rainless summer, would
occasionally retire to the mountains to avoid the enervating
heat and to breathe again the light fresh air of the heights.
Early in the June of 1899 I myself found it impossible to
sleep at nights in Tiberias, and on the 7th of the month I
rode up to Safed, where I was soon myself again.

A journey into the district adjoining Tyre was the occasion
when the Greek-speaking Phœnician woman sought Jesus'
aid for her possessed daughter (Mk. vii. 24 *ff.* ; Mt. xv. 21 *ff.*).
According to Mk. vi. 53 and Mt. xiv. 34, this journey started
apparently from the plain of Ginnesar ; according to Mk. vii.
31, Jesus returned to the sea of Galilee ; and according to
Mt. xv. 29, He returned from there. It is peculiar to the
Matthæan text that the objective of the journey is given as
the district of Tyre *and Sidon* ; in Mk. (not according to Syr.
Sin.) the return journey was through Sidon. This caused
Holtzmann to imagine that Jesus went from Tyre northward,
then, through the neighbourhood of Sidon, on the road over
the Lebanon, crossing the Leontes by the natural bridge in
the direction of Damascus, and finally arriving at the lake
from the east, by way of Decapolis. This exceedingly circuitous route—from which anyone cognisant of the district
would, in any case, omit the Lebanon and the natural bridge—
is, according to him, not indicated in the narrative itself, and
would presuppose an independent tradition concerning the
route taken by Jesus. Wellhausen simplified matters by
considering Sidon to be a corruption of Bethsaida. Spitta[1]
thinks it possible that a Tyre-narrative was mixed with a
Bethsaida-narrative. But it has to be kept in mind that the
Gospel tradition is not likely to have contained independent
accounts of the routes taken by Jesus, but only narratives
of His activities connected with certain places, which needed

[1] *Streitfragen der Geschichte Jesu*, p. 47 *ff.*

to be supplemented by the journeys. In this case the journey taken into the neighbourhood of Tyre was merely related in connection with the fact that this incident shows Jesus holding converse with a heathen woman. The return to the lake was unavoidable, since the succeeding narrative of the feeding of the 4,000 once more has it as a background. The mention of Sidon on the return journey, without giving any further explanation for it, probably originated in Mk. because his source, like that of Mt., had the district of Tyre and Sidon as the scene of the narrative concerning the Phœnician woman. The mention of *both* cities was meant only to leave the actual spot where the incident occurred vague. Mk. took it literally, and, realising that the event could have happened only in *one* district, chose Tyre for the narrative and reserved Sidon as a place through which Jesus passed on the return journey. A heathen Phœnician woman could, of course, also have met Jesus in a Jewish district. The Phœnician region is the more natural, as Mt. assumes. So that we have indeed to think of a journey of Jesus to the north-west, the exact purpose of which we do not know. Melania saw in Sidon[1] the supposed house of the Phœnician woman turned into a church dedicated to Phocas. In the time of the Crusaders a stone, built into the apse of a church near Sidon, was shown as that upon which Jesus had been wont to sit and teach.[2] Near Tyre was built a church over a stone with a like significance.[3] It was also thought that Jesus had eaten and drunk at the spring of the ancient Oktogon *Ras el-'Ain*, south of Tyre.[4] So evidently it was generally assumed that Jesus had actually passed through the cities of Tyre and Sidon, not merely skirted them. Since Kedes was Tyrian at that time[5] and the brook of 'Oba south of it, which runs into the lake of Simchu, is to be taken as a Galilæan frontier, then the Tyrian domain could not have been far off. It could be reached easily in a day from the lake of Tiberias. Between Merom and Zephath there are many roads radiating towards the north and north-west which lead into this region, and it is most likely that Jesus took one of these. From the northern shore of the lake He would reach the plain near Merom—via

---

[1] *Acta Græca* vii. (not in the Latin text). *Vita Melaniæ junioris* xxvi. ; *Anal. Bolland*, 8.

[2] Phocas (Migne, *P.G.* cxxxiii., col. 932).

[3] Fretellus (Migne *P.L.* clv., col. 1041).

[4] Phocas (*ibid.*, col. 933).

[5] Jos., *Bell. Jud.* ii. 18, 1.

Zephath[1] (now Safed, a town high up and visible fron the whole
of the lake)—which plain, according to a Jewish legend,
R. Shimeon ben Jochai once caused, by prayer, to be covered
with golden dinars.[2] In taking this way Jesus would have
passed the then most important city of Upper Galilee, the
high-lying *Gosh Ḥalab* ; the Gishala of Josephus, now *ed-Jish*—
which, from the ruins of two synagogues which it possessed
(one only now remains), is marked out even to the present
day as a Jewish settlement,[3] and was supposed to have been
the native place of the family of St. Paul—as well as *Kefr
Beri'im*, which also had a Jewish population.[4] He would here
have entered the Tyrian district.

The nearest way to Tyre would have led through the
Tyrian Cana and by the supposed tomb of Hiram. But the
privacy, which Jesus sought for Himself and His disciples,
He undoubtedly found everywhere as soon as He left the
Jewish districts behind Him. That His miraculous power
was well known is best explained if He had left Galilee not
far behind. He might have made His return journey to the
lake, following the "waters of Merom" (Josh. xi. 5)—a stream
which gushes out at the foot of *Jebel Jermak*—all the way to
the spot where it enters the lake of Tiberias. But if He
desired to avoid as far as possible the territory of Antipas,
and aimed at reaching the eastern shore of the lake, it would
have been very convenient for Him to descend from Kedes
or Zephath into the low ground of the *Arḍ el-Khet*, cross the
Jordan by the " Wailing Ford," south of the " bridge of the
daughters of Jacob " (built in the Middle Ages), and continue
southward towards Bethsaida. Should He still have desired
privacy, the shore of the lake below Hippos would have
afforded it, and food would have been obtainable along the
lake road from Capernaum. The barely mentioned return
journey of Mt. xv. 29 is, in Mk. vii. 31, described as a going
to the sea of Galilee " through the midst of the district of

---

[1] In Josephus Σέπφ. According to p. R. hash. p. 58a, flame-signs were
given from there announcing the appearance of the New Moon. Josephus
fortified the city, *Bell. Jüd.* ii. 20, 6.

[2] p. Ber. 13d; Ex. R. lii (118b). The olives of Merom, Thekoa and Gosh
Chalab were famous, Tos. Shebi. vii. 15 ; Men. ix. 5.

[3] Concerning the Aramaic inscription of one of the synagogues, see *PJB*,
1914, p. 48; and Klein, *Jüd. Pal. Corp. Inscr.* ii. 7 ; *cf.* Kohl and Watzinger,
Antike Syn. in Galiläa, p. 89 *f.*, for the synagogue.

[4] Concerning the Hebrew inscriptions of its particularly well-preserved
synagogue, see Klein, *op. cit.* ii. 8. Concerning the synagogue buildings,
cf. Kohl and Watzsinger, *op. cit.*, p. 107 *f.*

Decapolis." If the narrator had thought not only of the arrival at the centre of the eastern shore, then one would have to suppose a very circuitous route. Since Mk. previously mentions Sidon, the most likely route would have been across the Jordan north of the Ḥuleh district, reaching the Golan from Cæsarea Philippi, then turning south from el-Ḳuneṭra, and joining the Damascus road at *Tell Tshochadar*, which passes to the lake through the Hippos district.[1] That was exactly the route taken by our Institute in 1907, with the view of reaching Hippos from Cæsarea Philippi. However, only the most northerly portion of Decapolis is crossed by such a route, and is by no means a " coming through the midst of the district of Decapolis." The phrase in Mk. is thus apparently geographically inexact, and should not be taken literally.

The healing of the deaf mute (Mk. vii. 32 *ff.*) is in no wise connected by the Evangelist with the " midst of Decapolis," but rather set along with the miraculous Feeding, according to viii. 10, by the shore of the lake ; as is shown even more clearly in Mt. xv. 29 *f*. It is therefore most likely that the " Ephphatha " of Jesus (correctly rendered into its original form *itpattaḥ* in the Evangelarium Hieros.) was uttered there.

To the equipment of a traveller,[2] as well as of a shepherd,[3] belonged at that period a staff and a wallet ; the former was not merely for walking, but also for defensive purposes ;[4] the wallet (*i.e.* a small leathern pouch which was bound round the waist) held a small provision of bread, which was indispensable on a long journey, and, therefore, not forbidden as a " burden " even on the Sabbath, if the object of the journey was of a religious character.[5]

Money was carried tied up in the corner of a garment, or in a purse bound round the waist,[6] or hidden in the folds of the wide waistband.[7] Such arrangements Jesus forbade to His disciples when travelling to spread the Gospel (Mt. x. 9-10 ; Mk. vi. 8 ; Lk. x. 4). This does not mean that it was forbidden on all occasions. In any case travellers in Palestine,

---

[1] Proksch, *PJB*, 1918, p. 23, makes the return journey more intelligible by inserting here the Transfiguration, but the probability is that the narrator merely connected the two incidents geographically.

[2] Jeb. xvi. 7 ; Ber. ix. 5.

[3] Tos. Yomtob iii. 17 ; Bab. mez. viii. 17 ; p. Shebi. 38e.

[4] R. hash. i. 9, therefore at the period of New Moon permitted to be carried even on Sabbath.

[5] *Ibid.*   [6] Ber. ix. 5.

[7] Nowadays wide sashes with a lining are used, which can be filled with money.

in those days as now, depended a good deal upon the hospitality of the villagers.　If there was no particular territorial or racial animosity felt for the stranger, and if the company was not too numerous, gratuitous supper and lodging could be reckoned on, and, on the next day, food for the continuation of the journey.　So a journey could be prolonged for some time without much expense, particularly if there was enough in the "money bag" (Jn. xii. 6; xiii. 29) to enable the traveller from time to time to buy bread in the towns at a baker's shop, to consume on the way or during the midday rest (Jn. iv. 8, 31).

The narratives concerning the Messianic self-disclosure, the announcement of the Passion, and the Transfiguration point to their having taken place in the northern part of the east-Jordan district, the scene of which, according to Mt. xvi. 13; Mk. viii. 27, was in the region of Cæsarea Philippi, while in Lk. ix. 10 the neighbourhood of Bethsaida alone is mentioned,[1] yet *v.* 28 suggests the possibility of a long journey from there to Cæsarea Philippi.　The place is connected with the content of the narratives in so far as they assume that Jesus was there entirely alone with His disciples.　The Markan "multitude" (viii. 34), distinguished from the disciples, is evidently a misunderstanding, for, according to Mt. xvi. 24 and Lk. ix. 23, it could only mean the "multitude" of the disciples themselves.　Privacy such as this Jesus found only at a considerable distance from the scene of His public activities.　Spitta[2] rightly emphasises the fact that the scene of Peter's confession and of the prediction of the Passion is set on the way to a goal mentioned; from which it follows that the district of Cæsarea Philippi is intended to be the scene of the succeeding narrative, namely, that of the Transfiguration, and thus the neighbourhood of Bethsaida lying along the route is not excluded as the place of the confession. The "high mountain" of Mt. xvii. 1 and Mk. ix. 2 must be sought at a greater distance, which the six or eight days of the interval between the events (Mt. xvii. 1; Mk. ix. 12; Lk. ix. 28) doubtless intended to imply, although it cannot mean that the mountain of the Transfiguration actually lay exactly that many days' journey off.　Neither the attempted artificial harmonisation of the eight days in Lk. with the six days in Mt. and Mk., nor the reference to the Jewish six days working week and the Roman week of eight working

[1] *Cf.* above, p. 166 *f.*　　　　[2] *Streitfragen*, p. 111.

days,[1] is satisfactory. We have here, as frequently happens, a round number ; in Mt.-Mk. twice three days, in Lk. one, differently phrased.[2] It would have been possible in six days to travel from Jerusalem to Cæsarea Philippi (168 kilometres) without any excessive haste ; the period suggests a time in which a considerable distance could be traversed, without its being an exactly measured amount.

If the narrators had had in mind a journey towards the southern frontier of Galilee, taking Tabor to be the mount of the Transfiguration, they would not have failed to mention that mountain ; but just as little did they think of Hermon or one of its spurs, for in that case Hermon would have been mentioned as the goal of Jesus' journey. Cæsarea Philippi (in Christian Palestinian Aramaic *Kesaron de-Philippos*) was a city well known among the Jews under the name *Kesariyon* (Little Cæsarea).[3] Tradition, however, has never connected the present Banias with any incident in the life of Jesus, although in the time of Eusebius a statue of Christ was venerated there, which the woman with the issue of blood (Mt. ix. 20), a native of this district, was supposed to have dedicated, and which the emperor Julian replaced by one of himself.[4] So there is absolutely no foundation for the purely fanciful connection of the rock, the gates of hell, and the Church, of Mt. xvi. 18, with the mountain-wall above the Jordan spring, the wide grotto that is found in it, and the temple of Pan before it.[5]

To the Jews the cave of Paneas with its supposedly bottomless pool was merely the source of the Jordan which gushes out below it,[6] being therefore one of the " fountains of the deep " of Gen. viii. 2.[7] Legend has it that Moses desired to enter Canaan by means of this subterranean cave, but God refused his request.[8] Nor did the heathen look upon this

---

[1] So Schmidt, *Der Rahmen der Geschichte Jesu*, p. 223 *f.*

[2] Mt. xii. 40; xv. 32; xxvi. 61; xxvii. 63; Lk. ii. 21 (Gen. xvii. 12); Acts ix. 33; xxv. 6 *f.*; Jn. xx. 26. Lk. also has 18 (xiii. 4, 11, 16), Jn. has 38 (v. 5). Mt. and Mk. never have an 8. For the Jewish use of the number 6, *cf.* *Pahad Yizhak* under *shesh*, *shishah* (twenty-six examples). In the same work there are nine examples of the number 8.

[3] Tos. Sukk. i. 9; Mech. on Ex. xvii. 24; Targ. Jer. ii Gen. xiv. 14; Dt. xxiv. 1 (Cod. Lips. and Cod. Vat.).

[4] Eusebius, *Hist. Eccl.* vii. 18; Sozomen, *Hist.* v. 21; Virgilius, Pitra, *Analecta Sacra* v., p. 119.

[5] Immish, *ZNW*, 1916, p. 18 *f.*

[6] Jos. *Ant.* xv. 10, 3; *Bell. Jud.* i. 21, 3; Tos. Bechor. xii. 4.

[7] Gen. R. xxxiii. (87a).

[8] Mech. on Ex. xvii. 14 (ed. Friedmann, 55b), *cf.* Sifre on Num. cxxxv. (51a).

dwelling of the god Pan as the abode of a sinister power of Hades, but rather as a cave inhabited by the protector of the flocks and herds on the mountains. Exuberant life comes from the spring and nature wears a smiling face, bestowing never-failing refreshment. This was (and still is) the impression that the Paneion left upon the beholder. Herod's temple to Augustus, which stood between the cave and the spring, the water of which was used for purification from the defile-ment caused by contact with a corpse (Para. viii. 11), must have also meant to Jesus only a defiling of a God-given stream and not a symbol of men rallying round the Lord's Anointed.

Unfortunately, we have no information whatsoever con-cerning the extent of the Cæsarea Philippi district. In any case, the plain sloping to the *Huleh* marsh below the city with, possibly, the *Hasbani* river as a western boundary belonged to it ; and it must be assumed that part of the eastern highland area belonged to the young city, so that *Jolan* in the north-west—as far, one would conjecture, as the volcanic range, where *Phiala* lake lies—to *Tell Abu en-Neda*, belonged to it, in which case the *Via Maris* from Jacob's bridge to el-Kunetra was its most probable southern frontier. From the northern shore of the lake of Tiberias one could reach this district from either side of the Jordan. On the one side one could take the *Via Maris* or the more northerly way from Capernaum ; while on the other, the road above the Jordan, which at that time connected Julias with Cæsarea Philippi, could be used. In view of the Lukan mention of Bethsaida this latter is most likely the way that Jesus took. At the Ford of " Jacob's daughters " the road must have divided and one of the branches have kept on in the lowland and continued northward, passing between the lake and the marsh at the foot of the heights. This road, although quite practicable, is no longer much in use, and I, personally, have not travelled along it. Another branch followed the *Via Maris* for some distance towards the north-east, and turned northward in the highlands. Continuing over *Skek*, it descended into Cæsarea by way of *Za'ora* (which I am inclined to identify with the *Mis'ar* of Ps. xlii. 7).[1] On the way there are no " high mountains," at any rate not south of the Ford of " Jacob's daughters," for here the high plateau, with its westerly incline, reaches out as far as the narrow dale of the Jordan, above

[1] *PJB*, 1909, p. 101 *ff*.; 1913, p. 56.

which the road runs ; not until the neighbourhood of the
Simchu lake[1] is reached does the lowland plain begin, which
is clearly distinguishable from the ascent to the plateau (about
900 metres) of northern *Jolan*. Walking in the plain below,
the traveller has on his right the mountainous projections of
the plateau with their intervening valleys. Above, only the
200-300 metres volcanoes situated on the high plateau could
be singled out as mountains of any remarkable height. Therefore the heights *Tell el-Aḥmar* (1,238 metres), *Tell Abu en-Neda*
(1,257 metres) and *Tell esh-Shecha* (1,294 metres) may dispute
among themselves for the honour of being the mount of
Transfiguration. These heights far overtop Mount Tabor
in the view of the whole of Galilee which lies spread out
to the west. For him who would pray they afford the desired undisturbed solitude. However, the absolute solitude
assumed for the event was perhaps the reason for the notion
that the mountain was unusually high (Mt. xvii. 7 ; Mk. ix. 2),
and so the Lukan tradition (ix. 28) is correct when it represents
the mount of the Transfiguration as being one of those heights
around the lake which Jesus had been wont at other times to
ascend for prayer and meditation (*cf. v.* 18). In that case,
the miracle of the feeding of the multitude, narrated at the
beginning of the section, took place, presumably, not far
from the lake (*vide* p. 166 *f.*). But as Luke also assumes a
longer sojourn in the desert district of the Golan, north of
Bethsaida, by mentioning an interval of eight days before the
Transfiguration took place (ix. 28) (which even goes beyond the
six days of Mt. and Mk.), he must also have assumed the mount
of Transfiguration to be situated at a considerable distance from
the lake. Jesus was conscious that He was sent only to the lost
sheep of the house of Israel (Mt. xv. 24). His journeys beyond
the then Jewish domain, although not avowedly missionary,
were not, as Bultmann thinks,[2] without purpose. On the
contrary, they have to be accepted as facts. It is not likely
that these journeys extended as far as the coast of the Mediterranean, or to the foot of the Hermon, and in any case they
did not go beyond the borders of the land of Israel. The

---

[1] See with regard to this ancient name of the basin, erroneously called
" Meron Lake," p. Shek. 50a ; Bab. b. 15a ; Kil. 32c. A second form is *jamma
shel-Sibke*, b. Bech. 55a ; Bab. b. 74b, corrupted to jamma shel-Suphne, Tos.
Bech. vii. 4 ; Sifre Dt. on xxxiii. 23. Josephus calls it the " Semochonian
lake," *Ant.* v. 5, 1.
[2] *Cf.* S. E. Aurelius in *Theologiska Studier tillägnade Erik Stave* (1922), and
in *Lunds Universitets årsskrift* (1923), vol. xix., No. 4.

northern frontier of the district which, according to Jewish
tradition, was occupied by the returned exiles, excludes Tyre
and leaves the Mediterranean coast in the neighbourhood of
'Akka ; but it runs from *Nahr el-Mefshuh* in the west in a
north-easterly direction through *Ja'ter* and *Ber'ashit* towards
Merj 'Ayun, and encloses Cæsarea Philippi in the north-east,
where " Upper Tarnegola above Kesariyon " probably refers
to the stronghold of Banias—now *Kul'at Namrud.*[1] *Kenat* is a
fixed point in the east, *i.e.* most likely *el-Kanawat* at the foot of
the *Jebel Hauran,* which city must be taken to have been that
which Josephus, Plinius, and Ptolemy considered as the most
eastern of the Decapolis, in comparison with which the insignificant *el-Kerak,* lying in the plain, cannot be taken seriously
into consideration,[2] especially as its flat environment would
not fit in with what Josephus describes as being " rocky and
impracticable ground."[3] Moreover, a Nabatæan inscription,
found in *Si'a* above *Kanawat,* shows that the Judæan sphere
spread, in fact, as far as the mountainous region of Hauran, for
an altar was dedicated in that place in the year 33 (or 23) to
" our Lord Philip " (*marana philippos*).[4] This points either to
the year A.D. 19-20 or to 29-30, which was in either case in
the time of Jesus.

Thus the whole region of the Decapolis undoubtedly belonged to the land of Israel, to which, from the point of view
of rabbinic legislation, the law concerning the Sabbatic year,
both as regards the cultivation of the soil and the consumption
of its fruits, was applicable, and which was considered to be
" pure." Jesus never went beyond its frontiers. Within
these frontiers we also may wander over the high lonely
plateau of the Golan, on which are but few settlements ; may
delight in its green meadows sown with speedwell, daisies,
and ranunculus ; gaze with wonder on its volcanoes forced
upward by subterranean energy ; look with amazement down
into its ravines in whose far depths brooks rush wildly, dispers-
ing their waters into unseen caverns. Gazing at one such water-
fall at *Wady Ehrer,* it is easy to understand how in early times
the Stygian waters were thought to be here, and the conviction reigned that here indeed were the gates of the underworld.[5]

---

[1] See Sifre Dt. li.; Tos. Shebi. iv. 11.
[2] See Brünnow, *Provincia Arabia,* iii., p. 107.
[3] *Bell. Jud.* i. 19, 2.   [4] Littman, *Princeton Univ. Arch. Exp.,* iv. a, p. 78.
[5] According to Photius (Migne, *P.G.* cii. 3, col. 1290), the Stygian waters
were in the plain of Arabia and were visited from Bostra. They are described
as waterfalls violently rushing down from all sides, from an enormous height

Nor can we forget that in this wild solitude light was cast for His disciples upon the riddle of the Person of Jesus, until He threw a veil over it again with the announcement of His approaching Death and Passion, the deep meaning of which was as yet incomprehensible to them. The " gates of the realm of Death " (*sheol*) in Mt. xvi. 18 is a term not to be understood in the sense of a special entrance into the underworld, but must rather be taken in the Old Testament sense (Isa. xxxviii. 10) : as the insatiable power of Death (Hab. ii. 5) from which nothing earthly can escape, unless God as Saviour intervenes (Hos. xiii. 14). What is true of Christ's Church is also true of Him.

---

into a deep ravine, only accessible by a winding way, 15 stadia long, cultivated below, but eventually becoming a narrow and dreadful cleft from which great height the water is flung violently down, so that it disperses in volumes of spray. All this applies to the 50 metres high fall of *Wady Ehrer* but not to either *Tell ash-Shihab* or *Zezun*. Therefore it was at the former that gifts were in olden time thrown into the water to the subterranean gods.

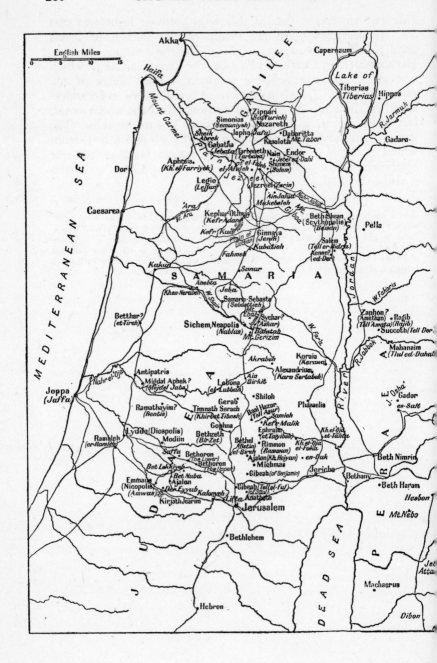

XII

FROM GALILEE TO JUDÆA

1. THE MIDDLE ROAD AND JACOB'S WELL

THERE are between Galilee and Judæa three roads to be taken into consideration in connection with the journeys of Jesus : a middle way, leading through the highlands of Samaria ; an eastern, through the Jordan valley ; and a western, along the coast. Josephus must have had these three in view when he designated the route through Samaria as the shortest between Galilee and Jerusalem, and one which could be traversed in three days.[1] Other reports, according to which one could reach the Temple in Jerusalem from Galilee in one day or one night, though of Palestinian origin, are legendary.[2] The middle road was used as a route from Jerusalem in the time of Josephus even to reach the lake of Tiberias, diverging in a north-easterly direction[3] at the plain of Jezreel over Dabaritta at the foot of Tabor. This road was also, according to Josephus, the route usually taken by the Galilæan pilgrims,[4] in spite of possible molestations at the hands of the Samaritans. Jesus must have been familiar with this route from His early years (Lk. ii. 41). There is in rabbinic literature also an instance of the route being taken by a Jew, who, passing by Mount Gerizim, " went up, in order to pray in Jerusalem."[5]

In Jn. iv. 4 this road between Judæa and Galilee is referred to as a matter of course. Its advantage must have consisted not merely in its shortness. It went all the time through inhabited localities, which meant for the traveller greater safety and easily obtained provisions and lodging for the night. On this road halts must also have been made in caravansaries at certain places for men and animals. On a good horse one could accomplish the journey between Japha, on the southern frontier of Galilee, and Jerusalem (200 kilo-

---

[1] *Vita* 52.   [2] p. Maas. sh. 56a.   [3] *Vita* 62.
[4] *Ant.* xx. 6, 1; *Bell. Jud.* ii. 12, 3.   [5] Gen. R. xxxii. (64a), lxxxi. (174a).

metres as the crow flies) easily in two days.　It is more convenient to do it in three days, in which it is a quite possible journey to do on foot.　As halting-places, *el-Lubban* at the frontier of Judæa and Samaria and *Ṣanur* north of *Sebaṣṭṭieh*, would divide the road into almost equal parts.　In any case it is necessary to spend the night in the Samaria district. St. Luke must have had this road in mind when he relates (Lk. ix. 51-56) that Jesus sent messengers to a village in Samaria to ask for a lodging (according to a custom which I also followed), in order to settle everything in advance and have a meal prepared.　The story of the ten lepers, one of whom was a Samaritan, whom Jesus met at the frontier between Samaria and Galilee (Lk. xvii. 11 *f.*), must also have been connected with this road.　And here it must first be determined where this frontier lay.　Josephus specifies Kesaloth as the southern border of Galilee, Ginaia as the northern frontier of Samaria,[1] and once considers the plain of Jezreel as belonging to Samaria,[2] and yet at another time he does not.[3]　The real frontier must have run through the middle of the plain, the territories of the border townships meeting therein.　If Nain, at the northern foot of the *Jebel ed-Daḥi*, was still Galilæan (p. 192), the frontier would have to be drawn at least in a line from the western foot of this mountain somewhere in the direction of *Sheikh Abrek*.　For what the towns Japha (*Jafa*), Gabatha (*Jebata*),[4] Simonias (*Semunieh*),[5] and Besara (*Beth Sharay*[6]) possessed in the plain naturally belonged to Galilee.　An outpost of Jewish Galilee was Tarbeneth, now *Ṭarbana*,[7] situated in the midst of the plain, south-south-west of Nazareth ; there, in the fourth century A.D., a Jewish elementary school existed.　Still further south was Kefr Othnay, of which more later.　Jezreel and Shunem must have been Galilæan at that time, in spite of the indications of Josephus referred to above, because in such cases he often thinks only of the routes on which the border places had their special practical significance.

The indication of place in Lk. is intended to make intelligible how it came about that at the entrance into a village, nine Jews and one Samaritan implored Jesus to heal them. But it is peculiar that the phrase " passed through the midst of

---

[1] *Bell. Jud.* iii. 3 ; i. 4.　　　　[2] *Bell. Jud.* ii. 12, 3.　　　　[3] *Ant.* xx. 6, 1.

[4] According to Jerome, *Onomasticum*, it lay at the frontier of the district of Diocæsarea (Zippori).

[5] According to Jos., *Vita* 24, at the frontier of Galilee.

[6] Jos., *Vita* 24.　　　　[7] p. Meg. 75b.

Samaria and Galilee " seems to suggest a journeying along the frontier, although it is not necessary to assume the exact frontier line. It is difficult to visualise the route along this frontier. It has been suggested that it was a road leading to the Jordan valley. In that case one might think first of the natural connection of the Jezreel plain with the Jordan valley *via* the valley of the *Nahr Jalud*, *i.e.* the line Jezreel-Beth Shean. But here, with the environs of the town of Jezreel at the frontier—which probably means 'Ain Jalud—the district of Scythopolis would have been reached, and in that case it could not be considered as a route along the Galilæan-Samaritan frontier. The same would be true if one took into consideration the next southern cross-road which runs from *Jenin*, over the Gilboa mountains, to the Jordan valley.

A " fairly ancient " tradition,[1] which, however, I can only trace to the fifteenth century,[2] is supposed to designate the north Samaritan frontier-place 'Ain Gannim—now *Jenin*, and in the time of Christ probably simply *Ginnin* or *Ginnaya*, " the gardens "[3]—as the village of the ten lepers. But it is not likely that a locality which somewhat later became notorious for its spiteful treatment of the Galilæan pilgrims[4] should have tolerated a company of nine Jewish lepers. Their presence points to the Galilæan district, or at least to a locality close to the real frontier. Small villages in the plain, like Tar-beneth, *el-'Afuleh*, *el-Fuleh*, also *Solem* (*Shunem*), may be taken into consideration, as in such places it was quite possible for Jewish lepers to have in their company a Samaritan fellow-sufferer and beggar. Locating the unknown village in the " great plain " probably gives us the key to the Lukan problem. This plain is neutral ground between Galilee and Samaria, which do not begin properly until the mountainous region on both sides is reached. If Jesus journeyed by it on His way to Jerusalem, it might be designated as a " passing through the midst of Samaria and Galilee," " passing " corresponding to the Hebrew and Aramaic 'abar, which may also mean merely " passing across." Syr. Cur. interpreted the Lukan place-datum in the sense that Jericho was the journey's goal.[5]

---

[1] Meistermann, *Guide*, p. 471.

[2] Rohricht and Meisner, *Reisebuch der Familie Ritter*, pp. 32, 83.

[3] In Josephus the readings are not uniform ; see Schlatter, *Die hebräischen Namen bei Josephus*, p. 86.

[4] *Ant.* xx. 6, 1 ; *Bell. Jud.* ii. 12, 3.

[5] Merx, *Die vier kanon. Evangelien nach ihren ältesten bekannten Texte*, on Lk. xvii. 11.

Luke himself scarcely had this in mind.   The Palestinian
Syriac translation most probably expresses the right meaning
of the Evangelist by rendering : " *bemis'at shamerayin ugelila* "
—" in the midst of Samaria and Galilee."   The Peshita translates : " *bet shameraye lagelila*," which evidently means : " in the
district of the Samaritans in the direction towards Galilee,"
but as the goal was Jerusalem, a journey through this district
towards Galilee is out of the question here.   K. L. Schmidt,[1]
however, does not consider it impossible that Luke did have
this extremely circuitous route in mind, and is even inclined
to locate the event as occurring nearer to Jerusalem, because
the quick return of the healed leper from the purification rite
of the priests excludes a long journey.   But the " being
cleansed "[2] means (as in Lk. iv. 27 ; v. 13 ; vii. 22) being
healed, and, according to Lk. xvii. 14, this had taken place
already on the way.   The most natural assumption is that the
grateful leper returned immediately, even before going to the
priest, being eager to give expression to his joy in praise to
God and gratitude for His messenger.   Not the completed
carrying out of the command of Jesus but the faithful obedience
was the condition of the cure.   In that case the meeting of
the lepers by Jesus in the neighbourhood intimated by Luke
is quite conceivable.   Just because it was a long distance
from the place where the healing was accomplished to Jerusalem, the return of the healed leper to Jesus is the more
explicable.   There was greater certainty of catching Him up
there and the postponement of the expression of gratitude
was the more burdensome.

The most direct route from Galilee to Jerusalem led from
Jenin through *Ḳubaṭieh* and *Jeba* to Nablus, without touching
Samaria-Sebaste, and from there to Jerusalem.   This road
must be assumed for Jn. iv. 4 *f.*, although the Judæan
baptising place whence Jesus came (iii. 23) must be thought
of as having been in the lower Jordan valley.   In that case
He might have gone up from Jericho to Bethel, or, at any
rate, have reached the district of Sichem directly from Phasael
through '*Aḳrabeh*.   If, in the first case, He spent the night
near *el-Lubban*, then Jacob's well at the foot of Gerizim was
a convenient place for the midday rest.   According to Jn.
iv. 35, Jesus was there four months before the harvest ; thus
presumably it was January, and mid-winter.

The city of Sychar (Pal. Ev. *Sukhar*) near which, according

---

[1] *Die Rahmen der Geschichte Jesu*, p. 261.   [2] *Cf.* 2 Kings v. 14.

to Jn. iv. 5, was the "parcel of ground that Jacob gave his son
Joseph," where the " deep " (v. 11) cistern called by his name
was situated, Jerome (and Syr. Sin.) identified with Sichem,
and, with Eusebius, differentiated from Neapolis, the Nablus
of the present day.   But the pilgrim of Bordeaux[1] knows of
Sechar, from which the Samaritan woman was supposed to
have come to Jacob's well, namely a place 1,000 steps
distant from Sichem, which he also considers as being outside
Neapolis, at the foot of Mount Gerizim.   The present-day
village 'Askar, with a well bearing the same name—about
$1\frac{1}{5}$ kilometres distant from Jacob's well—lying at the foot of
Mount Ebal, reminds us of the name of this Sechar, which,
however, seems to have been situated in close proximity to
Jacob's well.   This fits in with Askaroth,[2] which is situated
" above," in the domain of Ephraim, and with the well 'Ain
Sochar (or Sukkar),[3] the plain which, distinguished by its fine
early-ripening wheat, might well have been the plain of
Askar stretched out to the east in front of Ebal and Gerizim.
The Madaba map distinguishes by special pictures, left of the
church at Jacob's well, between Sichem (Συχεμ η κ[αι
Σικιμα]) and Sichar (Συχαρ ι[η] νυν Συχχωρα),[4] the latter
reminding one of the Jewish tradition, according to which
a deaf mute wanting to indicate 'An Sochar would put one
hand on his eye (Aram. 'ain) and the other on a lock (Aram.
sukkera).[5]   A site of undoubted age and importance, situated
between Ebal and Gerizim, and much nearer to Jacob's
well than 'Askar, is taken by Sellin, who began excavations
there in 1913, to be Sichem.[6]   If he is right, and if 'Askar
is identical with Sychar, then the larger might have been the
successor of the ruined, or at least quite decayed, Sichem,
until Flavia Neapolis, erected in A.D. 72, succeeded it.[7]   However, it is only the position of Jacob's well which seems
to have had an unbroken Church tradition, unchanged since
the time of the Bordeaux pilgrim, although the Samaritans
consider it as an invention of Christian priests !
    The three-aisled Crusaders' church now coming to light
again, under the high altar of which one can see the well in

---

[1] Geyer, *Itinera*, p. 20.
[2] Gen. R. xcviii. (214b), where the reading is Azkaroth.   In Midrash ha-gadol
on Gen. xlix. 25 it is Askaroth.   According to Epiphanius Hagiop. (Migne,
P.G. cxx., col. 210) Judas was from Skara.   [3] Men. x. 2.
[4] v. Jacoby, *Das geogr. Mosaic von Madaba*, p. 81.   [5] p. Shek. 48d.
[6] Sellin, *Wie wurde Sichem eine israelitische Stadt?* (1922), p. 14.
[7] See Haefeli, *Samaria und Peräa bei Flavius Josephus*, p. 52.

a crypt, succeeded a Byzantine cruciform building, with the
well in the centre, which Arculf saw and painted in the year
670,[1] and which perhaps was not the church which Jerome[2]
saw being erected.

In the neighbourhood of Jacob's well there are also
other wells. If the site investigated by Sellin be indeed ancient
Sichem, then the strongly flowing spring of the well *'Ain
Balaṭah*, which comes out below the town, and has sometimes
driven a mill, has the strongest claim to be considered the
town well. Near to it the plane-trees (*Platanus orientalis*,
which in Palestine grows only near water) must have stood,
which the pilgrim of Bordeaux saw not far from Jacob's
well, and which Jewish tradition[3] identified with the terebinth
near Sichem, under which Jacob hid the idols of his wives
(Gen. xxxv. 4). Besides the town well, *'Ain Defna* gushed
out at the north foot of Gerizim, and at the east foot of Ebal
the *'Ain 'Askar*. There must have been some special reason
why people went from that ancient site, also from *'Askar*,
to draw water from Jacob's well, and it may be assumed
that special powers were attached to a well supposed to have
been opened up by the patriarch. On the other hand, the
expression used by the Samaritan woman (Jn. iv. 11) suggests
that there was no other well near by.

The original design of this (seemingly superfluous) 32 metres
deep cistern would be reasonable if it was sunk by someone
who, possessing a piece of ground in the valley, above the
well surface, wished to have his own access to water. It was
called "Jacob's well" probably because it was assumed that
the ground round about was the piece of land which the
patriarch purchased (Josh. xxiv. 32).[4] It is, however, difficult
to harmonise this with the fact that the Bordeaux pilgrim saw
the tomb of Joseph, supposed to have been buried in this
ground, far from the well, namely at the foot of the descent
from Gerizim, *i.e.* near the present shrine of *Rijal el-'Amud*.[5]
Nor does the present position of Joseph's tomb, in greater
proximity to *'Askar*, fit in, because in either case a well would
have made the digging of the cistern superfluous.

[1] Geyer, *Itinera*, p. 270. According to Antoninus, the well was before the
altar railings. *Ibid.*, p. 162.

[2] Onomasticum, ed. Klostermann, p. 165.

[3] Gen. R. lxxxi. (174a); p. Ab. z. 44d, *cf.* Gen. R. xxxii. (64a).

[4] According to Gen. xxxiii. 18 (LXX) the estate was near Salem, which the
Madaba map as well as Eusebius consider as another name for Sichem.

[5] Geyer, *Itinera*, p. 20.

Apart from its position under Mount Gerizim, the peculiarity of Jacob's well is that it is near the crossing of the roads. To the east is the road running past the plain of *'Askar* from south to north—a straight continuation of that which comes from Jerusalem, to end at Beth Shean and the lake of Tiberias. Immediately south of the well runs, from west to east, the important route joining the Mediterranean and the Jordan valley, on which lay Neapolis, and from which the way led on towards western Galilee. Jacob's well has therefore the character of a road-cistern, which serves the convenience of travellers, and this, at any rate, fits in with the situation described in Jn. iv. Jesus came from the south, and turned off from the north road in order to bend round, at the foot of Gerizim, on the now " old " road to Nablus, into the valley between Gerizim and Ebal; because, according to Jn. iv. 43, His goal was the neighbourhood of Nazareth. The first water which He reached was Jacob's well, dear to every Jew. There He sat down for His midday rest, and sent the disciples to Sychar, which lay in a northerly direction, for bread, which He desired to eat with them by the well. In the meantime the Samaritan woman comes to draw water from the patriarch's well, and finds there " a well of water springing up into everlasting life."

When in the second century A.D. Rabbi Ishmael ben Jose passed here on the way to Jerusalem, a dialogue took place between him and a Samaritan, based on the contrast also mentioned in Jn. iv. 21 *f.*, but at the same time showing how our Lord's conception of true worship rises above the ideas of both contending parties. The Samaritan asks the Jew: " Where goest thou ? " The Jew answers : " I go up to worship in that Jerusalem." The Samaritan : " Would it not be better for thee to worship on this blessed mountain instead of that heap of rubbish ? " The Jew : " I say unto you : to whom can I liken you ? To a dog who is greedy of carrion, for ye know that idols are buried under your mountain, as it is written (Gen. xxxv. 4) : *and Jacob hid them* (under the terebinth) ; therefore are ye greedy of it (the mountain)."[1]

Further along on the way to Jerusalem was the place where the parents of Jesus, on the return journey from the feast of the Passover, hoped in vain to find their Son among the pilgrims

[1] Gen. R. lxxxi. (174a) ; p. Ab. z. 44d. A similar conversation is described in Gen. R. xxxii. (64a).

returning from Jerusalem. According to Lk. ii. 24, this happened a day's journey from Jerusalem, so that the parents required two days for the journey there and back, and only " after three days " (ii. 46), *i.e.* a day after their return, did they find Him in the Temple. In the time of the Crusaders, the *Mahomeria magna*, i.e. *el-Bireh*, 15 kilometres from Jerusalem, was thought to have been the place where the Boy Jesus was searched for by His parents, and where " close by a church dedicated to St. Mary stands a great cross of hewn stone, raised upon seven steps " (Theoderich). The ruins of the church are still preserved.[1] But this would have been at the most half a day's journey. The *khan*, which at that time served as a halting-place for caravans, may have occasioned the placing of the site here. A full day's travel was only accomplished by descending the other side of the height, by ancient Gerab,[2] not far from Shiloh, which lies away on the east ; coming down thus to the wide valley of *el-Lubban*, formerly *Lebona*, there, by a well, would be found a place of rest, which at present also is provided with a *khan*. Only 2 kilometres north from there, by *'Ain Berkit*, formerly perhaps *Enewat Borkay*,[3] where there is also a *khan* unused at present, was at that time the border between Judæa and Samaria. One can well understand that the Galilæans would have been eager to spend the night in Judæa. Then the proper place was by the well of *el-Lubban*, where the members of our Institute have often pitched their tents.

One of the most charming parts of Judæa would be traversed in taking this longer way to Jerusalem. Phocas in 1177 found the road from Sychar " all paved with stone, and, albeit the whole of that region is dry and waterless, yet it abounds with vineyards and trees." Especially lovely is the valley of the present so-called " Highwaymen Wells," with the remains of a mediæval *khan*. The road leads through hills well stocked with olive-trees, but eventually it must be abandoned, since the straight road has to turn southward to reach the height of the watershed, and then follows it practically the whole way.

---

[1] *Cf.* the charter of the Holy Sepulchre from the year 1164, Migne, *P.L.* clv., col. 1232 : " Birra, quæ a modernis Mahomeria major nuncupatur," this in contrast to the Parva Mahomeria in the district of Betsurieh (Bet Surik ?).

[2] Sanh. 103b, *cf.* PJB, 1912, p. 27.

[3] The place was called, according to Josephus, *Bell. Jud.* ii. 3, 5, *Anuath Borkeos* (Borkaios), which is perhaps to be traced back to *'Enewat* (or *Hanewat*) *Borkay*, *i.e.* the " wells " or " inns of Borkay."

Thus it comes into the immediate neighbourhood of Bethel, leaving it on the left, and very soon passes near to the former Ophra of Benjamin, which watches from its hill-peak by the mountain-chain of Baal Ḥazor. To this neighbourhood, moreover, belongs the city of *Ephraim* (Christian Palestinian *Efrem*), in the district near to the desert into which Jesus retired with the disciples from Bethany, according to Jn. xi. 54. Eusebius,[1] at the mention of this, points to the Judæan Ephron (Josh. xv. 9)—not found here at all—which Ephraim (Jerome : Ephræa), as a large village, is supposed to be situated 20 Roman miles north of Jerusalem. This estimate of the distance would lead as far as Shiloh, *i.e.* far beyond the district which Eusebius could reckon as belonging to Judæa. The Madaba map, which is closely related to the data of Eusebius, has, beyond Bethel (*i.e.* apparently in an eastern direction), first Remmon, then, immediately above it, " Ephron or Ephraia, whereunto the Lord went " ; at the right, close to it, " Ailaman, where the moon stood still over Naue " (*i.e.* Joshua the son of Nun). The latter is based on the identification, also found in Eusebius,[2] of Ajalon with Ailon (Jerome : Ajalon), now *Khirbet Ḥeiyan*, which lay 3 Roman miles east of Bethel. Remmon corresponds to the *Rammun* of the present day. Thus the Ephraim of the Gospel, identified by Eusebius with Ephron, is assumed to have been in the same neigh-bourhood farther north. This leads to *et-Ṭaiyibeh*, which lies 6½ kilometres north-east of Bethel (*Betin*), and therefore probably also to the village of Aiphraim (Jerome : Efraim), 5 miles east of Bethel, which Eusebius[3] considered to be the Benjaminite Aphra (Josh. xviii. 23). This *et-Ṭaiyibeh*—whose ancient name was, according to the villagers' own recollections, '*Afra*[4]—lies as the crow flies only 20 kilometres distant from Jerusalem, instead of the 30 kilometres which Eusebius would lead one to expect. But it must be taken into account that it does not lie on any north road from Jerusalem, where the distance could be measured, but 4 kilometres aside to the east of the great north road of the country, so that the notion of such a considerable distance is explainable. Had Eusebius have mentioned 16 miles instead of 20, he would have guessed correctly. To the neighbourhood of Bethel belongs also that Ephraim, through the desert of which Epiphanius in the fourth century ascended from Jericho to the highland, since

[1] *Onomasticum* 257, *cf.* 254.
[2] *Ibid.* 216.
[3] *Ibid.* 227.
[4] L. Einsler, *ZDPV*, 1894, p. 65.

he speaks of the "desert of Bethel and Ephraim."[1]   And
when in 2 Sam. xiii. 23 an Ephraim serves to define the position
of Baal Hazor, it also points to *eṭ-Ṭaiyibeh*, as Baal Hazor is
rightly identified with *el-'Aṣur* (1,011 metres), 3½ kilometres
north-east from it, on the highest summit in the neighbourhood.[2]   The Ephraim written with *aleph* is an error in spelling,
caused by the name of the tribe Ephraim, for *'Ephrayin*, which
the Masora (2 Chr. xiii. 19) demands instead of *'Ephron*.
Eṭ-Ṭaiyibeh, which stands on a dominating place on a hill
visible from afar, fits in with the district capital *Aphairema* of
1 Macc. xi. 34; *Ant*. xiii. 4, 9, bordering on Samaria, and
with the Ephraim near Bethel which was taken by Vespasian.[3]

Accordingly, there is no cogent reason why the Ephraim
of Jn. xi. 54 should be considered as other than *Ephron
eṭ-Ṭaiyibeh*.   In spite of this, Albright[4]—in the desire to find
an historical name for the ancient settlement of *Samieh*, in a
valley coming down from *Kefr Malik* east of *el-Aṣur* to the
Jordan plain, 24 kilometres from Jerusalem, which he
examined—distinguished this, as the Ephraim of the Fourth
Gospel and the Book of Samuel, from the Ophrah of Benjamin which is to be located in *eṭ-Ṭaiyibeh*.   As a proof of
this he points to the fact that Eusebius gives to Ephraim a
distance of 20 miles, of which *Samie* would also be 4 miles
short ; and to the colder position of the high-lying *eṭ-Ṭaiyibeh*,
which hardly fits in with a stay there at any time before Easter ;
and to the out-of-the-way and warmer position of *Samieh*,
which would appear to have been extraordinarily suitable for
Jesus' purpose.   The latter argument is correct, but it cannot
decide the question, for in that case one might also mention
other names.   One has rather to take the personal relationships of Jesus, or of one of the disciples, into consideration.
In any case this Ephraim, being situated off the main road,
would have been unsuitable for the determining of the position of Baal Hazor.   The Ephraim of 2 Sam. xiii. 23 would
have thus to be separated from it and be found towards
eṭ-Ṭaiyibeh.   Another identification suggested by Albright,
namely the Talmudic " Ephraim in a valley not far from
Michmas," is quite out of the question.   He evidently derived
this reference from Neubauer's *Géographie du Talmud*, p. 155,

---

[1] *Adv. Hær.* 133; Migne, *P.G.* cxli., col. 421.
[2] *PJB*, 1913, p. 15.   [3] *Bell. Jud.* iv. 9, 9.
[4] *Journal of the Pal. Or. Soc.*, iii., p. 36 f.; *Annual*, iv., p. 124 f.   See on the other
side Dalman, *PJB*, 1925, p. 31, note.

where, in fact, a Talmudical Afaraim is located in this neighbourhood, but in evident ignorance of its nature.   The second
best class of wheat, according to Mishna Menachot viii. 1,
comes from " Chapharayim in the plain."   The name is also
written in another passage in the Mishna (ix. 2) with 'Ain :
'Apharayim.   " Dost thou bring straw to 'Apharayim, pots
to Kephar Hanina, wool-shearers to Damascus, sorcerers to
Egypt ?" (*i.e.* taking " coal to Newcastle "),[1] it says in a
rabbinic text.   This 'Aphrarayim (Chapharayim) possessed
therefore a good and extensive wheat-land, because it lay in
a plain and not up on the highland.   This fits in with the
Chapharayim belonging to Issachar's tribe (Josh. xix. 19),
which Eusebius[2] identified with the village Aphraia, 6 miles
north of Legio, which most probably is the *Khirbet el-Farriyeh*,
at the edge of the plain of Jezreel, of the present day.   At
any rate, the narrow *Wady Samieh* has nothing to do with
" Chapharayim in the plain."   There is still less reason to
follow the reading in Codex D, which—probably because of
the Αφεραιμ of Josh. xix. 19a—transposed Ephraim to the
land of Samphurein, that is to say, Sepphoris.

Thus everything speaks for the identification of the
Ephraim in Jn. xi. 54 with *et-Taiyibeh*.   It had been Samaritan,
but it was added in the year 145 B.C. to Judæa.[3]   As, later, it
seems it was no longer the capital city of a district, it became a
part of the district of Gophna.   It was, in any case, a frontier-
place of the Judæa of the time of Jesus, outside the district
of Jerusalem.   The designation " near to the desert " is quite
consistent with the character of the neighbourhood, although
the prosperous *et-Taiyibeh* has well-cultivated land round
about it.   For only 3 kilometres farther east begins the slope
of the highland towards the Jordan valley, which can rightly
be described as " wilderness."   What can be seen from the
height of *et-Taiyibeh* (869 metres), moreover, is, as far as the
Dead Sea, the desert of Judah, on the northern edge of which
one finds oneself here.   A church, the ruins of which are still
in existence, was probably set up as a monument to the retire-
ment of Jesus there.   The bulk of the traffic of the land does
not affect *et-Taiyibeh*, since a deep valley in the south and a
range of hills in the north seclude the neighbourhood, and the
meridional road of the country had to pass farther to the west.
But this position made it also possible to go there and back,

---

[1] Gen. R. lxxxvi. 6 (186a) ; Men. 85a.   [2] *Onomasticum*, 223.
[3] 1 Macc. xi. 34 ; *Ant.* xiii. 4, 9.

from Bethany, by little-trodden ways, on the edge of the
desert, through Anathoth, Gibeah of Benjamin, Michmas, and
Rimmon, without attracting any attention.

Reaching the main road of the country from *eṭ-Ṭaiyibeh*, one
comes to the high ground of Bethel, and has here, for the
first time, a view of the Mount of Olives, which indicates
the neighbourhood of the capital. Yet only at *el-Bireh* did
the Galilæans, who came as pilgrims to the feast, enter
the actual environs of Jerusalem. Some of these pilgrims
would have turned off from the road to the nearly 893 metres
high peak of the *Ras eṭ-Ṭahuneh*, upon which, at the time of
the Latin Kingdom, a cross of hewn stone, raised upon seven
steps, was erected.[1] From here could be seen in the distance
the great towers which guarded the palace of Herod in Jerusalem, and a glimpse could be caught of the Mediterranean,
which had not been seen since the heights by Nazareth had
been left behind. Two and a half hours later the pilgrim
would stand on the " Lookers-out height " (*Safin*),[2] only
2 kilometres distant from Jerusalem, with the whole city
spread out before his eyes, and above all, the Temple, into the
area of which he now entered. His thoughts would be centred
on it. According to Josephus, it was here that the high
priest once greeted Alexander the Great, who arrived here
from Gaza.[3] The rabbinic law looked upon this spot (which
it calls " Hazzophim " in Hebrew) in its own way. The
fact that the sanctuary begins to be visible from here demands
that any sacrificial meat which has inadvertently been brought
from Jerusalem must be burnt here at the latest.[4] Coming
from the north, one must, from this point on, consider the
honour of the Temple when obeying a call of nature,[5] and
tear one's garments as a sign of sorrow over its destruction.[6]
Jesus was certainly not occupied with such thoughts, but a
grateful thanksgiving to His Father for the privilege of coming
again near to His earthly House was for Him as it were a
first joining in the hymns which, together with the smoke of
the festival-sacrifices, ascended to heaven before the altar of
the Temple.

---

[1] Theoderich, ed. Tobler, p. 92.
[2] In Josephus in the Aramaic form *Safin*, Greek σκοπός, *Ant.* xi. 8, 5 ; *Bell.*
Jud. ii, 19, 4, 6 ; v. 3, 2.
[3] *Ant.* xi. 8, 5. The rabbinic legend puts the meeting at Antipatris,
Megillat Taanith ix.
[4] Pes. 49a, *cf.* Tos. Pes. ii. 13.
[5] p. Ber. 14b, *cf.* Tos. Meg. iv. 26.   [6] p. M. K. 83b.

2. The Western Road and Emmaus

There is no ancient evidence that between Galilee and
Judæa the road was often taken through the Jordan valley,
but we know definitely that the route along the coast was
usual. "He who goes to Galilee from Judæa and reaches
Antipatris (the northern frontier of Judæa)—he who goes
from Galilee to Judæa and reaches Kefr Othnay (the southern
frontier of Galilee)," it says in Mishna Gittin vii. 7.[1] The
mention of Antipatris shows that the coast route is referred
to. Hence the road must have left Galilee, where the best
connection between Galilee and the coast was to be found.
A suitable place is *Wady 'Ara*,[2] in which case Kephar Othnay
will have been the native name for Legio;[3] this would tally
with the fact that it lay 16 Roman miles (23½ kilometres)
from Zipporin.[4] This is the connection given by the Bordeaux
pilgrim in his Itinerary for the route from Scythopolis over
Jezreel and Maximianopolis to Cæsarea, as Maximianopolis is
to be identified with *Lejjun*.[5] A connection more towards
the south and therefore shorter, which avoided Samaria proper,
ran through the plain of Dothan towards the coast, which
was reached by *Kakun*. In the fourteenth century the line
Zerin, Jenin, Fahmeh, Kakun, was a part of the way from
Damascus to Egypt;[6] but the Peutinger map already shows
the route Scythopolis, Caparcotani, Cæsarea, which must also
have run past this way, and even long before that the Ishmaelites
marched from Gilead to Egypt by this road (Gen. xxxvii. 25).[7]
The Caparcotani of the Peutinger map is, moreover, doubtless Kaparkotnei, considered by Ptolemy[8] as belonging to
Galilee, and will have been the above-mentioned Kephar
Othnay, the name of which might have been pronounced
Kaphar Gothnay, as Othni in 1 Chr. xxvi. 7 is Gothni in LXX A.
Kefr Kud, formerly suggested by Klein,[9] is out of the question,
because it lies away from the road, in the mountains, whilst
Kufr Adan at the edge of the plain, north-west of *Jenin*, fits
in every respect.[10] As *Adan* is the plural form of *Udn*, *Kefr*

---

[1] See also Gittin i. 5 ; Tos. Gittin vii. 9 ; Bech. vii. 3 ; Para x. 2.
[2] See Alt, *PJB*, 1914, p. 79 *f.* ; Dalman, *ibid.*, p. 34 *f.*
[3] So Quandt, *Chronologisch-geographische Beiträge*, ii. 1 (1873), p. 121.
[4] Tos. Bech. vii. 3.   [5] See Jerome on Zech. xii. 1 ; Thomson, *Loca Sancta*.
[6] P. Hartmann, *ZDMG*, 1910, pp. 689, 692 ; 1916, p. 489, 506.
[7] *Cf. PJB*, 1913, p. 42.   [8] *Geogr.* v. 16, 4.   [9] *Beiträge*, p. 29.
[10] So also Klein, *Pal. Studien* (Hebrew), ii., p. 67, who, however, has the place-
name erroneously with 'Ain.

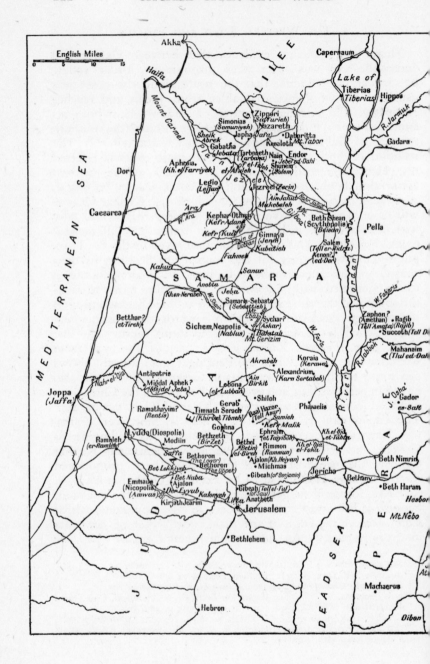

Udnay might easily have become *Kufr Adan*. Those who came from Galilee, as also those from Scythopolis, would then have turned off by *Mukebeleh* from the road leading directly southward, and may have gone up at *Kefr Adan* by the charming *Wady Ḥasan* to the plain of Dothan. That the distance from *Ṣaffurieh* is 30 kilometres, that is to say almost 20 Roman miles, instead of the 16 miles given by Jewish tradition (see above), may be disregarded. Also, from the neighbourhood of Nazareth, as well as by the way of the *Via Maris* from the lake of Tiberias, Kefr Othnay was easily reached. When Joseph and Mary returned with their Child from Egypt, and, avoiding Judæa, made Nazareth their home (Mt. ii. 21 *f.*), they must have reached Galilee by way of *Kefr Othnay*. But, approximately at the same time, Varus went, on the more northern military road, from Galilee to Jerusalem.[1] He came from Zippori and then encamped at the village 'Arus, which is to be located at *'Ara*, that dominated the road in the valley called after it.[2]

Then followed the road along the coastal plain which corresponded to the Biblical Sharon, a little distance from the highland, and was thus not a coast road. Since Josephus designates the district as " forest " (ὁ δρυμός),[3] and as Strabo (xvi. 27) speaks of the large forest between the Crocodile city and Joppa, the woodland—of which only the oak-wood *el-Rab*, east of Cæsarea, was still in existence before 1914, and has since quite disappeared[4]—must have been more extensive than in our day. The English map, even in 1880, marked a large wooded area behind the downs along the sea-coast, between *Wady el-Ḥauarit* and *Nahr el-'Oja*. Besides this " excellency of Sharon " (Isa. xxxv. 2), the white stars of its aromatic narcissus (*Narcissus Tazetta*, Arab. *Rundshus=Nurdshus*) were in bloom and lovely at the period of the winter solstice, which the Targum identifies with the *ḥabasselet* of the Sharon in Cant. ii. 1, and the Christian Palestinian with the *ḥabasselet* of Isa. xxxv. 1, while the meadow-saffron (*Colchicum lætum* and *C. Decaisnei*), which as the " harbinger

[1] *Ant.* xvii. 10, 9 ; *Bell. Jud.* ii. 5, 1.
[2] Haefeli, *Samaria und Peräa in Flavius Josephus*, p. 40 *f.*, looks in vain for it somewhere else. This *'Ara* lay in the direction of Samaria, which, however, Varus did not attack, if his purpose was to threaten the former from the mouth of the *Wady Shair* to the coastal plain.
[3] *Bell. Jud.* i. 13, 2 ; *PJB*, 1909, p. 15, 1914, p. 32, 1922-23, p. 15; *ZDPV*, p. 344.
[4] J. Löw, *Die Flora der Juden*, ii. (1924), p. 156 *f.*, thinks of the meadow-saffron. It is, however, uncertain whether originally *ḥabasselet* in Isa. xxxv. 1 and Cant. ii. 1 signified a special kind of flower at all.

of rain " clothes all the highlands at the conclusion of the summer, looks unassuming and modest, as befits the emblem of the Virgin.[1] If an autumn flower is wanted here, the sea-leek, with its metre-high blossoms, would be much more probable. But naturally the plain through which the road ran was, above all, arable land, which was terminated in the direction of the sea by the downs, and towards the south also by other elevations which shut out the sea from view.

After the road entered the coastal plain, it must have run at first southward in the territory of the city of Cæsarea. We have, however, no certain information concerning the extent of this area. According to Haefeli,[2] Antipatris lay at her southern boundary, and the Carmel formed the northern. But it is unlikely that Dor was included, and the rabbinic reference to the relation of Migdal Milcha and Kephar Saba to Cæsarea, referred to by Haefeli, speaks only of the extension of a legal precept and not of boundaries of a political district.[3] Nor can it be inferred from Acts xxiii. 23 (cf. 31 f.) that Antipatris was the frontier of the district of Cæsarea. It is, however, probable that the whole area of the *Wady el-Ḥauarit* belonged to Cæsarea. In any case, *Narbata*, to which the Jews, in A.D. 66, fled from Cæsarea, and the territory of which Testius caused then to be devastated, lay outside this district.[4] This Narbata, which so far has not been identified, is, most probably, *Khirbet en-Nerabeh* by *'Anebta*, in the north-west of Samaria. The Aramaic form of its name must be traced back to Neraba. Perhaps also the name *'Anebta* originated from *'Ain Narbata*. It is true, the distance given by Josephus does not fit in. His 60 stadia = 4,040 yards would have to be altered into 146 stadia. The distance given by him reaches only as far as the edge of the highland, and may in reality only refer to the western boundary of the territory of Narbata. According to Georgios Kedrenos,[5] the " plain under Parnas " and Narbathon (or Narbathos) were a part of the domain of Herod Antipas. By the former the Ḥuleh plain below Paneas[6] (= *Banias*) is meant, and the latter is the Narbatean toparchy, the Herodian possession of

---

[1] See *PJB*, 1922-23, p. 44 *f*.   [2] *Cäsarea am Meer*, p. 33.
[3] p. Dem. 22c, where it has to be read with Luncz (Jerusalem 1914) *kekesarin* instead of *bekesarin*.
[4] *Bell. Jud.* ii. 14, 5 ; xviii. 10.
[5] *Histor.* i. 333 ; Migne, *P.G.* cxxi., col. 369.
[6] Read Πανεαν instead of Παρναν. Hölscher, *Palästina in der pers. und hellenist. Zeit*, p. 80, thinks of Tabor or Hermon, but the text does not suggest it.

which would presuppose that the Jezreel plain was included in Galilee. In that case the whole route towards the coast ran through Jewish domain.

On the coastal plain Betthar (Betaro) was later an important road-station,[1] which is perhaps to be considered equal to *et-Ṭireh*. A second station of military importance was Antipatris, lying at the border of Judæa and founded by Herod,[2] at the wells of the *Oja* stream. An earlier Greek name for it must have been Pegai ("Wells"), as Alt has shown.[3] To this belongs the Jewish name Pega, which denotes a place where grain was cultivated,[4] as also the designation "water of Pega" for a stream whose water—because it issues from a swamp—could not be used for ritual purifications.[5] In contrast to Josephus, according to whom Antipatris was originally called Kephar Saba,[6] Albright[7] considers Aphek to have been its ancient name, differentiating this Aphek from the "Tower of Aphekos" (Migdal Aphek) of Josephus,[8] which Guthe[9] and I[10] located in the nearby *Mejdel Jaba*.

For the ascent towards Jerusalem Nature offered roads where a ridge between two valleys ran up in a gentle elevation to the watershed of the highland. The first possibility of this kind was opposite Antipatris, to the east. This road went through the fortified capital city of the district of Tamna[11] (Timnath Serach), now *Khirbet Tibneh*,[12] Bethzeth, now and even at the time of Josephus, *Bir Zet*,[13] and the capital of the district Gophna, where the north-by-south road was reached. This way Titus once traversed and this route later became a Roman road marked by mile-stones.[14] A little south from this road,

---

[1] *Itinerarium Antonini* 150 ; the Bordeaux pilgrim, Geyer, p. 25.

[2] *Ant.* xiii. 15, 1 ; *Bell. Jud.* i. 21, 8.

[3] *ZDPV*, 1922, p. 220 *f.* [4] Tos. Terum. i. 15.

[5] Para viii. 10. Together with the river Pega a second river of the same character is mentioned, called Qarmeyon. If it were Karseyon, the Crocodile-river would suit it, which Ptolemy V. (xv. 5 ; xvi. 2) mentions as Chorseos between Dora and Cæsarea, *cf. Khirbet el-Charashi* at the upper reaches of that river, Graf v. Mulinen, *Beiträge zur Kenntnis des Karmels*, p. 326. S. Klein, *Die Küstenstrasse Palestinas*, p. 6, locates Pega at Wadi Feddshas in Galilee, but there is no brook there.

[6] *Ant.* xiii. 15, 1 ; *cf.* xvi. 5, 2.

[7] *Bulletin* xi. 6.

[8] *Ant.* xiii. 15, 1 ; *cf.* xvi. 5, 2. [9] *Bulletin* xi. 5, 6 *f.*

[10] *Bell. Jud.* ii. 19, 1. [11] *MuN des DPV*, 1911, p. 33 *f.*

[12] *PJB*, 1912, p. 21. To its district Arimathæa certainly belonged ; it ruled over its own district when it was detached from Samaria to form part of Judæa (1 Macc. xi. 34 ; *Ant.* xiii. 4, 9).

[13] *PJB*, 1914, p. 29.

[14] *Ant.* xii. 10, 2; *cf. PJB*, 1914, p. 29 *f.*; Thomsen, *ZDPV*, 1913, p. 76.

and still in the hilly district below the highland proper, lay the native place of Joseph of Arimathæa (Mt. xxvii. 57 ; Mk. xv. 43 ; Lk. xxiii. 51 ; Jn. xix. 38), the present *Rentis* (Jerome *Remphtis*), once most probably the Ramathayim which was the home of Samuel and which the Madaba map marks as Αρμαθεμ η Αρι-μαθε(α), north of Jerusalem.[1] Thus that wealthy disciple had his estate there—perhaps as the representative of the whole neighbourhood—although his sepulchre shows that he trans-ferred his residence to Jerusalem.

The next southern way was the famous road of Bethhoron, starting from Lydda,[2] which in the hill country passed Modiin (Modiith), the native place of the Maccabees and their ancestral burying-place,[3] and came out below Gibeah of Saul (*Tell el-Ful*) into the road leading from Neapolis to Jerusalem. Here Cestius went in A.D. 66 from Lydda to Jerusalem,[4] and the importance of the road can also be seen from the fact that a Jewish scribe illustrated, from the district traversed, the sphere of three forms of legislation in connection with the law of the Sabbatic year.[5] Above Bethhoron the country is considered as royal highland (p. 53). The land below can be divided into three stages : from Bethhoron to Emmaus, from Emmaus to Lod-Lydda, and from there to the sea. Then followed the ascent over *Bet Lekki-yeh* and *el-Ikbebeh*[6] and, finally, the way over Em-maus, the later Nicopolis, now *Amwas*, where at Kirjath Jearim and at *Kalonyeh*, deep valleys had to be crossed.[7] This latter unmade, and hence a less convenient, road was, however—at least since Roman times—used by preference. Varus, coming from the north, marched up it, after passing Sappho=Saffa at the Lower Bethhoron, from Emmaus to Jerusalem.[8] The Bordeaux pilgrim came from Cæsarea over Antipatris, Lydda, and Nico-polis (Emmaus) to Jerusalem,[9] Theodosius reached the same goal from Joppa over Lydda, Emmaus-Nicopolis.[10] Even the Crusaders used this route.[11] This way, together with the next northerly route, is also presupposed when the points are named at which Hadrian set watches in order to capture the

---

[1] See *PJB*, 1913, p. 38.
[2] See concerning it *PJB*, 1913, 21 *f.*, and Gelgarte, *PJB*, 1918, p. 73 *f.*
[3] *PJB*, 1912, p. 19 *f.*
[4] *Bell. Jud.* ii. 19, 1.
[5] Pal. Shebi. 38d.
[6] *PJB*, 1916, p. 121.
[7] *PJB*, 1913, 1914, 1921.
[8] *Ant.* xvii. 10, 9 ; *Bell. Jud.* ii. 5, 1.
[9] Geyer, p. 25. Concerning St. Paula, see below, p. 231.
[10] *Ibid.*, p. 239. Also the monk Bernhard travelled through Lydda and Emmaus (Tobler, *Descr. T. S.*, p. 91).
[11] See *PJB*, 1913, p. 37; 1918, p. 35 *f.*

fugitive Jews.[1] Bethlehem (see above, p. 25), as well as Chammetha is mentioned there, which must be identified with Emmaus, and Kephar Lekitaya, which can refer only to the present *Lekkiyeh*.

The most northerly road is the one which St. Paul must have used on his journeys between Cæsarea and Jerusalem (Acts ix. 30 ; xxi. 15 ; xxiii. 31). The other roads lack New Testament attestation, unless the narrative of the appearance of the Risen Jesus on the way to Emmaus is to be placed here (Lk. xxiv. 13-31). It is not impossible that Cleopas, who according to Hegesippus (Euseb., *Hist. Eccl.* iii. 11) was Joseph's brother, and his companion were then on the way to Galilee ; the narrative itself (*vv.* 13, 28) indicates Emmaus as the goal, not as the first stage of a longer journey. Thus it may indeed have been the native place of Cleopas, as assumed by Church tradition. In bitter disappointment he had left the company of Jesus' disciples and was on the way to his home in Emmaus, when Jesus met him.

Since the fifteenth century the Franciscans have shown[2] this Emmaus as being close to *el-Ikbebeh*, $11\frac{1}{2}$ kilometres from Jerusalem, *i.e.* at a distance corresponding to the 60 stadia of the perhaps original Lukan text.[3] There, in 1878, they found westward below the village, to the left of the old road, the ruins of a three-aisled Crusaders' church, and in the front part of its north aisle the remains of a small house, which they believed to have been the sanctuary proper of the church, namely the house of Cleopas.[4] Meistermann[5] argues for the Byzantine origin of the original church and for the genuineness of the claim that the house was enclosed there from the first— which is not likely. The church only proves that in the time of the Crusaders this place, which could not otherwise have justified the construction of such a large church, was given a Biblical significance. It must have been taken for Emmaus ; although the Crusaders, when they came to Jerusalem in 1096, considered Nicopolis to be Emmaus (William of Tyrus[6]).

[1] Lam. R. i. 16 (34b).

[2] Schiffers, *Amwäs, das Emmaus des heiligen Lukas*, p. 184 *f.*, collects the often confused witnesses of the pilgrims.

[3] Sin. already has 160, agreeing with Eusebius and Jerome, and considered as genuine by Abel, *RB*, 1925, p. 347 *f.*

[4] *Cf.* Buselli, *Illustrazione del santuario d'Emmaus* (1888), p. 282.

[5] *Deux Questions d'Archéologie Palestinienne*, p. 116 ; *Durchs Heilige Land*, p. 278 ; *Guide* (1923), p. 397.

[6] *PJB*, 1913, p. 37 ; 1918, p. 36, whilst Lauffs, *ZDPV*, 1915, p. 286, tries to make it probable that Kirjath Jearim is meant.

Probably the distance of 60 stadia was decisive. The direction
in which the Emmaus of the older tradition was situated was
retained, and what was considered to be the right distance was
measured by the road, often used by them, running from the
neighbourhood of Emmaus to Jerusalem—over *Bet Nuba* and
by *Wady el-Brej*,[1] which latter is reached shortly before *el-
Iḳbebeh*, the head of the highland. Thus did the idea of this
Emmaus originate, whose beautiful church and the wonderful
garden of the hospice of the " Verein vom Heiligen Lande,"
planted, by German diligence, in a wilderness, with its rustling
pines, oaks, and arbutus-trees, form a charming walk from
Jerusalem, where it is pleasant to rest and meditate on the
Risen Christ who broke the bread and distributed it among
the disciples. Yet the name Emmaus (=Hamma[2]), which
elsewhere assumes warm wells, does not quite fit in here. For
el-Iḳbebeh has no wells, and the well *'Ain el-'Adshab*, which
emerges far away below the village on the slope, does not
justify that designation.

The older tradition, first attested by Eusebius, found Emmaus
twice as far from Jerusalem, where, without doubt, an old
Emmaus lay, and where, even to-day, the name *'Amwas* is
preserved. Virgilius[3] leads the way from Jerusalem through
Sinoda—the place where the ark of the covenant rested—to
'Amaus, " which is now called Neapolis." Sinoda, by the
way, is to be corrected—according to Theodosius, who gives
the same direction—into Silona (=Shiloh), and Neapolis into
Nicopolis, and Petrus Diaconus makes it clear that what is here
meant by Shiloh is Kirjath Jearim, *i.e.* the present *el-Ḳeriyeh*.[4]
There the ark of the covenant remained for a time before
David brought it to Jerusalem (1 Sam. vii. 1 ; 2 Sam. vi. 2).
Epiphanius Hagiopolita reached Emmaus from Bethlehem by
the " Mount Carmel, of the Forerunner," *i.e.* *'Ain Karim*, and
at a distance of eight miles the other side of Emmaus he found
Ramble (=*er-Ramleh*) and Diospolis=(Lydda[5]). Thus it is
sufficiently established that it was *'Amwas* on the way to
er-Rameh which ancient tradition identified with the Lukan

---

[1] *PJB*, 1911, p. 12 ; 1914, p. 21.

[2] Jewish literature also uses the semi-Greek form of the name (so also the
Pal. Evang. Cod. B.C.), while in regard to the thermæ of Tiberias and Gedara it
uses the Semitic form.

[3] Pitra, *Analecta Sacra*, v., p. 119.

[4] Only later was the height of the Samuel tomb considered to have been
Shiloh. *Cf.* Lauff, *ZDPV*, 1915, p. 249.

[5] Migne, *P.G.* cxx., col. 264.

Emmaus ; in fact, it knew of no other place.[1]   This Emmaus—
having had a much frequented cattle market[2]—was considered
to be a place of good water and pleasant situation,[3] lying as it
did at the transition from mountains to hills.[4]   The families
of the Temple flute-players had their home here.[5]   But its
position at a junction of important roads lent it a more far-
reaching significance, for which reason it came into prominence
at about the time of the Maccabees,[6] and also became the
chief centre of a district.[7]   At this place alone was an Emmaus
known at a later date in the neighbourhood of Jerusalem.
The tepid water of two cisterns at this place,[8] one of which
was considered to have miraculous powers because Jesus was
supposed to have washed His feet in it,[9] confirms, at the same
time, the justification of its old name.   So it is best to follow
the tradition and disregard the Lukan estimate of distance.
In fact Luke himself suggests this conclusion, in so far as he
tells that the goal of the journey was only reached in the evening,
and thus presupposed a full day's journey.   In that case the
60 stadia in St. Luke are not based on an exact knowledge of
the position of Emmaus, but merely on the supposition that
because the two disciples went there and back on the same day,
only the distance of a comfortable half day's journey was to be
considered.   The distance from Modiin to Jerusalem was
reckoned a long way which, when necessary, could be managed
in the time from midday onward ;[10] it is 27 kilometres, *i.e.*
140 stadia, and once has been measured as 15 miles ($22\frac{1}{2}$ kilometres[11]).   The way to Lydda was a full day's journey,[12] *i.e.*
37 kilometres (=192 stadia).   But there was also talk of a
twelve-hour day's march of 30 miles (=45 kilometres), to which
might also be added 5 miles for the twilight before sunrise
and after sunset.[13]   Emmaus-Nicopolis lay only 23 kilometres
(*i.e.* about 15 miles or 120 stadia) from Jerusalem, and this
must have made the return journey on the same day rather
difficult by reason of its distance, but not impossible.   One
can reach Emmaus from Jerusalem in five hours, and Abel
(*RB*, 1925, p. 366) may be right in his assumption that

---

[1] Also assumed by the Palestinian Evangelarium with 160 stadia.
[2] Chull. 91b.   [3] Eccl. R. vii. 7, 103a.   [4] p. Shebi. 38d.
[5] Tos. Erach. i. 15.
[6] 1 Macc. iii. 40 ; ix. 50; *cf. PJB*, 1914, p. 20.
[7] *Bell. Jud.* ii. 20, 4 ; iii. 3, 5.   It only received the name Nicopolis about
A.D. 200 ; *cf.* Schürer, *Geschichte*, i., p. 641.
[8] *PJB*, 1914, p. 20.
[9] Sozomen, *Hist. Eccl.* v. 21 ; Willibald (Tobler, *Descr. T. S.*, p. 69).
[10] Pes. ix. 2.   [11] Pes. 93b.   [12] Maas. sh. v. 2.   [13] Pes. 93b.

the 160 stadia are brought into the Lukan narrative only as an equivalent for a five-hour journey. That at the arrival of the disciples " the day was far spent " (Lk. xxiv. 29), need not mean the time of sunset. As early as the middle of the afternoon the Arab says : " *rabat esh-shems*," " the sun has set." Soon after their arrival the travellers would have refreshed themselves with an early supper. If they started on their return journey at 7 o'clock, they would reach Jerusalem at midnight, in the clear light of the Passover full-moon. Hesychius[1] has conceived this differently. At the eighth or ninth hour the disciples left Emmaus, because the sun begins to set at the seventh hour (1 o'clock in the afternoon). Therefore the journey there and back was quite possible in one day.

In order to find a much shorter road for the disciples, some have located Emmaus in *Kalonyeh*, which lies beautifully on the slope above its valley covered with olive-trees, only 6½ kilometres from Jerusalem; appealing to the fact that, according to Josephus,[2] Vespasian allotted a place called Ammaus, 30 stadia from Jerusalem, to the veterans as a settlement, which fits in with this *Kalonyeh*. But the reading *Amassada* in the Latin translation shows that various similarities of sound exercised an influence on the name here. The original name must have been Ammosa ; for doubtless it refers to the Benjaminite Hammoza of Josh. xviii. 26, which, according to Mishna Sukk. iv. 5, was the nearest place to Jerusalem where willows grew, and which according to the Palestinian Talmud was called later *Kelonia*,[3] and must thus have been a Roman colony. Had this been the Emmaus of St. Luke, it would mean not only that the name is incorrectly written there, but that the distance of 60 stadia would have to be reduced to half.

The way from Jerusalem to Emmaus-Nicopolis, as far as *Kirjath Jearim* (=el-*Kerieh*), with the exception of the bit between *Lifta* and *Kalonyeh*, where the old road ran somewhat more to the south, is in general the same as the modern road to Jaffa. Yet this road, like its first practicable predecessor and the road arrangements of Arab and Roman times, has lost all trace of its original shape. At the other side of Kirjath Jearim the road divided itself into two. Through the *Wady 'Ali* one branch went up into the hill and passed one kilometre south of Emmaus. The other, which became a Roman road in the

---

[1] *Quæstio* 1445, Migne, *P.G.* xciii.   [2] *Bell. Jud.* vii. 6, 6.
[3] p. Sukk. 54b. In b. Sukka 45a it says that Moza was " a kind of a colony."

second century,[1] was used for the ascent to a height north of *Wady 'Ali* and ran past Ajalon,[2] or possibly also directly over *Der Eyyub*, to Emmaus. Both ways certainly existed in ancient times, and were scarcely different in length and convenience. We cannot know for certain which way the two disciples took, or where Jesus met them.

In Emmaus, the church, the ruins of which still exist,[3] was evidently meant to commemorate the place where the disciples entered in; although its position outside the old town would suit better the spot where Jesus desired to go on, while His companions turned to the town. To a building with three apses of large stones a smaller building was later joined, to which the old middle apse served as choir. Meistermann[4] considers the older building to be a Roman bath into which a church was put in the Byzantine period. But it is much more likely that a larger Byzantine church was rebuilt in the time of the Crusade on a smaller scale. Perhaps the remains of the old building were not removed at the rebuilding, because it was thought that the house of Cleopas had become the first church here.[5] Only in later times, after Emmaus was identified with *el-Iḳbebe*, was the commemoration of the "seven Maccabæan brothers," previously attached to another place, transferred to this church. Even to-day the Emmaus tradition guarded by the Franciscans in *el-Iḳbebe* (so easily approached from Jerusalem) puts the *genuine* Emmaus into the shade. But its old church, in the choir of which the purple anemones blossom in the spring, is, just in its abandonment, a solemn spot, commemorating the last walk of the Risen One, and the house in which He broke bread with His disciples as He had done before His death.

That Jesus was then recognised *by* the breaking of bread is not stated in Lk. xxiv. 31, 35, but only that the recognition occurred at that moment. Yet the manner in which He did it might have contributed to the recognition. The essential

[1] That also a roundabout way from Jerusalem to Emmaus by the Bethhoron road was sometimes taken, is seen in p. Sheb. 38d, where the route Bethhoron, Emmaus, Lydda, is assumed, and also in Eusebius and Jerome in the *Onomasticum*, according to which both Bethhorons lay on the way to Nicopolis. This roundabout way was also taken by St. Paula from Nicopolis to Jerusalem (Tobler, *Palestinæ Descriptiones*, p. 14).

[2] At present the road goes over Ajalon, and Jerome also says in the *Onomasticum* that it lay by Nicopolis at the second stone in the direction of Ælia.

[3] *Cf.* Riemer, *PJB*, 1918, p. 41.

[4] *Deux Questions*, p. 52.

[5] Already, as it seems, Jerome in *Peregrinatio Paulæ*, then Willibald (Tobler, *Descr. T. S.*, p. 69).

element in the act of the " breaking of bread " was the benediction of God the Creator over the bread and the distribution
of it to all those participating in the meal. Before the benediction, he who says it " takes " the bread, seemingly holding
it in his hand during the benediction, though to-day the Jews
spread out both hands over it. When the benediction is re-
sponded to with " Amen," the one saying the benediction breaks
a piece of the bread lying before him for each of the participants
and puts it before each one. Then he first eats and the others
follow suit. It was a sign of politeness when Rab distributed
the bread with the right hand and then ate it using the left.
Whether the bread was " broken " or torn depended upon the
kind of bread; the Aramaic (also the Christian Palestinian)
expression *kesa* is neutral on this point. In the East, where
there are no thick loaves, the use of the knife is superfluous;
moreover, to the Orientals the application of a knife for the
cutting of bread would have meant a violation of God's gift.
When I asked why, the answer was: " *debihat elchubz mush
halal*," " The slaughtering of bread is not allowed." In the
Greek Church alone is the Host " cut," that is " slaughtered,"
for symbolic reasons.

The Jewish custom of " grace " before a meal is based on
the conception that the enjoyment of anything in this world
without thanking God for it is an embezzlement of God's
property. The distribution of the bread, at which each
participant must receive, if possible, a piece of the size of an
olive, or at least of a grain of coarse wheaten flour,[1] presupposes the participation of all who are present at the meal,
not in the loaf over which the benediction was said as such,
as if it were " blessed," but all participate in the benediction
itself, which each one would need otherwise to say for himself;
it is thus a participation in a religious duty. The same is
true of the benediction of the " Creator of the fruit of the vine,"
which has to be spoken before every drinking of wine, and
which Jesus will not have omitted at Emmaus, unless the wine
(always mixed with water) was not available. Our Lord at the
breaking of bread and drinking of wine, which was usual at every
meal, was not merely saying the benediction in order to observe
a legal duty, but as the Master who now invites His own to
share His communion with the Father. His eyes therefore were
turned to heaven at the benediction (Mt. xiv. 19; Mk. vi. 41).[2]

[1] Cf. *Jesus-Jeshua*, pp. 133-138.
[2] *Ibid.*, pp. 147-155. [The translation is here shortened, since a fuller
discussion is available in *Jesus-Jeshua*.—TRANSLATOR.]

3. THE EASTERN ROAD AND PERÆA

To-day no one would go to Jerusalem from the lake of Tiberias by way of the Jordan valley as far as Jericho, but would rather turn off at *Beisan* in a south-westerly direction, and at Jacob's well enter the great north-to-south road of the highland. In *Merj 'Ayun*, at the northern frontier of Palestine, a man was pointed out to me in the year 1900, who had done the journey on foot from there to Jerusalem and back in seven days, and on the return journey even visited Jaffa. He walked *via* Tiberias and *Beisan*, left the Jordan valley there and came *via* Nablus to Jerusalem. But this was an unusual achievement. Normally it would take three days from Tiberias to Jerusalem.

Only special reasons could at the present time induce anyone to walk from Galilee along the whole of the Jordan valley and thus prolong the journey by a day. In the summer in any case one would avoid the valley because of the heat ; in winter and early spring alone are its warm climate and lack of rain attractive, and sleeping in the open would be possible. At all seasons the Jordan valley might be a desirable road to persons not wishing to be seen in the towns, for fear of the government or of vendetta. But it would be otherwise if there were a special goal in view, or if the end of the journey was the southern Jordan valley. Anyone wanting to go from the lake of Tiberias to Jericho would naturally walk along the Jordan valley. Were Nazareth the starting-point, Jericho would be reached quickest if the road, well known to us, was used, running *via* Endor and Beth Shean, to the Jordan valley, this being followed as far as Jericho. The three days' journey from the Baptism-place in Judæa to Cana (Jn. ii. 1) is hardly based on exact knowledge of the distance, but rather on the fact that it takes three days to come from Jerusalem to Galilee (p. 209). But if it is to be understood literally, one would have to assume that the road just mentioned was taken. In that case, one may think of Koraia by the *Wady Far'a* and of Beth Shean as night-quarters, which would have meant a march of 37 kilometres a day, a rate not at all excessive for a vigorous walker.

On the well-irrigated plain of Beth-Shean[1] Jesus would pass by the *Tell er-Ridra*, which, according to Greek tradition,[2] will have been the Salem near which John the Baptist baptised,

[1] *Cf*. Gen. R. xcviii. (214b), where *Bet ha-Shakay* is to be read.
[2] Eusebius, *Ætheria* (Geyer, p. 56), the Madaba map.

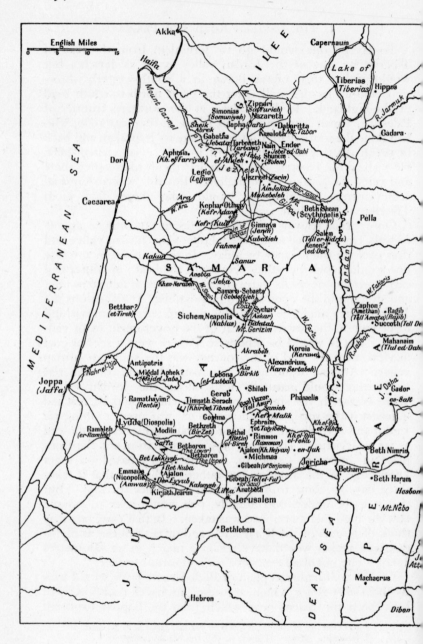

namely at the well-watered Ænon (Jn. iii. 23). But it was
not the well Salem itself but the five wells of *ed-Der* with their
brooks south of it that must have been the place of the Baptism,[1]
which was thus on an important thoroughfare and easy of access
from Judæa as well as from Galilee, but, being in the domain
of Scythopolis, was outside the jurisdiction of the powers
dominating those parts. South of Koraia (now *Ķerawa*) the
road crossed near high-lying Alexandrium (now *Ķarn Sartabeh*),
the boundary of Judæa,[2] and thus entered into a land filled
with memories of the last Hasmonean princes and the Herodian
family. In that case it was not *Phasælis* itself, lying away from
the road, with its palm-grove reaching to the road, which was a
convenient halting-place, but *Archelais* (also marked in the
Madaba map) with its palm-plantation—now non-existent—
which was a successful speculation of Archelaus.[3] Since
about A.D. 10 Herod's widow Livia was the owner of both
lucrative domains.[4] Formerly I considered *Khirbet el-'Oja
el-Foķa* as identical with the Naaran, half of whose water
Archelaus drained away, but since the discovery of the syna-
gogue-mosaic at *en-Duķ* in the year 1919 Naaran must be sought
there. In that case nothing else remains but to refer Archelaus'
aqueduct to an enlargement of the oasis of Jericho, and to
separate from it the foundation of Archelais. The palm-
plantations of Archelais are, in that case, only referred to in
Ant. viii. 2, 2. Probably *Khirbet el-'Oja el-Foķa*, lying like
Phasælis on the edge of the highland, was at that time the
proper centre of Archelais, which had the source of its waters
in her power. But she might have had a suburb by *Khirbet
el-Oja et-Taḥta*, 7 kilometres farther east on the road coming
from the north, a suburb which guarded the irrigated land
stretching out there. So one could rest there in the shadow
of the palms and drink from the water of the '*Oja* conveyed
to this spot and after a hot, though otherwise easy, journey,
which is all along the plains, with the exception of the short
stretch just before Koraia which passes over an outlying terrace of the highland, the goal would be attained in three days.

From Jn. (iv. 4 *f*.; *cf.* iii. 22) it follows that the journey from
Galilee to Jericho could also be made *via* Sichem, where perhaps the descent from Bethel to Jericho was entered (p. 217 *f*.).
It is certain that the last journey of Jesus to Jerusalem was
through Jericho (Mt. xx. 29; Mk. x. 46; Lk. xviii. 35). The

[1] *PJB*, 1912, p. 34 *f*.; *RB*, 1913, p. 222.   [2] *Bell. Jud.* i. 6, 5.
[3] *Ant.* xvii. 13, 1.   [4] *Ibid.* xviii, 2, 2.

Lukan account seems to assume a road which touched the
northern boundary of Samaria (p. 211), so that it remains uncertain where, according to this Evangelist, the descent into the
Jordan valley began.   According to Mt. xix. 1, Jesus had gone
before that to Judæa on the other side of the Jordan; according
to Mk. x. 1 to Judæa and Transjordania.   Nothing is said
about the route, and the events narrated only presuppose that
it was Jewish country in which He stayed, so that it can be
understood why the Jewish character of the country beyond
Jordan was specially stressed.   Therefore it is probable that
St. Mark either means the same, or that he wished, because of a
misunderstanding, to correct his source.

If the expression in Mk. is to be taken seriously, then, apart
from the already mentioned descent from Bethel, the way
to Peræa through Judæa could also be undertaken by the road
which came down into the Jordan valley already to the north
of Bethel, through the present *et-Taiyibeh*, which was once a
Roman road.[1]   Epiphanius in the fourth century walked
here once in the company of a Jew.[2]

From the Matthæan account it follows that Jesus went, on
the eastern side of the Jordan, southward, and remained for a
considerable time in Jewish Peræa.   As the way through the
Jordan valley was not the usual one for the Galilæans, one
must assume that there was a special reason for the choice of this
route.   The purpose might have been to remain as much as
possible outside the Judæan sphere and to avoid the usual road
in order not to fall prematurely into the hands of His Judæan
enemies.   At the same time it would have been in accordance
with His conception of His task to be active before His Death
in a part where there were Jewish people with whom He had
not until then come into contact.   Also the desire to be alone
with His disciples before His last journey to Jerusalem may
have been a factor in the choice of this route.   This may have
been the case, as we see from the Fourth Gospel, where a
passing visit to the Transjordanian place where John had
baptised is described as having been undertaken with a special
purpose.   Such intentions would in fact have justified the use
of the Jordan valley for the journey to Jerusalem.

From Capernaum Jesus might have chosen the road on the
western side of the lake and would then have gone through
Tiberias.   The crossing of the Jordan could have taken

[1] *PJB*, 1912, p. 61 *f.*; Thomsen, *ZDPV*, 1917, p. 75 *f.*
[2] See above, p. 217.

place in the south only, if the Samaritan and Judæan districts were not to be avoided. But there was also a possible route on the eastern side of the lake, through the district of Hippos. From there, after crossing the Yarmuk in the Jordan valley, Jesus would have taken the road which leads near to the foot of the eastern highland. He would thus have come through the domain of Gadara and Pella, without touching these cities,[1] until in the neighbourhood of *Wady Fakaris*, the Jewish Peræa, *i.e.* the domain of Herod Antipas, began. Rabbinic legislation divided the Transjordanian domain into three parts in regard to the law of the Sabbatic year : the highland, the lowland, and the low-lying plain.[2] The mountains about Mekhawer and Tabor were considered as highland; the localities on the Moabitic plateaus from Hesbon to Dibon as lowland; the Jordan valley with Beth Haram, Beth Nimrin, Der 'Ala, 'Amethan as low-lying plain. Beacons lit on the 30th day of the month on the Mount of Olives proclaimed to the mountains of Mekhawer and Gador, and thus to the *Jebel Aṭṭarus* and the *Jebel Osha'*, when this day should be considered to be the first day of the new month.[3] But in the whole Jordan valley the message was received from the Sertabeh summit on the frontier of the Samaritan land and visible from everywhere, in case it had not already been noticed on its first starting-point, the Mount of Olives. Therefore this land was also included in the legal considerations of the scribes.

Thus the question arises whether Jesus on His way through Peræa kept Himself to the Jordan valley only, or also went up to the wooded highland of Gilead. In the valley *'Amethan*,[4] now *Tell 'Ammata*, there was the most important and fortified city,[5] which would correspond to the ancient Zaphon (Josh.

---

[1] Also Pella lay away from the road in the Jordan plain, in the basin of the *Jurm* brook. Once I thought (*PJB*, 1910, p. 17) that *Dion* might be looked for in its immediate neighbourhood, but I have given up this notion long ago. It lay, according to Photius (Migne, *P.G.* ciii. 3, col. 1290), at the western edge of the Arabian plain, to which Bostra belongs. According to position and name *Edun* fits in well with it, which lay north of an important east-west road Aristobul (*Ant.* xiv. 3, 3) might have used.

[2] p. Shebi. 38d ; Tos. Shebi. vii. 11 (text corrupt).

[3] Tos. R. h. S. ii. 2 ; b. R. h. S. 32b, where, according to p. R. h. S. 58a, it must be read : *behare mekhawer wegador*. See also Ginzberg, *Jerushalmi Fragments*, p. 149.

[4] p. Shebi. 38d, where Amethu is most probably a slip. Josephus writes Αμαθους, where the ending is probably Greek and need not be based on anything corresponding to it. This Amethan is not to be confused with the 'Ammethan of p. Mo. k. 82a, which refers to Chammethan near Gader; see Klein, *MGWDJ*, 1915, p. 165.

[5] *Ant.* xiii. 13, 3, 5 ; *Bell. Jud.* i. 4, 2, 3.

xiii. 27 ; Judg. xii. 1),[1] but is not the same as the Asaphon of
Josephus, which is mentioned together with it.[2]   As Gabinius
in A.D. 57 instituted a Synedrion there and in Gadara,[3] it must
be considered to have been the capital of Jewish Peræa north
of the Jabbok.[4]   South of it and nearer the Jabbok lay, on its
large hill, *Der ʿAla,* now *Tell Der ʿAlla,* which was most
probably ancient Succoth.[5]   But if Jesus wished to go up
into the mountains, they were not far from Ragib, now Rajib,[6]
lying by its brook, during the siege of which king Alexander
Jannæus died of malaria in the year 76 B.C.,[7] and once famous
for her oil, which was the second best in Jewish Palestine.[8]
Farther south *Mahanaim,* crowning both banks of the Jabbok,
could also be easily reached.   This Mahanaim, now *Tlul ed-
Dahab,* was then perhaps called " Didymos," " Twin-City."[9]
South of the Jabbok, on the mountain near the summit of the
Neby Osha, lay Gador, whose successor in the valley below is
the present *es-Salt.*[10]   This was, according to Josephus,[11] the
capital of Peræa.   But Jesus would not have gone up there
without a special purpose.   On the other hand, He might have
visited the walled *Beth Nimrin,*[12] now *Tell Nimrin,* as the last
city on His tour, lying opposite to Jericho, where the brook of
Gador entered the Jordan plain.   From her irrigated fields the
Transjordanian Bethany (p. 89) which, according to Jn. x. 40,
was the next goal, could easily be reached.   The most southern

---

[1] p. Shebi. 38d.

[2] *Ant.* xiii. 12, 5.   This Asaphon (=*ha-Saphon*) may belong to the same
neighbourhood.   The battle between the Gileadites and Ephraimites would
then be connected with the same Jordan ford as the battle between Alexander
and Ptolemy.

[3] *Ant.* xiv. 5. 3 ; *Bell. Jud.* i. 8, 5.

[4] The " marital case " which, according to Schlatter, *Die hebräischen Namen
bei Josephus,* p. 87, came from there before the Patriarch Judah, might resemble
our Lord's *logion* in regard to divorce (Mt. xix. 3 *f.* ; Mk. x. 1 *f.*).   But it deals
in fact with the question of cutting beard and nails on half-festivals (p. Mo. k.
82a).

[5] p. Shebi. 38d.; *cf.* in regard to the reading *PJB,* 1913, p. 72.

[6] *PJB,* 1913, p. 67 *f.*, against Schürer, *Geschichte,* i., 3rd ed., p. 274.

[7] *Ant.* xiii. 15, 5.   [8] Mishna Men. viii. 3 ; Tos. Men. ix. 5.

[9] Midr. Tehillim iii. 1 ; *cf. PJB,* 1913, p. 72.

[10] That not *es-Salt* itself is ancient Gador, as even Haefeli, *Samaria und Peräa,*
p. 108 *f.*, holds, I have shown in *PJB,* 1910, p. 22 *f.*

[11] *Bell. Jud.* iv. 7, 3 ; *cf.* Schlatter, *Zur Topographie und Geschichte Palästinas,*
p. 44 *f.*   Josephus, it seems, called the city " Gadoroi " ; see Schlatter, *Die hebr.
Namen bei Josephus,* p. 34.   According to *Ant.* xiv. 5, 4, Gabinius made her the
centre of a special judicial circuit, which evidently reached as far as the Jabbok.
But in 218 B.C., the city conquered by Antioch the Great was already of importance ; see Polybius, *Hist.* v. 71, where Gadara appears together with Rabbat-
Amana.

[12] p. Shebi. 38d ; in Jos., *Bell. Jud.* iv. 7. 4, *Bethennabris.*

part of the eastern Jordan valley, rich in Christ-thorn trees and irrigated by brooks, is opposite to the steppes of Moab, from which Moses went up to Mount Nebo, in order to die (Dt. xxxiv. 1); that Moses whose fate (according to the Midrash)[1] was inevitable, because he who desired to die for Israel's sin refused to ask for forgiveness for himself.   It is not likely that Jesus visited this district, which stretched as far as the Dead Sea. Still more improbable is it that He should have gone up by Mount Nebo to that part of Jewish Peræa the centre of which was Machærus.   Farther in the north lay the Peræa of the Gospel story.   He was active there in order to escape for the moment a momentous decree.   Its towns, where He was probably more or less unknown, were, when He entered them, the scene of His activity, before He started on the way to His Death. It is significant that His words in regard to the indissolubility of marriage and His blessing of the children took place just at this time, and it is intelligible that Peter, in the name of the disciples, pointed out just here that they had " forsaken all " and followed Him (Mt. xix. 27 ; Mk. x. 28).

[1] Thus according to the Midrash of the Parting of Moses, Jellinek, Bet ha-Midrash i. 120.   Different, but also Jewish, is the Samaritan's Marqah narrative of the death of Moses (ed. by E. Munk), p. 15, according to which Moses, destined to die, praises God as the righteous Judge.   *Cf. Jesus-Jeshua*, p. 214 *f.*

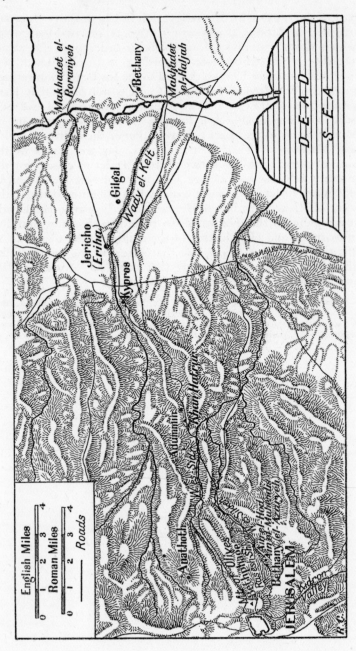

XIII

FROM JERICHO TO JERUSALEM—BETHANY
AND BETHPHAGE

To the list of those places and routes visited or traversed by
Jesus must be added the road from Jericho to Jerusalem,
which the parable of the Good Samaritan (Lk. x. 30 f.) presupposes as being generally known. Jesus, coming from
Galilee on the east side of the Jordan, would have to cross
the river before He could take this road. That there were
bridges across it was assumed already in early times.[1] Yet
no trace of a stone—or brick—bridge has come to light. In
any case, there could have been no lack of ferries. In Hebrew
a ferry was called, like a ford, *ma'boret*, in Aramaic *ma'bera*,
mabbera. There is a reference to ferry money which had to
be paid,[2] and to the danger of sitting on a ferry-boat together
with a heathen.[3] In the neighbourhood of the present wooden
bridge by the ford *Makhadet el-Roraniyeh* the Madaba map
shows a rope stretched across the river, and in the middle
of the stream a small boat, with its mast touching the
rope. At the upper part of the river, in the neighbourhood of Aenon by Salem, a second ferry is recognisable.
If Jesus came from the north, then the *Roraniyeh* ford would
have been the natural crossing-place for the Jericho road.
If, however, according to Jn. x. 40, He stayed in Transjordanian Bethany, He would have to cross the river farther
south, by the *Hajlah* ford (p. 88), and then pass by Gilgal.
Here were to be seen certain colossal blocks, which the
Israelites, according to Josh. iv. 7, 20, once brought from the
Jordan to this spot.[4] There is a legend that Jesus instituted
in the same place a peculiar memorial. In the sixth century
the *Ager Domini* was shown here, "in which the Lord sowed
with His own hand, casting in seed to the amount of three

[1] Tos. Para ix. 9.
[2] Bab. k. 116a; Yeb. 106a.
[3] Sabb. 32a (read *goy* instead of *kuthi*).
[4] Tos. Sot. viii. 6.

241

measures (*moaii*), which is still reaped twice in the year, but in the month of February, in order that it may be eaten as sacramental bread at Easter. When it has been reaped, it is ploughed, and a second time reaped together with the harvest from the other fields. Then it is ploughed again."[1] Also there is said to be a vine planted by Jesus, which yielded grapes as early as Pentecost.[2] The vine thus singled out grew in front of the church marked in the Madaba map near the twelve stones brought from the Jordan, which may be located close to the group of evergreen tamarisks, *en-Neteleh*,[3] now cut down. As Gilgal was the place where the Israelites ate for the first time from the corn of the land (Josh. v. 11 *f*.), a Jewish Joshua-legend may in this case have been transformed in time into a Jesus legend. The Rabbis pictured the army of Gog being overthrown in the plain of Jericho, Moses watching its destruction from Mount Nebo, and the view towards Zoar would mean to him a look into hell.[4] No one can draw near to Jericho without casting a glance towards the Dead Sea, although only from an elevated view-point is there more than a glimpse of its shining surface. Here also the fate of Sodom and Gomorrha would come to mind, though it was dwarfed by the judgment to come and by the great decision which Jesus puts before men (Mt. x. 15; xi. 23; Lk. x. 12).

The oldest Jericho lay off the Jerusalem road, near the fountain named by Christians after Elisha (as the Bordeaux pilgrim knew, who saw Rahab's house above this fountain). Sellin's excavations have shown that the hill by the fountain was no longer covered with buildings in the time of Christ. But the town had then spread out a long way to the south. The palace of Herod, intended as a winter residence,[5] in which this gifted but not truly great king died, lay probably at the *Wady el-Kelt*, between the present *Eriha* and the ascent to the mountain, whilst an older palace may at one time have existed on the site of the present village. One may assume that the amphitheatre[6] and the hippodrome,[7] to which clung sad memories of a mass-murder planned by the dying Herod,

[1] Thus Antoninus. According to Theodosius, Jesus ploughed only one furrow with His own hand, and nothing is said of the miraculous seeding.
[2] Theodosius.
[3] *PJB*, 1911, p. 30; 1914, p. 12; 1924, p. 76. It is the *Tamarix articulata*, whilst on the Jordan the foliage-changing *Tamarix Pallasii* predominates.
[4] Mech. on Ex. xvii. 14 (ed. Weiss 63b); Sifre on Dt. xxxiv. 3 (149b); Targ. Jer. Dt. xxxiv. 3.
[5] *Bell. Jud.* i. 21, 4.   [6] *Ant.* xvii. 6, 3; 8, 2; *Bell. Jud.* i. 33, 8.
[7] *Ant.* xvii. 6, 5; *Bell. Jud.* i. 33, 6.

stood in the space between the *Wady el-Kelt* and ancient Jericho. Above this royal new Jericho the citadel Kypros[1] crowned the summit of the hill which led towards the wilderness. This citadel probably took the place of the earlier castles Tyrex and Tauros, destroyed by Pompey.[2] All this Herodian splendour had disappeared by the fourth century. In the neighbourhood of the present village there was a settlement which in Arculf's time lay similarly in ruins.[3]

When Jesus passed this way, Jericho still stood in her full glory, though royal majesty no longer enhanced her fame. He turned off from the direct road towards Jerusalem, perhaps with the intention of resting a little. A blind man called to Him as He was come nigh unto Jericho (Lk. xviii. 35 *f.* ; according to Mt. xx. 29 *f.* there were two blind men who called to Him, and that after His departure from Jericho). One may visualise this incident as taking place before the south entrance to the town, on the way to the Jordan crossing. St. Luke also tells of a chief publican—probably set over all the custom-houses on the southern Jordan[4])—who climbed up a sycamore tree in order to see Jesus (Lk. xix. 1 *f.*). This tree is in fact native to Jericho, although Hasselquist did not find it in Jericho in 1751,[5] for it is a tree belonging to the warm climate of the coast and the Jordan valley, but not found in the higher mountainous region.[6] Its strong boughs spread out horizontally, permitting the climber to sit comfortably enough and look down, and in addition it was already in foliage, so Zacchæus could assume that he would not be observed in its thick leaves. However, in the small, walled town of ancient Jericho which then lay in ruins[7] there would have been no room for such trees, and it would have been more convenient for Zacchæus to climb up a roof. The passing through Jericho of which Luke speaks (xix. 1) fits in only with the widely extended settlement which was the Jericho of that time, where sycamore-trees could easily have stood here and there on the streets (*cf.* p. 13). Epiphanius gave to the Jericho of ancient times, probably judging by what she was in his time, a circumference of 20 stadia=

---

[1] *Ant.* xvi. 5, 2 ; *Bell. Jud.* i. 21, 4, 9.   [2] Strabo xvi. 2, 40.
[3] *Cf.* Eusebius, *Onomasticum.*   [4] *Cf.* pp. 5, 87.
[5] *Reise nach Palästina*, pp. 151, 560.
[6] *Cf.* Shebi. ix. 2, and Dalman, *Arbeit und Sitte*, i., p. 255 ; Klein, *Schwarz-Festschrift*, reprint xl. It is assumed in Lk. xvii. 6 as being an especially firmly rooted tree.
[7] Sellin and Watzinger, *Jericho*, p. 184.

3·8 kilometres.[1] This is not exaggerated, for the distance from the citadel at the Elisha fountain to the Herodian buildings at the *Wady el-Kelt* is 2 kilometres. Jericho appeared like a paradise even to the pilgrim Antoninus,[2] evidently because of her trees ; and for the dying Moses on Nebo the town of palms meant the Garden of Eden, according to the Jewish legend.[3] At present a sycamore-tree on the road to Jerusalem reminds one of the tree of Zacchæus. The Bordeaux pilgrim found one on the same road, but nearer to the descent from the mountain ; in 570 it was still revered, but was dried up.[4] The house of Zacchæus, into which Jesus invited Himself (Lk. xix. 5), most probably stood near the road from the Jordan ford to Jerusalem, in the Herodian Jericho.

The last journey of our Lord to Jerusalem, which signified for Him that the way to death was the way to " the Kingdom of God " (Mt. xx. 17 *f.* ; Mk. x. 32 *f.* ; Lk. xviii. 31 *f.* ; xix. 11 *f.* ; Jn. xi. 7), contrasted strangely with His traversing of the wilderness on the way to the Temple at the time of the Temptation. To the astonishment of the disciples, He was firmly resolved to take this road now. Mark x. 32 emphasises that He " went before them,"[5] by which the first departure from the Judæan Peræa is recalled. Thus it is seen that the renewed announcement of the Passion and the desire of the sons of Zebedee to sit one at the right hand and the other at the left hand of King Messiah, as well as the disclosure of the purpose of His Passion, took place east of the Jordan.

The first half of the road from Jericho to Jerusalem is clearly defined by local conditions. After He had accomplished the steep ascent of the lower mountain slopes, south of the *Wady el-Kelt*, He had to use the Adummim acclivity (Josh. xv. 7) in order to mount the greater heights of the eastern slope of the upland. This height, on which a Jew once thought that he observed the appearance of the new moon between two rocks,[6] ended at the summit of *Khan Ḥaṭrur*, a spot remarkable for its red stones, above which lay the ruins of a Templar stronghold,[7] on the site of an earlier road fort.[8] There must

---

[1] *Adv. Haer.*, Migne, *P.G.* xli., col. 157.   [2] Geyer, *Itinera*, pp. 168, 201.
[3] Sifre on Dt. xxxiv. 3 (149b).   [4] Geyer, pp. 23, 169 *f.*
[5] The ἔμπροσθεν (Lk. xix. 28) evidently also emphasises this firm resolution.
[6] p. R. h. 57d.
[7] Theoderich saw there on the way the *cisterna rubra*, which was given out to have been " Joseph's cistern," and a chapel, and above it the castle of the Templars ; see Tobler, p. 70.
[8] Eusebius, *Onomasticum*, 219.

have been a rest-house there, which probably supplied water from a cistern to man and beast, but was certainly not the inn of the Good Samaritan (Lk. x. 34), which must have been in Jericho. Jerome supposed that this place, stained with deeds of blood, was the spot where the man in the parable fell among thieves.[1] For here, in the midst of the wilderness, where the lonely traveller is unprotected even to this day, and where everything depends upon the people one happens to meet, is found the suitable background for the parable.

From the height, by the "Khan of the Good Samaritan," where the view of the Mount of Olives opened up anew, which the pilgrims had previously enjoyed from a greater distance between the Jordan and the Gilgal, the road descends to a wide, low plain, crosses the *Wady es-Sidr*, and there divides into two. The more northern route, later utilised for the Roman road,[2] first follows this valley, but later ascends to a ridge which leads up between two branches of that valley to the Mount of Olives chain. The more southerly way follows the *Wady es-Sikkoh*, an accessory valley of the *Wady es-Sidr*, thus remaining a valley road, until it rises about 250 metres directly before Bethany—now through a steep ravine, now encircling it—and so reaches the eastern promontory in front of the Mount of Olives. If Bethany was the next stage of the journey, as is assumed by St. John (xi. 1 *f.*), then naturally the latter road was taken. Epiphanius[3] testifies to this road over the Mount of Olives to Jerusalem being a well-known ancient road, though the Gospel of Marcion, by its omission of the whole narrative of the entrance of Jesus, seemed to witness against it. Therefore it seems justifiable to call the fountain issuing from that ravine, now discharged in the valley into a cistern, *'Ain el-Ḥod*, "Apostle's fountain."[4] However, the leeches infesting it might have prevented the Apostles from drinking there, as they did me.

As it was before Passover, the country here up in the mountain would be decked with spring flowers. The daffodil (*Asphodelus microcarpus*, Arab. *Khosalan, bosalan*), which vies with the autumn-flowering sea-leek (*Urginea maritima*) for the honour of being the "flower (*ḥabasselet*) of Sharon," would sway in the breeze, with its white, star-like blossoms, and the

[1] *PJB*, 1913, p. 18.   [2] Thomsen, *ZDPV*, 1917, p. 78.
[3] *Adv. hær.* xlii.; Migne, *P.G.* xli., col. 717, 757.
[4] Usually this fountain is taken to be the "Sun-fountain" (Ain Shemesh) of Josh. xv. 7, but see my objections in *Graf-Baudissin Festschrift*, p. 118 *f.*; *PJB*, 1918, p. 48 *f.*

rocket (*Erucaria aleppica*), which reminds one of our lady's-smock (cuckoo-flower), decked whole slopes with its lilac-coloured blossoms. But neither was there any lack of thorns, without which one cannot conceive Palestinian soil. The proper domain of the trees and shrubs of the Christ-thorn (*Zizyphus spina Christi*, Arab. *sidr*) the traveller has left behind with the *Wady es-Sidr*, called after it. But the thistles on the road and the thorny burnet-herbs (*Poterium spinosum*), which, like our heather, cover the heights, form in the Judæan highland a mass of thorns, which may well remind us of the crown with which the head of the Son of David, hastening towards Jerusalem, was soon to be wreathed. In autumn the burnet stands entirely barren with its tangled, thorny boughs, but later it grows dark-green feathery little leaves, and its red blossom-ears suggest drops of blood. This unassuming plant is industrially of importance, for it is gathered in great masses to heat the lime-kilns,[1] but it is also used, when there is a lack of brushwood, for heating the peasant fireplace for cooking (Arab. *mokade*). Because of its abundance I have often suggested that the Crown of Thorns was made of it.[2] For it could have been collected from this part and brought into the city for the watchfires of the Roman soldiers (Lk. xxii. 55), the warmth they afforded being still quite welcome at Easter time. "Whoso loads thorns (Aram. *kubbin*), from him all flee," we read in a dream interpretation, whilst in the parallel passage "fuel" is substituted for thorns.[3] One must, however, own that, frequently as thorn-weeds are used as burning material in lime-kilns and peasant houses, their use for heating purposes in Jerusalem is, at least nowadays, not customary. The thorn-crowns sold there are made sometimes of this *Poterium spinosum*, but more frequently of branches of *Lycium europæum* (Arab. *osaj*), which has sharper thorns, and which is a near relation of our poisonous goat's thorn, and as common in Palestine as the latter is in Europe. This high-growing thorn-shrub might have been found in the immediate environs of the city by the soldiers and brought in for firing purposes. It is much more probable than the Christ-thorn,[4] the latter being native to the warmer climate of the lower-lying Judæan desert, the Jordan valley, and the

[1] *Cf.* Mt. vi. 30; Lk. xii. 28, where, according to Pal. Evang. and Syr., it refers to the baker's oven.

[2] See also Linder, *PJB*, 1916, p. 119.

[3] Lam. R. i. 1 (23a); *cf.* Pal. Maas. sh. 55b.

[4] The Aramaic name must have been *kinnara*, Pes. 111b, Ber. 40b.

coast-plain, and having been, according to Lundgreen,[1] brought back by the soldiers as a curiosity from a journey to the region of the Jordan. However, the fact that occasional examples of this tree are also found near Jerusalem—I knew of one in the neighbourhood of the " gate of Herod "—makes it more probable than the thorn-shrub *Paliurus aculeatus* proposed by Fonk and Killermann,[2] who state that it is frequent near Jerusalem, though in fact it does not grow there at all, and according to Aaronson[3] is found only by the Jordan fountains and at one place in Galilee and one in Samaria.[4] There are also other kinds of thorn-plants near Jerusalem which might be taken into consideration, *e.g.* the jujube-tree (*Zizyphus vulgaris,* Arab. *ennab*), the hawthorn (*Crategus Azarolus,* Arab. *zarur*), and the prickly broom (*Calycotome villosa,* Arab. *kundel*). These are ruled out because it would not have been easy to wreath a garland of their stiff twigs.

All the above-mentioned plants are suitable only on the understanding that flexible wooden twigs with sharp thorns would have best suited the purpose. But the intention at the crowning of the condemned " King " (Mt. xxvii. 29 ; Mk. xv. 17 ; Jn. xix. 2) was not to give Him physical pain, as the representations of the Middle Ages emphasised,[5] but to mock Him. The ἄκανθαι of the garland put on Him were meant to signify the contrast with a golden royal crown. The Greek word is a general expression for " thorns " and " thorn plants." In Palestinian Aramaic *kubbin* is the corresponding word (also in the Christian dialect), of which a proverb says similarly to Mt. vii. 16 : " Whilst it (the thorn plant) was still unripe it brought forth thorns[6] (*kubbaya*)." In Arabic one would use *shok* for it, and think of the whole range of Palestinian thorny plants, especially thistles. The purpose of ridiculing the royalty of Jesus was certainly best accomplished if His crown consisted of the insignificant thistles which grow everywhere and could be easily fetched. A garland of olive-wood twigs may signify future greatness or approaching flagellation ; it all depends on whether one thinks of the blossom

[1] *Neue kirchl. Zeit.*, 1916, p. 840 *f.*
[2] *Streifzüge durch die biblische Flora* (1900), p. 100.
[3] *Die Blumen des heil. Landes*, ii., p. 3 *f.*
[4] *Bulletin de la Société botanique de France*, 1913, p. 591 *f.*; *cf.* Dinsmore in *The Jerusalem Catalogue of Palestine Plants*, 1912, No. 397.
[5] They painted thorns which I can identify only with the American honey-thorn (*Gleditschia triacanthos*), which was shown to me in my boyhood as Christ-thorn.   [6] Gen. R. ii. (4b).

of the olive-tree, or of the knocking off of its fruit.[1] A thistle garland cannot be misunderstood. The LXX have always translated the Hebrew *ḳoṣ* by *ἄκανθαι*, which must always be taken to refer to a troublesome field herb, especially thistles.[2] For one kind of thistles the name *ḳuṣ* and *kus* has also been preserved in Palestinian Arabic, namely for a common thistle with small violet blossoms, *Carthamus glaucus* v. *syriacus*, which covers particularly the reaped fields. But one would prefer to think of the thorny knapweed, *Centaurea pallescens* (Arab. *murrer, dardar*),[3] which grows everywhere on the road, a medley of stalks, frequently bluish in hue, starred with blossoms and bristling on all sides with thorns. Naturally at Easter its thorns are not yet hardened into wood ; but so much more easily could they be twisted into a garland, whilst most other kinds of thistle are useless for this purpose. In the year 1900 I brought to Leipzig a garland wreathed by me of *Centaurea pallescens* and *Poterium spinosum*. It was a particularly miserable contrast to a royal crown, and so could well claim to be considered a " genuine " crown of thorns. This " botany of the crown of thorns," which teaches us so much about the character of the country from which Jesus drew His parables (Mt. vii. 16 ; xiii. 7), appeared to Bultmann[4] superfluous. It may indeed be so for him, to whom a concrete visualisation of the sacred history is not a task for science, and to whom plants are perhaps only names. But it is different to one who encounters before the gates of Jerusalem thorns and thistles at every step. They all have much to tell him of the Divine words of punishment spoken to the first man (Gen. iii. 18), of the King to whom the soldiers called mockingly : " Hail ! King of the Jews " (*shelam lakh malkehon dihudaye*) (Mt. xxvii. 29), and of the final Judgment (Heb. ix. 27). Are they to signify something to the Christian, but nothing to theological scholarship ?

Upon the height above the Apostles' fountain there is a direct road to the summit of the Mount of Olives, which is separated from Bethany by a small valley lying in a northerly direction. If the direct goal of Jesus' journey from Jericho was Jerusalem, as stated in Mt. xxi. 1 ; Mk. xi. 1 ; Lk. xix. 29, He may have taken this road, and would have passed very

---

[1] p. Maas. sh. 55b; *cf.* Lam. R. i. 1 (23b).
[2] So also Mt. xiii. 7 ; Mk. iv. 7 ; Lk. viii. 7.
[3] This word also in Hebrew, Gen. iii. 18.   Aram., Targ. Jer. ii., *ibid.*; Pal. Evang. Mt. viii. 16 for τρίβολοι.
[4] *Wissenschaft und Leben*, 1922, col. 124.

near to Bethany; naturally He might also have kept further
to the left and actually gone through Bethany.

That Bethany[1] lay east of the Mount of Olives is firmly
established by the data of the Gospels. One comes nearer
to knowing its exact position by considering the Lazarus
tomb,[2] which was shown since about A.D. 300 at the same
place and over which a church was built before 380. This
tomb (Jn. xi. 38) was formerly a rock-chamber with tombs
in vaulted recesses on three sides. Its genuineness is uncertain,
but the tradition is undoubtedly based on reliable knowledge
of the position of Bethany, which is thus to be found in the
neighbourhood. The tomb lies on a very gradually sloping
declivity which descends, not from the Mount of Olives, but
from the *Ras esh-Shiyah* stretched out in front of it; and looks
towards a little valley which lies eastward. Above and close
to it the present village *el-'Ezaryeh*,[3] or *el-'Azaryeh*, " The Place
of Lazarus," grew up. The old village scarcely lay so near
the tomb. That Bethany extended farther east above the
ravine coming up directly from the *Wady es-Sikkeh*, might be
deduced from the fact that there are undoubtedly ancient
cisterns there, and from the nearness of the fountains *Bir
el-'Odd* and *'Ain el-Muhendis* in the upper part of that ravine,
as well as from the statement in Jn. xi. 18, according to
which Bethany was " about fifteen furlongs off Jerusalem,"
i.e. about 3 kilometres, which is more than the distance from
the tomb of Lazarus. But archæological finds have proved
that the present village, excluding its latest extension towards
the east, actually goes back to pre-Christian times.[4] Thus
within its borders stood the house of Mary and Martha (Jn.
xi. 1; probably also Lk. x. 38 *f.*) and the house of Simon the
leper (Mt. xxvi. 6; Mk. xiv. 3). The mention of the Mount
of Olives in connection with Bethany can be justified by the
fact that, after all, the latter faced the " wilderness " at the
ascent towards the Mount of Olives, and thus the Mount of
Olives, as a prominent and far better known feature than the
little village, and as being more important to the narrative,
could not be overlooked.

The neighbourhood has a considerable supply of olives,

[1] See concerning it Fenner, *ZDPV*, 1906, p. 151 *f.*
[2] First mentioned by Eusebius in the *Onomasticum* and by the Bordeaux
pilgrim.
[3] So the Moslem inhabitants call it after El'ezar (el-'uzer), who was supposed
to have been a brother of Lazarus. The Christians call it El-azariye.
[4] Vincent, *RB*, 1914, p. 438.

which is also noticed by Arculf. The village, like Anathoth, Bethlehem, and Tekoa, is one of the places on the edge of the semi-wilderness which extend their cornfields far into the wilderness. If the name, as the Christian Palestinian and Syriac rendering "*Bet 'Anya*" suggests, is derived from the Hebrew *'ani*, "misery," it would perhaps tell us something about the village. But it is probably the Ananiah of Neh. xi. 32, and its name is connected with the personal name Ananiah, and thus gives us no clue to the character of the village.

It is remarkable that, according to the description of Ætheria[1] (380) and Daniel (1106),[2] the place where Jesus and Martha met (Jn. xi. 20) was shown 500 steps west of the tomb of Lazarus, *i.e.* in the direction of the Mount of Olives. A church stood there which was already in existence in the sixth century ;[3] it also marked the spot of our Lord's mounting of the ass for His entry into Jerusalem, which was connected with the name Bethphage.[4] The mounting of the ass was permanently connected with this spot. According to the monk Epiphanius,[5] on Palm Sunday a branch from an olive-tree used to be taken here for the solemn procession to the city.[6] A monument dating from the time of the Crusaders referring to these facts was discovered in 1876, on the way between Bethany and the Mount of Olives, just where this mountain—at the ridge between the *Ras esh-Shiyah*—reaches its easternmost summit. It is a rocky cube[7] on which are presented the events of Bethany (on the east and the south sides the meeting of Jesus and the resurrection of Lazarus), as well as those of the entry into Jerusalem (on the north and west the bringing of the ass and apparently the procession of palms). A chapel was built over this memento which adopted the name Bethphage.

---

[1] Geyer, p. 82.

[2] Khitrovo, *Itinéraires Russes*, p. 22, where the meeting with Martha and the mounting of the ass are considered as taking place at this same point and on the same occasion.

[3] Theodosius (Geyer, p. 146). In the seventh century it was destroyed, as Sophronius does not mention it.

[4] Ætheria says nothing of Bethphage, but already in Origen on Mt. xx. it is the place of the mounting of the ass ; see also Petrus Diaconus.

[5] Migne, *P.G.* cxx., col. 268.

[6] The procession began at the time of Ætheria and also in the seventh century (Georgian Canonarium, *Or. Chr.* v., p. 218) on the Mount of Olives, but began later, according to the Typikon of the Anastasis, in Bethany. Then the olive branch was taken from there, not from Bethphage.

[7] Theoderich (1172) refers to the great stone in the chapel of Bethphage on which Jesus is supposed to have stood before He mounted the ass.

That the spot where Jesus met Martha was located between Bethany and the Mount of Olives is explicable only if He is pictured as reaching the Mount of Olives *via* the Roman road (p. 245). In that case He would have left it at the foot of the mountain, to take a road which led towards its southern flank, intending to turn towards Bethany just where this flank descends into the road from Jerusalem to Bethany. At that point Martha met Him. In fact, Antoninus actually reached Bethany from Jericho in 570 by this route. But it is not the usual way,[1] and probably the placing of the event at the Mount of Olives is merely an artificial combining of different traditions in one spot. If Jesus came by the proper road leading from the wilderness to Bethany, then Martha must have expected Him where this road comes up from the *Wady es-Sikkeh* before Bethany. This leads into the neighbourhood of a stone called *Jahsh el-'Azar*, " Colt of Lazarus," which is shown east of Bethany, in the neighbourhood of which the Greeks have erected their monastery *ed-Jeneneh*, which is said to be known also as *Burj el-Ehmar*, " Ass-tower." It may be the same stone which used to be shown in 1400, east of Bethany, at the house of Simon the leper, as the place where Jesus said (Jn. xi. 34) : " Where have ye laid him ? " In that case this would have been the place where He met Martha, and the meeting with Martha and the mounting of the ass may have been combined here.

In any case since the sixth century this stone between Bethany and the Mount of Olives, or a place near it, has been identified as Bethphage. One would therefore be inclined to imagine a place which might have been Bethphage on the summit of the *Ras esh-Shiyah*. But even before the present houses were built I was unable to discover there any trace of a genuine ancient site. Rock-tombs with tomb-troughs, also rolling-stones for the closing of tombs, were discovered in the immediate proximity of the Bethphage chapel. An especially extensive sepulchre with four chambers, with special arrangements for the corpses, drew one's attention, because on the cover of one of the eleven sarcophagi found there, there is a number of names in Hebrew. Twice, persons are designated as Galilæans.[2]

---

[1] It is rather strange that an inhabitant of Jerusalem like Meistermann should think it possible that the usual ancient road from Jerusalem to Jericho should have been *via* Anathoth (*Durchs Heilige Land*, pp. 235, 248).

[2] Orfali, *RB*, 1923, p. 253 *f.* Yet some of the difficult names require further examination.

In rabbinic literature there are many references to Beth
Page. It is particularly mentioned in connection with exact
definitions of the limits within which a sacred thing can be
prepared or used. In Mishnah Menachoth xi. 2 the shew-
breads and the two Pentecost loaves can be prepared, according to Rabbi Simeon, in the holy court as well as in Beth Page.
The bread of the thank-offering, in order to be sacred, must
not be found during the slaughtering of the thank-offering
" outside the walls."[1] According to the third-century Rabbi
Johanan, the wall of Beth Page is referred to.[2] The Passover
may be slaughtered for one who is within the walls of Beth
Page in a heathen prison, because in case of necessity he may
be permitted to eat it even there.[3] The rule in regard to
spending the night at the place of the sanctuary applies to the
second Passover (Num. ix. 10 f.) as to the first Passover.[4]
Only Rabbi Judah opposes this view, and thinks that after
the slaughtering of the Passover Lamb, if the father of the
family has died, it is permitted to arrange the lamentations in
Beth Page and leave the city.[5] He who brings his " sacred
things " from Beth Page to Jerusalem may eat them in
Jerusalem, but then he must spend the night in Beth Page,
with the exception of the eighth day of the feast of Tabernacles.[6]
In connection with the second tithe, which has to be consumed near the sanctuary (Dt. xiv. 23), a question arises in
regard to its being threshed " within the walls of Beth Page."[7]
As, according to Sanhedrin xi. 2, the rebellious scribe can
only be punished when he expresses his views before the
highest court—which is, according to Dt. xvii. 8 f., at the
place of the sanctuary—the question is whether Beth Page
is to be considered as such, and the answer is in the negative.[8]

All these references to Beth Page are based on the supposition that it lay outside the sanctuary proper, beginning
apparently where the latter ended.[9] It lay outside Jerusalem,[10]
and there is a reference to a wall which was supposed to have
formed its boundary.[11] It must have been a district situated
outside Jerusalem (in any case a suburb, but not a separate
unit),[12] beginning at the border of the sanctuary, i.e. before

---

[1] Men. vii. 3.   [2] Tos. Men. viii. 18.   [3] Pes. 91a.
[4] Pes. 95b.   [5] Tos. Pes. viii. 8.   [6] Sifre Num. cli. (55a).
[7] Bab. mez. 90a.   [8] Sanh. 14b ; Sota 45b.
[9] Estori happarchi (ed. Berlin, 1852), 20a, considers it therefore as a place near
the Temple mount. Isaak Dhelo (Carmoly, Itinéraires, p. 235) looks for it at
the Kidron.   [10] Tos. Pes. viii. 8 ; Sifre on Num. cli.
[11] Tos. Men. viii. 18.   [12] Thus Neubauer, La Géographie du Talmud, p. 149.

the eastern wall of Jerusalem. It is nowhere brought into connection with the Sabbath-day's journey.[1] But it is clear that an extension beyond it is improbable because Beth Page's nearness to the city of Jerusalem is taken for granted (with the probable exception of Tos. Pes. viii. 8).

In other rabbinic passages certain places in the neighbourhood of Jerusalem are only mentioned as examples for others —for instance, *Zophim*, the last possible place from which the Temple could be seen (see above, p. 220); *Migdal Eder* as the beginning of the pasture-land (p. 49), *Modiith* as the measure of a distant journey (Pes. ix. 2);[2] as the last point of the district in which the statement of the potters concerning the ritual purity of their vessels is to be considered as reliable (Chag. viii. 5); *Lydda*, together with others, as the goal of a day's journey (Maas. sheni v. 2). One is tempted to apply the same to Beth Page and mention, for instance, as an independent place of this name, the village Phicola of Josephus (*Ant*. xii. 4, 2), if Beth Page's close proximity to Jerusalem were not against it. Neubauer assumed that Beth Page was on the Mount of Olives. No wall enclosing the precincts of Jerusalem is to be assumed, so probably in those rabbinic passages where there is a reference to the wall of Beth Page, the expression arose from the fixed legal term "wall" in regard to the definition of distance, and did not imply that there was an actual wall surrounding Beth Page. The name of the district has usually been derived from *pag*, "unripe, juiceless fig," although it is generally written with *aleph* after the *pe*. It would be in accordance with its significance if the word were to be derived from the Latin *pagus*.[3] Then Beth Page would be=*Bet Page* (=*pagaiya*[4]), "the place of the *pagi*," *i.e.* the country district of Jerusalem, her suburb.[5]

Of the expansion of the Jewish Beth Page we learn nothing. The Sabbath district could be extended beyond its proper measure if round about Jerusalem dwelling-houses were scattered, the space between which did not extend beyond the Sabbath limit. Even Bethany could in this way be con-

---

[1] Thus Clermont Ganneau, *PEFQ*, 1878, p. 60; Warren-Conder, *Jerusalem* p. 400; Cheyne, *Enc. Bibl.*, "Bethphage."

[2] *Cf.* p. 229 *f.*

[3] For the writing of a long *a* with *aleph*, *cf.* Klein, *Corp. Inscr.* ii. 83.

[4] So it is also written in Pesh. and Pal. Evangel. As *paganus* has been assimilated as *pagan* in later Hebrew (*Gen*. R. L. 3 [106a]; p. Sabb. 13c), this derivation is not impossible. See also Dalman, *Die Worte Jesu*, p. 54.

[5] *Cf. bet sataiym*, "a space for two sea seed," 1 *Kings* xviii. 32; Erub. ii. 3 *bet ha-matbahim*, "slaughtering place," Midd. iii. 5; Ab. v. 4, *cf.* Kel. xv. 5.

nected with Jerusalem. Only if in regard to Jerusalem it
was considered as an independent locality, Beth Page would
have ended where Bethany's land-mark began. In that case
the eastern limit of the Mount of Olives on the way to Bethany
was the border of Beth Page, and the Bethphage of Christian
tradition was therefore accurately placed. When this tradition
identified the site of the mounting of the ass, it was based
primarily, it would seem, on the Fourth Gospel, according
to which Jesus arrived on that day from Bethany. The mention of the mounting at the reaching of the Mount of Olives in
the Synoptic Gospels naturally pointed then to the place west
of Bethany, where the Mount of Olives was reached, and where,
from other reasons, the meeting with Martha was also assumed
to have occurred.

In the Gospels, the form "Bethphage" shows that the
derivation of the name from *pagus* was not recognised. In
spite of this, the Jewish significance of the name would be
applicable where Bethphage is mentioned together with
Bethany, as in Lk. xix. 29, perhaps also in Mk. xi. 1. But
in Mt. xxi. 1 it is certainly the place from where the ass was
taken, as only this feature of the narrative demands the mention
of a definite place. In Mk., according to Origen, only
Bethany was originally mentioned, and the insertion of
Bethphage from Mt. was evidently meant to designate this
as the real place whence the ass was fetched. In Lk. it
might also have been the same, if the author did not originally
speak only of the Mount of Olives (*cf.* p. 261).

If we enquire after the natural presuppositions of the
Synoptic narrative, it is probable that the first village on
coming up from the desert supplied the ass for the journey
over the Mount of Olives, for, after a journey of five hours
from Jericho in the midday heat, Jesus would have been tired
and have had good cause to ask for an ass. Unintentionally
the Rider in the midst of the pilgrims to Jerusalem gave the
occasion for their act of homage. In that case Bethany was
the most likely place for the ass to be brought from. It is
different in Jn. xii. 14, where the ass, found on the way from
Bethany, might indeed be used by Jesus for a special purpose.
But Merx ought not to have called it a " Royal comedy,"
when Jesus, as a testimony concerning Jerusalem, thinking
of Zech. ix. 9, which to Him expressed the will of His Father,
desired to enter as a " poor King into Jerusalem," of whose
threatening tragedy He was as conscious as he was of His

own death.   As we have no certain knowledge of the position
of Beth Page, we can come to no decision ; only one thing is
certain, that the Synoptic narrative presupposes a real village,
within which—according to Mk. xi. 4, on the village street
through which the road led—the ass was found at the entrance
to some court, and that such a village, if it was not Bethany—
which seems to me to be the most probable—may have been
situated off the road towards the Mount of Olives, say at or
upon its eastern slope.

If the place whence the ass was fetched must remain uncertain, the road which Jesus took after Bethany lay behind
Him, is easier to determine.   It could only have been the one
which, after traversing the narrow pass between *Ras esh-
Shiyah* and the Mount of Olives, runs along the southern slope
of the Mount of Olives' eastern height, and then crosses its
elongated western summit on its southern shoulder.   On the
top the whole of Jerusalem, which from this point appears
especially as the city of the Temple, opened up to the view
of one coming from the east, very near at hand.   Nowadays
it surrounds the former site of the Temple from west to north
in the shape of a colossal theatre.   Then the city lay mainly
in the south and the south-west.   From the Mount of Olives
one could look into the courts of the sanctuary and observe
the cloud of smoke which rose from the great altar before the
high front-wall of the Temple.   But to the right of it were
also visible the four towers of the Antonia castle which
projected into the Temple area, and behind, at the western
edge of the city, the three high towers of the Herodian citadel
with its newer upper stories.   Both citadels signified the power
of the Roman eagle which gripped the holy city with its
talons.   To the majority of the Jews the close proximity of
Rome's imperial power to the house of God was an unbearable
discord.   In the mind of Jesus, God stood too high above
both these opposing factors to feel this discord in the same
way.   He saw in it, above all, the fate which hovered over the
city because it did not accept His message.   That He could
not prevent it, forced tears from His eyes (Lk. xix. 41).   For
He loved Jerusalem.

A later tradition has dedicated to the site of Jesus' weeping
over Jerusalem, at the descent from the Mount of Olives, a
chapel, which was afterwards replaced by a Moslem house of
prayer.   In the fourth century a procession came down here
from the Mount of Olives on Palm Sunday, to join which the

people gathered in the Mount of Olives' church, at one o'clock in the afternoon.   In the church of the Ascension the story of the entrance of Jesus into Jerusalem was read at five o'clock in the afternoon, and the congregation then went down the Mount of Olives on foot.   The bishop was accompanied by the people, who sang antiphonally : " Blessed is He that cometh in the name of the Lord."   The children, even those who were carried by the parents on their backs, had palm- or olive-branches in their hands.[1]   Thus the procession proceeded into the city, not to the Temple area, which was considered as rejected,[2] but to the church of the Resurrection.

For the descent from the Mount of Olives two ways were open to Jesus and His followers : an almost straight but steep one, on which it was difficult to ride downhill, and on which 537 steps were counted in the ninth century;[3] and one which twisted somewhat to the south but eventually led towards the same goal, and which to this day is used for descending in carriages.   Church tradition must have considered the former as the one taken by Jesus, for on that road a palm was seen in the fourth century in the neighbourhood of the present Gethsemane garden,[4] and was considered to have been a memorial of the palm-branches with which, according to Jn. xii. 13, the people of Jerusalem met the coming Jesus. The narrative itself assumes that for such purposes palm-branches were prepared in the city at festivals.   At the entrances of the solemn processions of pilgrims such a solemn reception may in any case have been customary.[5]   Of a different character were the branches which, according to Mt. xxi. 8 ; Mk. xi. 8, were broken off from the trees, in order to strew them in the way.[6]   These could only have been olive-branches, the breaking of which before blossoming time (May) could not have done any damage worthy of mention, which in any case the enthusiastic crowd would not consider.   The antiphonal chanting was improvised by using well-known psalm-verses, which the crowd repeated after the leader of the singing.   According to Lk. xix. 37, the jubilation of the people

[1] Ætheria (Geyer, *Itinera*, p. 83 *f.*).
[2] Even as late as the time of the Crusades the procession went to the rocky dome ; see Baumstark, *Oriens Christ.*, v., p. 219, note 6.
[3] *Commemor. de casis Dei*, Tobler, *Descr. T. S.*, p. 83.
[4] Bordeaux pilgrim ; Cyril of Jerusalem, *Cat.* xiii. 4 ; Petrus Diaconus.
[5] Nowadays they are brought in large quantities to Jerusalem for Palm Sunday. The Muslims carry them in front of their funeral processions.
[6] Traditional legislation protects only the root-shoots (*gerophiyoth*) of the olives (b. Bab. K. 81a).

began on the height of the Mount of Olives. Those who know the emotional potentialities of orientals, who were here roused to great enthusiasm at beholding the longed-for holy city and by the consciousness of leading into it a Son of David who was, at the lowest estimation, a Man of God above all others, will not be astonished at the phrases used on that occasion. They suggested wishes the immediate fulfilment of which probably no one expected.

As early as Eusebius[1] and Jerome[2] it was taken for granted that the valley between the Mount of Olives and Jerusalem is the plain of Jehoshaphat, where, according to Joel iii. 2, 12, the nations will gather for judgment. However, this plain is rather to be sought, with the "king's dale" (2 Sam. xviii. 18), to the north of the Jerusalem of that time. To this belongs, according to Jn. xviii. 1, the name "brook Kidron," rendered by the Pal. Evangeliarium *nahla dekatresaiya*, because it understood Kidron as meaning cedars, as the widely attested reading τῶν κέδρων shows. Already in the fifth century A.D. a brook ran here only in the winter, at times of heavy and sustained rain storms.[3]

Over the bottom of the Kidron valley a dam, with a path over it, was perhaps already in existence, provided with a contrivance for letting the winter-water pass through. At present the conditions have changed much on account of the sepulchre church of St. Mary which blocks up the valley, and because of this the water does not flow away immediately any longer, but the collected water is drawn off from the pool through the dam. On the far side there was formerly a stairway,[4] leading up steeply to the east gate of the Temple area, and also a direct ascent to the east gate of the city. Of the latter a few steps above the present road can be recognised. By edging northward, one eventually arrives by circuitous ways at the east gate. Just here it is not quite certain how the city wall ran in the time of Christ: whether it enclosed a space north of the Temple area, and the "sheep gate" (Jn. v. 2 ; Neh. iii. 32) belonged to this wall; or whether the northern extension of the Temple court joined its north corner also as far as the city corner, so that one would have to look for the sheep gate on the north side of the sanctuary. On one of

---

[1] *Cf. Die Worte Jesu*, p. 180 *f.*

[2] *Onomasticum* 273, 300. Also the Bordeaux pilgrim, Eucherius, Antoninus, Arculf. Also the reading τοῦ κέδρου in Cod. D. erroneously understands the expression as referring to the tree.

[3] Eucherius (Geyer, *Itinera*, p. 227).　　　　[4] Arculf, p. 224.

those two ways Jesus had then to ride to Jerusalem. Church tradition was divided in regard to this. In olden times the Palm Sunday procession moved from the Mount of Olives through the city gate, which was named "The gate of Benjamin," and, avoiding the Temple place, moved on to the church of the Resurrection.[1] Near the gate a halt was made by the sheep pool.[2] At this time (about 530) it is stated that the gate of Benjamin was the gate of our Lord's entry into Jerusalem.[3] It was only as late as the time of the Crusaders that the east gate of the Temple place became the gate of the procession as well as the supposed gate through which Jesus entered Jerusalem.[4] This so-called "golden gate of the Temple" has this advantage, that in its present building, adorned with late Roman art, which may perhaps be ascribed to the emperor Heraklius, there are found in thresholds and side-posts venerable relics of the time of Christ, which the Jews considered imperishable,[5] and to which also Antoninus draws attention. Rabbinic law demands reverent behaviour opposite this eastern gate because behind it was the Holy of Holies.[6] We cannot know which road our Lord took then. The way through the sheep gate might have been more suitable for riding. But the golden gate belonged to the Temple, where was heard the hosanna of the children, and which displeased the scribes (Mt. xxi. 15 *f.*). In its proximity, either outside or within the Temple walls, ended the last pilgrimage of Jesus to the feast of Passover.

---

[1] Ætheria. [2] Georg. Canonarium, *Typikon.*

[3] Petrus Diaconus, Theoderich, Daniel.

[4] The gate of the priests, by which is meant the east gate, should remain, like the Hulda gate and the western Temple wall, until God restores the Temple. Cant. R. ii. 9 (31a).

[5] Also Prudentius, according to Baumstark (*Byz. Zeitschrift*, 1911, p. 184), and the Madaba map. *Cf.* p. 287 *f.* [6] Ber. ix. 5.

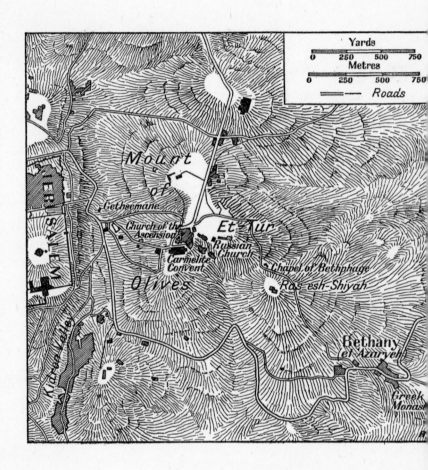

XIV

THE MOUNT OF OLIVES

THE road from Bethany to Jerusalem played a significant part in the Life of Jesus on more than one occasion. As, according to Mt. xxi. 17 ; Mk. xi. 11, He spent His nights in Bethany during His last stay in Jerusalem, He had frequently to take this road. Luke (xxi. 37) mentions the Mount of Olives as Jesus' night lodging : so does St. John on an earlier occasion. In Luke xxiv. 50 the road to Bethany is the scene of the last farewell, which in Acts i. 12 is the Mount of Olives. The one statement is not intended to exclude the other, for in the mind of the Evangelist Bethany lay on the Mount of Olives, although not on its peak.

In Mt. and Mk. the night quarters in Bethany are mentioned only in order to connect with them the narrative of the cursing of the fig-tree (Mt. xxi. 18 f. ; Mk. xi. 12 f.), which, as given in Mk., assumes that Jesus passed the tree at least twice. It is possible that on the road from Bethany there stood a withered fig-tree which, it was said, withered away by the almighty word of Jesus, because He had looked in vain for fruit on it. The fig-tree likes a warm position, whilst the olive-tree can stand cold weather ; therefore a fig-tree on the eastern slope of the Mount of Olives, in a sheltered spot, would be quite in place, and indeed there are a good number of them in that neighbourhood to this day. An early development of the first fruits, appearing at the same time as the leaves on the ends of the sprouts from the previous year, was to be expected.[1] But ripeness by the Easter season would be impossible. For in April there are only undeveloped figs (Arab. 'adshr or taksh), of which many fall off, or at the most fully developed yet still juiceless fruit (fajj), but not the ripe, juicy " early figs " (defur), which can be expected only in June, not to speak of the proper, less juicy " figs " (tin) of the chief harvest, which ripen in August out of the new sprouts of the same year. In Pales-

[1] Cf. Dalman, Arbeit und Sitte in Palästina, i., p. 378 f.

tine forty-five or fifty days used to be counted from the appearance of the leaves to the *paggim* (=*fajj*), then the same number
of days to the falling-off of the fruits, and lastly the same space of
time to the ripe figs.[1]   The figs remaining on the tree over the
winter may be disregarded, for they fall off at the sprouting of
the new shoots.   But the Oriental also eats the as yet juiceless
fruit and even the small '*adshr*, although they taste bitter.   For
one says of the first fruit : *Auwal etmar—bitauwil al-'amar*, " The
first of the fruits prolongs life."   That it was not the time of
figs yet (Mk. xi. 13), *i.e.* neither the time of the early figs in
June, nor the time of the chief fig harvest in August, can only
be meant to emphasise the fact that the tree's full adornment of
leaves at an unusually early period[2] led to the expectation of
something extraordinary in regard to its fruit also.   If the sprout
of the fruit was lacking, the tree was premature and promised no
good for the future.   Since the impending fate of Jerusalem
stood at the forefront of the thoughts of Jesus, the fig-tree was
to Him (as in Lk. xiii. 6 *f.*) an emblem of the City, which looked
so glorious but lacked the fruit of genuine righteousness.
But the disciples understood Him not, and the Evangelists
only thought of the power of faith which does wonders.

The Mount of Olives (Aram. *tura de-zetaiya*; in Pal. Evang.
Mt. xxi. 1; *cf.* Targum Zech. xiv. 4),[3] which was economically
important to ancient Jerusalem chiefly because of its olive-
trees, is the most southerly part of a mountain range ; its ridge
reaches its highest point (835 metres[4]) in the north, after which,
with several declines and ascents, it finally descends to 740
metres, and then to the level of the Kidron valley, which lies
about 600 metres above sea-level.   The last elevation of the
chain, which is connected with it only by a narrow ridge, forms
a threefold peak : two heights continue the chain, and a third
eminence stretches out in front of the more southern of the
two in the east.   The eastern peak, which looks towards the
desert, is the highest (817½ metres), but the ancient designation
of the Mount of Olives, now simply *et-Ṭur*, " the mountain," is
not applied to it, nor to the north-western heights (812½ metres),
which a tradition, attested since the sixth century,[5] erroneously
considers as the " Galilee " of the appearance of Jesus after the

---

[1] Tos. Shebi. iv. 20 ; p. Shebi. 35d.   [2] See also Mt. xxiv. 32.
[3] In Hebrew the mountain was later called *har ha-mishḥa*, " the mount of
anointing" (Par. iii. 6 ; Midd. ii. 4).
[4] Based mostly on my own measurements.
[5] *Brev. de Hieros*. (Geyer, p. 155).

Resurrection (Mt. xxviii. 16),[1] but solely to the south-western mountain running opposite to Jerusalem (with the mound, 815 metres) and its wide slope towards the Kidron valley, the level of which is here about 700 metres high. The olive-trees of this hill, from which, according to legend, the dove took her olive-branch after the Flood,[2] were formerly an important part of the possession of the old city, but now cemeteries, buildings, and gardens have reduced them to small dimensions. On the flat summit there is a small village which attached itself to the sanctuary of the Ascension.[3] In David's time there was some sacred spot there where people used to worship (2 Sam. xv. 32), and, according to rabbinic tradition,[4] at the time of the second Temple it was ploughed there, and this summit was found suitable to serve for the burning of the red heifer for the ashes of purification,[5] and so was in no danger of being thought impure. The ceremony is supposed to have taken place exactly opposite the Temple, a supposition which points to the proximity of the sanctuary of the Ascension. Also the beacon which used to signal between here and the Alexandrium on *Ḳarn Sertabeh*,[6] to mark the beginning of the month, presupposes an unoccupied summit, such as can best be found at the eastern top. Long cedar-laths, bound together with reeds, pine-branches, and tow, were lighted, and swung about up and down, right and left, until the same signal was seen on the next summit.[7] A legend tells of two cedars on the Mount of Olives, under the shade of one of which were four shops selling things suitable for sacrifices, and from the other emerged each month forty "*sea*" of young pigeons for the sacrifices brought by women after child-birth (Lev. xii. 8 ; Lk. ii. 24).[8] This legend, however, does not prove that there was a market-place on the Mount of Olives ; it is only intended to eulogise the once luxurious products of Jerusalem's environs. The phantastic exaggeration of the legend, which at one time was connected with a single tree on the "Royal mountain,"[9] has historic significance only for the time when affectionate imagination invented it.

[1] See *PJB*, 1916, p. 73.
[2] Gen. R. xxxiii. (67a).
[3] First mentioned in the fifteenth century.
[4] Pes. 14a.
[5] Para ii. 6.
[6] Rosh ha-sh. ii. 4.
[7] That the signal service as far as Mesopotamia, presumed by the Mishna, is not an impossibility, is shown by the light-signal line from Euphrates to Gaza which was constructed in the Mamluk kingdom in the thirteenth century. See Hartmann, *ZDMG*, 1916, p. 503 *f.*
[8] p. Taan 69a ; Lam R. ii. 2 (44a).
[9] Ber. 44a.

The top of the Mount of Olives was uncultivated; its busiest and most bustling part was certainly the south, through which runs the road to Bethany and Jericho. A convent of Carmelite nuns is there now. Because, according to Lk. xi. 1, Jesus seems to have taught the Paternoster to the disciples in the vicinity of Bethany, it is inscribed in the cloisters of the convent church in thirty-five languages. In the time of the Crusaders, under the altar of a church which stood here, the Lord's Prayer was shown, supposed to have been written by our Lord Himself.[1] Excavations have revealed what in all probability are the remains of the oldest church building at this place.[2] This was the basilica built by Constantine's mother.[3] It guarded the site where Jesus taught the disciples on the Mount of Olives the mysteries of the end (Mt. xxiv. 3 f.; xxv. 1 f.; Mk. xiii. 3 f.; Lk. xxi. 6 f.). There was under the altar, used as a crypt, a cave—now again cleared—which was then considered to have been the place where Jesus taught.[4] In the night of the Tuesday in Holy Week a solemn service took place there in the fourth century, when the bishop read Mt. xxiv. 3-xxvi. 6.[5] But the congregation also gathered there on Maundy Thursday evening, because Jesus was supposed to have taught the disciples there on that day also. The last meeting of our Lord with the disciples, as described by St. John, was located there, and therefore the discourses, Jn. xiii.-xvii., were read there.[6] This looks as if in spite of Jn. xviii. 1, according to which Jesus went over the Kidron only after these discourses, the Mount of Olives cave was considered to have been the place of the Last Supper. It is also conceivable, however, that originally the discourses were concluded at the place of the Meal with Jn. xiv. 31 ("Arise, let us go hence"), and Jn. xviii. 1 was understood in the sense that the contents of xv.-xvii. were spoken on the way to the Mount of Olives, which is grammatically permissible. The Palestinian Evange-

---

[1] Theoderich, cf. Petrus Diaconus, Phocas.

[2] See plan and description in Vincent and Abel, Jérusalem, ii., p. 337 f.

[3] Geyer, pp. 23, 77. See also Eusebius, Vita Const. iii. 43. The church was not, as usually stated, called "Eleona," but was the church "in Eleona," i.e. on the Mount of Olives, because in Lk. xxi. 37 the Mount of Olives is designated ἐλαιῶν.

[4] So Ætheria (Geyer, pp. 86, 91). Eusebius, Demonstr. Evang. vi. 1, 18, 23.

[5] Ætheria, p. 84 f.; Arculf, p. 251.

[6] Thus Ætheria, p. 86, and expressly the Armenian Lectionary; see Klameth, Die neutestamentlichen Lokaltraditionen ii., Die Ölbergtraditionen i., p. 40. Later this localisation was given up. According to the Georgian Canonar. (Or. Chr., v., p. 223) and the Typikon of the Anastasis, only the story of Gethsemane was read here.

liarium seems actually to have understood it thus.[1]   At a time
when there was only one Mount of Olives church, it is quite
likely that all that took place on the way to the Mount of
Olives and at its foot was read there, and in this wise appro-
priately introduced the progress back to the city.   In this way
the idea could arise, which is already expressed by Ætheria,
that those discourses were actually spoken on the Mount of
Olives.   Yet it is also possible that the belief attached to the
Gethsemane grotto as the place of the Last Supper (see
Chapter XVIII.) had something to do with it.   That a cave
was taken to be the place where Jesus taught on the Mount
of Olives, contradicts Mk. xiii. 3, according to which He
sat opposite the Temple.   It is possible that the Mithra
cult, where they " call the place where they teach the
initiation of them that obey him, a cave,"[2] and the Gnostics
of the third century who liked to describe the Mount of
Olives and its grottoes as the scene of Jesus' mystic instructions,[3] may have had some influence on this, as well as
the verse concerning the righteous one who " shall dwell
in the high cave of a strong rock " (Isa. xxxiii. 16 LXX).
However, the sanctuary was erected, after all, there where the
Bethany road ascended the Mount of Olives.   When Jesus
came in the evening from the Temple with His disciples, it
can be assumed that He stopped here for a while, and cast a
glance towards the city and its Temple illumined by the
setting sun.   On that occasion the disciples drew His attention
to the colossal stones of its eastern wall, seemingly erected
for eternity, the remnants of which excite our interest even now
(Mt. xxiv. 1 ; Mk. xiii. 1 ; Lk. xxi. 5).   A shimmer of the
ancient glory still lies upon the ancient sanctuary when
viewed from the Mount of Olives.   To Jesus the view gave
occasion to call the disciples aside, to sit down with them at
the edge of the height and there to speak at length to them
concerning the end which awaits not only this Temple.   The
glorious view of the Temple opposite made Him think of the
bitter earnestness of the time.   " Do not admire," but " watch,
for ye know not when your Master cometh " (Aram. *Hawon'irin
deletekhon ḥakhemin behayden yom marekhon ate*, Mt. xxiv. 42).

With what emotions the pilgrims approached the Mount
of Olives, Sophronius shows in his pilgrim song[4] (*cf.* p. 35 *f.*) :

[1] The Peshitta translates : " Thus said Jesus and went out "; Pal. Evang.:
Bema di de'amar halen-nephak, " In saying this He went out."
[2] Justin, *Dial. c. Tryph.* lxx., lxxviii.   [3] *Acta Johannis* xcvii.
[4] Migne, *P.G.* lxxxvii., 3812.

" Ascending the steps from the famous valley,[1] I would kiss the Mount of Olives from whence He ascended into the heavens. Oh, how sweet art thou, fair and lofty summit, whence Christ the Lord beheld the starry spheres![2] Magnifying with joy the awful depth of His divine wisdom, by which I was redeemed, I would swiftly run thither where He was wont to expound the mysteries of His Kingdom to His reverend companions, casting light into darksome depths. I would pass beneath the roof[3] and through the greatest gate, and at last, going out upon the terrace,[4] would gaze upon the beauty of the holy city as it lay towards the west. How sweet to behold thy loveliness from the Mount of Olives, O thou city of God ! "

Not far north from the church of Instruction on the Mount of Olives, on the highest point of the same mount, there has been since the fourth century a church dedicated to the Ascension. It must have been thought that Jesus was again in the grotto of the church of Instruction with the disciples ; then parted from them, and that on the mountain height he disappeared before their eyes. The Bordeaux pilgrim confused the site, on which, in his time, there was as yet no building, with the mountain of Transfiguration. He speaks of a " small mountain " in the proximity of the basilica of the Mount of Olives. Ætheria, who visited the same site in 380, differentiates between " the church in Eleona," *i.e.* Greek ἐν Ελαιῶνι, and the Inbomon—*i.e.* ἐν βωμῷ, " on the hill," not designated by her as a church. Yet this place, used for solemn services, must already have had some suitable arrangement, because the bishop, priests and congregation " sat " there during the lections and singing. The pilgrim Poimeria must thus have already then erected the building[5] where the Ascension was celebrated on the day of Pentecost. This was not a basilica but a round court, " having in its circuit three vaulted porticoes roofed over,"[6] the soil in the centre of which was considered to have been the site of the Ascension. There the footprints of Jesus were believed to be visible and the ever fresh turf excited wonder.[7] In the seventh century this centre

---

[1] The Kidron valley.   [2] Geyer, *Itinera*, p. 23.
[3] *Ibid.*, pp. 83, 86, 94.   [4] *Ibid.*, p. 94.
[5] Peter the Iberian, ed. Raabe, p. 30 ; *cf.* Clameth, *Lokaltraditionen* II. i., p. 96 *f.*
[6] Thus according to Arculf.
[7] Prudentius ; see Baumstarck, *Byz. Zeitschrift*, 1911, p. 183 *f.*, and Paulinus of Nola, *Ep.* 31. *Cf.*, as to the widely spread belief in holy footprints, Klameth, p. 196 *f.*

was covered by a hollow brass cylinder of large circumference, flattened at the top, " its height being shown by measurement to reach one's neck." If one entered through a door made in the western side, one saw through the open hole in the wheel the ground, now covered deeply with dust, in which was seen the impress of the footsteps of Jesus.[1] In the ninth century there was here only an altar surrounded by columns in the centre of a court, in which a second altar in a niche facing east served for a service conducted by the patriarch on Ascension day.[2] The Crusaders erected over the ruins of the first building an Oktagon, the ruins of which surround at present the site of the Ascension. In the centre an eight-cornered chapel covers a piece of marble with a footprint, which cannot have anything to do with the surface of the mountain. If the site had not been built on, one would have had the impression of being on the summit of the Mount of Olives, which was the site where our Lord was frequently present with His disciples until the last departure. But, as it is, one longs to be out in the open.

As the summit of the Mount of Olives was not covered with buildings in the time of Christ, there is nothing against the assumption that this was the scene of His last meeting with His disciples. According to Lk. xxiv. 50, this took place on the way to Bethany. When in Acts i. 12 the distance of the Mount of Olives from Jerusalem is given as a sabbath day's journey, i.e. 2,000 cubits (about 5 stadia), it must mean the summit of the mountain. Thus the traditional location somewhat north of the Bethany road, on the full height of the summit looking out towards Jerusalem, would suit all the data. But according to Vita Euthymii[3] there was another mountain near Jerusalem, occupied by a monastery, a height which the natives called " The Mountain of the Ascension," evidently without consideration of the official sanctuary. If this was not the Ras esh-Shiyah in the proximity of the Bethphage sanctuary, it could only be the eastern top of the Mount of Olives, which is now occupied by Russian buildings, and which had monasteries in olden times, as mosaic finds and old reports prove.[4] Also Hesychius Hieros. does not seem to have thought of the Inbomon, for he says in regard to the Lukan πρὸς Βηθανίαν that it points to the road towards Bethany, on which road the Mount of Olives is situated, and to that part of the mountain which

---

[1] Arculf. [2] Epiphanius Hagiopolita (Migne, P.G. cxx., col. 604),
[3] Migne, P.G. clxvi., col. 604. [4] Antoninus (Geyer, p. 170).

borders on Bethany.[1]   This can only be the eastern top.   Here
the eye wanders unchecked to the horizon, south, east, and
north, whilst Jerusalem is hidden from view by the western
summit, unless one ascends the high tower of the Russians.
In the west, the summit of the Ascension, with its sanctuaries
occupies the attention.   But above all one views the magnificent picture which opens up in the east and which has charmed
many a pilgrim disappointed with Jerusalem.   But we are not
at present considering the beauty of the view, in which the grey-
yellow waves of the desert-hills provide the foreground to the
dazzling-white Jordan valley, to the mild-blue surface of the
Dead Sea and to the high wall of the mountains of Moab—we
are seeking only the footprints of Jesus.   In the south, Bethlehem, with her white pinnacles above her green hill, greets us—
the place of His Birth ; in the north, Ephraim rises before the
mountain of Baal Hazor : His last peaceful resting-place before
the struggles of the end.   In the east, we see below us the road
from Jerusalem to Bethany, to which the account of the
Ascension points (Lk. xxiv. 50); but also the chapel of Bethphage, Bethany, the Greek monastery, and the road to the
desert with the pass of Adummim.   The position of the now
unseen Jericho is marked by the Quarantana mountain and
by the pointed height which keeps watch at the descent into
the Jordan valley.   In its desert plain the eyes seek the green
band which marks the path of the Jordan.   The first appearance of Jesus, His last way, and the departure from His own,
are visualised here at one and the same time.   Many problems
have yet to be solved in connection with the Gospel topography
and its relation to the Mount of Olives, but one thing is certain :
Jesus of Nazareth was here.

[1] *Quæstiones*, Migne, *P.G.* xciii., col. 1148.

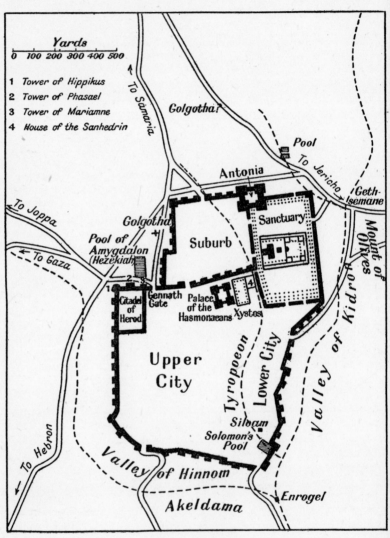

Plan of Jerusalem.
(Designed by Dalman.)

XV

JERUSALEM

" GOING up " to Jerusalem is the Gospel phrase (Mt. xx. 17 *f*.;
Lk. ii. 42 ; xviii. 31 ; xix. 28 ; Jn. ii. 13 ; v. 1 ; vii. 8 *f*. ;
xi. 55). The same expression is used in the Old Testament
and rabbinic literature : one " goes up " from Babylon to the
land of Israel ;[1] from Galilee,[2] from Bittir in Judæa,[3] from
Askalon,[4] to Jerusalem " in order to pray " (Aram. *lesallaa*).
Also in the parable of the Pharisee and the publican the
starting-point of their " going up " to the Temple " in order
to pray " (Lk. xviii. 10) is probably not the city of Jerusalem,
which certainly was not the home of the publican, but some
place in Palestine, although in Jerusalem this expression was
used (as in Acts iii. 1) even when, in fact, in the city itself
one went some way downhill first, and then just slightly up.
One might conclude from this that Palestine lay higher than
Babylon, Judæa higher than Galilee, and Jerusalem higher
than all the others, as the future Jerusalem is poetically
described by Isaiah and Micah (Isa. ii. 1 ; Micah iv. 1), or as
a certain rabbi pictured it to himself—which was that Sinai,
Tabor and Carmel together only equal the height of the mountain of the sanctuary and the area of Jerusalem.[5] In actual
fact the Jerusalem of the present age is quite different. True,
she is situated upon the Judæan highland, 740 to 770 metres
above the sea-level—not higher than Bethlehem, 160 metres
lower than Hebron (927 metres), 110 metres lower than
Bethel (881 metres), but higher indeed than Tabor (562
metres). She lies in a basin, which permits no wide view in
any direction. The Mediterranean Sea and the Dead Sea
are invisible even from the highest parts of the city. But the

---

[1] 2 Chr. xxxvi. 23 ; Ezra i. 5 ; p. R. h. S. 58b ; B. b. 45a.
[2] Lam. R. iii. 9 (50b). Joseph also " goes up " from Galilee to Judæa,
Lk. ii. 4.
[3] Lam. R. ii. 1 (43a).   [4] Cant. R. vii. 2 (67b).
[5] Pesikt. 144b ; Midr. Teh. xxvi. 6 ; lxxxviii. 3.

natural drainage of the basin towards the south-east in the direction of the Dead Sea has formed channels which in the immediate neighbourhood of Jerusalem sink to 600 metres above the sea-level, and leave high ranges standing up between them, which offer to an ancient city of moderate size a naturally strong site. The present Jerusalem, walled round by the Turks in the sixteenth century, like her predecessor the Ælia Capitolina of Hadrian, preferred to occupy the summits of the heights where they rise up higher towards the north-west. In this way the city took in a part which originally lay outside, as her centre, and so became, unwittingly, the city of Golgotha. The Jerusalem of the time of Jesus, on the other hand, was still directly connected with the city of the Israelitish kings, which Nehemiah, on his rebuilding of the walls, took in again. Consequently, the original starting-point of the foundation of the city in the neighbourhood of the Gihon well and the Rogel cistern, had the result that the southern slopes of both the city hills, which now lie outside the city walls, were entirely built upon, so that the city descended at one point to a height of 630 metres, and thus enclosed within her borders a difference in heights of about 140 metres. As a result, Jerusalem at the time of Christ was, much more than to-day, a hill city, where the streets had frequently to take the form of steps and were therefore impassable for carts and riders.

The fact that in the purlieus of the city a western branch of the eastern chief channel in the Jerusalem basin, i.e. the Kidron valley, ran almost parallel with the chief channel itself, was of significance in deciding the outer shape and the inner character of the city. This secondary valley, which Josephus calls the " Cheesemakers' Valley,"[1] but which must really have been called the " Valley of nakedness,"[2] or " Dung Valley,"[3] divided Jerusalem naturally into eastern and western parts, as is also assumed in the administration of the city in the time of Nehemiah (Neh. iii. 9, 12). In the time of Josephus these parts were known as the " Upper City " and the " Lower City."[4] This distinction consequent on height came about

---

[1] *Bell. Jud.* v. 4, 1 (φάραγξ τῶν τυροποιῶν), which was turned into " The Tyropœon " !

[2] See *PJB*, 1918, p. 63 f. (Hebrew *ge ha-Toreph*).

[3] Dalman in *Temple Dictionary*, p. 305 (Hebrew *ge ha-Asphot* ; cf. 2 Sam. xvii. 29, where *shephot*=cheese).

[4] *Bell. Jud.* v. 4, 1 ; cf., for " Jerusalem at the time of Christ," Mickley, *PJB*, 1911, p. 35 ff.

because the part of the city situated east of the valley is substantially lower than the western part, and it was even more obviously fitting since the sanctuary on the eastern hill—through the artificial terracing and walling of its foundation—became such an independent entity, both to outward appearance as well as from the point of view of administration and defence, that Josephus in writing of it separates the hill of the sanctuary, as the third hill, from that on which the Lower City was situated. At any rate, only the southern spur of the eastern hill came to be considered as the "Lower City," and it deserved this name the more, as an artificial removal of its highest summit[1]—the exact place of which has not so far been located—transformed it into the unbroken slope that it appears to-day. The natural boundary of both parts was the valley which lay between them, which was certainly a part of the Lower City. The Upper City was popularly called, according to Josephus,[2] the "Upper Market," a name which occurs also in rabbinic literature as *ha-Shuk ha-'elyon* in Hebrew.[3] In Aramaic it must have been *shuka 'illaa*. This name shows that market streets were found there, and were considered characteristic of that part of the city, where indeed they are in place, since the great traffic routes of the city from the north, west, and south passed through them; it may be assumed therefore that this part of the city was originally a marketing centre.[4] The Lower City—although Josephus does not say so—seems to have been called the "Lower Market," Hebrew *ha-Shuk ha-tahton*,[5] which is *shuka 'tahtaa* in Aramaic, although there are no definite references to its exact position. Josephus calls this quarter also *Akra*, after the former stronghold of the Syrians, whose retreat on Iyar 23, 142 B.C., was celebrated annually, long after the event, by a prohibition against fasting on that day.[6] That the stronghold was called *hakra* in Aramaic, is in accordance with the name given to the citadel of David on Mount Zion in the Targum,[7] but it must be traced back to the Greek word. It is due to the confused description of Josephus that, following others, Kirmis[8] again has defended the erroneous view that the position of the stronghold was an easterly projection of the western hill, north of

---

[1] *Ant.* xiii. 6, 9 ; *Bell. Jud.* v. 4, 1.   [2] *Bell. Jud.* v. 4, 1.
[3] Shek. viii. 1.   [4] See *PJB*, 1915, p. 82.   [5] Tos. Sanh. xiv. 14.
[6] 1 Macc. xiii. 51 ; Meg. Taanit ii. ; *cf.* Dalman, Aram. *Dialektproben*, pp. 1, 32.
[7] 2 Sam. v. 7, 9 ; xxiii. 14.
[8] *Die Lage der alten Davidstadt* (1919).

the Upper City, and that Pronobis[1] also locates it on the eastern part of the hill of the Upper City.[2]

The northern limit of the Upper City can be located with certainty by the way its wall runs from the Hippikus tower towards the western hall of the Temple area, which it reaches in the neighbourhood of the Xystus,[3] and by a western off-shoot of the great city valley—on a line which would, approximately, correspond to the present road from the Jaffa gate towards the Temple area, thus leaving two-thirds of the present walled Jerusalem outside. Thus it becomes certain that the *suburb* of Josephus, which probably dated from pre-exilic times,[4] lay north of that line. To judge by the number of the towers on its wall and its course from the " Garden gate " in the north wall of the Upper City towards the north-western corner of the sanctuary, it could not have been extensive.[5] The quarter between the market street and the Temple area in the west and east, and between David street and *Via dolorosa* in the south and north, must have corresponded to that of modern Jerusalem. A timber market, a market for wool and cloth,[6] and also copper-works, were situated there.[7] In the north-east the continuation of the Temple hill was covered with the buildings of a new city, not yet walled in the time of Christ, which was called simply *Bezetha*, the " Cut."[8] Here the Jerusalem of that time reached to the northern border of the present Old City.

The citadel of Zion on the southern part of the eastern hill was not replaced after the destruction of the Syrian Akra, so the city lacked an Acropolis in the antique sense, unless the Sanctuary could be considered one. The Hasmonæan palace on the eastern edge of the Upper City, from whose roof-terraces there was a fine view over the Sanctuary,[9] could not serve this purpose, because it was only secured in the east by the city valley, but otherwise was essentially dominated by the Upper City. Herod, therefore, erected for himself a castle at the other end of the Upper City, in its north-western corner, which

---

[1] *Akra und Sion* (1923), also Mommert, *Topographie* i. (1900).
[2] See, concerning the Zion citadel in general, *PJB*, 1915, p. 39 *f*.
[3] *Bell. Jud.* v. 4, 2.   [4] *Ant.* xiv. 13, 4; xv. 11, 5.
[5] Perhaps mentioned in 2 Kings xxii. 14; 2 Chr. xxxiv. 22; Zeph. i. 10; Neh. xi. 9 (?). The Targum on Zeph. (MS. Orient. 2210), however, thinks of Uphla, *i.e.* Ophel, so that Mishne would correspond to the Lower City.
[6] A market for wool merchants and the preparers of incense is mentioned in b. Erubin 101a.
[7] *Bell. Jud.* ii. 19, 4; v. 8, 1.   [8] *Ibid.* v. 4, 2; *cf.* under xvii.
[9] *Ant.* xx. 8, 11; *Bell. Jud.* ii. 16, 3.

was also his *palace*.[1] The native name seems to have been *ḳasṭra demalka*, " the camp of the king."[2] There had in fact been an important military camp in the precincts of the palace.[3] It was, however, less Jerusalem's refuge than a fortress for her coercion. From the great north-by-south road of Palestine and the connection towards the west, the city was almost cut off by Herod's citadel. A street running along within the wall, which traversed the city valley by means of a bridge,[4] was the way of approach to the Sanctuary. Three high and strong towers protected the palace and the city towards the north, in that part which lacked the protection of the suburban wall, and also afforded the possibility of a constant watch being kept over the city, the suburb, and the Sanctuary. This muzzling of Jerusalem and her Jewish life was made complete by a second smaller, but specially well built, castle on the northern boundary of the Sanctuary. It had once been the citadel of the Hasmonæans for the protection of the Temple, but now it became its fort, with entrances to the roofs of its pillared halls. That it bore the name *Antonia*, after Antonius, the Roman conqueror of Syria and Palestine, showed in whose interest this coercion was wrought. The keeping of the high-priestly vestments in its chambers, made even the solemn office of the high priest in the Temple service at festivals dependent upon the goodwill of the rulers (*Ant.* xv. 11, 4 ; *Bell. Jud.* v. 5, 8).

In the time of Jesus the Herodian foreign rule in Jerusalem had been followed by the Roman. Even on the Mount of Olives, a glimpse at the city must have sufficed to make the contrast between this power, and that of the God worshipped imageless in the Sanctuary, clearly visible (*cf.* above, p. 255). But every walk through the streets where, among thronging crowds, the Roman soldiers paraded even as far as the environs of the Temple ; every payment of taxes for the imperial exchequer—even though the payment was made to the native provincial office ;[5] and, finally, every time the coins with the image, or at least the name, of Augustus or Tiberius on them were used for payments in the shops, and even put into the boxes at the Temple, hammered into the soul of the Jew the

[1] *Bell. Jud.* v. 4, 3 *f.*
[2] Tos. Ed. iii. 2 ; b. Men. 103b. *Isṭratit* (*isṭaria*) must be traced back, after *ḳaṣram* (p. Shek. 51a) to *ḳasṭra* if στρατιά did not mean " camp."
[3] *Bell. Jud.* ii. 15, 5 ; 17, 8.   [4] *Ant.* xiv. 4, 2 ; *Bell. Jud.* ii. 16, 3.
[5] See Schürer, *Geschichte d. jüd. V.*, i., pp. 340, 474 ; ii., p. 235 ; *cf. Bell. Jud.* ii. 17, 1.

fact that all the splendour and all the luxuriousness which the
capital offered him, was only enjoyed in slavery, a slavery
most unbecoming to the people which alone among the
nations of the world was honoured by the name " the son of
God " (Hos. xi. 1).   Only to God's sanctuary, to its ministers,
and to necessitous fellow-citizens was the Jew obliged to
pay tribute, and this was made almost impossible for him
through the fiscal burdens put upon him by the Roman
emperor.   However, anyone who considers the history of the
Jews from the point of view of tyrannical Rome, and with the
eyes of the unprincipled Flavius Josephus, and, like Eduard
Meyer, declares that the Maccabees were fanatical brigand-
chiefs; and anyone to whom Israel's election as a medium of
Revelation culminating in Christ appears to be but an illusion;
will not be able to grasp the depth of this national, as well as
religious, conflict.   But one who does grasp it,[1] understands
also the weight of the question put to Jesus in the sanctuary
(Mt. xxii. 17) : " Is it right to give tribute unto Cæsar, or not ?"
and what was meant when He answered : " *Habun dilekesar
lekesar, wedile-elaha le-elaha*," " Render unto Cæsar what is
Cæsar's, and what is God's to God " (*v*. 21).   The Mosaic
Law does not even command that tribute be paid to Israel's
own king.   Jesus seems at first sight to acknowledge the
foreign ruler's equal right with God to Israel's property.   But
this cannot be seriously supposed.   Let the emperor get
back the coin with his image !   God demands what is His,
which for Jesus means the whole man, including his possessions.
He who ranged himself in this matter on the side of Jesus
could not but look at enslaved Jerusalem—which also for
Him was " the city of the great King " (Mt. v. 35 ; *cf*. Ps.
xlviii. 3)—with new eyes.   God's reign, as He proclaims it,
is not tied down to it.

In external appearance the Jerusalem of the time of Christ
must have been similar to the old city of the present day, in
the narrowness of her up- and down-hill streets, occasionally
provided with steps, on to which not the fronts but the plain
and almost windowless exteriors of the houses abut.   But
the flat roofs were not, as they now are, overtopped with the
dome-shaped vaulted rooms.   For the roofs, constructed of
plaster, rested on beams,[2] which at that time could be bought
at a special timber market in the suburbs.[3]   Also the orna-

---

[1] *Cf*. Klausner, *Jesus of Nazareth*, p. 318.
[2] Ohal. xii. 5 *f*.; Tos. Ohal. v. 5 ; *Bell. Jud.* v. 4, 4.   [3] *Bell. Jud.* ii. 19, 4.

mental buildings of the city did not at that time tower above the dwelling-houses with domes or pointed towers, but all the lines ran straight and level. Only step-like pinnacles—from early times usual in the East—must frequently have relieved the monotony of these lines in walls and towers. The towers built on the 10-15 metres high city wall would not greatly have overtopped the wall. But the three towers constructed by Herod on the north side of his palace in diminishing stages, after the pattern of the Pharos lighthouse, were a landmark of the royal city, visible from afar. The gates which certainly gave entrance to the city, not as now at the corners, but opening straight out of the centre of the wall, must have had particularly strong towers at their sides. The view of the whole was not oriental in our modern sense of the term, having in mind the present-day domes and slender minarets : but rather Roman, dignified and solemn, yet certainly not gloomy, since the white limestone of the country—which Josephus likes to call " marble "[1]—reflected the light of the strong sun then as to-day. The judgment once passed in regard to the city of the Temple, was true enough then: " He who has not seen Jerusalem in her beauty, has never beheld a beautiful city."[2]

The proper forms of Græco-Roman art were not absent in Jerusalem : even rabbinic literature is cognisant of the fact that, in harmony with the traditional understanding of the Decalogue, figured sculptures existed in Jerusalem, and only human representations were avoided.[3] But it would have been less evident from the outside, and even within they were probably more sparingly used than in a purely Roman or Greek city. The porticoes of the chief streets which the Madaba map has, to represent the Roman Ælia Capitolina, are not to be assumed for the Herodian Jerusalem, since there was not enough room for extensive ornamental sites. Only in the city valley, below the sanctuary, the small square of the Xystus—in which, perhaps, the gymnasium of the Syrian period, divested of its original purpose, was preserved[4]—will certainly have had its pillared halls. Mass meetings could be held there.[5] There was certainly no lack of columns and half-columns in the Herodian theatre, presumably situated in the upper city, whose ornamental trophies were regarded by the Jews with disfavour.[6] Outside the city, in the south,

---

[1] Bell. Jud. v. 4, 4.   [2] Sukk. 51b.   [3] Tos. Ab. z. v. 2.
[4] 1 Macc. i. 14; 2 Macc. iv. 9, 12, 14.   [5] Bell. Jud. ii. 16, 3.   [6] Ant. xv. 8, 1.

lay the hippodrome,[1] which presumably is identical with the
"very large amphitheatre,"[2] built, according to Josephus,
by Herod "in the plain." In regard to the royal palace,
Josephus speaks of "many porticoes, one beyond another,
round about, and in each of the porticoes different kinds of
pillars, with the open courts between, all green."[3] So one
must think of a number of pillared courts, each of which had
its own order of columns. The Temple had been hellenised
by the art-loving king, but the Corinthian style Josephus
only mentions in regard to the fourfold columnar rows of
its great basilica, built at the southern end of the antecourt.[4]
It seems as though it was found impossible to fit into any of
the classical styles the innumerable pillars which upheld the
long galleries of the sanctuary. Perhaps here there were
Corinthian and Ionian capitals embossed like those in Galilæan
synagogues,[5] in the southern temple of the Hauran Seeia,[6]
and, above all, at Petra,[7] by which the stone-mason's work was
made easier. Josephus' direct statement that painting and
carving were excluded from the Temple galleries,[8] probably
means only that all figurative representations on walls and
ceilings were prohibited, and that the more rigorous interpretation of the commandment with regard to images was
applied here,[9] while the roofs of the Basilica in the outer Temple
court had perhaps figured representations among their many
carved works.[10] No undisputed examples are preserved of
the capitals of the buildings of that time ; but the Ionian and
Doric capitals from three rock-tombs in the Kidron valley,
and the Corinthian embossed capitals lying before the tomb
of queen Helena, give an idea of the art-forms then in use

[1] *Ant.* xvii. 10, 2 ; *Bell. Jud.* ii. 3, 1.

[2] *Ant.* xv. 8, 1. Nothing is said about the erection of the hippodrome on
the other hand, he mentions chariot races in connection with the statement on
the building of the theatre and the amphitheatre, so that the amphitheatre must
be thought of as a hippodrome. Also in connection with Cæsarea he speaks
first of a theatre and amphitheatre and of races (*Ant.* xv. 9, 6 ; xvi. 5, 1 ; *Bell.
Jud.* i. 21, 8), while afterwards a hippodrome plays an important rôle (*Ant.*
xviii. 3, 1 ; *Bell. Jud.* ii. 9, 3).

[3] *Bell. Jud.* v. 4, 4.   [4] *Ant.* xv. 11, 5.

[5] Kohl and Watzinger, *Antike Synagogen in Galiläa*, pp. 48, 78, 122.

[6] *Princ. Univ. Exp. to Syria*, ii. A. 6, p. 394.

[7] Dalman, *Petra und seine Felsenheiligtümer*, p. 267 ; *Neue Petra-Forschungen*,
p. 20 *f.*

[8] *Bell. Jud.* v. 5, 2.

[9] *Ant.* xvii. 6, 2 ; *Vita* 12. *Cf.* Duschak, *Josephus Flavius und die Tradition*,
p. 34, where the stricter conception is explained by the conditions of the time
when there was more inducement to idolatry than in the time of Solomon.

[10] *Ant.* xv. 11, 5.

here. At the same time one observes that also in the use of cornices with grooves, and of pyramids and round tent-roofs, the sepulchral art of Jerusalem was akin to that of Petra. Apart from these rock-tombs, the foundations of a part of the outer walls of the Temple and the ground-floor of one of the three towers of Herod[1] are the only witnesses to the art of building of that time, in which royal power sought, by the immense bulk of its embossed stones, set one upon the other without mortar, to put up a monument to itself. Excavations undertaken in the area of the Herodian royal citadel and in the now blocked-up city valley, would probably help us to visualise the Jerusalem of the time of Christ even more distinctly.

Jerusalem, which God has set "in the midst of the nations and the countries that are around her" (Ezek. v. 5; cf. xxxviii. 12), and which the Jews liked to consider as the centre of the world (Jubil. viii. 19; Enoch xxvi. 1 f.), could indeed be called the hub of the ancient world, because of her connections with all the settlements of Jews in the coast-lands of the Mediterranean Sea, and anyone living there could hardly have limited his horizon to the narrow limits of Palestine. The many different nationalities of Palestine, which were reflected in her commerce, and the great influx of foreigners to Jerusalem at festival time, to say nothing of the varied trades of the city, caused a great variety of human types to be seen, and a variety of tongues to be heard, in her streets. St. Peter, in his Pentecost speech (Acts ii. 8 f.), gives us a vivid picture of all this. The inscriptions in Greek and Hebrew, or Aramaic, found on the ossuaria in the rock-tombs of Jerusalem, show which were the most important languages spoken there.[2] Our Lord, as is evident from Jn. xii. 20. f., belonged to the Aramaic-speaking "Hebrews," like St. Paul (2 Cor. xi. 22; Phil. iii. 5), although Greek could not have been entirely foreign to Him.[3] These "Hebrews," like the Hellenists who had been brought up entirely in Greek surroundings—one of whom was Stephen (Acts vi. 5)—will have had their own quarter in Jerusalem, and especially their own synagogues. That there were 480,[4] or 394,[5] such synagogues, is as exaggerated as the

---

[1] It is considered to be the tower called after Phasael because of the measure of its old ground-floor which fairly corresponds to that given by Josephus (Bell. Jud. v. 4, 4). Merril's description (PEFQ, 1886, p. 21) is archæologically valueless. [2] Cf. Jesus-Jeshua, p. 3 f.

[3] Ibid., together with Latin, Lk. xxii. 38 A.D.; Bell. Jud. v. 5, 2.

[4] b. Keth. 105a. [5] p. Meg. 73d.

legend of there being 500 elementary schools in Bettar,[1] which number is, however, taken seriously by Krauss![2]   But there is documentary evidence for the synagogues of the Alexandrians,[3] the Libertines, the Cyrenians, the Cilicians, and Asians.[4] For the synagogue of Vettenos, made known to us through an inscription, see Chapter XVII.   Only in the Temple did they all meet.   But even more striking than the differences in language was the variety in spiritual and mental outlook. There were pure heathen who, however, had no opportunities for the public practice of their religions in Jerusalem.   There were certainly also Jews like Herod, who found their ideal of life so far fulfilled in heathen culture that they lost all inner connection with the faith of Israel.   Among the genuine Jews there might be found distinguished Sadducees, who endeavoured to harmonise secular culture and political sagacity with the ancient Law of Moses ; pietistic Pharisees, whom it would be an injustice to consider mere formalists and literalists, but who considered the traditional interpretations of the Law to be an absolute necessity ; retiring Essenes, who laid less emphasis on legality of conduct than on ceremonial purity of physical being and behaviour.   If the Pharisees strove to form circles of those people among which the Law would receive its due position, the Essenes were compelled even more to join together in groups, in order to realise that higher holiness to which they aspired in monastic fashion and to avoid the polluting intercourse with the capital as much as possible. By the side of and among all these there were nationalists, often natives of Galilee, to whom God and people, God and Jerusalem, God and the Temple, were inseparable objects, and who burned with indignation over everything which was not in accord with this unity.   Jesus was not national enough for the nationalists, too old-fashioned for the Sadducees, too modern and liberal for the Pharisees, not "holy" enough for the Essenes, and for the ordinary man of the people He was too strict.   Yet He was convinced that He represented the cause of God, which hitherto the Law of Moses and the Temple of Solomon had been ordained to minister.

Jerusalem's being "the holy city" (Mt. iv. 5 ; xxvii. 53), *i.e.* the abode of God's Sanctuary, expressed itself practically in the care taken that he who visited the Temple should be ritually clean and not lose his cleanness, and that lodgings

---

[1] Lam. R. ii. 2 (43b).	[2] *Synagogale Altertümer*, p. 200.
[3] Tos. Meg. iii. 6 ; Acts vi. 9.	[4] Acts vi. 9.

should be provided for the multitudes of festival pilgrims. It is said that no one had to search in vain for a night's lodging.[1] The upper stories of the houses, especially the rooms erected on the flat roofs, are the " upper rooms " of which the New Testament speaks (Mk. xiv. 15 ; Lk. xxii. 12 ; ἀνάγαιον, Pal. Aram. *'illita* ; Acts i. 13 ὑπερῷον). They were not used as the usual family dwelling-rooms and could quickly be turned into guest-rooms. When they were provided with couches or cushions,[2] as is taken for granted for the Last Supper, they could be used for meals as well as for sleeping-places, since in both cases the Oriental has no liking for settling himself on the bare floor, and his minimum requirement is a mat or a carpet. Wooden stands under the cushions and tables proper were usual in the time of Jesus, at least in the towns. The meal-places, hewn out of the rock, as seen at Petra,[3] show at the same time that there was a fondness for constructing raised couches along three sides (*triklinia*) of a room, or round couches (*stibadia*), before the inner side of which was a narrow shelf on which were laid dishes.

There are also other indications that the Hellenistic custom of lying at a meal was widespread in Palestine. The exclusively used ἀνακεῖσθαι (Pal. Aram. *reba'*[4]) of the Gospels presupposes it. According to b. Berachot 42a, the reclining position at a proper common meal was taken for granted.[5] Eating in a sitting position was not the custom. At the Passover meal at least, even the poorest man must lie at his ease.[6] The head (*i.e.* the right-hand end) of the first couch was reckoned the place of honour (Mt. xxiii. 6 ; Lk. xiv. 7), when there were two couches ; when there were three, the head of the middle one.[7] Below such a couch (Pal. Aram. *'arsa*), which had a wooden stand, one could put a light (Mk. iv. 21). From the correspondingly high table (Pal. Aram. *patura*) the crumbs could fall (Mt. xv. 27 ; Mk. vii. 28 ; Lk. xvi. 21 ; *cf.* Judg. i. 7), to gather up which was a religious duty.[8]

---

[1] Ab. de R. N. xxxv.

[2] Christian Pal. *meschawya* ; *cf.* Jewish Aram. *shiwwaya*, " bolster, couch " (Targ. 1 K. i. 47 ; Gen. xlix. 9).

[3] Dalman, *Petra und seine Heiligtümer*, p. 89 *f.* ; *Neue Petraforschungen*, p. 28.

[4] See also p. Ber. 12b ; Taan. 66a.

[5] That it meant lying on the stomach is evident from p. Taan. 66a.

[6] It is strange that, according to p. Ber. 11d, the one who eats walking must stand up for the benediction, if he stands he must sit down, if he sits he must lie down, if he lies he must cover his face.

[7] Pes. x. 1 ; *cf. Jesus-Jeshua*, p. 108.

[8] Tos. Ber. v. 5 ; *cf.* Mt. xiv. 20 ; Mk vi. 43 ; viii. 8, 9 ; Lk. ix. 17 ; Jn. vi. 12.

For the ritual purifications of the Temple visitors, especially from defilement in connection with a corpse (Num. xix.), there had to be places outside the sanctuary where the necessary sprinklings and ablutions could be performed. In Egypt reference used to be made to a pool of David in Jerusalem into which the ritually impure entered on one ladder, the pure coming out on another.[1] The trough of Jehu, which the school of Shammai damaged in order that it might not in itself be considered as a vessel, supplied all the purifications of Jerusalem with the necessary water,[2] which evidently ran through this trough into a ritual bath. At the eastern gate of the women's court of the Temple were the ashes of the red heifer necessary for the purifications.[3] As Jesus and His disciples submitted themselves to the ordinances of the Law, they would not have considered themselves above undergoing such purifications as these, as an apocryphal *logion* of Jesus states.[4] On the contrary, the fact that Jesus arrived in Jerusalem five days before the Passover (Jn. xii. 1, 12), implies that His purpose was to be in time for the purification with the ashes on the third and seventh day (Num. xix. 12, 19; *cf.* Jn. xi. 55). Although the wandering through heathen—not to speak of Samaritan—districts within the land of Israel did not necessarily imply pollution, if one had guarded against visiting heathen dwellings and sitting on Samaritan seats[5] (for the impurity of heathen houses, which was based on the presumption that prematurely born children were buried in them, was not extended to tents and various huts),[6] yet to have managed to avoid defilement by coming into contact with a dead body was not so easy.

As the Passover could only be consumed in a ritually pure condition, it was important to guard against any defilement— which could be caused also by entering a heathen dwelling-place within the city (Jn. xviii. 28). The streets therefore were cleaned daily.[7] At festivals the ritually pure walked in the middle and the impure on the edges of the streets.[8] In the gates the pure ones used steps for passing through a higher

---

[1] Oxyrhynchus papyrus; *cf.* Zahn, *Neue kirchl. Zeit.*, 1908, p. 378.
[2] Mik. iv. 5.   [3] Par. iii. 3; Tos. Par. iii. 4.   [4] Papyrus Oxyrhynchus.
[5] Wandering on mountains and rocks in a heathen land, even the air of which is impure (Ohal. xviii. 6; Tos. Mikw. vi. 1), causes impurity (Ohal. xviii. 6). But heathen districts, like that of Hippos in the Decapolis, which lay within the domain of the land of Israel (Tos. Ohal. xviii. 4) were as little impure as that of the Samaritans (Tos. Mikw. vi. 1; p. Ab. z. 44d).
[6] Ohal. xviii. 7.   [7] b. Pes. 7a; Bab. mez. 26a.   [8] Shek. viii. 1.

passage, while the " impure " used the ordinary way.[1]   Saliva
on the pavements of the Upper City, where many heathen
lived, was defiling,[2] and in later times it used to be related with
horror that pilgrims who arrived in Jerusalem for the festivals
used to wade up to their knees in that part of the city through
the blood of the slaughtered wild asses.[3] From the point of
view of Pharisaism, no fowls might be kept in Jerusalem, and
no balcony was allowed to project, lest defilement might
occur.[4] The tombs of David and the prophetess Huldah,
at the south end of the Temple-hill, were the only sepulchres
tolerated within the city,[5] and a rose-garden was, from ancient
times, an object which caused qualms,[6] on account of the
manure used for it.

Our Lord would not have objected to these and similar
ordinances, had they not diverted the mind of the people and
their spiritual leaders from the essentials of the Law (Mt. xxiii.).
What were all these trivial regulations in comparison with the
stupendous question, What did God expect of Jerusalem
at this time ?   Jesus saw that there was a greater conflict than
the one between Rome's tyranny and the Jewish consciousness
of being the chosen people of God.   Jerusalem—such a
glorious frame for God's Sanctuary—considered not the things
which belonged unto her peace.   Hence the dirge :

> Jerusalem, Jerusalem, that killest the prophets . . .
> how often would I have gathered thy children together,
> even as a hen gathereth her chickens under her wings, and
> ye would not ![7]

[1] Letter of Aristeas, ed. Wendland, p. 106.
[2] Shek. viii. 1.
[3] p. Shek. 51a ; Tos. Eduy. iii. 2.
[4] Bab. k. vii. 7.   The Sadducees and the people were not likely to have bothered
themselves much about such ordinances ; cf. Mt. xxvi. 74 ; Mk. xiv. 68, 72 ;
Lk. xxii. 60 ; Jn. xvii. 27.
[5] Tos. Bab. b. i. 11; cf. PJB, 1915, p. 50 f.   See Büchler, Revue des Études
Juives, 1911, p. 201 f.
[6] Maas ii. 5.
[7] Cf. for the Aramaic expression Lev. R. xxv. (26b) : " The hen, when her
little ones are small, gathers them and takes them under her wings."   See also
Lam. R. Introduction (12a).

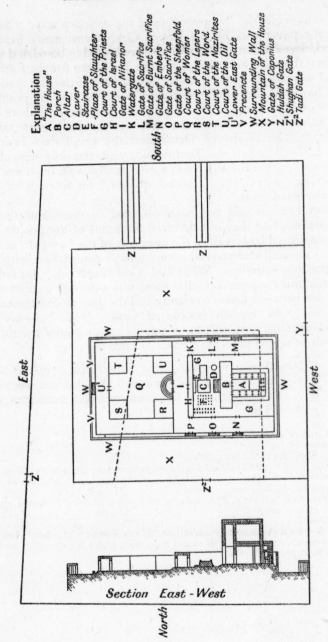

Explanation

A "The House"
B Porch
C Altar
D Laver
E Staircase
F Place of Slaughter
G Court of the Priests
H Court of Israel
I Gate of Nikanor
K Watergate
L Gate of Sacrifice
M Gate of Burnt Sacrifice
N Gate of Embers
O Gate of Sacrifice
P Gate of the Sheepfold
Q Court of Women
R Court of the Word
S Court of the Nazirites
T Court of the Oil
U Court of the Oil
U¹ Lower East Gate
V Precincts
W Surrounding Wall
X Mountain of the House
Y Gate of Coponius
Z¹ Huldah Gate
Z² Shughan Gate
Z³ Tadi Gate

South

East

West

North

Section East - West

XVI

THE SANCTUARY

THE Sanctuary of Jerusalem is in the Gospels always termed τὸ ἱερόν, as distinguished from the Temple edifice rising in its midst—ὁ ναός. Jesus teaches in the " sanctuary " (Mt. xxvi. 55 ; Mk. xiv. 49 ; Lk. xxi. 37 ; Jn. vii. 28), but will "destroy" the Temple " (ὁ ναός ; Mt. xxvii. 40 ; Mk. xv. 29 ; Jn. ii. 19), the veil of which was rent in twain at His death (Mt. xxvii. 51 ; Mk. xv. 35 ; Lk. xxiii. 45). The corresponding words in Aramaic are *makdesha*[1] and *hekhela*.[2] The Syriac translation, however, employs *haikela* throughout, and the Palestinian Evangeliarium translates both Greek words with *naosa*, whilst Jerome renders them with *templum*. It is necessary to keep the distinction in mind, as it is topographically indispensable.

In the present Jerusalem the still imposing site of the Ḥaram at the eastern boundary is undoubtedly the place of the ancient Sanctuary. That the originally much lower summit of the lesser of old Jerusalem's two chief heights was artificially extended by the construction of strong retaining-walls and the filling of the inner space, partly by earthen walls and partly by strong vaults, is evident from personal observation, which tallies with the descriptions of Josephus.[3] He speaks in exaggerated fashion of rocks 40 cubits (20 metres) in length, out of which the walls were constructed. The largest stones which are seen in them now measure only 11·81 (or 9·84 by 1 metre) and 7 by 1·85 metres.[4] But even if one thinks only of the average size of the stones in layers of between 1 to 1·20 metres high, the disciples' admiration of them is justified (Mk. xiii. 1 ; Lk. xxi. 5). Also worthy of admiration was the size of the place thus constructed. It measured

---

[1] Maas. sheni 56a ; Pea 20b ; Ber. 5a ; Targum Cant. iii. 11. Not as frequent is the purely Hebrew *mikdash*, p. Sukk. 55c.

[2] Trg. Cant. iii. 9 (*hekhal kudsha*) ; b. Kidd. 71a ; p. Taan. 67a (here as a designation of the ark for the holy rolls in the synagogue).

[3] *Ant.* viii. 3, 9 ; xv. 11, 3 ; *Bell. Jud.* v. 5, 1.

[4] Kuemmel, *Materialien zur Topographie des alten Jerusalem*, pp. 106, 118.

approximately 480 by 300 metres,[1] whereas the famous Altis of Olympia was only about 210 by 170 metres large, and the Acropolis of Athens 240 metres long and only in the middle as wide as 120 metres. The Sanctuary of the Jews was twice as large. Also the height of the outer walls was considerable. At the south-east corner old masonry was found, 42·20 metres high, measured from the rock, which is now at this point 24 metres under the present ground surface, and may give us the original level. If we assign to the back wall of the surrounding colonnades the normal height of about 7 metres,[2] we can speak of a height of 50 metres; it must, however, be remembered that some layers of stone were, from the beginning, certainly covered up by the soil outside. At the south-west corner an ancient street-pavement was found, 6·07 metres above the surface of the rock, at the fifth layer of the blocks which, up to this point, are only roughly squared on the outer surface between the smoothed edges. Then followed layers of stones which were designed from the beginning to be seen. Their middle surface is smoothed, but is enclosed as by a frame by the edges, which are recessed to the depth of 1 centimetre.[3] The street-pavement referred to is 23·44 metres below the surface of the present *haram*. The retaining-wall must thus have risen here to this height and, including the superimposed enclosure-wall, was at least 30 metres high. On the western side towards the north and in the middle of the south and east sides, the nature of the ground caused the outer wall to be lower. On the north, where the Sanctuary was higher, the western part was occupied by the Antonia citadel, which jutted into the Sanctuary with a part of its quadrangle, and gave occasion thereby for a peculiar interpretation of a prophecy, when the Jewish destruction of Antonia was followed by the heathen destruction of the whole Sanctuary:[4] when the Sanctuary became quadrangular, city and Temple would be destroyed. The reference is evidently to Daniel ix. 27, as interpreted by the Rabbis. This citadel was the "castle" which once protected St. Paul from the rage of the Jews, who believed that their Sanctuary was desecrated through him; it was also his first Roman prison.

[1] The exact measurements in Kuemmel, *loc. cit.*, p. 103.

[2] Josephus asserts (*Bell. Jud.* v. 5, 1 *f.*) that the pillars of the halls were 25 cubits high, the superstructure of the circular wall 300 cubits. In Gerasa the columns of the columnar streets measure only 6 to 9 metres.

[3] See Mitchel in *Annual of the American School of Orient. Research in Jerusalem*, i., pp. 15-17, 25, 34 *f.*

[4] *Ant.* xv. 11, 4; *Bell. Jud.* v. 5, 8; vi. 5, 4.

The entrances to the Sanctuary were unusual, being conditioned by the site. A bridge, corresponding to the present so-called " Wilson's arch," served as a means of communication with the palace of Herod in the Upper City, which was reached through the city valley. The gate belonging to it must have been the Coponius gate of Jewish tradition,[1] which is now superseded by a gateway ornamented with pillars, dating from the time of the Crusaders, which was once held to be the " beautiful gate " of Acts iii. 10.[2] Anyone coming from Bethlehem, like Joseph with Mary and the Child (Lk. ii. 22 f.), would have entered from here into the Sanctuary. However, there was within the old city of Jerusalem at that time another ascent by steps from the valley,[3] which corresponded perhaps to the present Barclay gateway, the mighty lintel of which (south of the bridge entrance which has now become a dam) is still visible. The ascent then ran one-third outside and two-thirds within the outer wall, probably with many twists, towards the height of the inner " place." But a strongly-built archway near the south-west angle of the wall, the so-called " Robinson's arch," to which an ascent, resting on several arches, seems to have belonged, may have corresponded to the steps mentioned by Josephus. The southern part of the Upper City was connected by it with the Sanctuary. If the Last Supper took place in the south part of the city, this must have been the way taken thither after the slaughtering of the Passover lamb in the Sanctuary.[4] Also when Peter and John went up from this quarter into the Temple for the afternoon prayers (Acts iii. 1), they would have used this western approach. Of the two entrances which connected the suburb with the Sanctuary, one has to locate with Warren the more southerly one at the cistern which cuts the outer wall. Still recognisable as ancient approaches are gangways— which recall the " Huldah gates " of the Mishna[5]—rising gradually from the so-called " double " and " triple " gates in the south wall, in a flight about 80 metres long, to the height of the inner ground-surface. That the " double " gate is discernible even to-day as an old gateway, fits in with the Jewish tradition that the Huldah gate outlived the destruction

---

[1] Midd. i. 3.
[2] La Citez de Jherusalem (Tobler, Descript. T. S., 207) ; Fretellus (Migne, P.L. clv., col. 1047) ; John of Würzburg (Tobler, p. 125) seems to identify it with the western entrance of the rock-dome.
[3] Ant. xv. 11, 5.   [4] Cf. Jesus-Jeshua, p. 112 f.
[5] Midd. i. 3; cf. Ant. xv. 11, 15.

of the Sanctuary and would remain until it was rebuilt.[1]   On
the east, the Mishna knows only an eastern gate leading
directly to the Kidron valley, which will have corresponded
to the old double entrance of the present golden gate.   It
was perhaps used only by the priests, and was certainly the
gate of the priests in which the Jews saw a witness of past
and future glory.   A north gate had once been there,[2] but,
according to the Mishna, had fallen into disuse, which would
mean that when Jesus came from the Mount of Olives,[3] if
the east gate was not a public thoroughfare, He would either
have gone round by the north and entered the Sanctuary from
the suburb, or else have used one of the southern entrances.
This would mean that from outside the city no direct communication with the Sanctuary was permissible, as indeed is
still the case to-day.

Entering through the outer gates from any side, one came,
as Josephus puts it, to the " first,"[4] " outer,"[5] or " lower "[6]
sanctuary, also the " first enclosure " ($\pi\epsilon\rho\iota\beta o\lambda os$.)[7] No
Hebrew or Aramaic equivalent expression is known.   In
rabbinic literature this space is always called in Hebrew ḥar
ha-bayit; ha-bayit being short for bet ha-mikdash, so that it is
to be rendered: " the mountain of the Sanctuary." This
designation was a conscious avoidance of the name 'azara,
which was a substitute—occurring only twice in the Old
Testament (2 Chr. iv. 9 ; vi. 13)—for the earlier ḥaser, " court,"
which Onkelos renders (e.g. Ex. xxvii. 9) daretha, and the
Targum on the Prophets often (e.g. Ezek. x. 5) renders 'azarta.
This was merely the mount of the Sanctuary, not the Sanctuary
itself.   Therefore Israelites who had been defiled by contact
with a corpse, as well as non-Jews (in this respect of the same
category as " defiled " Jews), were permitted to enter it.   Of
the ten grades of holiness, the tenth of which was ascribed to
the Holy of Holies,[8] the first is applied to the city of Jerusalem,
from which lepers are excluded.   The second grade is applied
to the mount of the Sanctuary, from which sufferers from

---

[1] Cant. R. ii. 9 (31a), also in ed. Pesaro 1519.   The same is said there of the
" gate of the priest " and the " western wall," i.e. the present " wailing wall " at
the west side of the Sanctuary.   The parallel passages mention only the western
wall.

[2] Midd. i. 3 ; Bell. Jud. ii. 19, 5.   [3] Cf. above, p. 257 f.

[4] Bell. Jud., v. 5, 2.   [5] Ibid. iv. 5, 1 ; vi. 2, 7.   [6] Ibid. v. 5, 1.

[6] Ant. xv. 11, 5 ; Bell. Jud. iv. 3, 12 ; cf. c. Ap. ii. 8.

[8] Thus after Kel. i. 6-9.   According to another opinion, the space above the
Holy of Holies was even holier than this ; cf. PJB, 1909, p. 33 f.   According to
Num. R. (37a), there were even more grades.

an issue, male or female, and women not purified after child-
birth, are to keep away, whilst persons made impure by coming
into contact with dead bodies, and heathen,[1] are allowed to
enter. The third grade was reckoned to be the so-called
ḥel, i.e. the narrow space, which enclosed the ascent to
the Sanctuary proper, which Israelites whose time of purification after bathing was not yet completed (Lev. xv. 5) could
enter. The court of the women, situated on the east before
the innermost court, was the fourth stage from which the
above-mentioned persons were excluded (this, however, was
considered to be an innovation, not demanded by the written
Law[2]); entrance to it was permitted to those whose offering,
as a last act of purification, was still due (Lev. xiv. 20). Only
then, with the enclosure of the innermost court, began the
Sanctuary proper, permitted only to the ceremonially pure.
The traditional Law, which was based on the command to
keep the camp in the wilderness pure (Num. v. 2), divided
this tent into the three grades of sacredness : the camp of
Israel, that of the Levites, and that of God, and thus reckoned
three corresponding divisions of the holy city.[3] From the
gates to the Temple mount was regarded as the camp of
Israel ; thence to the " court " (of the sanctuary) represented
the Levites' court ; while from the entry of the court to the
rest of the Sanctuary was Shekinah's camp.[4] Within the
camp of the Levites it was originally only the women's
camp that constituted a division by itself, but later the
scribes also separated the space of the ḥol as a special division
(see above). In this way the three sanctity-grades within the
Levites' camp were arrived at. As from the point of view
of scribal interpretation these demarcations were based on
Divine ordinance, an unwitting transgressor was obliged to
offer a sacrifice, whilst the Divine judgment of " extirpation "
(caret, being " cut off from the people ") befell him who sinned
intentionally against these regulations.[5] It was not in the
power of any tribunal to deal with such cases, except that it
could order scourging.[6] Josephus speaks of the exclusion of

[1] Goyim in the Venice ed. 1522.
[2] b. Yeb. 7b ; Pes. 92a ; Zeb. 32b, with regard to the " new court " of 2 Chr.
xx. 5.
[3] Sifre on Num. p. 3 (English translation).
[4] Thus according to Sifre on Num. 1 (1b). Tos. Kel. Bab. k. i. 12
mentions here the Nicanor gates—Zeb. 116b. the Nicanor gate—as a border.
Num. R. vii. has the double tradition.
[5] Kerit. i. 1 ; Men. 27b ; Tos. Kel. Bab. k. i. 10.
[6] Makk. iii. 2 ; Tos. Kel. B. k. i. 8 ; b. Pes. 67a.

lepers and sufferers from an issue from the whole city of
Jerusalem—a considerable extension of rabbinic prohibitions.
Women during their periods, and strangers, were permitted,
according to him, to enter the outer enclosure: he makes no
second division.[1] It is surprising that tablets were put up
before the entrances to the inner Sanctuary which threatened
strangers with death if they should enter it,[2] or, more precisely,
proclaimed, according to the Greek inscription found in
Jerusalem[3]: "That no stranger (ἀλλογενής) should enter
within the limit and enclosure of the Sanctuary. He who is
caught, will carry the guilt on himself, because death will
follow." This did not imply sentence of death passed by a
tribunal, but was a reminder that the transgressor would, when
found out and fallen upon by the incensed populace, be merely
suffering a just and self-invoked punishment. That this
popular "justice"—not founded on any Mosaic ordinance—
was not uncommon among the Jews, is seen by the tumult
which the charge that Paul had led Greeks into the Temple
(Acts xxi. 28) aroused. At the same time the Mishna reports
as something in accordance with the Law that a priest who
officiates in an impure condition, although he is not brought
before a tribunal, should nevertheless be killed by the young
priests.[4] And a heathen (goy) who ate in Jerusalem of the
fat-tail of the Passover lambs[5] was, on discovery, killed by
zealots—evidently without a judicial verdict (b. Pes. 3b).

Notwithstanding the admission of "impure" to the
Sanctuary mount, it was considered desirable that also this part
of the Sanctuary in the wider sense should not be treated
as profane ground. Staff, shoes, and pouch, that is to say,
travelling equipment, had first to be put aside and the feet
freed from the dust; no spittle was allowed to pollute the
plaster floor, in order that no one should become defiled by it.[6]
Cautious ones left their shoes outside the doors of the entrance
gate.[7]

[1] Bell. Jud. v. 5, 6 ; c. Ap. ii. 8.
[2] Ant. xv. 11, 5 ; Bell. Jud. v. 5, 2 ; vi. 2, 4.
[3] Thomsen, Lat. und Griechische Inschriften, p. 27 f. ; Klein, Jüd. pal. Corpus
Inscriptionum, p. 86.
[4] Sanh. ix. 6 ; cf. Tos. Kel. Bab. k. 1, 6.
[5] No stranger may eat of the Passover lamb (Ex. xii. 43). The fat-tail
belongs to the parts offered at the altar in connection with peace offerings (Lev.
iii. 9). The Samaritans, however, did not apply it to the Passover lamb ; see
PJB, 1912, p. 127 ; Samaritanernas Päskfest, pl. xlviiii,-l.
[6] Ber. ix. 5 ; b. Yeb. 6b. Special instructions for the carrying of money are
given in b. Ber. 14c ; Tos. Ber. vii. 19.
[7] p. Pes. 35b.

That the lame man who was laid daily at the Beautiful Gate of the Sanctuary (Acts iii. 2) was, for legal reasons, not in the inner court, is assumed by J. Jeremias.[1] Because, according to Sab. vi. 8, the cripple may enter the fore-court ('azara) with a stilt but not with a seat, Jeremias concludes that the lame man, who had to be carried, was prohibited from entering the fore-court, because of his bolster-seat. Also the blind and the lame who approached Jesus in the Sanctuary (Mt. xxi. 14) are supposed to have been in the outer court, and the blind beggar of Jn. ix. 1, at a southern outer gate of the same. Of the latter, however, it is only certain that Jesus encountered him outside the Sanctuary (Jn. viii. 59). Because Jesus sent him to the pool of Siloam, it does not necessarily mean that it was on the south side that Jesus found him. The mention of the blind and the lame in Mt. xxi. 14, in connection with the casting out of the traders in the Sanctuary, may point to the outer court. In any case, however, there is no Biblical or traditional ordinance excluding blind and lame as such from the inner courts. Naturally, they were under the same purity regulations as everybody else. When Sab. vi. 8 (p. Sab. 8c) discusses the purity or otherwise of the substitutes for missing feet or bones, this is not directly concerned with the entrance into the Sanctuary. It concerns only the question, whether the possible impurity of a cripple imparts impurity also to his implements. In connection with this it also says that one kind of such implements is allowed on Sabbath and in the fore-court, and another not. The difference is based on this : that one set of implements are a substitute for the missing feet, and the others are not, because they only make sitting, not walking, possible. On the Sabbath, only what belongs to the body and to clothing may be carried, and in the fore-court, travelling equipment is prohibited, and may not even be carried unto the Sanctuary mount (Ber. ix. 5). A blind person is forbidden to walk on a festival with a staff (Tos. Yom Tob, iii. 17; b. Bez. 25b). Naturally this is true also of the Sabbath (Orach Chayim, 301, 18), and is to be applied to the Sanctuary. This presupposes that the blind person as such was able to walk, so that his staff belonged to the same category as the prohibited travelling staff. It was different with the lame, if he could not walk without a staff. Although there is no ancient reference to such a case, later Jewish legislation (Orach Chayim, 301, 17) permits him the

---

[1] *Jerusalem zur Zeit Jesu*, ii. A., p. 34 f.

use of a staff on the Sabbath. With crutches, a lame person
would have been allowed to enter the Sanctuary. Naturally
it would have also been allowable to carry him there, but
hardly to bring a special couch or seat. So the analogy between
the lame and the cripple would justify the theory of Jeremias.
It remains, however, more probable that the real cause of this
sitting at the Sanctuary gate was the good opportunity it
afforded for begging. There the lame could not be overlooked, and it could be taken for granted that those who went
to the Temple to pray would not let the opportunity slip to
attain merit by the exercise of charity (*sedaka*).

Jeremias bases his argument on the LXX of 2 Sam. v. 8,
which excludes the blind and the lame from the house " of
the Lord," but this is foreign to Jewish Law. In Pirke Rabbi
Eliezer xxxvi. it is indeed hinted that one might hold such a
view, but only in order to refute it as erroneous. It says
there : "Perchance thou mightest say, 'the blind and the lame
entered not into the Sanctuary.' Perish this interpretation !
It refers to idols which have eyes but see not, feet and walk
not." The Targum on the passage in 2 Sam. does not interpret
the words " the blind and the lame should not come into the
house " as referring to the Temple at all, but to sinners and
guilty ones, who may not enter a house. That blind and lame
priests were prohibited from appearing at the holy place
between the Temple edifice and the altar (*cf*. Lk. xi. 51 ; Tos.
Kel. B. k. 16),[1] as well as at the altar and in the Temple
itself, is based on the exclusion of physical defectives from
service in the Sanctuary (Lev. xxi. 21). But proves again that
such a physical blemish excludes neither priests nor laity from
the Sanctuary in its wider compass.

That the beggars could assume that a visitor in the Sanctuary would carry with him "silver and gold" (Acts iii. 6)
does not seem to fit in with the prohibition of carrying a
pouch (bag) in the Temple (Ber. ix. 5). But in order to
offer gifts at the Sanctuary (p. 299) one had to be able to
bring money there. And, according to Tos. Ber. vii. 19, one
only needed care to carry the money unostentatiously. In
regard to shoes, which were also prohibited in the Sanctuary,
as also belonging to travelling equipment (*cf*. Mt. x. 10 ;
Lk. x. 4 ; xxii. 35 ; Mk. vi. 9 has " sandals," which might
have been permitted), the Mishnah emphasises the reason :
not to bring the dust of the street into the Sanctuary. As in

[1] Kel. i. 9 ; *cf*. Zeb. 16b. 1 ; Sifra on Lev. xxi. 21 (95b).

the East of to-day the shoes are put off before the entrance alike of the cottage and the mosque, so it must have been in connection with the Temple in Jerusalem. The priests were therefore obliged to officiate barefoot (p. Shek. 48d), and, according to Midrash Num. R.V. (29a), even the Levites whose duty it was to carry the holy vessels in the wilderness—where the ban had no sense or significance—had to walk barefoot.

One cannot fully appreciate the character of the Jerusalem Sanctuary unless one considers the current conceptions of its " sacredness " and the ritual preparations which those who desired to " appear before the Lord " had to undergo. There were times when pious Israelites banded themselves together not to enter the Sanctuary at all, because its ministers did not make the required division between sacred and profane and thereby aroused God's wrath.[1] They, on their part, by punctilious observance of the Law, sought to preserve unbroken the link between God and His people. Thus they extended the purity-ordinances, prescribed in the Mosaic Law in connection with the sacrificial system, into everyday life; washed the hands before every meal, achieved full ceremonial purity before eating or drinking anything, and avoided defilement from contact with the dead, unless it was absolutely necessary.[2] The views of Jesus were different (Mt. xv. 2; Mk. vii. 2). He did not differentiate between ordinary and holy food, nor would He have agreed with Rabbi Pinchas ben Jair in making the following ladder of virtues : " cleanliness (ceremonial), purity, separation, holiness, humility, fear of sin, piety, the gift of the Holy Spirit, and resurrection ";[3] nor again would He have thought the eating of fruits in ritual purity essential for a " son of the world to come."[4] The various stages of holiness in the Sanctuary did not possess for Him the importance attached to them by His pious contemporaries. But that at the feast one must be pure to enter the Sanctuary and partake of the sacrificial meat,[5] must assuredly have been for Him one of the ordinances of the Law, to which He silently submitted Himself. He even thought it important to show that in such matters He was more sensitive than the then guardians of the Sanctuary. They saw nothing wrong in the selling of pigeons[6] there for the sacrifices brought by women

[1] Staerk, *Die jüdische Gemeinde des Neuen Bundes in Damascus*, p. 25 (vi. 12, 17).
[2] Hag. ii. 5.
[3] Sot. ix. 15. Cf. Büchler, *Types of Jewish Palestinian Piety*, p. 42.
[4] p. Shek. 47d.   [5] Sifra on Lev. xi. 8 (49a).
[6] The oxen and sheep in Jn. ii. 14 are probably a later addition.

after childbirth and by the poor, and in the changing of money
for the purposes of the Sanctuary, whilst He burnt with holy
zeal when He saw it (Mt. xxi. 12 f. and parallels). Klausner[1]
sees in that act of Jesus a lack of the humility which Christians
so frequently praise. But Jesus, like Jeremiah, whose words
He quoted (Jer. vii. 11), thought of the unavoidable rejection
of the Sanctuary by Him after whose Name it was called.
He spoke and acted in the Name of Him who alone was Lord
there. What is the use of all the purity of the Sanctuary, when
the hearts of all the worshippers are not even here undis-
tractedly lifted up to God, but are absorbed in the market-
bustle of work-a-day life? According to rabbinic tradition,
the collectors of the half shekels (Ex. xxx. 13) put up their
tables before the Passover feast in the " Sanctuary," *i.e.* in
the court of the women.[2] It is not likely that this would
have appeared unseemly to Jesus, who Himself (under protest)
discharged this tax (Mt. xvii. 27), although there was a great
deal of exchange business carried on with those who did not
pay the exact sum in silver according to the Tyrian currency.[3]
To a trade in sacrificial animals carried on by the priests there
is no reference anywhere.[4] The punctilious rules of the scribes
in regard to cleanliness even on the Sanctuary mount, not
to speak of the Sanctuary itself, would have tolerated such a
trade as little as the carrying of things through the Sanctuary
(Mk. xi. 16), which must not be used for short cuts (*com-
pendiaria*).[5] But the Sadducees, who controlled the Temple in
the time of Jesus, were probably of a different opinion in
regard to the outer court, and did not consider the trade in
pigeons, supervised by them, and an exchange business for
the benefit of the pilgrims who required small coins for the
payment of Temple taxes, as unseemly.

The whole length of the south end of the Sanctuary
mount was occupied by a three-aisled basilica with raised
central portion, the magnificent ornamentation and vast
pillars of which are mentioned by Josephus with rapturous
delight, though certainly not without exaggeration.[6] He says
nothing of the special purpose of this, in any case tremendous

[1] *Jesus of Nazareth*, p. 315.   [2] Shek. i. 3 ; Tos. Shek. i. 6.
[3] Bech. ix. 7 ; Shek. i. 6 ; p. Shek. 46b.
[4] The cattle-dealers of Shek. vii. 2 ; Tos. Shek. iii. 9, were not in the Temple.
Formerly I erroneously assumed that the cattle trade was in the hands of the
priests (*PJB*, 1909, p. 39). The tickets that were given out in the Temple
(Shek. v. 3 *f.* ; Tos. Shek. ii. 16) referred only to the spending for the different
sacrifices, not to the sacrificial animals themselves.
[5] Ber. ix. 5.   [6] *Ant.* xv. 11, 5.

creation of Herod. One may assume that it was not only designed to protect large crowds of people against sun and rain, as there would be no special reason for their congregating here, but also to attract trade ; and it may also have been the *ḥanut* (merchants' store) to which the Synhedrion is said to have moved forty years before the destruction of Jerusalem, before it descended into the city.[1] The place of the present *Aksa* mosque would in that case have been the historic site of the driving away of the traders and money-changers, in which act Jesus dealt according to the principle that, once the Sanctuary mount was brought—no matter by whom—into the sphere of the Sanctuary itself, and had become the place of worship for the Gentiles (Isa. lvi. 7), it participated in the sacredness of the Temple, just as the Temple " sanctifies the gold " used in it (Mt. xxiii. 17). In this neighbourhood the later church will have been situated which was dedicated to the driving out of the traders from the Temple.[2] On the Madaba map it seems to be marked at the south end of the Temple " place." Perhaps the old Huldah gate under the *Aksa* mosque was connected with it. Although this gate is now, like the east gate, ornamented in Byzantine fashion, it still shows traces of its ancient architraves (see above, p. 288).

The basilica at the south end of the large enclosure took the place, on this side, of the vaulted galleries with double rows of columns, which elsewhere, except at the spot where the citadel of Antonia jutted into the enclosure (p. 286), formed the inside of the enclosing walls (*Bell. Jud.* v. 5, 2). The pieces of armour captured in wars, which were hung up here, were probably meant to be dedication gifts to God who gave the victory, although Josephus seems to think them only a display.[3] Not the west side, but the east, *i.e.* that facing towards the Kidron valley, of the pillared hall bore the inscription : " Hall of Solomon." It was, according to Jn. x. 23, a place where Jesus taught in the winter, and later a centre where his followers used to gather (Acts iii. 11 ; v. 12). Here, on the mount of the Sanctuary, there was no lack of space in the long stretch of galleries, and entry was allowed

---

[1] b. R. h. S. 31a; *cf.* b. Sabb. 15a; Sanh. 41a; Ab. z. 8b. This *ḥanu* could not have been identical with the *ḥanuyot* of the sons of Hanan or Hanun, which were destroyed three years before Jerusalem.

[2] *Brev. de Hieros.* (Geyer, p. 154). The church in the form of a cross, mentioned there on p. 155, could have belonged here.

[3] *Ant.* xv. 11, 3.

even to those whose ritual purity was not complete. He who said his prayers daily in the Sanctuary (Acts iii. 1) could not have always been in the state of perfect ceremonial purity demanded for entrance into the inner parts. Josephus reckoned this eastern hall with its substructure as a work of Solomon, and the only structure which remained at the time of Herod and which was not even later rebuilt by Agrippa.[1] Here he was in error. In reality its middle part was, at the earliest, a remnant of the Temple of Zerubbabel, but the rest, with its substructure, may have originated in pre-exilic times, though popular belief traced the whole back to Solomon. We can realise how the Jews revered and loved this hall. It lay exactly opposite the Temple and the altar, offered protection against the cold east wind of the winter, and was to some extent warmed by the sun, although it was open on the west to the rain. The basilica of Herod, which Hasak identifies with the hall of Solomon,[2] and which he thinks had a decisive influence on the architecture of the Christian basilicas, would have given more complete protection.[3] Unfortunately, so far no excavations have determined the depth of the pavement in the outer Temple court in the time of Christ. To-day we walk in that court between cypresses and olive-trees, but just in the south, where we tread on paved ground, it is most certain that this was not the old court.

Whilst the earliest Church tradition did not point to any sacred sites in the Temple enclosure,[4] standing as it did in pagan property, and, according to the conviction of the time, abandoned by God, it nevertheless referred to the remains of an ancient corner-tower, standing at its south-east angle, and recognisable even to-day between more recent masonry, the rough foundation of which has been preserved. In the fourth century this towering ruin was taken to be " the pinnacle of the temple " upon which the Tempter set Jesus (Mt. iv. 5 ; Lk. iv. 9).[5] This supposition was not without justification,

[1] Ibid. xx. 9, 7 ; viii. 3, 9 ; xv. 11, 3 ; cf. Bell. Jud. v. 5, 1.

[2] Das Heilige Land, 1915, p. 24 f. ; 1921, p. 157 f.

[3] Zeitschrift für christliche Kunst, 1913, col. 129 f., 165 f. In that case Herod must have called it so because Solomon's palace stood in its environs. But no one would have projected the new structure of Herod back into the time of the first Temple, and one can well conceive that the pious among the people rather shunned this luxurious structure of Herod.

[4] The Presentation of Jesus was in the fourth century celebrated not there but in the church of the Resurrection, according to Ætheria (Geyer, p. 77).

[5] The Bordeaux pilgrim (Geyer, p. 21) ; Eucherius (ibid., p. 126) ; Breviarius de Hier., p. 155 ; Theodosius, p. 142 f. ; Petrus Diaconus, p. 108 ; Prudentius (450), according to Baumstark, Byz. Zeitschrift, 1911, p. 179.

for the narrative does not speak of the actual Temple (τό ἱερόν
is the word used), and as *pterugion*, " corner " (not " pinnacle ")
of the Sanctuary, in this case, where a specially great height
was in question, may well have been the south-east corner of
the outer court which projected into the Kidron valley, and
which rose, including the part covered by the ground, to a
height of about 50 metres.[1] In the interior of the corner-
tower there is now a space which Meistermann[2] considers to
be the crypt of Justinian's church of St. Mary. In 1165 it
was the crypt (provided with a wooden cradle of Jesus) of
a building considered to be the dwelling of Simeon the Just,
in which he entertained Mary, and where he was buried.[3]
Neither tradition fits the place. But the substructure of the
crypt, with its huge stones, as may be seen from the inside,
takes us back to the Temple, in which Simeon was the first
of the inhabitants of Jerusalem to greet the Child Jesus as
Redeemer (Lk. ii. 25).

Whilst the site of the outer enclosure of the Sanctuary can
be determined with certainty in present-day Jerusalem, and
doubts remain only in regard to the north side, the exact
placing of its inner, higher-lying terraces is impossible to
determine. Although the present Temple enclosure contains
—somewhat nearer the northern boundary than the southern,
and much nearer the west than the east—a higher terrace,
which narrows considerably towards the southern end, yet in
its confined space there is scarcely room for all that should
belong here. Excavations, which make at least some cross-
sections, east to west and north to south, are necessary before
any assured results can be obtained. The only fixed point is
the holy rock, which lies in the middle of the entire enclosure
(although not of the higher terrace) from north to south, being
nearer to the western than the eastern boundary, thus supplying
in the eastern direction the wider space necessary there, if it
corresponds to the site of the altar.[4] However, the descriptions of Josephus and the Mishna, on the whole, give
a sufficiently attested conception of what it looked like.
According to these authorities, the old Sanctuary proper was
set approximately to the centre of the outer court, but near to
its west side,[5] and its boundaries were supposed to correspond

---

[1] See above, p. 286.   [2] *Durchs Heilige Land*, p. 186 *f.* ; *Guide*, p. 207.
[3] John of Würzburg (Tobler, *Descr.*, p. 130 *f.*) ; Petrus Diaconus (Geyer,
p. 108).
[4] *Cf.* Dalman, *Neue Petra-Forschungen und der heilige Felsen von Jerusalem*, p. 137.
[5] *Cf.* Midd. ii. 1.

to the "curtains" (*kela'im*) of the Tabernacle court. The
Rabbis had special traditions concerning their exact position
in relation to the former outer walls, which must have been
meant in reality for the pre-exilic Sanctuary, that was authori-
tative for the extension of the sacred area.[1]   On the east side
there was a special court before the Sanctuary proper, the
entrance to which was forbidden to Gentiles and even to such
Jews as still needed to bring the required sacrifice for their
purification to be complete (see above in connection with the
fourth grade of sacredness).   This space was designated *'azara*,
"court," and was known by the name "court of the women,"[2]
not because men were excluded from it, but because women,
whose ritual purity was often doubtful, were not allowed to
proceed farther.   So at least says Josephus,[3] but rabbinic law
knows nothing of an exclusion of women as such from the
inner Sanctuary.[4]   An adulteress, who might be "pure"
ritually, was not excluded from the court of the women, and
in case of suspicion (Num. v. 11-31) had even to be brought
there for the Divine judgment,[5] as the woman taken in adultery
was brought before Jesus here (Jn. viii. 2).

A stone screen, on which were the aforementioned tablets
warning Gentiles not to proceed further, enclosed from the
outside the ascent to the outer walls of both the court of the
women and the Sanctuary proper, and prevented heathen as
well as ritually impure Jews from proceeding further.   The
space which lay between it and the wall of the Sanctuary was
called (like the space between the outer and the inner wall of
a fortified city) *Chel*, and was invested with a special grade
of sacredness.   A flight of high steps then led up within this
alley to a narrow terrace, in front of the wall of the inner
precinct, and special flights of stairs with low steps led to the
entrances.[6]   These "steps," from the top of which St. Paul
once spoke to the people (Acts xxi. 35, 40), from which also
Gamaliel announced that the Aramaic Targum of the Book of
Job should be immured,[7] and proclaimed the edict concerning
the intercalary month,[8] and where his son Shimeon saw a
beautiful heathen woman,[9] still existed, at least in part, in

---

[1] Tos. Kel. B. K. i. 9.   [2] Midd. ii. 5.
[3] *Ant.* xv. 11, 5 ; *Bell. Jud.* v. 5, 2.
[4] At a sacrifice offered for herself a woman could be present in the inner
Sanctuary (Tos. Er. ii. 1), except that she could not—according to many Rabbis—
lay her hands on the sacrificial animal (Men. ix. 8).
[5] Sota i. 5.   [6] Midd. ii. 3 ; *cf. Bell. Jud.* v. 5, 2.
[7] b. Sabb. 115a.   [8] Tos. Sanh. ii. 6.   [9] b. Ab. z. 20a.

Roman Jerusalem. Jerome, on Ps. cxix., points to "some signs" of steps running round the Temple, which were still visible in his time. And the δωδεκάπυλον, which was also called "the steps," of which the *Chronicon Paschale* speaks, certainly means, together with the *kodra*, not three quadruple gates in the market street of Ælia Capitolina, but rather the higher platform of the former sanctuary of the Jews (which perhaps still retained a triple gateway on all sides) in the middle of the quadrangle, from which the intruding Antonia citadel had now been removed.[1]   An old pavement, which was traced back to the time of the Temple, must have been visible here in the fourth century.   Small holes were seen there, in which were considered to be the marks of the shoe nails of the soldiers who slew Zacharias (Mt. xxiii. 35 ; Lk. xi. 51),[2] or of the Roman conquerors of Jerusalem![3]

The east entrance to the court of the women was distinguished by folding doors of Corinthian brass,[4] and may most probably be identified with the "Beautiful Gate" of Acts iii. 2, 10, before which the lame beggar sat.[5]   From Josephus we gather that occasionally public gatherings took place in front of it, and that it was so massive that it needed the united strength of twenty men to open and close it.[6]   In the court of the women, we presume, were placed the thirteen trumpet-shaped chests into which rich and poor put obligatory or voluntary gifts for the needs of the Sanctuary or the equivalent in money for certain offerings.[7]   It was probably into one of these that the poor widow dropped her "two mites" (Mk. xii. 41 *f.* ; Lk. xxi. 1).   The gift would be intended either for wood for the altar or for incense, but might also have been put into one of the six chests for the receipt of voluntary gifts, without a specially defined intention.   Billerbeck[8] assumes that Jesus could hear from the portico of the court of the women,

[1] Schlatter, *Zur Topographie und Geschichte Palästinas*, p. 159, thinks of twelve single gates on the site of the old ones belonging to the women's court and the court of the priests, with the addition of two western gates.

[2] Bordeaux pilgrim (Geyer, p. 22).

[3] Lam. R. xi. 7 (46b, reading according to Aruch).

[4] Jos., *Bell. Jud.* v. 5, 3.

[5] According to Schlatter, *Zur Topogr.*, p. 198, Solomon's Hall (Acts iii. 11) lay within the "Beautiful Gate." But the Apostles went first through this door into the inner Sanctuary to pray, and might afterwards have found themselves in the usual meeting-place of the disciples of our Lord.

[6] *Bell. Jud.* vi. 5, 3 ; ii. 17, 3.

[7] Shek. vi. 5 ; Tos. Shek. iii. 1 *f.* The first seven were for the receipt of specific objects ; the last six for general voluntary gifts.

[8] *Kommentar zum N.T.*, ii., pp. 41, 44.

before the open door of the " chamber of the chests," *i.e.* the
" treasury " of the Evangelist, how the widow negotiated with
a priest concerning her small gift, supposed to be destined
for the thirteenth chest. But the narrator has certainly
nothing so complicated in mind, apart from the fact that
the rabbinic sources say nothing of the special objects to
which donations placed in these six chests were devoted.
With the aid of the contradictory assumptions of certain of
the rabbis,[1] the commentators, of whom Maimonides was the
first, attempted to prove that only the thirteenth chest was
for the receipt of voluntary gifts. Of a chamber of chests
tradition says nothing. But a " chamber of the silent " is
mentioned, into which devout persons secretly deposited money
for deserving poor.[2] So there must have been some special
arrangement here, too, which would make it possible to give
without undue display. Josephus speaks quite vaguely of
chests behind the single, not the double, colonnade of the inner
Sanctuary,[3] but leaves it doubtful whether this refers to both
inner courts of the Sanctuary, nor does he say where in the
inner Sanctuary the " treasury chamber " was, over which
Agrippa hung up the emperor's present of a golden chain.[4]
The Temple treasury was called in Aramaic *korbana*,[5] because
all that was put there had a sacrificial character.[6] But the
sha'ar ha-korban, lying opposite the slaughtering-place in the
innermost court of the Sanctuary, according to which Holtzmann[7] is inclined to determine the place of the treasure-house,
is undoubtedly the " gate of sacrifice," as opposite to it, on
the other side of the altar, was the " gate of the firstlings,"
through which the firstlings fit to be offered were brought.
Thus one can only say concerning the position of the " treasure-
chamber," over against which Jesus sat (Mk. xii. 41) and in
which He taught (apparently sitting, Jn. viii. 2, 20), that it
was in the court of the women, because in both cases a
woman entered it. That He taught sitting is quite in accord
with Jewish usage,[8] but it is not easy to say on what He could
have sat in this case, whether, for instance, there were stone

[1] p. Shek. 50b; b. Men. 104a, 107b.   [2] Shek. v. 6; Tos. Shek. ii. 16.
[3] *Bell. Jud.* v. 5, 2.   [4] *Ant.* xix. 6, 1.
[5] *Bell. Jud.* ii. 9, 4; Mt. xxvii. 6. Also the Pal. Evangel. calls the γαζοφυλάκιον
(Mk. xii. 41; Jn. viii. 20) *bet kurbanaya* (*kurbana*). Rabbinic literature has no
corresponding name for it.
[6] *Cf.* Mk. vii. 11; Ned. i. 1, 2, *korban* in the formula of a vow; Neh. x. 35, for
the supply of wood for the altar.
[7] Middot, p. 52 *f.*   [8] *Worte Jesu*, i., p. 18; *Jesus-Jeshua*, p. 42.

wall-benches in the ante-courts of the Temple; for sitting
on the floor would not have seemed appropriate for a teacher.
In any case it was permissible to sit in the court of the women,[1]
but there were serious misgivings later in regard to sitting in
the inner court.

As a boy also, Jesus once "sat" in the Sanctuary, when
He was in the midst of the doctors, both hearing them and
asking them questions (Lk. ii. 46). Here one may think of
Him as a pupil sitting on the floor.[2] Besides a synagogue,[3]
there was in the Sanctuary also a house of study, both designed
for the ministers in the Temple, who cannot be conceived of
as neglecting obligatory synagogal worship. According to
Krauss, this Temple-synagogue and the hall of Solomon
where Jesus taught are both identical with the place in the
Sanctuary where He learnt.[4] But it is more likely that it was
some place in one of the porticoes where teachers gathered
disciples around them.[5] When the Boy Jesus in His answer
to His Mother, who was seeking Him, emphasised the fact
that He had to be "in the things of His Father" (Lk. ii. 49),
He did not refer merely to the Temple, which was not of essential significance for this place of study. Ἐν τοῖς τοῦ πατρός μου
(Christ. Pal. *bide-abba*) signifies the word and will of the Father
from which the Son cannot separate Himself.[6]

A semicircular stair[7] led from the court of the women up
to the great gate[8] which opened on to the avenue leading to the
innermost court of the Sanctuary. To this gate, which is
to be thought of as being in the vicinity of the present chain-
dome, came the lepers, not in order to show themselves to
the priest (Mt. viii. 4; Lk. xvii. 14), which had to be done,
according to Lev. xiv. 3, "outside the camp," *i.e.* outside
Jerusalem, say at the east gate of the outer court, but for the
last acts necessary to the completion of their purification.[9]
So also did the mothers who, like Mary (Lk. ii. 24), brought
purification offerings, which was first possible on the thirty-
fourth day after the birth of the child (Lev. xii. 4),[10] and all others

---

[1] Tos. Yoma iv. 12; *cf.* Yom. vi. 10, where waiting crowds are assumed to
have sat on the floor.
[2] p. Yom. 40b.   [3] *Cf.* Acts xx. 3; Aboth i. 4.   [4] *Synag. Altert.*, p. 68.
[5] Tos. Sukk. iv. 5.   [6] *Cf. Jesus-Jeshua*, p. 37.
[7] Midd. ii. 6; *Bell. Jud.* v. 5, 3.
[8] The Mishna (Midd. i. 4; *cf.* Tos. Yom. ii. 4; p. Yom. 41a; b. Yom. 38a)
places here the iron gate of Nicanor, which according to Josephus formed the
eastern approach to the court of the women. See Klein, *I. Pal. Corp. Inscr.*,
pp. 17 f., 89.
[9] Neg. xiv. 8 f.; Tos. Neg. viii. 10.   [10] Sot. i. 5.

whom incomplete purification prevented from entering the innermost court and who announced the completion of their purifications here.[1] On the other hand, Joseph was hardly called upon " to present to the Lord " at this place the Firstborn of Mary, as is recounted in Lk. ii. 22 *f.* For the custom of such presentations, which might be deduced from Ex. xiii. 2, 12, is not documented. The redemption-money, namely the five shekels prescribed by the Law (Num. xviii. 16), was delivered, when the child was thirty days old[2] (in Tyrian currency[3]), to any priest, at any place.[4] A priest's daughter, if Mary was such, was not obliged to pay it at all.[5] It was, however, natural for the mother to take the child with her, and pious parents would not have missed the opportunity of commending the child in prayer to God, to whom the firstborn belongs in a special sense.

All visitors to the court of the women could observe through its wide eastern gateway the immense and massive altar, occasionally made white, with the Temple building behind it. They could see how the priests mounted on the left side by a long ascent to the height of the altar, and with a bold sweep laid hold of heavy bullock's legs with both hands, and cast them surely on the fire, so that they might with certainty fall into the flames of the altar,[6] which were kept perpetually fed with fuel of fig, nut, and pine trees. But he who had a right to do so, entered this holy spot in order to perform his devotions or bring his offering. Jesus may have visualised the self-righteous Pharisee standing there (Lk. xvii. 11), whilst the publican stood afar off (*ibid., v.* 13), *i.e.* in the court of the women, or even outside on the Sanctuary mount, because he considered himself equal to the heathen and the impure.

The innermost court, compressed in the north and the south by buildings with cells for various purposes, and walled on all sides, must have been *the* court (Hebrew *ha-'azara*) *par excellence* of the Sanctuary. But even here there were demarcations of the various grades of sacredness. A stone balustrade[7]—according to rabbinic tradition consisting only of raised stones or a step laid crosswise[8]—separated the narrow

---

[1] Concerning the duties of the Nasireans, *cf.* PJB, 1909, p. 41 *f.*, and Acts xxi. 26.

[2] Bech. viii. 6. [3] *Ibid.* viii. 7 ; Tos. Bech. vi. 12.

[4] Mech. on Ex. xxii. 28 ; Chall. iv. 9 ; p. Chall. 60b.

[5] Bech. viii. 1 ; Tos. Bech. vi. 5.

[6] The Letter of Aristeas, ed. Wendland, 93. Concerning the wood for the altar-fire, of which olive wood was excluded, see Mishna Tam. i. 3.

[7] *Bell. Jud.* v. 5, 6 ; *Ant.* xv. 11, 5, *cf.* xiii. 13, 5. [8] Midd. ii. 6.

strip, as the " court of Israel," from the space enclosing the
altar, which formed the " court of the priests " and was open
to Israelites only when presenting their sacrifices.[1] Rabbinic
tradition imagined the court of Israel to have been only
11 cubits broad from east to west, like a front section of the
innermost court, whilst according to Josephus the former
surrounded at least three of the latter's sides. One coming
here in order to pray at the time of the evening sacrifice,[2]
i.e. at the ninth hour (three o'clock in the afternoon, Acts iii. 1 ;
cf. Lk. i. 10), would see first of all the slaughtering and cutting
up of the sacrificial lamb, and would then notice that a priest
went to the Holy Place to burn incense (Lk. i. 9). Both these
were acts at which the Israelite was not merely an onlooker,
for they were performed in the name of the people, of whom
the priest was a representative, in order to affirm daily Israel's
relationship to God, according to His command ; and when,
after the censing from the steps to the ante-hall was accomplished, the priests pronounced the blessing with outstretched
hands (Num. vi. 22 *f.*) and " put God's Name upon the children
of Israel,"[3] it was like an answer to the offering in the Sanctuary.
For it meant that God had " nothing but blessing for Israel,
for the proselytes, for the women, for the slaves," and that it
was " not the priests who blessed, but God," who poured
out the whole treasury of His gifts.[4] It was for the reception
of the blessing that the people " bowed themselves " (Ecclus.
l. 21) to the ground on hearing the ineffable Name, the pronunciation of which was not permitted in ordinary life.[5] This
was followed, in the consciousness that God would graciously
accept the gift, by the bringing of the sacrifice to the altar.
The attached meat-offering and wine-offering completed the
act of devotion. At this juncture the Temple music began.
The clash of a cymbal preluded the singing of the Levites from
their special place near the altar. The psalm of the day was
sung in unison by the choir of the Levites, with which mingled
the voices of boys.[6] At the close of each of the three sections
of the psalm, trumpet blasts gave the people the signal for
renewed prostration, which was now done as a sign of praise
and worship of the Lord.[7]

[1] Kel. i. 8.   [2] Pes. v. 1.
[3] Tam. vii. 2 ; Sot. vii. 6.   According to Schürer, *History of J. P.*, ii. 4, p. 24,
at the evening sacrifices the incense was burnt after the burnt offering.   But
this was only on Passover eve.   See Sifre Num. 143 (53b), ed. Horowitz, p. 143.
[4] Sifre on Num. E. p. 43.   [5] Yom. vi. 2.   [6] Erach. ii. 6.
[7] Tam. vii. 3 ; *cf.* Ecclus. l. 14 *ff.*

It is inconceivable that Jesus should not also have stood worshipping before the altar. According to rabbinic law, three sacrificial duties were incumbent on every adult pilgrim appearing in Jerusalem for one of the three great festivals—the sacrifice of the "Presence" (before God), that of the "Chagiga," and that of "Joyousness."[1] Jesus might even at one time have first put His hands on a Passover lamb at the slaughtering place on the right side of the altar, then slaughtered it, Himself turning towards the Temple, whilst the lamb was directed north and south, with its face twisted towards the Temple.[2] The altar on whose wood-pile the fat of the lamb was then burnt, and upon whose lowest base its blood was poured out, was also to Him that which "sanctifies the gift" (Mt. xxiii. 19), because He knew that there was a Divine purpose in the service of the altar. In fact, He never spoke against the sacrificial system, although of course insisting on the offerer's first becoming reconciled to his brother (Mt. v. 24). One has to think of Jesus as being present in the innermost court on the seventh and greatest day of the Feast of Tabernacles,[3] and that it was after the priest had returned from Siloam with his golden pitcher, and for the last time poured its contents on the base of the altar ; after the "Hallel" had been sung to the sound of the flute, the people responding and worshipping as the priests three times drew the threefold blasts from their silver trumpets ; after the high priest had poured with raised hands water on the altar at the sevenfold circuit round it of the people praying for rain for the thirsty land[4]—after all this that He raised His voice, saying : "If any man thirst, let him come unto Me, and drink" (Jn. vii. 38). Only upon this circuit could an "Israelite" (*i.e.* a layman) have found himself between the altar and the Temple building. To enter into the latter was prohibited to a layman. It was a naive error of the time of the Crusaders to imagine that, at the presentation of the Child, Mary stood at the place of the Ark of the Covenant, and the Child impressed His foot in the holy rock, when Simeon took Him in his arms.[5]

---

[1] Chag. i. 1 *f.* ; Tos. Chag. i. 4 *f.* ; Sifre on Dt. cxxxviii. (102a).

[2] Tam iv. 1 ; Tos. Men. x. 12.

[3] According to Jn. vii. 37, the greatest day of the feast was at the same time the last one, whilst in Mishna Sukk. iv. 3, 5, the seventh day was distinguished by the sevenfold circuit round the altar, and the eighth day, as "the last day of the feast," has no special distinction (Sukk. iv. 8 ; Tos. Sukk. iv. 17), probably also without the water-pouring.   [4] Sukk. iv. 9, Pal. text.

[5] This footprint was then shown on the left, that is to say north of the altar erected upon the rock. See Peter the Deacon (Geyer, *Itinera*, p. 107 *f.*) ; Theoderich (ed. Tobler), p. 41 [*cf.* Jn. of Würzburg, xiv,—TRANSLATOR].

The lofty Temple building in the background of the inner
court stood in striking contrast to the courts with their
Hellenistic decorations. For, instead of a large peripteros,
with its simple gabled long-house surrounded by columns, such
as a Greek would have expected to find here, he would have
discovered a long-house with adytum, cells, and vestibule
indeed, but all strikingly surmounted by an upper story, overhanging in the front and covered by a 50 metres high and
wide, 10 metres deep front-building without divisions, on all
other sides enclosed by a low three-storied superstructure of
chambers, above whose height of 30 metres the chief building
towered to a greater height of still another 20 metres.[1] Jewish
imagination compared this peculiar building, after Isa. xxix. 1
(*ariel*, *ari*=lion), with a lion, who is narrow behind and wide
in front.[2] The purpose of Herod, who here particularly was
bound by the form once laid down by Solomon, could only
have been that the Temple should be visible from a long
distance off, and that it should dominate its surroundings.
Snow-white limestone, which Josephus calls marble,[3] was the
building material, and the square front was entirely covered
with gold, according to Josephus, which was at any rate
meant to divert the attention from all the rest. It was therefore quite natural to swear by the gold of the Temple: Jesus
pointed out that the Temple and He who dwelt therein were
what mattered most (Mt. xxiii. 17, 21), and it might have been
expected that every pious Israelite would look back from all
the grandeur of the Herodian building to what the Temple
really stood for. The high entrance of the vestibule did not
remind him of the open heaven, the curtain behind—of the
elements of the universe—as Josephus interprets them—but he
was conscious of being present at the place which Israel's
God had chosen in order "to put His Name there" (Dt.
xii. 5), or as Onkelos understood it, "to let His Shekinah
dwell there." The Midrash comments thereon that the
similarity of these expressions to those used in connection
with the "putting of the Name" referred to in the priestly
blessing (Num. vi. 27), indicate that this Name may be uttered
only in this place.[4] It ought rather to have pointed to the
blessing which this "putting of the Name" in a material

[1] *Bell. Jud.* v. 6; *Ant.* xv. 11, 3; Midd. iv. 6, 7.   [2] Midd. iv. 7.
[3] According to b. Bab. b. 4a, Sukk. 51b, the Herodian Temple was built
of alabaster and marble, perhaps also of a dark kind of stone, but not covered
with gold, of which the Mishna also knows nothing.
[4] Sifre on Dt. lxii. (88a); Hoffman, Midrash Tannaim, p. 49.

building meant, and to the joy in God expressed in the use of His gifts in His Presence (Dt. xii. 7, 12).

It was only really the entrance to the Temple that was visible to the people, for its fore-part and its projecting buildings covered it on all sides. Only the large opening of the fore-building, which could not be closed and which was covered above with oak beams,[1] permitted a view of the narrow front of the long-house and its door, framed in a gigantic vine of pure gold, and covered by a rich curtain of the four colours of the Temple (fine linen, blue, scarlet, and purple) which moved in the wind.[2] This curtain hid the gilded inside and its contents from all laymen. The eyes of all visitors to the Temple must have hung in awe and in longing on this curtain. It was an awful event[3] when at the Crucifixion this curtain was " rent in twain from the top to the bottom " (Mt. xxvii. 51). Opposite this curtain Mary stood in the distance of the east gate with her Child, later the twelve-year-old Boy stood there likewise, and lastly the Man Jesus, when after His solemn entrance into Jerusalem He "looked round about upon all things " (Mk. xi. 11). This all pilgrims for the feast may have done, when their journey to appear before God (Ex. xxiii. 17) ended before the Temple building. To Jesus it meant more, not because He knew that this was His last visit to the Temple, but because in the foreground of His thought was the destruction which threatened the Sanctuary (Mt. xxiv. 2 ; Mk. xiii. 2 ; Lk. xix. 4). It must disappear, because God had something better in mind. The adversaries of Jesus may have thought, like Jeremiah's enemies (Jer. vii. 4, 10), that the Temple of the Lord would protect them from misfortune, of which, indeed, the last defenders of the Sanctuary were convinced.[4] This was the occasion when Jesus uttered the words which were afterwards used to prove His guilt (Mt. xxvi. 61 ; xxvii. 40 ; Mk. xiv. 58 ; xv. 29) : " *Ana satar hekhela haden ubitelata yomin nibne horana* " ("I destroy this Temple, and in three days I build another").[5] It is possible

---

[1] Midd. iii. 7.

[2] Shek. viii. 4 ; Tam. vii. 1 ; *Bell. Jud.* v. 5, 4. *Cf.* the Letter of Aristeas 86, where it speaks of this curtain, not of the curtains, of the vestibule doors.

[3] This is also the Matthæan conception of it, not as a sign of a higher symbolism, as if it referred to one of the two curtains of the entrance to the Holy of Holies.

[4] *Bell. Jud.* vi. 2, 1 ; 5, 2.

[5] This after Mk., leaving out the interpretatory additions. In Pal. Evang., which has only the Matthæan parallel, *shera* is used for " bringing to naught." But for the destruction of the Temple *setar* (LXX καταλύειν) is used in Ezra v. 12 ; also in b. Bab. b. 4a *setar* is used for destroying the Temple, and *bena* for the restoring.

to understand the " I " in a prophetic sense, *i.e.* as referring
to God, as in Jeremiah's announcement of the destruction of
the Temple (Jer. vii. 14), and like the " I " in our Lord's
logion concerning the fruitless gathering of Jerusalem's
children (Mt. xxiii. 37).   If so, then Jesus referred to God as
the Builder of the Temple of the future.[1]   Or He may have
regarded Himself as destroyer and restorer of the Temple, as
it is presumed in Acts vi. 14.   In truth, God is not bound to
the nearly fifty years old Herodian building (*cf.* Jn. ii. 20).
If it be His will, He can at any time substitute another one for
it, and the Builder whom He has appointed to accomplish this
wonderful work is already here.[2]

[1] In the Book of Enoch xc. 29, God is the Builder of the new Temple at the
old place.   In Midrash on the Psalms God stands as the Builder of the future
Temple in contrast to the past human builders, a parallel to the Marcan contrast
between the Temple made with hands and the one not made with hands.

[2] There are many rabbinic references to Messiah as Builder of the future
Temple : " The Messiah will come from the north and build the Temple in the
south," Lev. R. ix. (23a).

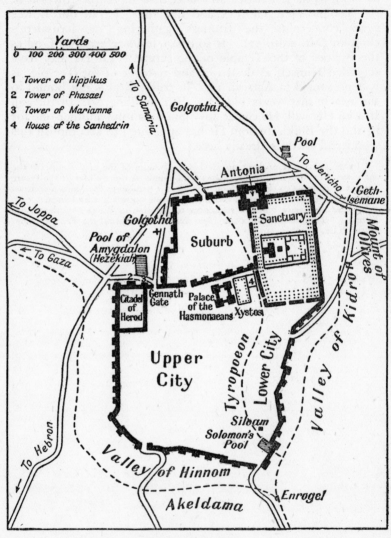

Plan of Jerusalem.

(*Designed by Dalman.*)

XVII

BETHESDA AND SILOAM

THERE are various readings of the name of the pool in Jerusalem referred to in the Fourth Gospel (Jn. v. 2). Besides Βηθσαιδα, which is probably due to a confusion with the town of that name, Βηθζαθα and Βηθεσθα are found.[1] The last reading, which is that of the Palestinian Lectionary, is doubtless based on the attractive interpretation of the name as signifying " House of mercy " in Hebrew : " bet ḥisda " ; although it is also possible that ḥisda was taken to be a proper name : " The House of Hisda." But the better supported Βηθζαθα reminds one so much of the similarly sounding Βεζεθα, Βεζαθα, or Αβεσσαθη, by which Josephus distinguishes the most northern suburb of Jerusalem,[2] that the two must be connected.[3] It must have been called bez'ata in Aramaic and ha-biṣ'a (" The Section ") in Hebrew.[4] In that case the pool would have been known in the time of Christ as the " pool of Bezatha," after the not yet walled city quarter, which name the Evangelist applied to the pool itself. In the vicinity of the " sheep-gate " referred to in the Gospel, which must be sought north of the Temple (Neh. iii. 1), a double pool as shown in the fourth century, which was named " Sheep-pool "; the explanation of its peculiar shape (it had five porches) was that four of these surrounded it, " and one was in the middle."[5] Eusebius says : " Bethesda . . . is now identified by the twin pools (ἐν ταῖς λίμναις διδύμοις), of which one is supplied by the periodic rains, whilst the

[1] Also represented by the Palestinian Evangeliarium.
[2] Bell. Jud. ii. 15, 5 ; v. 4, 2 ; 5, 8.
[3] Formerly I traced it back to Bet Zaita, " Place of Olives," or to Bet Sata, " Sheep-house," which is perhaps also the interpretation of Eusebius, because the Hebrew se, " sheep," occurs in the Aramaic form as sita. But as two suburbs of Jerusalem are designated bisin in plural (Tos. Sanh. iii. 4), the sinular bis'a, to which the Aram. biz'a, det. biz'ata, would correspond, is more probable.
[4] See below, p. 315.
[5] Cyril of Jerusalem, Hom. in Par. 2 ; Migne, xxxiii. 1133.

water of the other is of a ruddy colour—a trace, they say, of
the carcasses of the sacrifices which were formerly cleansed
in it before offering; whence also it was called προβατική,
'sheep-pool.'"[1]   Similarly Eucherius (A.D. 440): "Bethesda
is visible and remarkable by its double pool (*gemino lacu*): the
one is commonly filled by the winter showers; the other is
distinguished by its red waters."[2]   The Bordeaux pilgrim saw
there peculiar whirls.[3]   Virgilius actually found in the pond
near a church dedicated to St. Mary the bed of the palsied
man who was healed![4]   Also Sophronius in his Anacreontic
verses refers to this pond: "Entering into the holy church
of the sheep-pool, where renowned Anna bore Mary . . . I
would behold the steps whereon the palsied man took up his
bed and walked."[5]   Already in the fourth century a church
had been built over the pond,[6] which the Madaba mosaic
seems to indicate close to the church of St. Anne.[7]   Near
this church, under the ruins of a chapel, a spacious cistern
(6 by 16 metres) was found,[8] which will be the remains of one
of the twin ponds.   Further excavations showed the traces of a
second reservoir south of it, which may be taken to be the
second pond of the Byzantine period.[9]   Both are on the slope
of a valley, now completely covered, running towards the
Kidron valley, in which it was most natural to construct a
pond for rain-water outside the city.   Whether an intermittent flow of water into the tank caused the water to be
occasionally disturbed, or whether merely the wind, and how
the belief in its miraculous quality originated, we cannot
know.[10]   The cellar-shaped cistern, to which one now descends
by many steps, makes it difficult to visualise the former pool
surrounded by waiting patients, as is assumed in the Gospel.
Nevertheless, it is the Jerusalem of Jesus with which one
comes into contact in the depth under the ruins.

---

[1] *Onom.* (*s.v.* Βηζαθα).   [2] *De Loc. Sanct.* (Geyer, p. 127).

[3] Geyer, p. 21.

[4] Pitra, *Analecta Sacra*, v., p. 120.

[5] Migne, *P.G.* lxxxvii. 3, col. 3817, *cf.* under xx.   The same place is
mentioned by Petrus Diaconus (Geyer, p. 108); Theodosius, *De Terr. Sanct.*,
viii.; Antoninus (Geyer, p. 177).

[6] Peter of Sebaste; Peter the Iberian; Georgian Canonar. (*Or. Chr.*, 1915,
p. 219); in the time of the Crusading of Perdica; Migne, *P.G.* cxxxiii., col. 964.

[7] The ponds are not visible.   [8] See Schick, *ZDPV*, 1888, p. 178 *f.*

[9] See Vincent, *Jérusalem*, ii., p. 685 and plates.

[10] The outlet of the ponds runs towards the great reservoir *Birket Israin*, at
the north side of the Temple enclosure, which Burchard (1283) identified with
sheep-pool, from which he distinguished the pond adjacent to the church of St.
Anne as *piscina interior*.

Jerusalem does indeed possess an intermittent spring, the constantly recurring movement of which has always been a subject of great interest,[1] and might well seem miraculous. It has therefore in recent times often been proposed as being the pool of Bethesda.[2]   It is, however, the Gihon of the Old Testament,[3] whose water, owing to the stopping of its proper channel, was only approachable at the south end of Jerusalem, at the exit of a long channel excavated by Hezekiah through the rock.[4]   This explains why Josephus found the spring at the outlet of the Cheese-makers' valley,[5] and why the Targum calls the Gihon *Shilo-ha*.[6]   It was also the reason why Jesus sent the man blind from birth to the pool of Siloam (Jn. ix. 7), which was at the lower end of the channel, to wash off the clay from his eyes.   Thus it is certain that the Evangelist could not have identified Siloam with the pool of Bezetha. This pool was not a proper reservoir for the spring-water of the Gihon, but only a pond 1·22 metres deep, used for drawing water and perhaps also for washing (laundry).   It used to be praised as sweet and pure water for drinking,[7] even as being excellent as a digestive.[8]   From here was the water taken in a golden can for the libation at the Feast of Tabernacles,[9] as well as the water for the ashes of the red heifer (Num. xix. 17).[10]   Its purifying effects used to be compared with the primæval water of creation.[11]   And it was the Siloam water with which the blind man washed his eyes and came back seeing.   All this is in contrast to what it is to-day. Now the women of the village Silwan wash their laundry here, and would not even drink the water from the spring above, which now flows again, because it is unpalatable and suitable only for the watering of their gardens.   A native of Jerusalem would not even bathe here.

In close proximity to the pool of Siloam stood, according to

---

[1] The Bordeaux pilgrim, Eucherius, Bede, Jerome on Isa. viii. 6.

[2] See Mickley, *PJB*, 1911, p. 58 ; Pronobis, *Akra und Sion*, 1923, p. 48.

[3] *Cf*. Dalman, *PJB*, 1918, p. 47.

[4] Josephus, *Bell. Jud.* ii. 16, 2 ; v. 4, 1 ; 12, 2, according to whom the spring was at the south end of the city.

[5] *Bell. Jud.* v. 4, 1.

[6] 1 Kings i. 33. So the name is also formed in Aram. Pal. Ev. Jn. ix. 7. The position of the Solomonic gardens is defined by it, Targ. Eccl. ii. 5.

[7] *Bell. Jud.* v. 4, 1 ; Lam. R. Intr. xix. (7a).

[8] Ab. de R. N. xxxv. (ed. Schechter 53a).

[9] Sukk. iv. 9.   [10] Par. iii. 2 ; *cf*. Tos. Par. iii. 3.

[11] p. Taan. 65a ; *cf*. Targ. 1 Chr. xi. 22. In the same neighbourhood the "fountain opened . . . for sin and for uncleanness" (Zech. xiii. 1) is located, p. Shek. 50a ; b. Yoma 78a.

Lk. xiii. 4, a tower, which tumbled down in the time of Christ.
R. Weill, during the course of his excavation at the southern
point of the Zion hill in the winter of 1913-14, thought he
had found it, when, below the eastern slope of the hill, he
came across the remains of a round tower fully 7 metres in
diameter.[1] This tower stood at a point near which two
channels of the Gihon fountain make their way underground,
one running above the other. But this fact could scarcely
have been so generally known that the tower would therefore
be called "The Tower of Siloam." This name clung at that
time to the neighbourhood of the pool where the channel of
king Hezekiah issued. It is there that the fallen tower must
be sought, and most probably at the southern point of the
hill of Zion, where its sloping rock-base would easily explain
its fall. Now at this point Weill found that the extreme
corner of the wall seems to terminate in a bastion 10 metres
wide and about 13 metres long,[2] which is better described as
a tower. So, just above the rocky steps, over which one
ascends at present to the hill, above the mouth of the older,
and the outlet of the later, Siloam channel,[3] stood this tower
which, at this spot where the city joined the basin of the
valley,[4] killed eighteen persons (Lk. xiii. 4). Their death, in
which a judgment of God was seen, gave Jesus an opportunity
to oppose the attitude of mind which readily assumes the guilt
of other people,[5] but hesitates where itself is concerned.

Not far from the pool of Siloam, on the hill of Zion, some
distance above the south-east corner of the old city, Weill
in 1914 found, upon some cisterns provided with steps, a
Greek inscription.[6] It runs : " Theodotos, son of Vettenos,
priest and synagogue-overseer, grandson of a synagogue-
overseer, built the synagogue for the reading of the Law and
instruction in the commandments, and the home for strangers
and the houses (rooms), and the receptacles for water, for the
housing of strangers who are in need of them, which (*i.e.*
synagogue) was founded by his fathers and the elders and

---

[1] *La Cité de David* (1920), p. 118 ; *cf.* Dalman, *PJB*, 1915, p. 71, pl. v., fig. 2.
[2] *Ibid.*, p. 120 *f.*; *cf. PJB*, 1915, p. 68 ; 1918, pl. iii.
[3] *PJB*, 1918, pp. 53, 69.
[4] The tower protected the " Fountain gate " of Jerusalem (Neh. ii. 14), *PJB*,
1915, p. 69 *f.*
[5] Seeing a blind or a lame person one says : " Blessed be the true judge,"
p. Ber. 13b.
[6] See Weill, *La Cité de David*, p. 186 ; Clermont-Ganneau, *Syria*, i., 1920,
p. 190 *f.*; Klein, *Jud. pal. Corpus Inscriptionum*, p. 101 *f.*; Thomsen, *Die lat.
u. griech. Inschriften der Stadt Jerusalem*, p. 134 *f.*

Simonides." So Greek-speaking Jewry in the time before the destruction of Jerusalem had here one of those centres from which sprang opponents to St. Stephen. It has been connected with the " synagogue of the Libertines " (Acts vi. 9), because the name of Theodotos' father, Vettenos, is Roman. Jesus is not likely to have ever entered this synagogue, but His Name must certainly have been a cause of great agitation, calling for combat against the supposed enemy of the Law and the Temple, here as elsewhere, and St. Paul might well have proclaimed this same Name boldly here before the Hellenists (Acts ix. 29).

Close to the synagogue of Theodotos two ancient rocky vaults were discovered during Weill's excavations ;[1] they may be regarded as the last remains of the tombs of the kings of Judah, in which David was the first to be buried (1 Kings ii. 10). Peter said of him : " His sepulchre is with us unto this day " (Acts ii. 29), in order to contrast him with his greater Son, who did not remain in the grave.

---

[1] Weill, *op. cit.*, p. 157 *f.* ; Dalman, *PJB*, 1915 p. 76 ; Vincent, *RB*, 1929, p. 247 *f.*

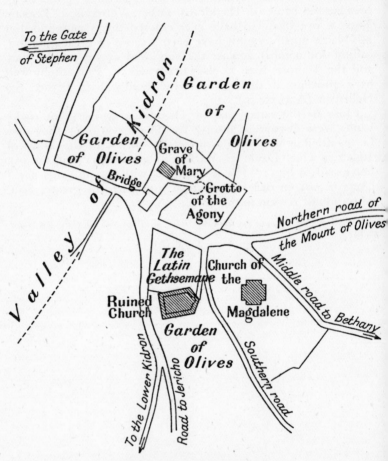

Environments of Gethsemane.

XVIII

THE UPPER ROOM AND GETHSEMANE

THE Gospels assume that our Lord did not lodge in Jerusalem during the feasts (*cf.* above, p. 261). The Passover, according to the Synoptists, was the cause of the Last Supper taking place in Jerusalem, whilst in St. John it is not clear why this was inside the city, as is none the less assumed.[1]

The Passover meal, like all sacrificial meals of a lower grade, had, according to the ruling of the time, to be consumed only in the area within the walls of Jerusalem.[2] It seems that the neighbourhood (*ibbur*) of a city was not considered part of it where such meals were in question; the practice was different in regard to vows, where the usage of ordinary speech was followed.[3] In Jerusalem, however, a distinction was made between a " lower section "—generally considered a part of the city proper, because its " sacredness " had been established before the exile—and an " upper section," which only the unlearned equated with the other part, whereas the scholars ruled it out. The reason given (the exposure, lit. " nakedness," of that part, Tos. Sanh. iii. 4) points to the north, where, in fact, there were two sections of Jerusalem's eastern hill, and excludes the locating of the upper section on the Mount of Olives.[4] There was, however, a view that the " wall of Beth Page " (see above p. 252) might rank with that of Jerusalem in regard to the eating of the Passover,[5] although only in the case of a person forced to remain outside the city. It must have been the normal thing for visitors arriving for the feast but stopping outside the city as well as for the inhabitants of the outer suburbs to provide a house for themselves in the city for the Passover evening, where the

---

[1] *Cf.*, for a full discussion on this subject, *Jesus-Jeshua*, pp. 86-184.
[2] Kel. i. 8 ; Zeb. v. 8 ; Makk. iii. 3 ; Sifre on Num. lxix. (18a).
[3] Ned. vii. 5 ; *cf.* Erub. v. 1 ; b. Erub. 22d.
[4] *Cf.* A. Schwarz, *Jüd. Monatsschrift*, 1917, p. 404.
[5] Pes. 91a.

lamb slaughtered in the Temple could be roasted[1] in an oven,[2] and where the necessary regulations concerning the exact manner of the solemn reclining at table could be complied with easily.[3] The other requirements for the meal (bitter herbs, sweet sauce, unleavened bread, and wine) would have been brought to the place thus chosen. So the place of the Last Supper is one of those things which stamp it as a Passover meal, as is also the hymn at the end (Mt. xxvi. 30 ; Mk. xiv. 26), of which an Aramaic proverb says : " Even if the Passover is only as big as an olive (*i.e.* for the individual participant) the *Hallel* cracks the roof."[4]

Nowhere in the New Testament is it suggested that the later meeting-place of the disciples in Jerusalem (Lk. xxiv. 33 ; according to Acts i. 13 an upper chamber)[5] was the upper room (Mk. xiv. 15 ; Lk. xxii. 12) of the Last Supper, or that their meeting-place was always, as in Acts xii. 12, the house of the mother of John Mark. Our Lord, when choosing a place, had purposely put personal relationships on one side, probably in order to be safe from His enemies during the meal, perhaps also in order that the " traitor " should not know about it beforehand. Thus it would follow that, even later, there was nothing to identify the house. There is, however, no doubt that the Christians in the fourth century were convinced that a certain building, south of the Roman Jerusalem, dated back to the time of the Apostles, and that its upper floor was their first meeting-place. According to Antoninus,[6] it was the house of James ; according to Virgilius, the house of John Mark ;[7] according to Epiphanius Hagiopolita, the property of the Apostle John, with whom lived the Mother of Jesus.[8] They were certain that here they were within the borders of old Jerusalem, and therefore spoke of this place as being in Zion, partly because they liked to apply the honourable name of the City of God just here outside Ælia Capitolina[9] and partly because they were convinced that David's citadel of Zion was connected with the towers of the Herodian palace left standing at the destruction of Jerusalem by Titus.[10] Josephus had already given a lead by connecting the Upper City with the citadel of David.[11] The pilgrim of Bordeaux, indeed, speaks only of a synagogue preserved

---

[1] Pes. vii. 2.   [2] Pes. v. 10.   *Cf.*, for the Passover ritual, *Jesus-Jeshua* iv.
[3] Pes. x. 1.   [4] b. Pes. 35b.   [5] *Cf. Jesus-Jeshua*, p. 114.
[6] Geyer, p. 174.   [7] Pitra, *Analecta Sacra*, v., p. 120.
[8] *Cf.* below, p. 334.   [9] *PJB*, 1915, p. 78 *f.*
[10] *Cf.* under xx.   [11] *Bell. Jud.* v. 4. 1.

there,[1] without mentioning its importance for the Christians. Epiphanius, however, records that at the destruction of Jerusalem, " apart from a few houses, the small house of the community of God alone remained, where the disciples ascended to the upper room after the return from the Ascension of the Saviour from the Mount of Olives."[2]   He goes on to tell of some other houses and of seven synagogues, one of which was preserved even in the time of Constantine " as a tent in the vineyard " (Isa. i. 8, LXX). This must have been identical with the one which the pilgrim of Bordeaux saw.   He does not say anything about a Zion *church*.   But in the year 370 Ætheria knows of such an one as being the place of the appearances of Jesus after the Resurrection and of the outpouring of the Holy Spirit.[3]   It was not yet held to have been the place of the institution of the Eucharist, because on Maundy Thursday Holy Communion was not celebrated there but " behind the Cross "[4]—that is to say, on Golgotha—and this, moreover, against usual practice, and so merely for want of a more suitable place.   But already in the same century the *Doctrina Addæi* designates the church of Zion with its upper story as the place of the institution,[5] and in 460 at least one celebration took place there on Maundy Thursday.[6] Since the seventh century there has been a general conviction that this church contained the site of the Last Supper.[7]   The original space was too small for the great number of Christians in Jerusalem, and towards the end of the fourth century a basilica was already erected at the north side of the two-storied house, which became their chief sanctuary.   Arculf gives a plan of it,[8] without making clear whether he means the old annex of the basilica or the basilica itself.   The Madaba map shows on the right, close to the Zion church, an annex, behind which is a higher square house with a dome-shaped roof. This must have been the presumed place of the Last Supper and of the outpouring of the Holy Spirit.   As late as the time of the Crusaders one here climbed 30 steps to a vaulted room

[1] Geyer, p. 22.

[2] *De mensuris et ponderibus* xiv.; Migne, *P.G.* xliii., col. 261.

[3] Geyer, pp. 92, 94; *cf.* Petrus Diaconus, p. 108; Theodosius, p. 141.

[4] *Ibid.*, p. 85 *f.*   [5] See Vincent and Abel, *Jérusalem*, ii., p. 453.

[6] According to an Armenian Lectionary, *Or. Chr.*, 1915, p. 222.

[7] According to Sophronius, the washing of the feet, the Last Supper, the appearance of the Risen Christ, the outpouring of the Holy Spirit, and the death of Mary took place here.   Later, Epiphanius added the Prætorium and the house of Annas and Caiaphas (Migne, *P.G.* cxx., col. 261).

[8] Geyer, p. 244.

with a dome-shaped roof, where the place of the Last Supper, and behind it that of the outpouring of the Holy Spirit, was shown, whilst the washing of the disciples' feet was supposed to have taken place on the first floor.[1] When Bernardino Amico in the year 1600 drew a plan and section of the chapel of the Holy Supper,[2] it referred to the still existing Franciscan building, which was built in the year 1350 on ancient remains as a reconstruction of the ancient sanctuary.[3] The division of the rooms remained the old one. A part of the eastern wall probably dates back to Byzantine times. In this way the Last Supper has retained its definite site in Jerusalem! The upper room of the gathering of the disciples (Acts i. 13) began to be identified closely with the upper room of the Last Supper.

The place which is now shown as the *Cœnaculum* of Jesus[4] looks like the refectory of an old monastery. Two columns support the vault of a room measuring 9 by 14 metres. Much simpler in reality was the chamber, provided with cushions, in which Jesus uttered wonderful words : *Den hu gufi* and *Den hu admi* ("This is My body, this is My blood") (1 Cor. xi. 24 *f.*; Mt. xxvi. 27 *f.*; Mk. xiv. 22 *f.*; Lk. xxii. 17 *f.*), giving to the bread distributed at the beginning of the meal and to the cup of blessing at the end (see above, p. 232), namely the third of the four cups of the Passover meal,[5] an unexpected significance which without the thought of the saving power of the slaughtered Passover lamb and its blood (Ex. xii. 13, 23, 27) could not have been understood.[6] God is represented in the Midrash as saying[7] : "I behold the blood of the Passover lamb and reconcile you, so that your joy may be full, even those of you that be poor and afflicted." The interpretation of the Passover rites prescribed in Ex. xii. 26 *f.*; Pes. x. 4 *f.*, with which the old Aramaic explanation of the unleavened bread as *ha laḥma 'anya* ("behold the bread of affliction") is connected, must have had some influence on our Lord's words. But even if the Eucharist was not instituted in the present *Cœnaculum* the propitiatory death of Christ was commemorated here at an early date. The Cup which the disciples of Jesus bless, and the Bread which they break,

[1] Theoderich (ed. Tobler, p. 55 *f.*) ; Phocas (Migne, *P.G.* cxxxiii., col. 941).
[2] *Trattato delle Piante ed Immagine* (1620), fig. 14.
[3] Lemmens, *Die Franciskaner im Heiligen Lande*, i., p. 48 *f.*
[4] *Cf.* Vincent and Abel, *Jérusalem*, ii., p. 421 *f.*
[5] Pes. x. 7 ; *cf. Jesus-Jeshua*, p. 148.
[6] *Jesus-Jeshua*, p. 166.   [7] Ex. R. xv. (35b).

had here their first users. But this means that for them
Israel's Passover has been succeeded by something quite
different. Many Jews expected the Messianic Redemption
on a Passover night.[1] The scribes based this hope on the
significance which is given in Ex. xii. 2 to the first month
and on the expression " the night of observation," used in
Ex. xii. 42 of the Passover night. Whether this connection
of the future Redemption with the Passover night was already
current in the time of Christ is not certain. It is, however,
likely that in the time of subjection the remembrance of the
first redemption on the Passover night awakened the thought
of a new redemption which might be expected from God,
the Redeemer of Israel. How this new redemption was conceived, the hymns of Kalir, appointed for the Passover, show.
He says in " Omez gebur-otekha," a hymn for the Passover
evening :

Those two[2] Thou wilt suddenly bring over those from Uz,[3]
Thine hand will be strong and Thy right hand high (Ps. lxxxix. 14).
In the night when the sacrifice of Passover was sanctified.

And in the Keroba " Asirim asher " for the second day of
Passover he prays :

Destroy them who are made like straw being bound[4]
As punishment to the ten horns,[5]
Set them in flames like straw burning in a dry place (Amos i. 10)
As a sign of the completion of the ten plagues.[6]

These imprecations flung at Byzantine Rome were occasioned
by the deeds of ancient Rome, whose heir Byzantium was.
But their root lies farther back in the history of Herod and the
Roman governors of Palestine. He who celebrated the
Passover in the time of Christ could not but long for re-
demption from the yoke of Rome. Jesus also thought of
Redemption, but there, in the upper room of His last meal,
He turned His mind to the Redemption from guilt, which

[1] See above, p. 117.
[2] Loss of children and widowhood, Isa. xlvii. 9.
[3] According to Lam. iv. 21, the daughter of Edom. Lam. R. on iv. 21 refers
" the daughter of Edom " as Cæsarea, " who dwells in the land of Uz " as
Rome.
[4] The house of Edom (Rome), Ob. v. 18.
[5] Of the fourth beast of Dan vii. 7, which is referred to Edom. Lev. R. xiii.
(34b).
[6] The plagues of Egypt should come over Edom (Rome); *cf.* Jer. xlix. 17
and *Jesus-Jeshua*, p. 168.

the people needed, before the actual work of Redemption, the establishment of the reign of God, which means something greater than a broken Roman yoke, could begin.

From the chamber of the Last Supper Jesus went to the place Gethsemane on the Mount of Olives (Mt. xxvi. 30 ; Mk. xiv. 26 ; Lk. xxii. 39), the other side of the Kidron (Jn. xviii. 1). It has seemed strange to some scholars[1] that Jesus left the scene of the Passover meal, since it is prohibited, according to Ex. xii. 22, to leave the house on Passover night " until the morning." The scribes, however, limited this prohibition, with much else, exclusively to the Egyptian Passover,[2] and it was only considered a duty, based on Dt. xvi. 7, not to leave the city of the sanctuary at least before the next morning.[3] For this duty of spending the night within the city, Beth Page, being in the precincts of Jerusalem (see above, p. 315), was considered by most as included in the city.[4] Jesus was certainly not bound by the " ordinances of the elders," but He would hardly have spent the night on the Mount of Olives, if this action had involved any breach of the Law. If Bethany had not been within the confines of Jerusalem, the Sabbath regulations—apart from the duty of remaining in Jerusalem throughout Passover night—would have hindered Him from returning to the mount on the most holy first day of the feast.

It is not difficult to determine the way from ancient Jerusalem to the Mount of Olives. He who would not use the sanctuary as a passage, which was considered as a profanation,[5] would most likely have avoided it by skirting its south side. At present one has to follow the outside of the southern city wall, from the point where it bends towards the south wall of the Temple area, and descends then in a north-easterly direction to the valley. In ancient times Jerusalem had to have an exit in this neighbourhood, which made it possible to come down to the Gihon fountain.[6] If the Gihon was stopped (see above, p. 311), it needed an eastern outlet all the more, as farther north the sanctuary barred the way to the east for the city.

[1] See Weiss on Mt. xxvi. 30, and *Jesus-Jeshua*, pp. 94, 95.
[2] Tos. Pes. viii. 14, 17.
[3] Tos. Pes. viii. 8 ; Sifre Dt. 134 *f.* (ed. Friedmann 101).
[4] Sifre on Num. cli. (ed. Friedmann 55a), whilst R. Jehuda (Tos. Pes. viii. 8) did not consider Beth Page as belonging to Jerusalem in regard to the duty of spending the night within the city.
[5] See above, p. 294.
[6] Near it must have once been the Water Gate of Neh. iii. 26.

The eastern gate of the Lower City thus served the whole of ancient Jerusalem for those who desired to reach the Mount of Olives. If the room of the Last Supper was somewhere about there, an exit at this place was obvious. It is therefore not fanciful to imagine Jesus, in the consciousness of the destiny appointed for Him, coming down here with His disciples into the Kidron valley—the same way which David took when he fled from Absalom (2 Sam. xv. 17). David wept because of his uncertainty concerning the decision which God had made in regard to him ; Jesus was certain of it.

A small bridge now leads over the bed of the Kidron brook which flows here in the winter. Opposite this rises a rock-tomb with a tent-shaped roof, which is now called after Absalom, but in the fourth century was said to be the tomb of Isaiah.[1] This peculiar structure originates from the Jerusalem before the Roman destruction, and might well have been a witness of our Lord's walk towards Gethsemane.

If one wanted to go from here to Bethany one would have to ascend at the left near this monument and travel along a way, lately blocked by walls, leading in an easterly direction, in order to reach the southern Mount of Olives road (see p. 256). Only when, from the foot of the mountain, one aimed at an objective farther north could one remain on the way leading towards the north-east, which does not leave the valley. Below the so-called " Tomb of Isaiah " the bottom of the Kidron valley is narrow and consists only of its river bed. Above, it widens and so can be planted with olive-trees. At present olive gardens fill the valley ground here as far as the point where it narrows down again, opposite the present gate of St. Stephen ; they also continue for some distance on the slope of the Mount of Olives, but soon become scarce. Only at the summit is there again a proper olive garden. To the foot of the mountain, at the point where the Bethany road descends, and to the country stretching northward from there, the name Gethsemane has been demonstrably attached since the fourth century, its mention in the Gospels causing its site and its name to be cherished among the Christians.

The name of the place on the Mount of Olives where Jesus spent His last night is best attested as " Gethsemani " in Mt. xxvi. 36 ; Mk. xiv. 32, and can therefore be traced back to the Hebrew *gat shemanim*, " oils-press " ; " oil-press " would

---

[1] Geyer, p. 23.   Later it was considered to be the tomb of Jehoshaphat ; see *ibid.*, p. 241.

have been "*gat shemen.*" *Shemanim* is sometimes used for kinds of oil,[1] for gifts of oil,[2] and for oil stores.[3] The η of the reading Γεθσημανει would in that case have been influenced by the Greek σημαίνω, σημεῖον, and the reading of Codex D (Γεθσαμανει) would be the correct one. The possibility, however, remains that the second part of the word does indeed go back to σημεῖον, "sign," which in the form of *seman* has become of frequent use in post-Biblical Hebrew and Aramaic. The Palestinian Lectionary has, in fact, in Mt. xxvi. 36, *gesemanin*, and the Peshita *gedsiman*. In that case the name would mean "press of signs" or of "forebodings." One has, moreover, to consider that *gat* as the Hebrew for a place of the preparation of oil is rare.[4] In the Mishna it is mostly called *bet hab-badd*,[5] as also to-day the Arabic *badd* designates an olive mill, whilst the oil-press is called *ma'sera*. "Press of signs" might have been the figurative name for a piece of ground, as is Jerome's interpretation according to the reading *gesamani*, after Isa. xxviii. 1, *vallis pinguedinum* = *ge shemanim*. But it is more probable that there was a press after which the neighbourhood was called. If it was an oil-press it might have been a cavern, because caves were used for oil-presses on account of their warmth. On the other hand, I have not heard of any winepresses in caves.

The exact position of Gethsemane, which, according to Jn. xviii. 1, was a garden, the Synoptists do not define. Mt. (xxvi. 30) and Mk. (xiv. 26) only state that "they went out into the Mount of Olives" and thence "came to a place which was named Gethsemani." In Lk. xxii. 39 it looks as if Jesus went up to the usual place where He abode at night "on the Mount of Olives" (Lk. xxi. 37). Only St. John (xviii. 1), who does not mention the Mount of Olives, points to the garden lying on the other side of the Kidron at its foot. At any rate, it is here, namely north of the three roads leading towards the summit of the Mount of Olives, of which the northern one has hitherto not been mentioned, that tradition has found the name Gethsemane, in connection with a spacious 17 metres long and 9 metres wide cave, which is now only accessible by means of a narrow passage, and

---

[1] Sabb. ii. 2.   [2] p. Bez. i. 9.   [3] Midd. ii. 5.
[4] Yet see Pea vii. 1 ; Tos. Ter. iii. 6.   *Cf.* Godmann, *Der Ölbau in Palästina*, p. 38.
[5] Tehar. x. 1 ; Bab. b. iv. 5.

which, before the present blocking up of the valley ground, about 7 metres above it, must have had an opening towards the front.   It might well have been found useful as an oil-press.   This cave is now shown as the site of the Agony, whereas up till the time of the Crusades it was considered to have been the place where Jesus was wont to be together with His disciples (Jn. xviii. 1), and three or four flat stones were supposed to have served as resting-places or tables.[1]   Without doubt it was thought that this was also the place where our Lord was with the disciples on the last night, as on so many others.[2]   In the time of the Crusaders it was referred to as the " four places in the grotto in each of which three of the Apostles lay and fell asleep."[3]   Yet it was also thought that the beginning of our Lord's prayer (see Mt. xxvi. 37 ; Mk. xiv. 34) was spoken there.[4]   Near the grotto the betrayal, *i.e.* the arrest, is supposed to have taken place,[5] under the assumption that the cave was the place which Judas knew (Jn. xviii. 2).   This assumption has its foundation in the fact that the cave lies on the way from the Temple to Bethany. Jesus must have passed there daily, and it was likely that on the way to or from the Temple He rested near the road with His disciples in order to be alone with them, which was not possible in the Temple.   At night the cave might also appear attractive as a sleeping-place.   As an oil-press it would have been used only in the autumn.   If Jesus went to meet Judas and his band (Jn. xviii. 4), this junction of several ways from the Mount of Olives and from the city, at the foot of the mountain, and in proximity to the cave, would have seemed the appropriate place, in order to spare them all further searching.

Naturally, the place to which Jesus retired with three of the disciples to pray (Mt. xxvi. 37 ; Mk. xiv. 33 ; Lk. xxii. 41), lay somewhat farther off.   A piece of land south of the Bethany road and acquired by the Franciscans in 1681, on which grew eight olive-trees, old already at that time, has since then been considered by many as Gethsemane proper. Rock benches outside the garden, at its east side, were taken

---

[1] *Virgilius* (Pitra, *Analecta Sacra*, v., p. 120) ; Theodosius (Geyer, p. 142); Antoninus (*ibid.*, p. 171) ; Arculf (*ibid.*, p. 242).

[2] Virgilius and Theodosius even speak of the washing of the feet.

[3] Theoderich (ed. Tobler, p. 61) ; Phocas (Migne, *P.G.* cxxxiii., col. 945).

[4] Phocas.

[5] The pilgrim of Bordeaux (Geyer, p. 23) ; Ætheria (*ibid.*, p. 86 *f.*); Antoninus (*ibid.*, p. 170); Cyril of Jerusalem, *Cat.* x. 19.

to have been the sleeping-place of the three disciples, and the walled garden of the Franciscans was looked upon as the place where Jesus prayed. Eusebius and Jerome do indeed designate Gethsemane as the place where Christ prayed before the Passion; but for Cyril of Jerusalem and the pilgrim Ætheria Gethsemane was the place of the betrayal at the foot of the mount.[1] Thereto descended in the middle of Good Friday night the solemn procession of Christians from the place of Jesus' prayer, and the weeping and crying of the people over the shame of the betrayal was heard from this place as far as the very gates of the city. Hesychius of Jerusalem[2] distinguishes Gethsemane at the foot of the Mount of Olives as the place where the disciples slept and where the betrayal took place, from the site of the prayer, a stone's throw from there towards the top of the mountain. And as late as the time of the Crusaders the name is applied above all to the tomb of Mary—pointed to with certainty since the fifth century—and the grotto of the betrayal;[3] it is only later that the name moved southward.

The position of the tomb of Mary has led to the plausible conjecture that John Mark, the son of a certain Mary (Acts xii. 12), was the owner both of the house in the Upper City where the disciples met, and of Gethsemane. Therefore, so it is suggested, Jesus often stayed there, and the tomb of Mary may have originally referred to that Mary. Epiphanius Hagiopolita thought of something similar when he related that Jn. the theologian, i.e. the Evangelist, bought, together with James, the land of the church of Zion, after having sold the parental property of Zebede.[4] The Last Supper was supposed to have been held there, and Caiaphas also was thought to have lived on that piece of land, and thus become acquainted with John (Jn. xviii. 15). There John took the Mother of Jesus (Jn. xix. 27), there she died, and was interred on the land belonging to John.[5] An old rock tomb, to which

---

[1] Cyril, *Cat.* x. 19 ; Ætheria (Geyer, p. 86).

[2] Migne, *P.G.* xciii., col. 1423.

[3] Daniel (Khitrovo, p. 22) ; John of Würzburg (Tobler, p. 171) ; Theoderich (ed. Tobler, p. 61) ; Phocas (Migne, *P.G.* cxxxiii., col. 944, where the name is extended as far as the place of prayer) ; Perdicent (*ibid.*, col. 969) ; also Bucchard (1283) of Laurent, *Peregrinatores*, p. 68 *f.*

[4] *Vita B. Virginis*, Migne, *P.G.* cxx., col. 208.

[5] According to the expression in the above-mentioned *Vita*, col. 212, Zion and Gethsemane were one and the same, but in the *Enarratio Syria* of the same author, *ibid.*, col. 261, 268, the death-place of Mary on Zion is differentiated from the place where she was buried, the " holy Gethsemane " in the Kidron valley.

a traditional connection with Mary has long clung, must have been the sepulchre upon which Arculf saw a rotunda,[1] which was probably erected in the year 450.[2] Later the sepulchre was described as a four-vaulted rock-chamber which had the recess on its east side.[3]

At the place of the prayer a church was built not long before 380, which was, however, not mentioned by Eusebius.[4] Its exact position was for a long time unknown. Only in 1909, directly south of the Franciscan garden, about 100 metres south of the tomb of Mary and the Gethsemane grotto, were the foundations of a church discovered, probably dating from the time of the Crusaders,[5] and in 1920 the traces of an older building under it,[6] which must have been the first church upon that spot. Unfortunately a new church has been built there since 1924, after a different plan. All traces of the church of the fourth century, as well as the remains of the Crusaders' building above it, have thus disappeared, and the Gethsemane garden has been reduced to a modest court before the church. The latter church, three-aisled like its predecessor but appreciably larger, measuring about 2·85 by 3·60 metres, included with its chief apse the spot at the end of the road to the Franciscan Gethsemane, which the Greeks have always shown as the spot where Jesus prayed. About 12·5 metres further north was situated the vertex of the middle apse of the older building, the axis of which faced north, and so reached nearly to the traditional sleeping-place of the three disciples (see above). Below it the rock is cut away, first 1½ metres, then about 3 metres, perpendicularly, in order to give the vertex of the church—measuring, according to Orfali, 18·24 by 24·50 metres, including the apse—the necessary level foundation. From this it follows that the surface of the rock, which was perhaps visible before the altar of the church, could not have been that actual soil on which the prayer of Jesus was thought to have been made. Before the entrance to the church there was, according to Meistermann's plan, an atrium of 16 by 16 metres, but this seems to be assumed only from the existence of a cistern. After the destruction

---

[1] See Baumstark, *Nichtev. syr. Perikopenordnungen*, p. 139.
[2] Geyer, pp. 240, 309.   [3] Phocas (Migne, *P.G.* cxxxiii., col. 944).
[4] First mentioned by Ætheria and Jerome.
[5] *Cf.* the plan of this church in Meistermann's *Gethsémani* (1920), p. 151, *Guide*, p. 236; Orfali, *Gethsémani* (1924), pl. i. and ii.
[6] Plan in Meistermann's *Guide*, p. 239; Orfali, pl. iii. A description of the finding in *La Terre Sainte* (1921), pp. 8, 15.

of this church by the Persians, Arculf saw on the "right wall" of the church of St. Mary a stone "above which, on the night when He was betrayed by Judas into the hands of sinful men, the Lord prayed in the field of Gethsemane, on bended knees, before the hour of His betrayal : and in this rock are seen the marks of His two knees, as if they had been very deeply impressed upon the softest wax."[1] John of Würzburg in 1165 found in the then new church of the Crusaders three "unwrought stones, upon which it is said that the Lord prayed, kneeling thrice,"[2] and Burchard in 1283 saw on one of these stones the marks of the knees and hands of the Saviour.[3] It is possible that something of this kind determined the place of the first church.

To us such considerations cannot be of much import. If the name Gethsemane clung to the neighbourhood of that grotto, its extension over the Mount of Olives road southward is too improbable, and it is equally improbable that our Lord, who sought solitude, would have expected to find it in the neighbourhood of that road. It is more likely that He retired into the depths of Gethsemane grounds, that is to say north-wards, for even at the present time one could remain undis-turbed there. A peculiar chain of circumstances has in recent times converted the cavern of Gethsemane into a place of prayer. Considered as a memorial in an historic spot, it is in fact in the neighbourhood of the most probable spot.

Here, on the slope, at the far side of the grotto, one is not disturbed, as one used to be not long ago in the garden of the Franciscans, by flower beds, artificial baths, and protecting railings. The olive-trees with their dappled shadows stand, as is fitting, on unplanted soil, and the grey limestone rock appears between the green of the Judæan spring flora. The luxuriant large leaves of the squills (*Urginea maritima*), to the autumnal growth of which high, withered stalks still testify, and the humbler bushes of mandragora, in which violet blossoms hide, stand here and there, whilst the rose-coloured *Silene atocion* spreads a veritable carpet. The tender yellow *euphorbia* (spurge) grows here too, and mingled with it, the purple-flowered Palestinian ranunculus, peculiar to the Easter season. The terraced olive garden, the quiet of which is not broken by the soft chirping of titmice, ascends the slope of the Mount of Olives. In these surroundings, unchanged for

[1] Geyer, p. 240.   [2] Tobler, *Descriptiones T. S.*, p. 137.
[3] Laurent, *Peregrinatores*, p. 69.

thousands of years, with the Passover full-moon shedding her dazzling light, " His sweat was as it were great drops of blood falling down to the ground " (Lk. xxii. 44[1]) and from His lips came the prayer which, although it was not answered, sought and found God's heart :

Abba, in yakhel, te'bar minni hada kasa,[2] beram la hekh deba'ena ana, ella hekh deatt ba'e.

My Father, if it be possible, let this cup pass from Me ; nevertheless, not as I will, but as Thou wilt (Mt. xxvi. 39).

And the disciples slept.

[1] R. Akiba plucked his hair in sorrow over the death of his master, he rent his garment, his blood streamed and fell to the ground, and he cried and wept : " Woe to me because of thee, my master, woe to me, my lord, for thou leavest thy contemporaries as orphans." Ab. de R. Nathan, xxv.

[2] The expression in the Aramaic prayer *Yekum purkan* does not run in an exactly similar fashion. According to the Yemen Prayer Book it is : " *Ya'de minekhon kasa dimerira,*" " May He let pass from you the cup of bitterness."

XIX

THE PALACE OF THE HIGH PRIEST AND THE "FIELD OF BLOOD"

IF the palace of the high priest to which Jesus was led (Mt. xxvi. 57; Mk. xiv. 53; Lk. xxii. 54) was in the Upper City, then the road thither was the same by which He went up to Gethsemane (see above, p. 320 f.). There, outside the city wall, as it was then, and is now, the Bordeaux pilgrim[1] saw about the year 333 ruins supposed to be those of the palace of Caiaphas. Curiously enough, a scourging pillar was shown there, although the scourging did not take place in Caiaphas' palace but in the Prætorium (Mt. xxvii. 26; Mk. xv. 15). In the sixth century a church of St. Peter was built there,[2] which the Madaba map represents as being behind the Zion church. This church was called after Peter because his denial, the crowing of the cock, and the look of Jesus (Mt. xxvi. 74; Mk. xiv. 72; Lk. xxii. 60 f.) were associated therewith. The scourging pillar was used to hold up the porch.[3] Later the pillar was taken to the church of Zion[4] and venerated there for some time.[5] In the seventh century it was not there any longer,[6] but a stone outside the church was considered to be the one on which Jesus had been scourged.[7] The striking features of that pillar were the supposed impressions on it of the chest, arms, hands, and fingers of one bound to it, and which

---

[1] Geyer, p. 22; *cf.* Cyril of Jerusalem, *Cat.* xiii.; Prudentius (Baumstark, *Byz. Zeitschr.*, 1911, p. 179 f.).

[2] Theodosius, *ibid.*, p. 141; *Brev. de Hieros.*, *ibid.*, p. 155; Georgian Canonar. (*Or. Christ.* v., 1915, p. 224).   [4] Theodosius (Geyer, p. 141).

[3] Jerome.

[5] Ætheria (Geyer, p. 88); Prudentius (according to Baumstark, *Byz. Zeitschr.*, 1911, p. 179 f.); *Brev. de Hier.* (Geyer, p. 154); Antoninus (Geyer, p. 174).

[6] The origin of the three columns which are still venerated in Jerusalem is quite uncertain: the "flagellatum column" in the chapel of St. Mary by the church of the Holy Sepulchre, the "mocking column" in the latter church itself, and the column guarded by the Armenians in the chapel of St. John, supposed to have come from the palace of Caiaphas.

[7] Arculf (Geyer, p. 243); Sophronius.

were later considered to have been due to the scourging of
Jesus at Pilate's command.   Probably the assumed impressions
were the cause of the assumption of a scourging in the high
priest's palace, the position of which was believed to be known.
The belief in such an origin of marks in stone was widely
spread in early times, and is not extinct in Palestine to-day,
even among the Moslems.   It is an advantage that the present
church of Caiaphas belonging to the Armenians, lying only
about 50 metres north of the Cœnaculum, has nothing of this
kind.   Its huge altar slab is supposed to have once closed
Christ's tomb.   Of the remains of the palace of Caiaphas
there is nothing discernible ; the remnant of a mosaic floor
outside the present church may have belonged to its Byzantine
predecessor.

In the time of the Crusades another church of St. Peter
existed in the same neighbourhood, which had the additional
name of *in gallicantu*, because of the crowing of the cock.[1]
Below it, a dark cavity used to be pointed out as the hiding-
place of the penitent Peter (Mt. xxvi. 75 ; Mk. xiv. 72 ; Lk.
xxii. 62).   There he was depicted as sitting, resting his head
upon his hand while he weeps over his holy Master's sufferings
and his own denial of Him, while the servant-maid threaten-
ingly leans over him, and the cock stands and crows before
his feet.[2]   The site of this church was presumed to have been
in the proximity of the city wall, on the eastern slope of the
western city hill, where in fact, according to Epiphanius
Hagiopolita, there was in the ninth century a church of " Peter's
weeping."[3]   Germer-Durand discovered on this slope, but
further south, a deep cistern marked with crosses and fragments of a church,[4] which some held to have been this church
of St. Peter, though Meistermann considers a former cistern
near the corner of the city wall *Burdsh el-Kibrit*, in the neighbourhood of the traditional place, as the more probable spot.[5]
At any rate, it may be that a cistern which was originally only
a help to the pilgrims' imagination became a sanctuary.   Its
being called after the crowing of the cock suggests that the
church was really at the spot where the house of Annas stood,
where, according to Jn. xviii. 13 *f.*, the denial of Peter took
place.   Yet there is no old tradition concerning it, and in

---

[1] *La Citez de Jherusalem* (Tobler, *Descr. T. S.*, p. 214) ; Innominatus I., ed.
Tobler, p. 122.

[2] Theoderich (Tobler, p. 63), Phocas, Perdicas.

[3] Migne, *P.G.* cxx., col. 264.

[4] *R.B.*, 1914, pp. 71 *f.*, 222 *f.*   [5] *Guide*, p. 190.

St. John it looks as if the palace of the high priest (xviii. 15),
where Jesus was first brought before Annas, was that of his
son-in-law, Caiaphas, who was high priest that year (*v.* 13).
In that case one would not have to look for a special palace
of Annas.   However, since the fifteenth century the house
of Annas has been shown within the present city wall, north
of the church of St. Zion.[2]   To an olive-tree, outside the
church built on the site, Jesus is supposed to have been bound.
The place of Christ's imprisonment, approachable from the
church, is supposed to be the place where He was struck
(Jn. xviii. 22).   We have no means by which to judge these
traditional sites.   That ruins of Caiaphas' palace were preserved
is in itself not impossible, the question is how they could
have been recognised.   From Josephus we only know that
the high priest Annas lived in the Upper City,[3] whilst in the
Lower City the place of the high-priestly house of the time of
Nehemiah (Neh. iii. 20 *f.*) was probably occupied by the
palaces of the princely family of Adiabene.

St. Luke (xxii. 66 *f.*) assumes that the condemnation of
Jesus by the Jews took place in a building not identical with
the house of the high priest, namely the place of the council
of the elders, the chief priests, and the scribes.   Christian
tradition has never troubled itself about this place ; probably,
in view of the different account given in the other Gospels,
it was thought to have been a part of Caiaphas' house.   Otherwise there would have been reason to look for this council
house of the highest Jewish court, following Josephus, below
the sanctuary, by the bridge leading from there to the Upper
City, *i.e.* where the present Moslem court of justice (*el-mehkama*)
is housed, although Jewish tradition also speaks of a court of
justice which was situated at the entrance to the mount of
the Sanctuary.[4]   But this was the lowest of the three courts
in Jerusalem, the higher being held at the entrance to the inner
court, the highest at the south side of the same in the holy
precinct itself, in the so-called " Hewn Chamber,"[5] where the
judges sat in a semicircle round their president, and in front

---

[1] So Zahn.
[2] Epiphanius Hagiopolita (Migne, *P.G.* cxx., col. 261) huddles together
the house of Caiaphas with the house of Annas, Pilate, and the emperor (!);
similarly Ricoldus (Laurent, *Peregrinatores*, p. 108) ; Perdicas thinks of the pool
of sheep (Migne, *P.G.* cxxxiii., col. 964 *f.*).   Poloner (Tobler) probably thinks
of the place shown at present ; certainly Sebald Rieter, jun. (1493), *Reisebuch der
Familie Ritter*, p. 65.
[3] *Bell. Jud.* ii. 17, 6.   [4] Sanh. xi. 2 ; Sifre Dt. clii. (104b).   [5] Midd. v. 4.

of them three rows of disciples, *i.e.* adepts in law.[1] This ideal meeting-place, which connected the power of the Law with the authority of the Temple, is, however, supposed to have been given up forty years before the destruction of Jerusalem. The court of justice moved first into the " market house " (see above, p. 294 *f.*), then, evidently even before A.D. 70, into the city of Jerusalem. There, at the place given by Josephus, must one look for the place where Peter, Stephen, and Paul were judged (Acts iv. 5 *f.* ; vi. 12 ; xxii. 30).

Thus the exact place where Jesus was condemned by the Jews remains uncertain. Among the traditional sites only the Caiaphus church has any claim to consideration. It is situated upon the height of the old Upper City of Jerusalem, the most important part of the city in the time of Christ, and there, outside the Roman and the present city, in the cemeteries and gardens which cover the sites of ancient Jerusalem, one remembers best the words of Jesus, which resulted in the sentence of death (which, from the point of view of rabbinical Judaism unjustified, was in keeping with Sadducæan custom) :

Tihmon bar enasha yateb leyammina digebureta weate 'im 'ananehon dishemaya.

Ye shall see the Son of Man sitting on the right hand of power, and coming in the clouds of heaven (Mk. xiv. 62 ; Mt. xxvi. 64 ; Lk. xxii. 69).

This forces us also either to acquit or to condemn.

The field of blood ('Ακελδαμάχ,[2] Aram. *hakel dema*) had a sad connection with the history of Jesus. According to Acts i. 18 *f.* Judas purchased a field " with the reward of iniquity," and there he perished ; whilst according to Mt. xxvii. 7 *f.* the high priests bought it with the money which Judas returned to them, " to bury strangers in." In any case a sinister connection with the betrayal of Jesus clung to it, and no native wanted to be buried there. The name of the field, known to the city, which was perhaps the starting-point of the narrative, has for obvious reasons been preserved. Papias already speaks of the smell of decay attached to it,

---

[1] Sanh. iv. 3, 4 ; Tos. Sanh. viii. 1, 2.
[2] In regard to the form of the name, *cf.* Dalman, *Grammatik des jüd.-pal. Aram.*, 2nd ed., pp. 137, 202 ; *Jesus-Jeshua*, pp. 28, 29.

that no one could pass it without holding his nose.[1]   Since
the fourth century we have evidence for the position of the
field opposite the hill of the former Upper City, at the south
side of the valley of Benhinnom,[2] where it was still used for
the interment of strangers.

At the time of the Crusaders a church of St. Mary was erected
here[3] which the patriarchate assigned in the year 1143, together
with the whole estate of the field Akeldemach, to the Johannites.[4]   These then built in front of and upon old rock tombs,
as a pilgrims' cemetery, the large vault, still preserved,[5] which
appropriated the name "Hakeldama" (by the Arabs *hakk
ed-damm*, "blood price," but also known by the name *esh-
sharnen*=French *charnier*,[6] carnarium).   The corpses were
thrown into it through nine openings made in the roof.[7]
However, a further extension of the field of blood is
recognisable in the name " esh-shama," which is attached to
the whole land lying above, and which comes from the French
champ demar.[8]   Originally the terrace below, between the
hill slope facing east and the bottom of the valley, may have
been the blood field.   A row of rock tombs lies there.
It is natural that later the Christians did not know exactly
who had bought the field, but its connection with the
blood-money of Judas was certain to them, and made
it a witness to the wickedness which caused the death of
Jesus.

The tree on which, according to Mt. xxvii. 5, the traitor
hanged himself, was shown to Antoninus as a stem of a fig-
tree protected by stones, near the eastern city gate, the gate
" which adjoins (*cohæret*) what was once the beautiful gate."[9]
Probably people were inclined to look for it in the proximity
of the Temple, because Judas came from there on his way to
commit his desperate act.   A hundred years later a fig-tree
on the west side of the city was considered to be the Judas
tree.[10]   Now it is a nettle-tree (*Celtis australis*),[11] resembling
a pine-tree which, standing not inappropriately on the hill of
Evil Counsel, south of Jerusalem, admonishes the passer-by,

---

[1] Theophylact on Acts i. 18 *f*.
[2] Eusebius, Jerome, Antoninus, Arculf.   [3] Theoderich.
[4] Rohricht, *Regesta Regni Hierosolymitani* Nu. 55.
[5] Plans and descriptions by Schick, *PEFQ*, 1892, p. 283 *f*.; Macalister, *ibid.*,
1901, p. 151 *f*.
[6] *Citez de Jherusalem* (Tobler, *Descr. T. S.*, p. 215).   [7] Poloner.
[8] *Citez de Jherusalem*.   [9] Geyer, p. 170.   [10] Arculf.
[11] The " Judas' tree " of botany (*Cercis siliquastrum*) does grow in Palestine,
although not near Jerusalem, but is not there connected with Judas.

reminding him of the disciple who delivered his Master to the enemies.

But still another reminiscence of the death of Jesus clings to the neighbourhood of the field of blood. Josephus says of the circular wall with which Titus encompassed the besieged city, that it "then turned towards the south, and encompassed the mountain as far as the rock called Peristerion, and that other hill which lies next it, and is above the valley which reaches to Siloam; where it bent again to the west, and went down to the valley of the fountain, beyond which it turned upward again at the monument of *Ananos the high priest*, and encompassing that mountain where Pompey had formerly pitched his camp, returned back to the north side of the city. . . ."[1] This necessarily points to the outer eastern slope of the hill south of the valley of Benhinnom, *i.e.* to the groups of rock tombs in and near the present Onuphrios monastery, east of the field of blood. *Ananos* is certainly identical with *Annas* (Pal. Lect. *Hannas*) of Lk. iii. 2; Jn. xviii. 13 *f.*; Acts iv. 6, the father-in-law of Caiaphas, who officiated as high priest A.D. 6-15, but exercised great influence even later. His Hebrew name was doubtlessly *Chanan*. His tomb looked towards the Temple-mount in the north, and may have been the same one which was considered in the fifteenth century to have been the hiding-place of the disciples after Jesus was taken prisoner.[2] In any case, in one of the tombs which my son and I examined in 1925 rested the powerful man who saw the coming of John the Baptist and Jesus, and who heard Peter bear testimony to the Risen Messiah (Acts iv. 6, 10).

The treachery of one disciple, the denial of another, the condemnation of the Master (with whom God's honour came first and foremost), for blasphemy, and that, too, by the guardians of the Law—these were the historic events which rightly have their monuments before the south wall of the present Jerusalem, even if none of them took place exactly on the spot which commemorates it. To our Lord these events did not come as a surprise (*cf.* Mt. xxvi. 31; Mk. xiv. 27).

To these monuments, however, also belongs the church of St. Zion, the mother of all churches, which indicates the place where, only seven weeks after the death of Jesus, the

[1] *Bell. Jud.* v. 12, 2.
[2] Poloner (1422) in Tobler, *Descriptiones*, p. 238.

wonder of the community of Jesus in Jerusalem, firm in its faith, became also an historical fact. Klausner makes the history of Jesus end with the closing of the tomb ; from then, he thinks, begins the history of " Nazarenism"; but this is a part of the history of the life of Jesus, which did not end with the tomb.

XX

THE JUDGMENT HALL OF PILATE

THE *Prætorium* is the name given in the Gospels (Mt. xxvii. 27; Mk. xv. 16; Jn. xviii. 28) to the judicial seat of the Roman governor Pontius Pilate. According to Jn. xix. 13, it was more exactly a place in front of the prætorium which was called in Greek "paved" (λιθόστρωτος), in Aramaic "*gabbatha*." The latter may be traced back to *gabbaḥta*, "bald upper-head," but better to *gabbeta*, "height."[1] Less probable is *gabbeta*, "bowl," in Christian Palestinian, as it is rather late, and in Jewish Aramaic unknown in this meaning.[2] There can be no doubt that it was intended by the Evangelist to define the place topographically. As a prætorium may be any place which the prætor chooses as a place of judgment, the question arises where Pontius Pilate resided. Diverging from the earliest Church tradition, this site was placed in the time of the Crusaders in the neighbourhood of the church of St. Zion, where, on the way to the city, in a chapel—perhaps on the site of the palace of Caiaphas—a flagellation column, and before its entrance the place of the *lithostrotos*, was shown.[3] It is possible that the flagellation column formerly revered in the church of St. Zion (see above, p. 328) gave rise to this. It was more justifiable that soon after that time the castle of Antonia was taken to be the prætorium of Pilate.[4] The purpose of this castle, situated at the north end of the outer Temple court, was to keep a watch on the Temple.[5] Hence at the feasts a considerable Roman guard must have been

---

[1] *Cf.* the Hebrew *gab*, together with *rama* of artificially erected heights, Ezek. xvi. 24. See also Dalman, *Gramm. des jüd.-pal. Aram.*, 2nd ed., p. 160.

[2] Schulthess, *Das Problem der Sprache Jesu* (1917), p. 35 f. *Gabata*, "dish," is also late Latin.

[3] Theoderich; John of Würzburg (not mentioned by Phocas); but see also Epiphanius Hagiopolita (Migne, *P.G.* cxx., col. 261).

[4] Perdicas (Migne, *P.G.* cxxxiii., col. 964); Ricoldus (1294); Laurent, *Peregrinatores*, p. 111; Poloner (Tobler, *Descr. T. S.*, p. 230); *cf.* Vincent and Abel, *Jérusalem*, ii., p. 578 f.

[5] *Bell. Jud.* ii. 12, 1; v. 5, 8.

placed there.   In recent times the situation has been recon-
structed thus : the crowning with thorns took place in the
citadel, that is to say within the confines of the present old
barracks ; the condemnation in the ante-chamber, at its north
side and towards its western entrance ; and farther back, the
flagellation.[1] Chapels built in recent times commemorate
these three sites.   A paved surface of a street—dating from
the Roman period and supposed to have been called " Gabbatha," now visible in the cellars of a Greek hospice, and
in the convent of the Sisters of Zion, as well as in the chapel
of Condemnation—and a contemporary gate, originally triple
but now only double, the so-called *Ecce Homo* arch—assumed
to have been the west entrance of the outer court of the citadel,
but which actually goes back probably only to the time of
Hadrian—are supposed to be witnesses of these events.[2] The
Greeks have in recent times added to the sacred objects
venerated here a " Prison of Christ," lying west of this gate,
by providing subsequently, as it seems, a rock tomb which
they excavated with a contrivance for the chaining of a prisoner.
In contrast to all these suppositions stands the isolated account
of Josephus[3] concerning the residence of the Roman procurator.   Gessius Florus used the fortified palace of Herod
at the north-west end of the Upper City, which was connected
with a " camp," that is to say, with a fairly large barracks,[4]
and which, because of its position, was very suitable for a
seat of government.   In front of its entrance, at the city side,
negotiations with the people took place, for which purpose
a βῆμα was erected there.   Pilate also stood up once on a
βῆμα to address the people,[5] probably on the same spot.
So Gabbatha is best located here.

The eastern boundary of this palace is unknown, but one
would be inclined to place it on the other side of the row of
houses to the east, opposite the tower of David.   In that
case Gabbatha would have been south of the eastern shore
of the pool of Hezekiah, where one must also assume the
presence of a city gate, because the city must have had an
outlet for the traffic passing west and south.   It is most likely

---

[1] See Meistermann, *Le Prétoire de Pilate et la fortresse Antonia* (1902) ; *Durchs
Heilige Land*, p. 136 f.; *Guide*, p. 149 f.   Cf. Dressaire, *Échos d'Orient*, 1904,
p. 366 f. ; Eckardt, *ZDPV*, 1911, p. 39 f.
[2] Vincent and Abel, *Jérusalem*, ii., p. 24 f.   Antoninus thinks of the arch as
belonging to an old city gate.   Only exact examination can show whether the
plaster is older.
[3] *Bell. Jud.* ii. 14, 8.
[4] *Ibid.* ii. 15, 5.   *Cf.* above, p. 275.   [5] *Bell. Jud.* ii. 9, 4.

that Gabbatha was a paved terrace, erected for the purpose of public transactions, upon which the $\beta\hat{\eta}\mu\alpha$ of the judge could be set, as is supposed in Jn. xix. 13. This would then have been the place where Pilate negotiated with the priests and the people (Jn. xviii. 29 f., 38 f.), where he showed Jesus to the people, crowned with thorns (xix. 5 f.), and where, by his cowardly judgment, he finally yielded to the clamour of the mob (xix. 13 f.). There, within the palace, most probably in the " camp," which we must assume to have been at its entrance, Jesus was kept bound, mocked by the guard (Jn. xix. 1 f.), and finally scourged (Mt. xxvii. 26 ; Mk. xv. 15). The substructure of one of the three towers on the north side of the Herodian palace is preserved till this day as a dumb witness of these events in the so-called tower of David.[1] In front of the bridge leading to it above the present citadel trench, is found now to the east an ascent from which General Allenby caused the proclamation to be read to the populace at the taking of Jerusalem on December 11, 1917. Thus it served the same purpose as did once the " pavement " in front of Pilate's prætorium. To this spot is rightly assigned the occasion by which Roman power and politics thought to subordinate to its purposes—by sacrificing Him to the crowd —the Son of God who stood by in a crown of thorns and did not defend Himself, while that crowd demanded as a boon at the feast not the Prince of Peace but, instead, the rebel (Mt. xxvii. 21 ; Mk. xv. 11 ; Lk. xxiii. 18).

That Church tradition did not connect the judgment seat of Pilate with the Herodian tower[2] can only be explained by the fact that it had long been called the " Tower of David." It was thought to have been king David's palace,[3] where he composed and sang his psalms.[4] Besides, Pilate's prætorium was looked for at a different spot—not on the west side of the city, but farther east, nearer the Temple, where the ruins of a considerable building were seen.

This supposed prætorium the Bordeaux pilgrim reached

[1] Meistermann, *Durchs Heilige Land*, p. 153, thinks that Hadrian built it from old material. But there is no reason to ascribe the tower—which according to Josephus was left standing by Titus—to Roman Jerusalem, in the defensive line of which it does not stand. *Cf.* the Madaba map.

[2] Only Epiphanius Hagiopolita saw the *lithostrotos*, as well as a small church commemorating the treachery of Judas, " at the right hand from the tower of David " (Migne, *P.G.* cxx., col. 261).

[3] Geyer, p. 22. Josephus already states that David called the hill of the Upper City " citadel " (*Bell. Jud.* v. 4, 1).

[4] Geyer, p. 173.

from the house of Caiaphas, so that he must have turned off
to the right from the great market street of the city, before
he came to the Golgotha church. Some walls stood there
" below, in the valley, where was the house or prætorium of
Pontius Pilate."[1]   About a hundred years later (A.D. 450),
this spot " in front of the ruins of the Temple of Solomon,
near the street, which on this side of the porch of Solomon
runs down to the fountain of Siloam,"[2] was occupied by a
church of St. Sophia.   In it was shown not only " the seat
upon which Pilate sat when he tried our Lord," but also the
square stone upon which our Lord was placed at the trial,
on which " the marks of His feet still remain."   The portrait,
" which was painted during his lifetime and placed in the
prætorium, shows a person of medium height, with beautiful,
small, delicate feet, a handsome face, hair inclined to curl, and
a beautiful hand with long fingers."   Near that church of
St. Sophia Justinian erected in 543 " upon the projection of
the hill "[3] the basilica of the Blessed Mary,[4] which the Madaba
map represents on the east side of the southern end of the
great Market street of Jerusalem.   The older church of
St. Sophia is most likely indicated by the mosaic on the left,
close to the church of St. Mary, where an entrance leads into
a court, in the background of which a gable is visible.   It is
also possible that the building standing diagonally on the left
by this court represents this church,[5] although according to the
previously given indications it was situated nearer to the valley
of the Roman Jerusalem, and thus it seems to be behind the
church of St. Mary.   Thus one is led to think of the neighbourhood of the bridge leading from the old Upper City to
the Temple,[6] and one comes thus either to the site of the old
council-house of Jerusalem in the valley directly below the

[1] *Ibid.*, p. 22.   Also Cyril of Jerusalem, *Cat*. xii. 29, knows the desolated
prætorium and the lithostrotos within (*Homil. in Paralyt.* 12).

[2] Geyer, p. 175.

[3] So is ἐν τῷ προέχοντι τῶν λόφων in Procopius to be understood according
to the context, not " on the highest," neither " at the foot," as Hasak, *Das
Heilige Land*, 1918, p. 115, translates.

[4] So by Antoninus.   Concerning its consecration in the year 543 (November),
see Vailhe, *Echos d'Orient*, 1903, p. 278.

[5] Abel, *Jérusalem*, ii., p. 573 *f.*, is of this opinion.   Besides, between the two
market roads of the mosaic there are three buildings of which there is no other
explanation and which must yet have some Church significance.   It is
impossible that the church of St. Sophia should have not been indicated in
the map.

[6] *Cf.* also Germer-Durand, *La Palestine: Guide historique et pratique*, 1909,
p. 101 and plan to p. 128.

Temple area,[1] or to the east side of the hill of the Upper City,[2] where, according to Josephus, the palace of the Hasmonæans was situated,[3] which remained in the Herodian family when Herod's palace at the western edge was occupied by the Romans. That Pilate resided there is not likely. On the other hand, Herod Antipas, when in Jerusalem for the feast, would have stayed there. In that case, although the site played a part in the Passion—because Jesus was sent to Herod by Pilate to be examined (Lk. xxiii. 7), yet He was not there condemned to death, but proclaimed innocent. The error of tradition, which is perhaps based on statements made by Jerusalem Jews, may be due to this palace's being held to have been the proper palace of Herod and therefore considered to have been the residence of the Roman Procurator, or to the fact that the Roman prætorium was confused with the council-house of the Jews.

The marble steps of the *Scala sancta* in Rome, which are supposed to have been brought there before the year 326, and were built up in 845,[4] are thought to be monuments of Pilate's hall of justice. Unfortunately there is no record whatever concerning the exact origin of these steps. In Jerusalem one would be inclined to connect them with the castle of Antonia. There, not indeed the too low ascent to the present barracks, but one of the original rocky scarps, 5 metres in height, would have allowed the necessary space for them. But in that case they must have come from the prætorium of the oldest tradition, if they came from Jerusalem at all, and may be thought of as an ascent from the valley of the city to the city itself.

With what emotions the pilgrims in 610 visited the prætorium, among the sacred sites of Jerusalem, the following verses of the often quoted Anacreontica of the patriarch Sophronius show :

> Thence would I ply my steps until I came to Zion, to the place where the grace of God came down in the likeness of tongues of fire ; where the Lord of all cele-

---

[1] *Cf.* above, p. 331.

[2] In this neighbourhood Vincent examined remains of buildings which may belong to the substructures of the eastern part of the church of St. Mary ; see *RB*, 1914, p. 429 *f.*

[3] *Ant.* xx. 8, 11 ; *Bell. Jud.* ii. 16, 3, according to which Agrippa II. resided there later.

[4] Kraus, *Geschichte der christlichen Kunst*, ii., p. 506.

brated the mystic Supper and washed His disciples' feet, in order to imbue them with His own humility. Mary it is who pours forth salvation for all men, like a river, for its fair waters flow forth from that stone whereon the child of God[1] was laid. Hail to thee, Zion,[2] O thou splendid sun of the worlds, with sighs and groans do I yearn for thee both by day and by night. When He the bonds of hell did burst and caught up into His own ascent the dead whom He rescued from thence, it was here that He graciously manifested Himself. Now leaving Zion and the heights, and having embraced the stone whereon my Creator was scourged on my account,[3] I would fain pass into the house and weep with sighs above the stone that marks the spot where the royal Virgin was born in her father's house.[4] Entering into the holy church of the sheep-pool, where renowned Anna bore Mary,[5] and going into the church, the church of God's holy Mother, I would embrace and kiss its beloved walls. I would behold the steps whereon the palsied man took up his bed and walked, being made whole at the bidding of the Word. I would rejoice with heartfelt joy whenever I sang of the field which received the body of God's mother Mary, the glorious field of Gethsemane, wherein was made a tomb for the Mother of God.

Oh, how sweet art thou, most noble mount from whence Christ the King ascended into Heaven!

The church of St. Zion, the prætorium, the sheep-pool, and Gethsemane—in connection with which no reference is made to our Lord[6]—all these places mentioned by Sophronius, the last representative of the old Greek tradition, demand serious consideration. That tradition still held good so far as knowledge of the localities of Roman Jerusalem was concerned, whilst the later Latin tradition often does not even deserve the name of a tradition. The Aramaic or Hebrew place-

[1] St. Mary is meant, who was supposed to have died near the church of St. Zion (Geyer, p. 111 ; Khitrowo, p. 36).

[2] The church of St. Zion as the place of Christ's appearances after the Resurrection.

[3] The stone of flagellation was revered, as in Arculf's description, at the outer side of the church of St. Zion.

[4] Referring to the church of St. Sophia with the *lithostrotos*.

[5] Mary was supposed to have been born in the still existing crypt of the church.

[6] This is connected with the position of the tomb of St. Mary in Gethsemane (p. 324). But neither does he mention the place of Christ's prayer in connection with the Mount of Olives (p. 266).

names of the Gospels—Siloam, Bezatha, Gethsemane, Hakeldama, Gabbatha, Golgotha—come from a still older time,
when even before the erection of the Ælia Capitolina the
Christians thought of the events in the life of their Saviour
in connection with these localities. It is quite possible that
the site of the high-priestly palace was also known then.
Occasional mistakes were not impossible, as the name Gabbatha
shows; but they do not prove that no real knowledge of the
localities was preserved. The destruction of Jerusalem by
the Romans—at which, after all, the ruins of the city were
not carried away—could not have obliterated all the traces of
the past to those who knew the locality. Titus left standing
the three towers on the north side of the Herodian palace
and its western border.[1] Some of this must have been removed
after the Jewish rebellion in the time of Trajan. It was the
building of Ælia Capitolina in 135 which caused the old
Jerusalem to be entirely obliterated within the borders of the
new city and by using the old stones for the new edifices
demolished for ever most of the old buildings. Yet even so,
besides a Herodian tower, some ruins remained, like that of
the supposed prætorium and of the Temple. However, the
churches of the Christians and the Jewish attempt to restore
the Temple under Julian, when they even removed the stones
of the ancient sanctuary as having been desecrated, made
an end of most of these remnants in the fourth and fifth
centuries. The southern half of old Jerusalem remained
outside the new city and was used by the latter as a convenient
quarry. A few modest houses and the ruins of Caiaphas'
palace were here the sole witnesses of the old glory. Through
excavations, on the height of the western hill as well as on its
eastern slope, only a few remains of ancient buildings have
been found, mostly merely cisterns, cellars, and old hatchways.[2]
Research cannot create certainties here, when all the foundations of our knowledge have been lost. But one fact remains,
viz., that southern Jerusalem, which has not been restored
since the year 70, and in which some memorial sites are now
prominent as monuments, was a part of the city of Jesus and
of His first community. He predicted her extinction—
visible even to-day—and connected it with the fact of His
rejection (Mt. xxiii. 37 f.; Lk. xiii. 34 f.; xix. 42 f.). One
must needs be moved with a sense of awe when one passes
amid vegetable-fields, gardens, and cemeteries, where once

---

[1] *Bell. Jud.* vii. 1, 1.   [2] See Germer-Durand, *RB*, 1914, pp. 71, 222.

the holy and glorious city of the Jews lay, which was to them, not without reason, the centre of the world.[1]   And yet it is not her destruction which is the chief tragedy but her desertion, which came because He left her, who visited her as God's last Messenger.   Jesus said at the conclusion of His dirge (Mt. xxiii. 38 *f.*; Lk. xiii. 35; *cf.* p. 383): " *Ha mishtebek lekhon betekhon weamar ana lekhon delatihmon yati min kaddun 'ad ma detemerun barukh ha-ba beshem adonay,*"[2] " Behold your house will be abandoned unto you, and I say unto you, Ye shall not see Me henceforth, till ye shall say, Blessed is He that cometh in the name of the Lord !"   The " abandoned " can only refer, in connection with the " not seeing henceforth," to the " going away " of the Person who had averted for so long the threatening doom, and ἔρημος, originally probably found in Mt. but lacking in Lk., means, as often in Greek,[3] " abandoned," " deserted," thus elucidating the sense, and does not add anything new with " desolate."   " Your house " is, according to the context, not the Temple, but Jerusalem. To be Saviourless is her misery.   To welcome the Saviour would mean Redemption to her.

[Vincent, in his recent excavations in the convent of Notre Dame de Zion, shows that the *Ecce Homo* arch, admittedly of Hadrian's date, stands on a pavement belonging to an earlier period, namely Herodian, and forms, in fact, the central court of the castle of Antonia, that court being some fifty yards square.   Further, beneath this level, also below the convent, a series of magnificent cisterns, which formed the original water-supply of the fortress, have come to light, and have been cleared.   It is now admitted that the prætorium of the governor was not necessarily a " Government House," but was the spot where he happened to be exercising his judicial office at any particular time ; and it is quite natural that during a time of tension, such as the Passover, Pilate should reside where he could best control that focus of probable riot—the Temple.   In his day this would be the fortress Antonia.— Translator.]

[1] Sanh. 37a ; Yoma 54b.
[2] Ps. cxviii. 26, as a well-known blessing, our Lord must have said in Hebrew.
[3] *Cf.* for the expression Mt. xxii. 22 ; Mk. xii. 12, and *The Words of Jesus*, p. 17.   Probably based on Jer. xii. 7.   See also Jer. xxxiii. 12 LXX.

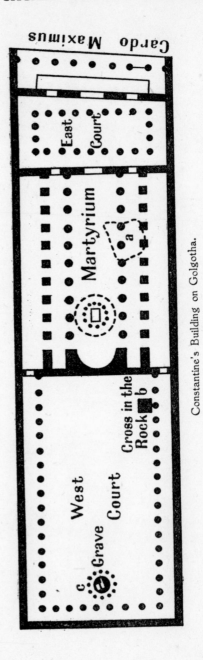

Constantine's Building on Golgotha.

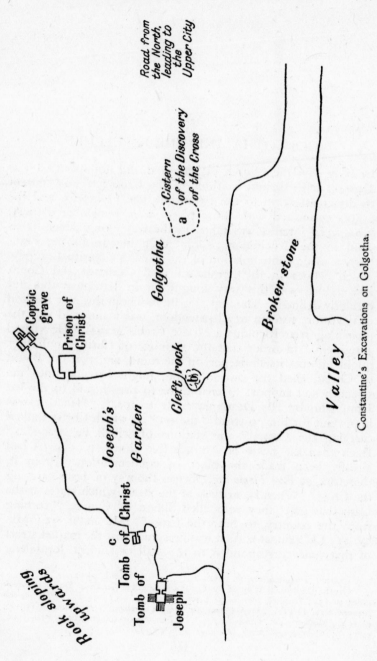

Constantine's Excavations on Golgotha.

XXI

GOLGOTHA AND THE SEPULCHRE

IN early days the Church in Jerusalem did not specify a *Via Dolorosa* with definite stations of the Cross : it was content to direct attention to the prætorium and Golgotha, and the events connected with those places were remembered there. No special interest was taken in the way along which Jesus went to the Crucifixion. Only when in Europe the Franciscans made contemplation of the Passion a spiritual exercise which echoes in the hymns of Paul Gerhardt and Count Zinzendorf, was this way sought for in Jerusalem too and carefully defined. The first pilgrim in whom this new method of devotion, foreign to Christendom, was manifested was the preaching friar Ricoldus a Monte Crucis (1294). He visited Jerusalem " in order that the memory of Christ's sufferings might impress itself deeper on the mind, and that the Blood of Christ, shed for our salvation, might become unto me strength and support to enable me to preach and to die for Him, who by His Death gave life to me."[1] Hence it was important for him to tread " the way on which Christ walked carrying the Cross,"[2] the stations of which he describes.[3] Even then the castle of Antonia (see above, p. 335 *f.*) had already been made the place of condemnation. From it, therefore, at *Ecce Homo* arch, began the way of Jesus carrying the Cross. When He arrived at the street which starts at the Damascus gate, they compelled Simon of Cyrene, " coming from the country, to bear the Cross " (Mt. xxvii. 32 ; Mk. xv. 21 ; Lk. xxiii. 26). As it was presumed that the market street of that time corresponded to the wall of ancient Jerusalem,

---

[1] Laurent, *Peregrinatores*, p. 105.   [2] *Ibid.*, p. 111.
[3] On the traditional Way of the Cross see Kneller, *Geschichte der Kreuzwegandacht*, p. 133 ; Dunkel, *Das heilige Land* (1915), pp. 40 *f.*, 93 *f.*, 158 *f.* ; on the present way, Höpfel, *Die Stationen des heiligen Kreuzweges in Jerusalem* (1914), p. 10 *f.* ; Meistermann, *Guide*, p. 142 *f.* ; my article on the subject in *PJB*, 1906, p. 15 *f.* ; Vincent and Abel, *Jérusalem*, ii., p. 610 *f.*

the remains of what was perhaps an old tetrapylon on a street ascending westward (where it crossed the market street) marked the gate through which Jesus left the city. The whole route was then correctly mapped out, presupposing that the streets of that time corresponded to the ancient streets, once the starting-point and goal were firmly established. But if the judgment hall was not Antonia but the castle of Herod, then the route to the place of Crucifixion must have begun in the west and not in the east of the city, and must necessarily have been quite different. However, the site of Golgotha[1] as the goal of the route (Mt. xxvii. 33 ; Mk. xv. 22 ; Jn. xix. 17 ; Lk. xxiii. 33 only κρανίον) must be determined first.

In accordance with the Evangelists' explanation, the name *Golgotha* must be traced to the Aramaic *golgolta, gulgulta,* " skull." In fact, the translation of the Palestinian Lectionary shows that the Palestinians actually called it so in Aramaic. According to Origen[2] and Epiphanius[3] the name was derived from the skull of Adam, who was buried there. To Jerome there was significance in the thought that the blood of the second Adam dripped down upon the skull of the first Adam,[4] but nevertheless he preferred to interpret the name as " The place of the beheaded ones."[5] As, according to the Jewish legend, Adam lived on Mount Moriah,[6] a place in Jerusalem called after Adam's skull would not, in itself, have been impossible. There must have been there a cavern or a ravine, similar to that under the altar of the Temple where the skull of Ornan was supposed to have been found.[7] It is, however, more probable that a bare rock formation, several examples of which are to be found in the environs of Jerusalem, suggested the name " Skull." Epiphanius found it strange that there was no summit or high watch-tower there to have occasioned the name, and therefore suggested the higher Mount of Olives and the mountain of Gibeon (now *en-Neby Samwil*). He did not, however, realise that such a name did not necessarily require a mountain and that the original natural formation of a hill-slope could hardly survive when once a temple and a city had been built on it. Moreover, in

[1] On the reading *Golgotha*, appearing in Latin texts only since the year 1200, see J. Herrmann, *Studien und Kritiken* (1916), p. 381 *f.*

[2] *In Matth.* 126 *Cat.* (Migne, *P.G.* xiii., col. 1717), where it is given as a Jewish tradition.

[3] *Adv. hær.* xli. 5 ; Migne, *P.G.* xli., col. 544 *f.*

[4] *Ep.* 46 ad Marcellam.   [5] *In Ephes.* v. 14 ; *in Mt.* xxvii. 33.

[6] Pirke R. E. xx. ; Midrash Tehil. xc. 5 ; Targ. Jer. i., Gen. iii. 23.

[7] Pal. Ned. 39d.

a neighbourhood where vaults formed of rocks are found, the
rocks are always visible and the rocky walls, either natural or
quarried, can always be used as entrances into the sepulchral
chambers, and there a formation resembling a skull would
not be at all extraordinary. So there is no reason for tracing
the name Golgotha, in contrast to the Gospel explanation,
back to the composite word *gal go'ata*[1] and explaining it as
" the hill of Goa,"[2] which is mentioned in Jer. xxxi. 38 as a
place in the north of ancient Jerusalem, situated probably in
the north-west.[3]

Both explanations can be harmonised if we consider the
hill of *es-Sahira*, north of Jerusalem, which was originally
connected with the eastern city hill, to be Golgotha, as suggested by Otto Thenius.[4] Its southern slope, made by
quarrying, with some grottoes might have suggested a skull.[5]
The fact that it lies outside the present city, and is only occupied
by a Muhammedan cemetery, makes the Gospel narrative of
the route to the Crucifixion (*cf*. Heb. xii. 12) and its occurrence
at a spot which was passed by many people (Mt. xxvii. 39 ;
Mk. xv. 29) particularly vivid. In support of this is the fact[6]
that Jews in later times, without any old tradition, spoke of
this place as of a *bet ha-sekila* (" stoning place "), which,
perhaps, was connected with the Church's tradition that the
stoning of Stephen took place here.[7] This description was
based on the Jewish Law according to which the one who was
to be stoned must first be thrown down from a height, so

---

[1] *Gal* in that case would have become assimilated in popular etymology, by
the influence of folk-etymology, with the vowel of the following syllable and
turned into *gol*.

[2] The name *Goa*, " the roaring one," might have been caused by a rock formation. The Targum translates " the pool of the young cow," and seems to have
known a pool of that name in the north of Jerusalem.

[3] This explanation was adhered to by Vitringa, Hengstenberg, Kraft, and lately
by Boehmer, *ZAW*, 1914, p. 300 *ff*. ; the position on Goa was already considered
by Baldensel (1336), according to Quaresmius, *Elucidatio* v. 2, 14.

[4] Illgen's *Zeitschrift für hist. Theologie*, 1842, No. 4, p. 18.

[5] General Gordon, who, like Conder (since 1879) before him, identified this
hill with Golgotha, did not think of this, but of its appearance on the map and
of its position in relation to the city hill, which he compared with a skeleton ;
see *PEFQ*, 1885, p. 79 *ff*.; 1904, p. 38 *ff*. Aversion to the forms of worship
in the church of the Holy Sepulchre and the difficulty of recognising the original
reality behind it must have been the motive of these two men, as well as of
others, in searching after the " genuine " place of the Crucifixion. The rocky
grave at the western foot of this hill, which is pointed out as the " Gordon
tomb," but of which Gordon did not think of originally, cannot seriously be
considered as " Jewish." See Vincent, *RB*, 1925, p. 401 *ff*.

[6] So also Klausner, *Jesus of Nazareth*, p. 352.

[7] Theodosius (Geyer, p. 141) ; Antoninus (*ibid*., p. 176).

that, if possible, he should already be dead when the stones were cast at him. By "stoning place" was understood an artificial terrace of the height of two men,[1] which, however, does not fit the steep slope—about 20 metres high—of the Sahira hill. Church tradition might have settled on this or any other place outside Roman Jerusalem on the north, east, or west, as the place of the Crucifixion, but instead of that it chose as Golgotha another hill, which was situated in the centre of the city of that time, above its greatest thoroughfare, and which must surely have been specially improbable. Here, on an artificially erected terrace, stood at that time a temple of Aphrodite, as the protecting goddess of the city,[2] probably at the back of a long court surrounded by colonnades. As the area was about 37 metres wide by 130 metres long, one must visualise the eastern half as a spacious outer court leading from the actual temple, which was on a higher terrace, to the propylæa in the market street, similar to the temple of Artemis at Gerasa.[3] Vincent[4] conceives the whole structure as being the capitol of the city (Ælia Capitolina), the temple of which, the *trikamaron* of the *Chronicum Paschale*, was really dedicated to Jupiter and was joined in the south to a forum, a remnant of the triple entrance-gate of which is preserved in the Russian Alexander hospice. But through Eusebius we have positive information only of the terrace of the temple, and that remnant of the gate could as well have stood originally at a street crossing.

Eusebius says in the *Onomasticum* that Golgotha, "the place of the skull," where Christ was crucified, was shown in Ælia, north of Mount Zion. In his account of the finding of the sepulchre[5] he does not mention the name Golgotha, nor does he mention any Christian tradition in regard to its position, but only relates that after the Council of Nicæa (A.D. 325) the emperor Constantine felt it a duty "to make that most blessed spot, the place of the Resurrection, visible to all and given over to veneration," and that therefore he commanded that a house of worship be built there. "As he saw with concern that that place ($\chi\tilde{\omega}\rho o\varsigma$), which through the plotting of impious men was entirely covered over with most impure things, might in time become merely a thing of the past and be altogether forgotten, he commanded that it should be cleansed,

---

[1] Sanh. vi. 4 ; Tos. Sanh. ix. 6 ; Sifre on Num. cxiv. (34a, English trans. p. 104).
[2] *Cf. PJB*, 1913, p. 102 *f*.
[3] *PJB*, 1908, p. 17.
[4] *Jérusalem*, ii., p. 7 *f.*, pl. i.
[5] *Vita Constantini* iii. 25 *ff*.

in the conviction that (the place)[1] now defiled by the heathen
must then enjoy the special benediction of the Most Gracious
One through him." Thereupon the temple of Aphrodite,
which had been erected in order " to deliver that monument
of immortality unto perpetual darkness and forgetfulness,"
was demolished in 330, and the whole terrace upon which it
stood was broken up ; " and its rubbish, defiled by demonic
contamination, was removed." " Then appeared, like a new
order of things, the place hidden in the depths of the earth,
the venerable and most sacred monument of the glorious
Resurrection was made visible against all hope, and the most
holy grotto revealed again the image of the Redeemer's restora-
tion to life in all its splendour." The expression $\pi\alpha\rho'$ $\dot{\epsilon}\lambda\pi\dot{\iota}\delta\alpha$
$\pi\hat{\alpha}\sigma\alpha\nu$ (against all hope) has often led to the conclusion
that only by chance was that tomb found, the site of which,
according to Eusebius' own admission, had been forgotten.[2]
If that were so, then the monk Alexander must have given later
a very necessary supplement to the Eusebian account when he
narrates that bishop Makarios, when the emperor commanded
search to be made for the wood of the Cross, and that the
blocked-up holy places should be brought to light again, called
those about him to prayer and then received a Divine revelation which pointed him to the temple of the impure demon.[3]
And the real course of events, veiled by Eusebius, would in
that case have been that either the excavations on the site of
the temple of Aphrodite were undertaken haphazard, in order
to comply with the command of the emperor to disclose the
tomb, or the emperor's command did not refer to the forgotten
tomb at all, but to replacing the heathen temple by a Christian
church. In doing so the persons concerned with the digging
were surprised actually to find a rock-tomb, which, to please
the emperor, was declared to be the sepulchre of Christ, and
also—a thing which Eusebius does not record—a stake that
was found there was also given out as the Cross. But we
have no right to suspect the truth-loving author of the
Onomasticum of participating in such a gross deception, by
which the miracle of the appearance of that grave is made of
equal importance with the Resurrection of Christ. Rather
must one assume that the temple of Aphrodite was considered
by the emperor, on the information sent to him from Jeru-

---

[1] The feminine subject is missing.
[2] So, for instance, Paton, *Jerusalem in Bible Times* (1908), p. 144.
[3] *De inventione sanctæ crucis*, Migne, *P.G.* lxxxvii. 3, col. 4061.

salem, as being undoubtedly the place where Jesus had been
buried (according to Jn. xix. 41 f., the Sepulchre was near
the place of the Crucifixion), for which reason he desired
that it should be cleansed and then adorned with a church ;
but that in Jerusalem it was thought extremely doubtful that
the actual tomb could have been preserved, though the emperor
took it for granted that it had been. In this way one can
understand the surprise at finding it and also the recognition of both the tomb and the cross, which would have been
unthinkable without the assumption of certain knowledge
concerning Golgotha. The source of this knowledge was at
the end of the fourth century considered to be Divine illumina-
tion (thus Rufin), or Jewish information (thus Paulinus of
Nola). The latter was certainly not in itself impossible, and
the Jewish legend concerning Adam's skull on Golgotha,
which Jewish literature has not preserved, would indeed
prove that the Jews had regard for this locality. Be that as
it may, nothing could have hindered Palestinian Christians—
who, after all, possessed the Gospels and naturally had always
an interest in knowing where Golgotha was—from preserving
reliable information on the subject, the first authority on
which would have been Judas Kyriakos, the bishop of Jerusalem at the time of the destruction of the city.[1] Had a place
like the Sahira rock, which had the semblance of a skull,
been taken as Golgotha, then one would be justified in
thinking that a mere conjecture lay behind the information
given to Constantine. But as this was not the case, one has
every reason to examine this view seriously, and should there
be decisive arguments against it, rather give up all attempts
to seek other sites, since it would then be quite impossible to
arrive at a certain decision.

That after the removal of the temple of Aphrodite they
revealed the place of both the Crucifixion and the Burial,
is of greater importance to us than it seemed then, because
the significance of the discovered tomb put everything
else in the shade at the time. How Golgotha looked we
can imagine more or less from the accounts of Eusebius and
Cyril of Jerusalem, as well as from present-day investigations.
The whole entirely rocky ground was a part of the eastern
slope of the western hill of Jerusalem north of the northern
wall of what was then the Upper City. The natural boundary
in the north-east was formed by the chief valley of the city,

---

[1] Schlatter, *Die Kirche Jerusalems vom Jahre* 70-130, pp. 59 f., 66.

and in the south by a secondary branch of the same. There was a wide declivity cut into it, probably due to quarrying, which had, on the west and the north, steep walls. In this Joseph's garden was supposed to have been, the traces of which it was later believed were discovered in the west court of Constantine's building.[1] Broken stones were also found at the southern boundary of the place at the edge of the valley. In the east, towards the south, rose what appeared to be a single disrupted rocky mass,[2] which Peter the Iberian in 500 still designated as an altar of unhewn stones,[3] behind it; farther east lay a deep cistern. Between the two, according to Vincent,[4] there ran from north to south a ditch approximately 15 metres wide, which might have served as the protection to the suburban wall of old Jerusalem, but which so far has not been identified. In the west, entrances led through the rocky wall into two rock-tombs. The one lying farthest west consisted, as far as is at present discernible, of a chamber of 2·24 by 2·16 metres, with three sliding hinges each on three sides. The other one, situated somewhat farther east, had, as it seems, only a half-made chamber half the size of the first, with a single place for a tomb on the right-hand side. There was an antechamber before the low entrance which faced east-north-east, and had a closing stone.[5] In the north also there were rocky chambers; the remains of one such,[6] which since the eighth century was connected with the Passion, said to have been used as a " prison " during the preparations for the Crucifixion;[7] one which was only discovered in 1885, originally consisting of probably three chambers, one above the other, of which the second must have been on the right, and on the left an open grave shelf; and a third showing a bench running on three sides. But it is questionable whether the ditch extended so far northward in the time of Constantine. The " Prison of Christ " was brought into the domain of the western court of the basilica probably only since the building

[1] Cyril of Jerusalem, Cat. xiv. 5.

[2] Pictured with a cross on it on the apse mosaic of San Pudenziana in Rome, also on an ampulla of the dome in Monza. See also Wulff, Altchristl. Bildwerke, No. 1117, 1467.

[3] Raabe, Petrus der Iberer, p. 38.

[4] Jérusalem, ii., pl. xii.

[5] Cyril, Cat. x. 19 ; xiii. 29.

[6] That there was really a sepulchre here is probable but not certain ; the remains of a rocky north wall, given by Vincent in pl. xii., I have never been able to recognise.

[7] Epiphanius Hagiopolita (Migne, P.G. cxx., p. 261); Typikon der Grabeskirche ; Petrus Diaconus (Geyer, p. 107); Innomin. I. (Tobler, Pal. Descr., p. 114); Daniel (Khitrovo, p. 16).

of Modestus, after the destruction by the Persians in the year 614,[1] in which case that third burial-place might have been quite unknown in ancient times. Of the tombs in the west, however, the one with the single burial-place was, according to the conviction of Eusebius, with which all agreed, considered to have been the grave used for the Redeemer, to the astonishment of Christendom come to light again.

The assertion of Heisenberg[2] is absolutely without foundation, that the deep cistern behind the massive rock, which later was considered to be the place where the Cross was found, was the original sepulchre of Jesus in Constantine's building. A heathen cultus-grotto, he says, was given a Christian name here, as in Bethlehem; only after the destruction of Constantine's building by the Persians in the year 614 was the place of the sepulchre altered, when the building was restored by Modestus. Originally, so he says, it lay on the east, not on the west. Against this, to start with, it is improbable that in a city which, even to-day, is surrounded by rock graves, a cistern about 6 metres deep should have been taken to be a rocky tomb. Then the account of Eusebius which sets out from the tomb in the west and proceeds eastward, as well as the Madaba map which has the tomb-rotunda in the west, speaks against it. Finally, it is unthinkable that in the ten years that passed between destruction and restoration the site o the tomb should have been forgotten. Neither does the Lateran sarcophagus No. 174 give any proof of the eastern position of the tomb through the sculptures on its narrow right side, as Heisenberg[3] imagines. It may indeed be that Jerusalem churches are represented on it,[4] because the Risen Jesus and Mary Magdalene, after Jn. xx. 17 (not Jesus and Martha, as Heisenberg thinks), are evidently portrayed there. But the sculptor has put the Martyrion basilica and the tomb-rotunda (of which more will be said later) with the entrances towards the front, one beside the other, not the rotunda in front of the basilica. From the position of the former in relation to the right side of the latter, the eastern position of the rotunda might indeed have been deduced, if the sculptor knew that the Jerusalem Basilica had, contrary to custom, its entrance on the east. But the relation to the Mary-scene

[1] So also Vincent, *Jérusalem*, ii., pl. xiii.
[2] *Grabeskirche und Apostelkirche* (1908).
[3] *Ikonographische Studien* (1922), 108 f.
[4] Schmalz, *Mater Ecclesiarum*, p. 124, supposes, however, buildings of Paneas by the source of the Jordan.

represented by him on the right side must have been the
determining factor for him, which caused him to set the tomb-
rotunda in the middle.   If, for the sculptor, the basilica had
the usual entrance from the west, he would even be a witness
for the western position of the rotunda.   Thus, in fact,
everything here remains uncertain.

Again, that Christ's sepulchre is called by Eusebius ἄντρον,
by the pilgrim of Bordeaux *cripta*, proves nothing for the
tomb-cistern of Heisenberg, for Arculf also calls the sepulchre
in the building of Modestus *spelunca*,[1] just as the rocky chambers
of Pharan are called *cryptæ* by Petrus Diaconus.[2]   The official
designation of a hewn tomb in Jewish Law is *me'ara* in Hebrew,
i.e. cave.[3]   The fact must also be remembered that in the
building of Constantine all the people surrounded the cave
of the sepulchre on festivals and the bishop spoke to them
in front of the entrance ;[4] a consideration which does not fit
in with that narrow cistern (about 7 metres square), into
which one must descend by a narrow staircase, nor tally in
the least with the chapel of Helena which is situated at present
above the staircase.   Both of these are excluded when Eusebius
says of Christ's tomb hewn in the rock :[5] " Wonderful to
behold, the rock stood out, lonely and straight, in the flattened
land."   And the " descending " to the church of Christ's
sepulchre referred to by Ætheria[6] does not sound strange to
anyone who knows that monks and laity, even to-day, go
down into it as a rule because the street situated nearest to
it is 12 metres higher.

Of discoveries other than that of the one tomb Eusebius
says nothing, but Cyril found the massive rock in the south-
east remarkable also.   He considered it to be Golgotha,
because its disruption seemed to testify to the earthquake
which occurred at the Death of Christ, when the rocks were
rent (Mt. xxvii. 51).[7]   Antoninus and Arculf speak particularly
of a wide cleft near the foot of the rock.[8]   Since the times of
the Crusades, when the rock, probably looking very much
as it does to-day, was almost entirely covered up, a crack
has been shown in the surface as well as below, into which
entered, it is said, the Lord's Blood which ran down from the

---

[1] Geyer, p. 229.   [2] *Ibid.*, p. 118.
[3] Bab. b. vi. 8 ; Tos. Bab. b. vi. 22, 23.
[4] Ætheria (Geyer, p. 71, *cf.* 72 : Ante cancellum, id est, ante speluncam).
[5] *Theoph.* iii. 30 ; Migne, *P.G.* xxiv., col. 620.
[6] Geyer, p. 71.   [7] *Cat.* xiii. 39.   [8] Geyer, pp. 204, 233.

Cross.[1] Cyril saw in the designation Golgotha, " Skull,"
only a symbol of Christ's being the Head of the Church.[2]
But if that rock-mass was Golgotha, or at least belonged to
it, would not the Cross of Christ have stood on it ? Near
this mass of rock pieces of wood were found, which, it was
believed, had to be taken into account in connection with
it. According to a tradition, which can only be traced with
certainty to Theoderich, 1172, the present chapel of the Finding
of the Cross, an ancient cistern situated in a rock had been
the place of the miraculous discovery, and a miracle was related
which confirmed the genuineness of the presumed wood of
the Cross.[3] Perhaps also the interest of the emperor, who
five years before made the Cross of Christ his battle ensign,[4]
played a part in it. At any rate, the splinters of the supposed
Cross wandered, as witness of the Death of Christ, into all
parts of the Roman Empire, as Cyril, twenty years later,
proclaimed exultantly.[5] But the chief piece remained in
Jerusalem[6] and was decorated with gold and precious stones,
the chief relic of the new church,[7] to which others were soon
added—namely, the title of the Cross, the reed with the sponge,
and the spear.[8]

Eusebius could not ascribe any special significance either to
the rock mass or to the wood of the Cross. To him the chief
thing was the tomb. But to the emperor, the bishop of
Jerusalem, and Christendom in general, the golden basilica
with double side-aisles in two stories,[9] the so-called Martyrion
—built over the place of the finding of the Cross and dedicated
in the year 336 on the day of the finding of the Cross,
September 14[10]—was, as the guardian of the wood of the

---

[1] John of Würzburg, in Tobler, *Descriptiones*, p. 144 ; *cf.* above, p. 347.
[2] *Cat.* xiii. 23.
[3] A pillar in the north of the city, which is supposed at the same time to represent the centre of the world (Geyer, p. 239), is mentioned by Arculf as erected
on the spot where the miracle took place. Perhaps it was the road-pillar of the
Madaba map on the place within the north gate.
[4] See concerning the Labaron of Constantine, Schönewolf, *Die Darstellung
der Auferstehung Christi*, pp. 9 *f.*, 44 *f.*
[5] *Cat.* xiii. 4.
[6] Cyril, *Cat.* x. 19.
[7] Even at present the treasure-chamber of the Greeks in the church of the
Holy Sepulchre possesses a wooden cross enclosed in a golden one ; the former
seems to me to be nut-wood, as Antoninus (Geyer, p. 172) describes the wood
of the Cross as being.
[8] Ætheria, Antoninus, Petrus Diaconus, in Geyer.
[9] *Brev. de Hier.* (Geyer, p. 153) ; the earliest representations are found on
the Madaba map, and Kraus, *Gesch. d. ch. Kunst* i., fig. 336.
[10] Ætheria (Geyer, p. 100).

Cross discovered under it, at least as important.[1] There, on the day of the finding of the Cross, on the ambon before the altar, the Cross was lifted high with both hands by the bishop and displayed, being turned in all directions.[2] What was felt at the time, an old Greek poem referring to the celebration reveals :[3]

> O the great miracle !
> The life-giving wood,
> the all holy Cross,
> raised to the heights,
> to-day made visible.
> All the ends of the earth give praise,
> the demons all are affrighted.
> Oh, what a gift is granted to mortals !
> Herewith, O Christ,
> save our souls
> as the only Saviour !

There was a conviction that the basilica stood upon Golgotha,[4] and the rough rock-mass in its western court—standing up about 5 metres, surmounted by a valuable cross—was from early times considered as the place on which Christ once suffered death, and therefore the real Golgotha, yea, the centre of the world.[5] Arculf, in whose time a two-storied chapel had been erected above the rock,[6] even takes it for granted that the silver cross on its summit stands upon the same place as did the Cross of Christ. The empty hollow where that votive cross stood then, was since the times of the Crusades revered as the site of the Redeemer's Cross.[7] Even in the fifth century it was provided with stairs and a platform, so that one could ascend to the place of the Cross.[8] However, it is very probable (at least from the present appearance) that, so far as can be judged, the Persians also destroyed the Golgotha rock, and that the chapel only contains its ruins, although Vincent still describes it as a compact mass.[9]

---

[1] See particularly Schmalz, *Mater Ecclesiarum* (1918), and Dalman, *ZDPV*, 1919, p. 167 f.

[2] After a Typikon of the eighth century, see Vincent, *Jérusalem*, ii., p. 232 f.

[3] Christ and Paranikas, *Anthologia Græca Carminum Christianorum* (1871), p. 81.

[4] Ætheria (Geyer, p. 74 f., 78, 83) ; also Cyril, *Cat*. iii. 10 ; Theodosius (Geyer, p. 141).

[5] Cyril, *Cat*. xiii. 28.   [6] Geyer, p. 233.

[7] Daniel (Khitrovo, p. 14); Theoderich (Tobler, p. 29).

[8] Petrus the Iberian, ed. Raabe, p. 40 ; Theodosius (Geyer, p. 141) ; Antoninus (*ibid*., p. 172).   [9] *Jérusalem*, ii., illustr. 54.

Here, at the newly found rock of the Cross, Good Friday began henceforth to be celebrated. " On Golgotha behind the Cross," *i.e.* between the site of the Cross and the basilica, where at present the lobby of the refectory of the Greeks and the western area of the chapel of St. Michael are situated, the faithful passed in an unbroken line, from eight o'clock in the morning till noon, by the wooden cross which, taken out from its receptacle, lay on a table, and was held by the bishop with both hands. All bowed before it, and were allowed to touch it with forehead, eyes, and lips, but not with the hand. From twelve o'clock till three they then stood at the foot of the rock, at its western side, and listened to the Gospel narrative of the Death of Christ and to the Old Testament predictions concerning it.[1] The bitter weeping of the whole congregation over the sufferings of our Lord for our sake, which Ætheria records, was certainly connected with the feeling of having experienced again, as it were, the events of the Passion, at the place which but lately had come to light again.

However, the rock-tomb, standing diagonally opposite the rock of the Cross, in the background of the western court of the basilica, was, after all, the sanctuary proper, the climax of the whole building. Originally the tomb, isolated from its rock, was merely a separate object in the court, like the rock of the Cross, surrounded by columns.[2] This follows from the description of Eusebius, who would not have failed to draw attention with his usual rhetoric to the splendour of this royal building also. His proceeding from the tomb to the court, with its halls, does not here mean a going from west to east, in the sense that the tomb must be excluded from the court, but rather a progress from what was of primary importance to what was of secondary importance. Besides, Ætheria shows, by her emphasis on the Constantinian origin of the basilica, that the tomb-rotunda existing in her time was not Constantinian in her opinion.[3] About the year 380 she found over the tomb a church[4] which, according to later descriptions, must be thought of as a two-storied rotunda, and which, in contrast to the Martyrion basilica, was given the name *Anastasis*, " Resurrection." It may have been in

---

[1] Ætheria (Geyer, p. 88 *f.*).
[2] Eusebius (*Theophania* iii. 30 ; Migne, *P.G.* xxiv., col. 620).
[3] See also Schmalz, *Mater ecclesiarum*, p. 31, against Vincent, *Jérusalem*, ii., pl. xxxiii., who provides even the Constantinian buildings with a tomb-rotunda.
[4] Geyer, pp. 75, 98, 100.

existence already in the time of Cyril, and must soon have become a necessity, because the daily services at the tomb demanded protection from sun and rain.[1] The tomb did not stand in the exact centre of the rotunda,[2] but immediately behind it, probably because in front of the tomb an enclosed space was provided for the clergy (see below), and, moreover, the congregation gathering there also needed the space. When the chamber was isolated, the open antechamber, which had been there formerly, as testified by Cyril,[3] was at once removed, and the rest of the space was given the form of a low, round tomb-tower, terminating above in a point,[4] examples of which can be found elsewhere in Roman Palestine and in many other places.[5] The exterior was kept simple, and later was covered with marble,[6] but as an adornment and also for protection a precious sparkling gold and silver polygonal alcove (*ciborium*)[7] was put up on it. Pillars with lily-capitals, probably twelve in number, joined by lattice-work, bore a pointed roof of gilded beams, which was crowned by a cross.[8] To reach the inside one had first to pass through an antechamber surrounded by a rail,[9] which contained an altar. Then a lattice-work door led into the interior of the alcove, and there one found, before the entrance into the rocky tomb itself, the stone lying which had once been the cover to close it.[10] Probably the space in which it was originally fixed was formed by the straight back wall of the tomb's antechamber having been

[1] Later the rotunda had a conical roof without a point, with an opening in the centre. The roof shown in the mosaics in the apse of San Vitale, also on the old models of the church of the Holy Sepulchre and on the Madaba mosaic, is conical.

[2] Vincent, *Jérusalem*, ii., fig. 119, pl. xxxiii., has got an exact central position of the tomb by providing it with an antechamber situated in the rock, and even shown in pl. xxxiii. as closed ; such an antechamber Cyril excludes.

[3] *Cat.* xiv. 9.

[4] The round form which was essentially preserved till 1555, is testified to by Antoninus (Geyer, pp. 171, 203) and Arculf (Geyer, pp. 228 ff., 304). The earliest witnesses are the reproduction in Augsburg (in about 1120), Eichstätt (1160), and Görlitz (1500). See Dalman, *Das Grab Christi in Deutschland*, pp. 45, 57, 82, pl. xiii., xvii., xxiii.

[5] See *Princeton Univ. Arch. Exp. to Syria* ii a. 6, p. 400.

[6] Arculf (Geyer, p. 228).

[7] *Cf.* the reproduction of the ciberium as polygonal in Garucci vi. 434, 1, 5, 6, and Dalman, *Das Grab Christi in Deutschland*, p. 32 f., pl. v., vi., vi a.

[8] The ciborium is mentioned in *Brev. de Hieros.* (Geyer, p. 154) ; Antoninus (*ibid.*, p. 171); and illustrated on the ampullas, of Jerusalem origin, of the cathedral of Monza (sixth century). *Cf.* Garucci, *Storia della arte cristiana* vi. 433, 8; 434, 1, 2, 4, 5, 6, 7 ; 435, 1.

[9] Cyril of Jerusalem, *Cat.* xiii. 29 ; *Brev. de Hieros.* (Geyer, p. 154) ; Antoninus, p. 171.

[10] See Dalman, *Das Grab Christi*, pp. 76, 82, 96, 199.

covered by an apsidal building, as the plans of Quaremius and Horn, and the best reproductions of the tomb in later times, show. Bending low, one reached by a door, at the utmost only 1 metre high, the tomb-chamber, which was a narrow space of 1 metre wide by 2 metres long and about the same in height. In the right (the northern) wall was the tomb, 60 centimetres high, 2 metres long, and 90 centimetres wide, which at the time of Arculf was under a built vault, originally certainly under an arch hewn out of the rock.

Formerly I believed from Arculf's description of the tomb that it could be definitely concluded to be not a trough but a shelf.[1] But when he says that "it had, after the fashion of a cave, the entrance from the side, and a low, artificially constructed vault above it," he does not imply that this tomb had not the appearance of an ordinary tomb. Rather he means that it was not hollowed into the floor of the chamber, as might be expected, but rose with its edge three spans above it, and that it was not like a sarcophagus either, standing freely in it, but was connected with a low niche, therefore it had its entrance at the side. Later he differentiates also between the lowest part of the tomb and its upper edge, as previously he did not speak of the surface of the tomb-shelf but of "the edge of the side of the tomb." Antoninus, too, would have called special attention to the unusual appearance of the tomb of Christ had there been anything about it to strike him as peculiar. A remark in his text seems even to designate the tomb as *puteus*.[2] It is true that Daniel, later when the tomb was already covered over with marble and the rock was only visible at the side through three holes, thought of it as a shelf. But Theoderich, who saw the same three holes, speaks only of the tomb "in" which Christ "has rested," and the representation of the tomb of that time in Eichstätt which reproduces those three holes, made it out to be a trough, and certainly thought that the bottom of the tomb, that is the actual resting-place of the Saviour's Body, could be seen through the holes.

Photius[3] must also have supposed the tomb to have been a trough when he describes it as a "rock formed with parallel surfaces such as are appropriate for the reception of the form of man, into which the faithful Joseph put the undefiled body of the Lord." On the other side, the testimony of the unusual

[1] Arculf (Geyer, p. 229).   [2] Geyer, p. 171, present reading *potus*.
[3] Vincent, *Jérusalem*, ii., p. 237.

chamber in the catacomb of Domitilla, which goes back to
the second century and is compared by de Rossi[1] to the tomb
of Christ, is without any value. For the shelf before the
single arkosolium of its north wall, which appeared to de Rossi
to be the mark of a trough set before the wall, can be otherwise explained, and the narrow entrance to the chamber—
the form of which is considered by Marucchi[2] to provide the
most important proof that it was an intended copy of the tomb
of Christ—must, on the contrary, from its high situation in
the wall, be considered as un-Palestinian; only the arkosolium
of the chamber, as a Christian burial form, could be taken as
an ancient testimony to the shape of the tomb of Jesus. At
any rate, all the old representations agree with this conception,
in so far as they delineate the tomb as a sarcophagus.[3]

This rock tomb, not embellished within, lighted by a
brass lamp at the head,[4] and later by twelve lamps (four of
which stood on its floor, eight hanging in two rows over its
edge)[5] lying in a cavity, the unpolished and bare red and white
rock of which showed even in the year 670 distinct traces of
quarrying,[6] was the revered monument of the Resurrection.
From its perpetual light all the lamps of the rotunda built
over it were lighted every evening; at its entrance the bishop
every Sunday morning read before dawn the story of the
Resurrection.[7] On Easter Eve the bishop kindled—evidently
in the tomb where the lamp had been extinguished—a new
light with steel, stone, and tinder, from which the lamp of the
tomb, as well as all the lamps of the rotunda and the basilica,
received their light. At midnight he proceeded with the newly
baptised, first to the tomb, then to the Martyrion, which was
brightly lighted by the new light and where a congregation
was gathered, and there held the chief service of the night,
then returned with the congregation to the tomb, where the
Resurrection account was again read and Mass offered.[8] Thus
the Resurrection of the Redeemer of the world was celebrated
as a feast of the heavenly light, illuminating anew the darkness of the kingdom of death.

[1] *Bulletino di arch. crist.* iii. (1865), p. 38 *f.*; *cf.* the plan, p. 35.
[2] *Roma sotteranea cristiana*, Nuova Seria i., p. 91, Tav. xxv.
[3] See Garucci, *Storia della arte cristiana* v. 350, 4; vi. 446, 3.
[4] Antoninus (Geyer, p. 171).   [5] Arculf (Geyer, p. 229).
[6] *Ibid.*, p. 232.   [7] Ætheria, p. 72.
[8] Ætheria, p. 90 *f.* For a miracle which caused the light to be kindled in
the grave, only mentioned since the sixth century, *cf.* B. Schmidt, *PJB*, 1915,
p. 85 *f.*; 1916, p. 76 *f.*; 1917, p. 55 *f.*

[The edifice of Constantine, which we have taken for granted in the foregoing descriptions of its most important sacred sites, is in its leading features well known from the account of Eusebius,[1] a witness of its origin.   From the great market street of Jerusalem which, framed by colonnades on both sides, traversed the city from north to south,[2] one entered towards the west through high propylons first into an atrium surrounded by arcades, then through three entrances into a five-aisled basilica with double-storied arcades and gilded ceilings.   This was followed on the west again by a court with arcades on three sides, and in the background of it was the tomb surrounded by columns.   But it is not clear how one should visualise the conclusion of the hinder court, whether as being round or, as is more probable, angular, so that the west, south, and north sides of the court led into the three arcades recorded by Eusebius.   It is also uncertain how one should conceive of the " half-globe " circled by twelve columns, which, according to Eusebius, was arranged at the peak of the basilica.   Mikley[3] would make it a cupola surmounting the tomb, which, however, is impossible, in view of what is recorded in the *Breviarius de Hierosolyma* of the twelve columns round the altar of the basilica.[4]   According to Schmalz[5] it refers (as indeed is the literal meaning) to a cupola which had under it an altar-space surrounded by columns, directly before the apse of the basilica, when the question still remains whether the apse is to be imagined as being within a rectangular termination of the basilica or projecting beyond it.

On the basis of the existing accounts of it, it is possible to make a design of the whole building, as I have attempted to do (see illustrations), but insuperable difficulties arise when one desires to construct a real plan which would correspond to the knowledge that we possess at present.   In spite of the labours of Wilson, Schick, and Vincent, we still have no reliable and exact plan of the present church of the Holy Sepulchre and its eastern environs, such as my own (for the most part unpublished) investigations of the remains of the edifice of Constantine to the east, the environs of the Golgotha rock, and the sepulchre rotunda, have yielded me.   It is true, we know the eastern wall of the atrium with the three entrances, but its local relation to the church of the Sepulchre is not

---

[1] *Vita Constantini* iii. 33-40.   [2] See the Madaba mosaic.
[3] *Die Konstantinkirche im Hl. Lande* (1923), pp. 39, 51.
[4] Geyer, *Itinera*, p. 153.   [5] *Mater Ecclesiarum*, p. 38 *ff*., 46 *ff*., 53 *f*.

established with certainty, and nothing is known about the position of the entrance and back wall of the basilica. Over his plan of the present church of the Holy Sepulchre Vincent has sketched in the Constantine building,[1] putting in right angles everywhere, in spite of the fact that the still existent south-eastern corner of the atrium is obviously obtuse-angled, a point that he simply ignores on his plan.[2] Probably the

Church of the Holy Sepulchre at time of Crusades.

front wall of the atrium had to turn towards the market street, and the atrium itself was not rectangular, while the basilica certainly was rectangular and the west front also may have been so. Moreover, it does not fit the description of Eusebius when Vincent encloses the basilica in the western court, so that it is connected by narrow passages with the eastern atrium. Without a thorough examination of the present eastern front of the church of the Sepulchre, every plan of the Constantine

[1] *Jérusalem*, ii., pl. xiii., *cf.* pl. xxxiii.   [2] *Ibid.*, pl. iii.

building is only hypothetical. The only established points are the tomb and the Golgotha rock in the western court, and in the eastern atrium the entrance wall (about 37 metres long), which fits in more or less with the width of the tomb-rotunda, and, most probably, gives in this way the width for the western court and basilica also ; but which, if the wider building be rectangular, must be taken as somewhat shorter, assuming an oblique position of the entrance wall, projecting from left to right eastwards. The extremest western limit of the basilica is the Golgotha rock, while for its eastern façade it lacks any firm point.

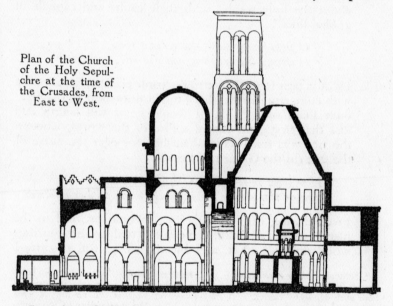

Plan of the Church of the Holy Sepulchre at the time of the Crusades, from East to West.

In spite of all these uncertainties, with the help of the already used *Anacreontikon* of the patriarch Sophronius we can visualise Constantine's building, which was destroyed soon after it was composed. The emotion which the song reveals is important as disclosing what a Christian then felt on reaching this centre of the Church. It runs :

O thou holy city of God, Jerusalem, I would that I were now at thy gates, that I might enter in rejoicing.

For pure Salem God-devoted fire
stirs continually in power my heart.[1]

[1] The distichs inserted between the tetrastichs signify the refrain (κουκούλιον), see *Petit Dict. d'Arch. Chrét.* i., col. 1866 *f.*

As I walk over thy ground I would draw near to the
church of the Anastasis, from whence the Lord of all
rose again, having subdued the power of Death. I
would kiss the earth, the sweet earth, and would behold
the holy dome (ἱερὸν κύβον),[1] and the vast sublime
rotunda,[2] the rotunda with four apses.[3] Crossing the
glorious choir,[4] I would go to the tomb of God in the
midst thereof, and would kiss with deep devotion that
stone (whereon the Lord was laid), and would dance for
joy to my heart's content as I kissed the columns round
about the holy tomb,[5] with their vaults and capitals of
golden lilies.[6]

> O light-giving tomb, the ocean stream
> of eternal life art thou, and true river of Lethe.[7]

I would pass from thence to the triple portico,[8] all adorned
with colourful marble, that I might draw near to the well-
built Place of a Skull. I would lie at full length and
kiss that stone, the sacred centre of the world, wherein
the tree was fixed which banished for ever the curse of
the tree (in the Garden of Eden).

> How great is thy glory, O exalted rock,
> wherein was set the cross whereby mankind was redeemed.

From thence, thrilled with joy, I would proceed to the
place[9] where all faithful people worship the glorious
wood divine.[10] Yet, as I hurried along, full of care, I

---

[1] Schmaltz, *Mater Ecclesiarum*, p. 37 *f.*, renders κύβος by " cube " and concludes
from it that the tomb-rock had the form of a cube, but probably κύβος is connected
here with κύμβος, " cavity." It may moreover be that the reading is ἱερὸν
κύβην with the poetic treatment of ἱερός. As to the comparison of the tomb-
rock with a mill-stone by Antoninus, see my arguments in *ZDPV*, 1919, p. 172 *f.*
It may be added that a round vertebra is called κύβος, and hence the round
tombstone could also be so called.

[2] Read with Christ-Paranikas, *Anthologia*, p. 45, οὐρανόστιγον.

[3] I add : (θείαν) τετρά (κογχον θόλου). Arculf (Geyer, p. 227) speaks of three
apses with altars, but the eastern chief altar which he mentions, p. 232, had its
apse also.

[4] The enclosures before the entrance into the sepulchre, *vide* p. 358.

[5] Read with Paranikas : "'Επ' ἀναξίου δὲ τύμβου."

[6] The pillars round the tomb had gilded capitals and bore frontons with
apses.

[7] This refrain stands in Migne and Paranikas behind *v*. 6, but from circum-
stantial and formal considerations it belongs here.

[8] The court between the Resurrection rotunda and the Martyrion basilica,
in which the Cross rock stood.

[9] The space " behind the cross " is meant.   [10] See above, p. 357.

would show respect to the picture wrought by the painter,[1] and eagerly bow my knee before it. Then joyously I would pass down from the splendid floor (of the church) to the glorious high choir ($\beta\hat{\eta}\mu\alpha$), where the noble Empress Helena found the holy beams of the cross, and would then, with a heart full of contrition, ascend to the chamber wherein I should behold the reed, the sponge, and the spear, kept there.[2]   Then as a new beauty I would carefully examine the church,[3] where a band of monks sing hymns all the night through.

The rock-tomb, together with Constantine's building re-stored by Modestus, was destroyed by the caliph Hakim in the year 1009. Since that time only a few remnants of it have existed under the artificial substitute erected over it in the year 1045, these being now no longer visible. When one visits the church of the Sepulchre at present—which actually stands on the building of the Crusaders dating from the year 1149 but is disfigured by an unintelligent and tasteless restora-tion after the fire of 1808—one finds a rotunda at the western end still ; unfortunately it has ugly massive pillars and an iron dome, and, within, a chapel, standing independently, crowned with a clumsy pavilion. Entering the front room one finds a pedestal, enclosed in a recess, the supposed remnant of what was once the slab closing the rock-tomb, a cube of 26 to 32 centimetres wide and 28 centimetres in height ; in the narrow back room, to the right, is a marble trough, 1·88 metres long, 63 centimetres high, and 88 centimetres wide, the lid of which cannot be opened. In the dome of the Crusaders—which has no aisles but is joined by a transept to the rotunda—one ascends from the south arm of the transept to the Calvary chapel, which is situated at the corner of the transept and the chancel, in the background of which a marble step covers the rock of the Cross, which here, behind walls, reaches a height of 4·92 metres above the floor of the church. Through a narrow cleft and a round hole in the cover of the step one can

---

[1] There was a picture of Mary above the western door of the basilica; cf. Antoninus (Geyer, p. 173).

[2] Antoninus saw the sponge and the reed "behind the Cross," the spear in the Zion church (Geyer, p. 173).   Arculf also saw the sponge there, but the spear in the eastern antechamber of the basilica (Geyer, p. 243 f.).   According to an Armenian description (Vincent, Jérusalem, ii., p. 235), the sponge and the spear were in the seventh century kept in the upper story of the Anastasis.

[3] I.e., the Martyrion basilica which has not hitherto been properly observed.

discern rocks, and also in the space under the chapel it is possible, through an opening in its back wall, to convince oneself that a cleft rock does in fact soar up behind the walls. The rock, however, shown by Vincent[1] in the plan and cross-section as being behind the chapel, is nowhere to be seen. One must be content with seeing but the smallest fragments of the rock of Golgotha and from these deducing its existence ; and on that account one would be indignant with those who cover up everything here were it not for the knowledge that the rest of the rock would also long ago have vanished into the hands of pilgrims bent on finding relics, had it been left visible. To one despairing of evidence the Angel's words to the women recur (Mk. xvi. 6 ; *cf.* Lk. xxiv. 5 *f.* ; Mt. xxviii. 6) : " Ye seek Jesus the Nazaræan, who was crucified ; He is risen again, He is not here. Why do you seek the living One among the dead ?"[2] The direction : " Behold, there is the place where they laid Him " (Aram. : *Ha atra han deshaw-won leh*), raises anew the question : " Did the Body taken down from the Cross really lie in the confines of the present chapel of the Sepulchre ?" Before answering this question it must be considered whether the rock-tomb, of which only a reproduction is to be seen, at least corresponds with the facts presumed in the Gospel accounts. This requires an investigation of the types of Jewish rock-tombs, for which the extensive necropolis of Jerusalem affords ample opportunity.

Among the various forms adopted for places of interment the one most frequently represented is that of the vaulted trough-tomb, or *arcosolium*, in which the corpse was laid on a stone shelf which ran along the sides of the rock and which was often hewn breadthwise into it, so that a sort of overhanging vault was formed. The measurements of these show only slight differences. A tomb in the north of Jerusalem measured by me consisted of a trough 1·97 metres long, 54 centimetres high, and 63 centimetres wide (outside measurement) ; and 1·75 metres long, 47 centimetres wide, and 37 centimetres deep (inside). The vault above it was 83 centimetres high, and its back wall above was somewhat bent towards the front. In another tomb the corresponding measurements were somewhat larger : the outside of the trough was 2 metres,

---

[1] *Jérusalem*, ii., illus. 55, 56.
[2] *Cf.* for the expression Lev. R. vi. (18b) : " Thou incomparable fool ! Usually the dead are sought among the living : are the living sought among the dead ? " This was said by a wise man to a father who was searching for his lost son among the tombs.

74·5 centimetres, 65·5 centimetres; the interior 1·80 metres, 49 centimetres, 46 centimetres, and 1·10 metres in the vault. Both measurements are very much the same as those of the tomb found in the time of Constantine (see p. 359).

This type of grave is closely related to another, together with which it is frequently found in the same burial grounds, namely the vaulted shelf grave. Here the vault-shaped niche has under it only a shelf, which is occasionally provided at the front with a low edge and at one end with an oblique elevation, meant as a pillow for the head. A tomb-shelf of this kind, for example, is 79 centimetres high above the floor, 2·21 centimetres long, and 86 centimetres wide, with a 1·12 metre high vault. It is clear that as the corpse lies quite exposed it is not as well preserved as in the trough-shaped tomb, the trough of which was certainly usually covered, although I have never found any remains of any of these rock-lids. Both types of graves are an improvement on the mere *bench-tombs*, also found fairly often in the vicinity of Jerusalem, where an open bench of 30 to 40 centimetres height to 1 metre width surrounds the sepulchre chamber on three sides and allows only a little free space in the middle. It was an advance when the place for the corpse was arranged to fit into the wall and a free space was allowed in the chamber itself, and the improvement was still greater when the advantages of a sarcophagus were combined with the new arrangement. The vaulted bench-tomb served as an important intermediate stage between the bench-tomb and the vaulted trough-tomb, but Wulff[1] and von Sybel[2] consider that the arcosolium was the direct development of the sarcophagus set in a niche. Sybel also refers to the tomb of Darius; but many more ancient niche interments of a crude kind were to be found in Palestine.[3]

Quite different from all these is the thrust-in grave where the place for the corpse does not lie parallel to the wall, but runs into it, shaftwise. These tomb-shafts, which are always vaulted on the top, are about 1·80 to 2·35 metres long, 52 to 72 centimetres wide, and 65 to 86 centimetres in height. The entrance—often very narrow—can usually be closed by a board set to run into grooves. While the tomb-bench and the trough-tomb are always elevated, the thrust-in tombs are mostly arranged level with the ground, and only occasionally are they found to have been constructed

---

[1] *Die altchristliche Kunst*, p. 22. [2] *Christliche Antike*, i., p. 124.
[3] See for instance, Vincent, *RB*, 1912, p. 445 *f*.

above a bench running round the sepulchre, by means of which they are protected from water which might run into the chamber. This type of tomb, apart from the safety for the corpse which it provided, made it possible for good use to be made of the chamber space also, for in the three walls nine or twelve bodies could be accommodated instead of three, and when two rows of these thrust-in tombs were made even double the number could be put there. However, the thrusting of the coffin-less bodies into the shaft was inconvenient, and the resting-place of the dead became very unlike that of the living, of which it was meant to be a continuation, and rising from the dead would be quite unimaginable from such a tomb. This type is rightly termed Jewish, for the Mishna considers it to be the normal kind, although Jewish traditional Law also accepts the trough-tomb hewn out of the rock and covered over.[1] The Mishna calls these thrust-in tombs in Hebrew *kokh*,[2] plural *kokhim*, and gives their normal length as 4 ells (nearly 2 metres), height 7 ells (or with the vault 8 ells), and width of 6 fists wide (about 72 and 54 centimetres), and assumes that two of them are put in a 4 ell wide wall,[3] and that in each *kokh* only one corpse was placed.[4] The real origin of this type of grave, occurring only since Hellenistic times,[5] is still unknown. The Christ tomb in the Constantine edifice was not such a one (p. 359), but, as we believe, a vaulted trough-tomb, and therefore had also a form which, in the necropolis of Jerusalem, appears only in later times.[6] The burial vault of the royal family of Adiabene, from the first century A.D., contains, together with thrust-in tombs, also vaulted bench-tombs ; the so-called Absalom sepulchre, dating probably from the same period, also contains vaulted bench-tombs. And yet one would have to suppose that the rock-tomb blocked up in the year 135, on

---

[1] This kind can also occur built into the wall of a grave above the ground (Hebrew *nephesh*) (Tos. Ohal. x. 7, where Kraus, *Talmud. Archäol.*, i., p. 76, speaks of sunk graves. There are also cases known of stone sarcophagi standing independently and interments in plaster, in marble, or on wooden planks (Tos. Ohal. ii. 3, p. Naz. 56b ; according to Kraus, bench-tombs, which is certainly wrong), and there have been coffins found in ploughing which were sunk in terraces or in among stones (Tos. Ohal. xvii. 1 ; according to Kraus, trough-tombs).

[2] Is it perhaps derived from " κογχ " ? The Nabatæan form is *Giha*, the Palmyrian, *Gimha* which is related to the Syrian *Gurha*, Arabic *kirh*, " monk cell." But the changed form in the Hebrew suggests that it is a foreign word.

[3] Bab. b. vi. 8.
[4] p. Bab. b. 13d, Sem. xiii.
[5] See Macalister, *The Excavation of Gezer*, i., p. 395.
[6] So also in Gezer ; see Macalister, p. 400.

the erection of Ælia Capitolina, survived from the necropolis
of Jerusalem (which was destroyed in the year 70), or at
the latest from the first century, so that the tomb of Christ
must be considered as an early example of the vaulted trough-
tombs. It may be that the vaulted bench-tombs and the
vaulted trough-tombs were only in that century introduced
in Jerusalem. It can be assumed with certainty that the
wealthy Joseph of Arimathæa (Mt. xxvii. 57), who, according
to Mk. xv. 43 ; Lk. xxiii. 50, was a counsellor, had made for
himself a tomb as perfect as possible. That since the second
century the fashion of the arcosolium spread in the Roman
world as an essentially Christian form of interment, may have
been connected with this tomb which he put at the disposal
of Him who died on the Cross. As the " Tomb of Christ "
it appeared in Germany also in the twelfth century.[1]

The sepulchre, called in Hebrew *me'ara*, " cave,"[2] in all the
three types of tombs, is in very many cases a full 2 metres
square and the same in height.[3] The Mishna[4] gives the
normal size as 4 to 6 ells, where, in each of the two long walls,
there would be three thrust-in tombs provided, and in the
narrow back wall two. But according to another view, the
normal size was 6 to 8 ells, with four tombs in each of the
long walls, and three tombs in the back wall, and also two in
the wall of the entrance. The height is given as 4 ells.[5]
When, as sometimes happens, a sepulchre is only half this size,
with a place for the corpse on one side only, it conveys the
impression of incompleteness. The walls and the flat cover
are as a rule unadorned, and seldom are there traces of painted
plastering or sculpture.

The square *entrance*,[6] level with the ground on the outside
and somewhat higher than the floor of the chamber on the
inside, is always very small. I found that measurements of
82 to 71, 64 to 58, 56 to 49 centimetres were usual, while 1·75
to 1·13 metres were rare. To close up the tomb, which for the
elimination of dirt was of great importance, grooves were
provided—it seems without exception—which extended round
the entrance along the sides and above, and to which an equally
large border, on the square closing-stone, corresponded, so
that when it was set in the opening, it covered it and the

---

[1] See *Das Grab Christi in Deutschland*, p. 40 f.
[2] See, apart from the above-quoted passages, Tos. Ohal. xvi. 2
[3] The vault which Vincent draws, *Jérusalem*, ii., fig. 53, is contrary to usage.
[4] Bab. b. vi. 8.   [5] Tos. Bab. b. vi. 22.
[6] Hebrew *petah*, Tos. Ohal. xvi. 44.

enclosure entirely, without projecting beyond it at all. To this outer flat cover, which is entirely without a lock, we find, in very rare cases, on the inner side of the entrance a *stone door*, the former existence of which can always be recognised from the holes for its hinges. Inner bolts, which could be opened with a "key" from the outside, have also been discovered. Finally, although among several hundreds of sepulchres there were only three of these[1]—there is also a type with an arrangement for a *roller-closing*, where, set in a deep groove which runs over to one side of the entrance, is a flat slab of stone like a mill-stone, which can be rolled before the entrance. It is generally set on a slant, so that it can glide in of itself—unless it is hindered by something on the way—but can only be pushed back into its groove by using a certain amount of exertion. A much more primitive method of securing the tomb entrance was to roll a cylindrical stone in front of the flat outer cover, an example of which Schick found near Jerusalem,[2] and as I have seen occur in Beth Shemesh in some of the tombs.

The Hebrew phrase *golel*, "roller," used in rabbinic literature for the usual closing of the sepulchre, fits this method of securing the entrance with a rolling stone. But it soon becomes evident that such a perfect arrangement was not meant. A beam, or even a cask, a heap of stones, and, it would seem, even temporarily a live animal, could serve as a *golel*.[3] The usual one must have been a large stone block, which was supported by another, and at times even by a third, as a *dophek*—"the knocker."[4] It is related that once a certain person died on the day before the Passover, and the men who came to bury him—in order to save themselves from defilement—pushed away the *golel* from the entrance and left the rest of the burial to the women.[5] It is assumed that the stone was very heavy, so that the women would not have been able to manage by themselves; it could certainly not have been a rolling stone made for the purpose, which would not have been drawn away but pushed back. But another case is assumed when two stones of four hands' width square were used as a *golel*,[6] which presumes that there was an extra

[1] At the tomb of Helena, the so-called "Tomb of Herod," and at a grave in Wady 'Ain Nar.
[2] *ZDPV*, 1878, p. 12.
[3] Ohal. xv. 8, 9 ; Tos. Ohal. xv. 8, 9.   [4] Ohal. ii. 4.
[5] Tos. iii. 9, where *nashim* must be read for *anashim* ; *cf.* Tos. on b. Kethub 5a.
[6] Tos. Ohal. iii. 10.

small entrance to the tomb. As the *golel* was the proper closing of the tomb,[1] one has to assume that even the flat covers of the rock-tombs of Jerusalem were also considered as *golel*, and the cylindrical stones placed before them as *dophek*. The name *golel*, however, was probably derived from the stone-block, as it was originally used for rolling before a tomb entrance and also used later where no provision was made for an artificial cover, or where such provision was as yet incomplete.

The simplest form of sepulchre, which consists only of one chamber with an *anteroom*, has a wide opening at the front, this being of varying measurements, generally only as wide as the sepulchre chamber itself, but usually less deep than wide and about as high as deep; 3 by 2 metres, 5 by 3 metres are the sizes that are usual. In the wide entrances, which are occasionally provided with columns, sculpture is possible, though rare. Sometimes the side walls have had a tomb-chamber constructed in each, and outside the antechamber there may also be a fore-court hewn in the rocks. When the Mishna refers to the *ḥaser*, "court," before the opening of the sepulchre, which is normally supposed to measure 6 by 6 ells,[2] and in this way offers the space necessary for the bier and its carriers, or even for two biers, it seems to include the fore-hall in the fore-court and also even the central chamber.[3] For this "court," which is also sometimes called *gat*, "wine-press," can either be open overhead, or covered;[4] it can be approachable from above, but also, we learn, from the side,[5] but it is not known how. Sepulchre chambers may be found on two sides, but also on all four sides.[6] They can also occur one upon the other.[7] Some rabbinical references to these chambers seem to be only theories, especially the assumption of an extension of only four hands' breadth.[8]

The application of the law of defilement caused by the dead in the rock-tombs was of great importance in connection with entering a sepulchre. According to Num. xix. 11, 16, touching

[1] b. Sanh. 47b ; Mo. k. 27a ; Keth. 4b ; Sem. iv. 11, x.
[2] Naturally it can also be larger. On Naz. ix. 3, where a distance of 8 ells between two tomb places is assumed, p. Naz. remarks that then it refers to the turning of the bier, as well as to the double number of carriers.
[3] Bab. b. vi. 8 ; Tos. Bab. b. vi. 23.   [4] Tos. Ohal. xv. 7.
[5] b. Sot. 44a.   [6] Bab. b. vi. 8.   [7] Tos. Ohal. vii. 9.
[8] Ohai. xv. 8 ; *cf.* Tos. Ohal. xv. 7. All this is not made entirely clear by Kraus, *Talm. Archäologie*, ii., p. 74 *f.* ; see Klein, *Tod und Begräbnis in Palästina zur Zeit der Tannaiten* (1908), p. 70 *f.*

a corpse, or the bones which belonged to the dead body,
caused defilement. But according to *v.* 16, the same was
true of touching a grave, and, according to *v.* 14, even being
in the place where a corpse lay was defiling. Now rabbinic
legislation explains that a tomb which is provided with a door
does not spread defilement on all sides.[1] So that anyone
could walk on the surface above a rock-tomb without being
defiled, but should he touch the door of a sepulchre[2] he is
defiled, and naturally defilement follows on entering into it.
In a fore-court closed from above one would remain undefiled,
if it measures at least four hands' breadth, or ells, square ;
while in an open fore-court there is no limit set concerning
the dimensions of the court, for as long as the lintel of the
tomb entrance is not touched[3] there is no defilement.

With these facts, with which the tomb discovered in the
time of Constantine can easily be made to harmonise, one
must compare the Gospel accounts. According to the
description of the Gospels it was possible to enter the sepulchre
and yet be in front of the entrance to the tomb (Jn. xx. 1, 3, 5 ;
cf. xi. 38), so that the entrance into the actual tomb chamber
was still to follow (Jn. xx. 6, 8). Thus the sepulchre must have
had an open anteroom. Then it was necessary to stoop on
entering the sepulchre from the outside, in order to perceive
that which was inside (Lk. xxiv. 12 ; Jn. xx. 5, 11). So the
entrance must also have been very low. When, according
to Lk. xxiv. 12, Peter, and, according to Jn. xx. 5, John, and
again, according to Jn. xx. 11, Mary only looked into the
sepulchre but did not enter, it may also have been due to the
desire to avoid defilement in view of the feast. At the same
time they immediately saw inside it the place where the Body
had lain : that is to say, the door must have led directly into
the tomb chamber, not first into an anteroom.[4] The cavity
must also have been narrow if a tomb which lay sideways
could have been surveyed completely at once. At the right
hand there was room to sit (Mk. xvi. 5), this being actually

---

[1] See Sifre on Num. cxxvi., cxxvii.

[2] Ohal. ii. 4 ; xv. 8 ; Tos. Ohal. xv. 8 ; Targum Jer. Num. xix. 16.

[3] Ohal. xv. 8 ; Tos. Ohal. xv. 7 ; *cf.* Maimonides, Hilch. Tumat Met. vi. 9,
and on Ohal. xv. 8 ; Derenbourg, *Commentaire de Maimonide sur la Mishna Seder
Tohorot,* ii., p. 79.

[4] Vincent, *Jérusalem,* ii., fig. 53, draws, without sufficient proof, instead of
an anteroom a closed antechamber, which, after all, the term σκέπη, " pro-
tective roof," applied to it by Cyril, *Cat.* 9, does not justify. Hesychius,
Questio 1437, did indeed imagine an inner and an outer room between which
the door with the stone upon it was found.

the place for the corpse to lie upon, at the head and foot-ends of which a person could sit (Jn. xx. 12) and where the napkin and the linen cloth could be placed separately (Jn. xx. 7; cf. Lk. xxiv. 12). The tomb of Christ must therefore have had the place for the corpse on the right hand, and it could not have been a tomb in the form of a shaft bored into the rock, nor is it likely to have been a shelf; for it is not emphasised that when the tomb was looked into through the door it was found empty, but that the linen cloth was seen to lie there. So it must have been the trough type of tomb, into which it was not possible to look from the door.[1] The tomb of Jesus was new and hitherto unused (Mt. xxvii. 60; Lk. xxiii. 53; Jn. xix. 41), so that this may have been the reason why it probably lacked an extensive chamber system, which, as a rule, grew out of an increased necessity for space.

To all these conditions among all the tombs found on Golgotha only the tomb with an anteroom will answer : this being the only one with an incomplete chamber, the tomb in the form of a trough being on the right side. Even if one should ascribe some of the details in the Gospel accounts rather to the narrators than to the eye-witnesses, the coincidence is none the less striking. Even that which the narratives do not actually demand, but which must, nevertheless, have been a very welcome fact, a single burying-place, is here found. The nearby burial-place with the shaft graves which might possibly have had an outer chamber[2] can hardly be seriously taken into consideration, because the place for the linen cloth and the seat for the angel would have been described differently. The sepulchres in the north, even when they were known, could not have given the impression of a new tomb, for they also lay outside the heathen temple, under which the tomb was suspected to have been. How striking it was that in the spot where it was believed that the tomb of Christ should be sought, a tomb actually was found which corresponded in every detail with that described in the Gospels, and, by its very isolation as a burial-place, seemed to point

[1] Gatt, *Das Heilige Land* (1880), p. 199, concludes from κατέθηκεν, Mk. xv. 46, that it was a trough-tomb. But this is the usual expression for " burying," from which the kind of tomb cannot be derived. Appel, *PJB*, 1907, p. 22, on the other hand, concludes from τόπος, Mt. xxviii. 6; Mk. xvi. 6, that it was a bench-tomb. But τόπος, like " locus," signifies any kind of tomb-place.

[2] This because its entrance would have otherwise presumably had a large inlet (bight) of the rocky wall.

to the only One, whose Body had rested there. Even the
sober Eusebius could not permit of any doubt here. The
very monument of the Resurrection of Jesus, which, with His
Death, forms the crux of the Christian faith, seemed to have
been found.

The *stone*, which closed up the entrance of the tomb, was,
after all, something comparatively unimportant. That in the
Gospels (Mt. xxvii. 60; xxviii. 2; Mk. xv. 46; xvi. 45; Lk.
xxiv. 2) we find mention of " rolling " and the " rolling back "
of a " great " (in Mt.) stone, was taken as a proof that the
tomb had had a proper closing in the form of a rolling stone
(see above, p. 370). But these rolling stones were not *rolled*
to and fro, but *pushed* forward and backward. The Gospel
of Peter therefore has not without cause spoken of a stone
which many persons, with their united strength, conveyed
and put before the tomb. Codex D speaks (Lk. xxiii. 53) of
a stone which could scarcely be rolled by twenty persons,
so it could not have been an easily movable rolling stone.
Also the idea of the angel sitting on the stone which he rolled
back (Mt. xxvii. 2) does not fit in with a " rolling stone "
pushed back in its groove. Therefore the " rolling stone "
which closed the tomb of Jesus was, for the Synoptic narrators,
most likely a rough, rollable rock block, which was perhaps
conceived of as a temporary closing, as is mentioned sometimes in rabbinic legislation (p. 369). But it is also possible
that the Jewish designation of that which was used to stop
up the mouth of a tomb as *golel*, " roller " (p. 370), gave rise
to an erroneous idea. Unfortunately it is not known what was
the shape of that door-stone found by the tomb of Golgotha.
In the seventh century it was severed into two rectangular
pieces, both of which served as altars. According to Arculf
the original stone could only be moved by many persons.[1]
This points to a considerable size and thickness. On old
reproductions of the stone[2] one sees it in cubic form. Even
if the opening was a flat one, which could easily be sealed
(Mt. xxvii. 66), it is possible to harmonise it with the Synoptic
narrative, if it is conceived of as specially thick and heavy.
But in John the stone by the sepulchre of our Lord and that
by the grave of Lazarus is not " rolled back " but " taken

---

[1] Arculf (Geyer, p. 232). Yet Willibald describes the then shown stone as
being only a reproduction of the old one, which must have been destroyed by
the Persians (Tobler, *Descr. T. S.*, p. 30).

[2] See a censer of the sixth century (*Échos d'Orient*, 1904, p. 150).

away " (Jn. xx. 1 ; xi. 38 f.), which is no indication of an unusual heaviness or shape of the stone, and the intensifying of the conception of the stone in Mt. and the Apocrypha looks suspicious. An ordinary flat closing-stone would have been in keeping with the idea of the narrator.

If the discovered tomb fits in with the tomb of Jesus, its position in relation to the Jerusalem of His time requires a special examination.[1] To those who in the time of Constantine sought to place Golgotha on the site of the present church of the Sepulchre it was certain that in the ancient city this place was left outside her walls. Cyril of Jerusalem pertinently asks something which is recognised by all : " Where is the rock (of the tomb) with the protecting roof (of the antechamber) ? Does it, by chance, lie in the centre of the city or near the walls and the outer parts ? Is it within the old walls or in the walls constructed later? It says in the Song of Solomon (ii. 14 LXX) : ' In the protecting roof of the rock, in the neighbourhood of the ante-wall.' "[2] From Josephus we know that the oldest northern city wall of Jerusalem remained about 200 metres south of this Golgotha. The wall of the suburb, lying in a northerly direction from it, which extended from Gennat gate (evidently making access to the gardens possible) to the citadel of Antonia[3], would have enclosed Golgotha only if a widely projecting arch and a beginning were given to it in that northern wall, but far in the west of it. Now Josephus would not have referred to the otherwise never-mentioned garden gate as the startingpoint had it been situated near one of the three towers on the north side of the citadel of Herod. Also his emphasis[4] on the weak protection of the western part of the old north wall would have had no sense if it were a question of only a few metres. It follows from this that the old piece of wall which was found in 1885, running from the north a distance of 50 metres from the assumed position of the Hippicus tower at the outer corner of the citadel of Herod towards the tower of David, could not have belonged to the suburban wall, as was conjectured by the first observers of it.[5] It is more likely, and it would also agree better with the inscriptions found there,[6]

---

[1] Cf. Appel, PJB, 1907, p. 25 f. [2] Cat. xiv. 9.
[3] Bell. Jud. v. 4, 2. [4] Ibid. v. 6, 2.
[5] Merrill, PEFQ, 1886, p. 21 f., 64 f. ; Schick, 1887, p. 217 f. ; 1888, p. 62 f.
[6] The most important is the dedication pillar of one or two stratores to the legate M. Junius Maximus from the end or beginning of the third century,

that it belonged to the western wall of Ælia Capitolina, which was rebuilt here after the destruction of the Hippicus tower, and from which the so-called third wall,[1] lacking in the time of Christ, branched, being joined to the Phasael tower, if this is the tower of David. But if the beginning of the suburban wall was not near the citadel of Herod, but farther east, then one must at least pass over the so-called pool of Hezekiah, the Amygdalon pool of Josephus,[2] at the east side of which Schick has seen old remains of a wall,[3] but which could not, at their height of 15 degrees above the present road here in the domain of the Ælia Capitolina, have belonged to the destroyed suburban wall. Both the siege walls of Titus at the Amygdalon pool and the tomb of John[4] point to a position even farther east ; for they must be located east of the citadel of Herod, and west of the suburban wall, which still stood on the southern part of it when the walls were erected.[5] So one would arrive somewhere in the neighbourhood of the street leading now to the German church of the Redeemer. A piece of wall running from east to west, and found during the building of this church,[6] may indeed be connected with a corner of this wall. Owing to the almost level crown of the hill reached from the wall, and the short range of ancient arrows, there was no necessity whatever for a higher and more western position for the wall. The tomb of the high priest John (Hyrcanus) mentioned by Josephus shows, together with the sepulchres near the church of the Holy Sepulchre, that there was a burial ground, *i.e.* that there were perpendicular rock-trenches belonging to ancient quarries, which could have been used for tombs. The "Gate of Gardens" points to a site occupied by olive gardens, which would fit in with the gardens of Joseph of Arimathæa (Jn. xix. 41 ; *cf.* Mt. xxvii. 60). If the cistern in the rock at the place where the Cross was found (see above, pp. 352, 355) was old—and there is nothing against this supposition—it might have been the reservoir of a garden.

If we are right in assuming that the Prætorium of Pilate was in the palace of Herod, then the *Via Dolorosa* could not

exhibited in the environment where it was found in the Court of the Grand New Hotel. See Thomsen : *Die lateinischen und griechischen Inschriften der Stadt Jerusalem* (1922), No. 5.

[1] *Bell. Jud.* v. 4, 2.   [2] *Ibid.* v. 11, 4.   [3] *PEFQ*, 1902, p. 55.
[4] *Bell. Jud.* v. 11, 4.   [5] *Ibid.* v. 8, 2.
[6] Mentioned by Schick, *PEFQ*, 1902, p. 46.

have been long. It was about 150 metres from there to the garden gate, and about 250 metres from the latter to Golgotha. In the neighbourhood of the garden gate Simon of Cyrene, according to Mt. xxvii. 32 ; Mk. xv. 21 ; Lk. xxiii. 26, relieved Jesus of the Cross. Kolmodin[1] thinks that the Gospel narratives presume a fairly long way, and that Heb. xiii. 12 points to the position of Golgotha outside the third northern wall of Jerusalem which existed at the time when the Epistle was written, with which the position of Golgotha assumed by Thinius (see p. 350) would tally. But, according to the findings of the last years, this third wall enclosed that hill, and the Epistle to the Hebrews intends, by the words " without the gate," to refer to what was true at the time of the Crucifixion, and the Evangelists, in their reference to Simon of Cyrene, only had in mind that the Cross was too heavy for Jesus to carry, and were not thinking of the distance.

There must of necessity have existed an important connecting road outside the suburban wall from the north road of the country to the garden gate of the old city, as well as a direct connection between that road and its continuation towards the south. This would supply for the neighbourhood of Golgotha that publicity which is presupposed for the judgment place of our Lord (Mt. xxvii. 39 ; Mk. xv. 29 ; Lk. xxiii. 35), and the nearness of the city which is testified to by St. John (xix. 20). Directly before the suburban wall one has to visualise a strip of uncultivated land, which was public property, and by which the road ran towards the garden gate. If our Lord was condemned in front of the palace of Herod, then there were two directions in which the place of the execution of the verdict could be sought. In the west, say on the height opposite the palace of Herod, the city proper and its traffic would be left behind. The greatest publicity for the execution of a threefold judgment would, on the contrary, be found without doubt in the north, in that corner which was formed by the wall of the old city and the suburban wall. Golgotha, which lay on a small eminence, at the other side of the low ground which begins before the gate of the garden, must have been the nearest place appropriate for it. When the suburban wall east of the church of the Sepulchre, in the neighbourhood of the present market street, is passed, the tomb would be at a distance from it of about 120 metres. Thus there was here, between the garden of the tomb and the city wall, sufficient

[1] *Johannesevangelist* (1926), p. 417 f.

space for a road and the uncultivated strip by the wall. Also the Jewish ordinance which demands that tombs should be 50 ells from the town[1] was complied with, although not Akiba's demand that the west side of the city should be free from tombs because of the prevalence of the west wind.[2] The spot where the cross was put up by Constantine upon the massive rock which was discovered, lies only 40 metres from the tomb and 80 metres from the presumed part of the city wall. Yet there is nothing against fixing the place of the Crucifixion nearer to the city wall, and accepting in this way the double distance. The Martyrion basilica of Constantine and the cistern of the Finding of the Cross would, in that case, designate its site. In this way the knowledge assumed by the Jerusalem Church at the beginning of the fourth century of the position of Golgotha and the Tomb of Christ seems to have been sufficiently justified. Joseph Klausner, who avoids forming his own conception of the walls of ancient Jerusalem, reproaches me with a desire merely to justify the traditional idea.[3] This is, of course, out of the question. What is involved is the testimony of the natives of Jerusalem at the beginning of the fourth century which we must admit in connection with the preservation of the place-name Golgotha. The neighbourhood of Golgotha seems therefore to be sufficiently identified; while the genuineness of the tomb that was discovered is only a probability but not a certainty, and the attempt of J. Jeremias[4] to prove its authenticity from the legends bound up with it is unconvincing. The church of the Sepulchre in the Jerusalem of to-day is therefore not merely the guardian of sacred sites, but—on the historical spot—a monument of Christian tradition almost sixteen centuries old. Surely we do not expect any " blessing " from a physical contact with the Cross—the rock of the Cross and the Tomb, as they are exhibited in the church of the Sepulchre—and we have no longing to kiss, with the thousands of Russian pilgrims, the holy relics. We find that the church which rises above these objects, stately as it may be, only disturbs our devotion, and would be inclined to wish Golgotha to be, for instance, on the *Sahira* hill outside the city, with the tomb at its foot in its natural condition, which tomb is since 1883 considered by many Englishmen to be the real tomb of Christ, but which is, in reality, of late date. But just here the external

[1] Bab. b. ii. 9 ; *cf.* Tos. Bab. b. i. 11.   [2] Bab. b. ii. 9 ; Tos. Bab. b. i. 8.
[3] *Jesus of Nazareth*, p. 352.   [4] *Golgotha* (1926), p. 28.

visualisation signifies very little, for, after all, we are not concerned merely with seeing how a man hung upon the Cross before the walls of Jerusalem, how he called (Jn. xix. 28), "*Sahena*," "I am thirsty,"[1] and then died and was buried in a rock-tomb between olive-trees. It would be something more if we comprehended that this Man knew how to die for the kingdom of God as we know how to die for the fatherland. But the mystery that is hidden in the fact that an unrighteous verdict here wrought righteousness is only revealed to one who, in the following of the Man of Nazareth and Capernaum, has found it to be the way to the Father, and recognised in all that He did and said God's power against sin and guilt. Only the eye which is turned inward and upward sees here the fact which signifies a new beginning in the history of the world. Is it therefore to be a matter of indifference to us to know where that supreme act took place?

Against the traditional view it is argued that the rare spiritual atmosphere of the early Church makes it doubtful whether she would have paid special attention to such material facts as the place of the Death and the Tomb of Jesus. And, again, it is said that the destruction of Jerusalem by Titus and the dispersion of the Community destroyed also its knowledge of all the localities of Jerusalem. But this is not only a question concerning what the early Christians recollected, but has to do with the old place-names, as, for instance, Golgotha; and there was as little reason for such names to disappear as there was for the names Mount of Olives, Siloa, Bezatha, etc., since Jerusalem and her environs were not entirely divested of their population and Jews as well as non-Jews lived there. The Gospels themselves, and not least the Fourth, prove what value was placed on the knowledge of the names of certain localities in and near Jerusalem in their original form. This shows that it seemed of importance at that time also to know the place where certain events in the life of Jesus occurred. This must not lead us to the conclusion that Christians began eagerly to venerate these places in a superstitious way, although one is not justified in drawing too sharp a line between the first Christians and the Jews who built "the tombs of the prophets and garnished the sepulchres of the righteous" (Mt. xxiii. 29; *cf.* Lk. xi. 47).[2] But she who not only shared

---

[1] *Cf. Jesus-Jeshua*, p. 208.

[2] Concerning the tombs of patriarchs and prophets revered by Christians in early times, see Schlatter, *Der Märtyrer in den Anfängen der Kirche*, p. 23 *f*.

in the events of those days (Lk. xxiv. 18) but also in the struggles, she who built on them the whole direction of her life and thought : the Church, which would not have come into being without those events, and to whose essence it belonged to recall and visualise them always anew—she could never have passed by with indifference the sites of the Cross and the Tomb.

Justin, in the second century, emphasised that the Birth of Jesus in the cave of Bethlehem was the fulfilment of Old Testament prophecy ; Origen, in the third century, pointed out that the truth of the Nativity narrative is confirmed by the local tradition connected with that cave.[1] It is unthinkable that at the same time there should have been no desire at all to know anything about the places of the Crucifixion and the Tomb. As long as the Church had to prove to Jews and heathen her right to existence above all from the fact of the Resurrection of Jesus, she could not have felt it unnecessary to point out where her roots in the Palestinian soil were established. The Gospels with their place-references ministered not so much to archæological curiosity as to the confident assuring of the faithful, as a defence against unbelief. What the Christians proclaimed was not a new philosophy or theosophy which can traverse the earth, spaceless and timeless, but the history of Jesus of Nazareth, which would be a myth if it had no connection with actual places. The same Eusebius who greeted with exultation the discovery of the tomb of Christ as a monument to the Resurrection, was also the author of a Church History; and his *Onomasticum* is the first Biblical Geography, which is an inestimable mine of knowledge concerning most places of the Bible. The concern to establish where in Palestine these places were to be sought rested on the sound sentiment that reliable history must also have its particular locality which can be demonstrated.

Even now we cannot advance beyond this point. Our faith in the Redeemer of the world is not dependent upon the knowledge of the sites of His Death and Burial, least of all on the actual point at which they occurred. But even mere reproductions of the Jerusalem tomb, of which Germany once possessed at least forty, and even now possesses twenty-four,[2] do not leave us entirely indifferent, and we feel at once that our faith would lack a certain support if the place-references of the Gospels merely hung in the air, as it were, and no

[1] See above, pp. 38, 43.   [2] See *Das Grab Christi in Deutschland* (1922).

actuality in Palestine corresponded with them. Christianity is, after all, not the mere blossoming forth of our own needs and thoughts, and is as little the teaching of one who has fallen from heaven or the work of an highly imaginative gnostic, but is rather the product of a God-wrought history, culminating in the Person of Jesus, apprehended by His Apostles who desired to show forth the right way to the thought, will, and activity of that humanity which, without Him, is lost. The contributions which Palestine supplies for understanding it, the vividness with which it aids our perception, are valuable to us, but, after all, the most important thing is the strong realisation to be gained upon its soil that this history stands in an indissoluble connection with our planet, that we are not its fashioners, and that nothing remains for us but to decide : either to fight against its actuality, or to let it become for us the Rock to which our mortal life may cling, for time and eternity.

INDEX OF PLACES

INDEX OF NEW TESTAMENT PASSAGES

INDEX OF OLD TESTAMENT PASSAGES

LIST OF CHURCH AUTHORITIES

Justin Martyr, 150
Origen, 248
Bordeaux Pilgrim, 333
Eusebius, 335
Cyril of Jerusalem, 350
Ætheria, 380
Epiphanius, 390
Jerome, 400
Nonnus, 400
Melania the younger, 430
Eucherius, 440
Prudentius, 450
Armenian Lectionary, 450
Peter the Iberian, 500
Theodosius, 530
Antoninus, 570
Madaba Map, sixth century
Breviarius de Hierosolyma, 590
Hesychius, 600
Sophronius, 610
Arculf, 670
Georgian Canonarium, 670

Bæda, 720
Willibald, 726
Commemoratorium de Casis Dei, 808
Bernhard, 865
Photius, 870
Epiphanius Hagiopolita, ninth century
Typicon of the Anastasis, tenth century
Innominatus I., 1094
Sæwulf, 1103
Daniel, 1106
Petrus Diaconus, 1137
Fretellus, 1148
John of Würzburg, 1165
Theoderich, 1172
Phocas, 1177
La Citez de Jherusalem, 1187
Perdicas, 1250
Burchard, 1283
Ricoldus de Monte Crucis, 1294
Marino Sanuto, 1308
Poloner, 1422

PRINTED IN GREAT BRITAIN BY
BILLING AND SONS LTD., GUILDFORD AND ESHER